Unification Through Division

Unification Through Division

Histories of the Divisions of the American Psychological Association

VOLUME II

EDITED BY

Donald A. Dewsbury

AMERICAN PSYCHOLOGICAL ASSOCIATION
WASHINGTON, DC

Published by
American Psychological Association
750 First Street, NE
Washington, DC 20002

Copies may be ordered from
APA Order Department
P.O. Box 92984
Washington, DC 20090-2984

In the UK and Europe, copies may be ordered from
American Psychological Association
3 Henrietta Street
Covent Garden, London
WC2E 8LU England

Typeset in Goudy by WorldComp, Sterling, VA

Printer: TechniGraphix, Reston, VA
Cover Designer: Minker Design, Bethesda, MD
Production Manager: Debbie K. Hardin, Reston, VA

Library of Congress Cataloging-in-Publication Data
Unification through division : histories of the divisions of the
   American Psychological Association / Donald A. Dewsbury, editor.
      p. cm.
   Includes bibliographic references and index.
   ISBN 1-55798-430-1
   1. American Psychological Association—History.   I. Dewsbury,
Donald A., 1939–
BF11.U55   1997
150′.6073—dc20

96-41480
CIP

British Library Cataloguing-in-Publication Data
A CIP record is available from the British Library.

Printed in the United States of America
First Edition

CONTENTS

CONTRIBUTORS

Herbert Barry, III, University of Pittsburgh

Ludy T. Benjamin, Jr., Texas A & M University

Mathilda B. Canter, Phoenix, AZ

Donald A. Dewsbury, University of Florida

B. Angela Dumont, Arizona State University

Paul R. Kimmel, Los Angeles, CA

Ronald W. Mayer, San Francisco State University

Carol L. Philpot, Florida Institute of Technology

Wilbur K. Rigby, Shawnee Mission, KS

Donald K. Routh, University of Miami

Nancy Felipe Russo, Arizona State University

Kenneth A. Wallston, Vanderbilt University

INTRODUCTION

DONALD A. DEWSBURY

This is the second volume in a set that will include the histories of as many of the American Psychological Association's (APA) 49 divisions as possible. About 50 years ago the APA was reorganized around a set of divisions structured to represent the diverse interests of constituent groups of psychologists within the organization at that time. Although the number of divisions has grown since, the basic structure remains intact. It is through these divisions that the unity of the APA was reestablished. By providing homes for groups with similar interests in research, practice, and policy, the divisions can work more effectively on many problems of local interest than can the association as a whole. Further, because they are smaller, they are more flexible and can change more readily as fields change. So effective have these divisions been that some psychologists identify more closely with these interest groups than with the organization as a whole.

In Volume I we presented the first nine division histories of the set. The project began with a survey of existing divisions histories, some of which had just been written for the 1992 centennial of the APA. From that survey, and word of mouth, we located authors for chapters dealing with many of the divisions. The first volume includes chapters the authors of which could meet the first possible deadline for inclusion; the second volume includes contributions from a second group of authors. We considered the possibility of holding chapters in order to publish a set of volumes with coherent themes, rather than the mix of diverse divisions as in the present volume. However, the advantages of such coherence seemed outweighed by the disadvantages of holding some chapters for several years as other authors work and the original chapters grow stale. The diversity of each volume will be characteristic of the wonderful and mystifying complexity of psychology itself.

We hope that these chapters will be of interest to diverse readerships. Division members should be aware of the histories of their divisions and understand where they stand in the webs and cascades of developing psychology. Historians of psychology and nonpsychologists will find much information with which to help understand the evolving fabric of the discipline of psychology. The hope is that any reader interested in understanding the complexity of this field will benefit from these chapters.

THE APA BEFORE WORLD WAR II

The APA was founded in G. Stanley Hall's living room at Clark University in July 1892 and held its first annual convention in Philadelphia in December of that year. Throughout its history, the APA has been the primary organization of psychologists in North America (see Evans, Sexton, & Cadwallader, 1992). However, throughout its history various interest groups of psychologists, on the sides of both basic research and practice, have formed their own organizations either within or outside of the APA. Beginning in 1904 Edward B. Titchener's Experimentalists, later the Society of Experimental Psychologists, was one such alternative organization for experimental psychologists (Boring, 1967). During the 1920s another group of experimental psychologists formed to conduct roundtables within the framework of the APA.

From the practice side, the American Association of Clinical Psychologists was founded in 1917 and became a section of the APA 2 years later. When the American Association for Applied Psychology (AAAP) was founded in 1937, the APA clinical section was disbanded and joined sections on consulting, educational, and industrial psychology as the clinical section of the AAAP.

Thus, when World War II broke out psychology lacked a unified presence. The Emergency Committee in Psychology was formed by the Division of Anthropology and Psychology of the National Research Council in 1940 to help mobilize psychologists for the war effort. It was from the Subcommittee on Survey and Planning of the Emergency Committee that Robert M. Yerkes and other psychologists began a push to reunify the APA, the AAAP, and various other smaller organizations into a single voice for psychology. An Intersociety Constitutional Convention was convened on May 29, 1943, in New York City to effect the reorganization. The result was a revised constitution and set of bylaws for the APA, which became an organization the stated purpose of which was not only to advance psychology as a science but also as a practice that could be used in the promotion of human welfare. Membership requirements were changed in order to accommodate practitioners whose efforts often did not lead to publication. The divisional structure was conceived as a way to maintain diverse interest groups within the broader structure of the new APA. Both the APA and the AAAP officially approved the reorganization in September 1944, and the new APA was inaugurated on September 6, 1945.

Psychologists were canvassed for their division interests with a preliminary list of 19 proposed divisions (Recommendations, 1943) and the results used to modify the proposed list into a revised set of 19 charter divisions arranged in a modified hierarchy (Doll, 1946; Hilgard, 1945a). Temporary division chairs and secretaries were appointed (Hilgard, 1945b), and elections of the first officers were held in 1945. The divisions were up and running.

This basic structure has seen minor modification over the past 50 years but has remained largely intact. Perhaps the greatest challenge to the integrity of the APA has come with the formation in 1988 of the American Psychological Society (APS), a group of academic, applied, and experimental psychologists that has challenged the hegemony of the APA. One can only hope that another unification will soon come to pass.

FROM 1945 TO THE PRESENT

Psychology in North America has changed dramatically in the 50 years since the division structure was adopted. I would summarize the changes as follows:

1. *Growth.* The membership has grown from approximately 3200 in 1943 to more than 80,000 more than 50 years later.
2. *Specialization.* Psychology has become more specialized, with few general psychologists and many psychologists limiting their interests to relatively narrow areas.
3. *Fractionation.* With increased specialization there have emerged many smaller societies and organizations that vie with the larger, umbrella groups for psychologists' loyalties.
4. *Professionalization.* There has been a dramatic shift from a dominance of basic science in psychology to an overwhelming numerical dominance of those with practice interests.

5. *External politization.* Psychologists have become more involved with matters of policy outside of the APA and psychology in general, including interactions with governmental agencies at all levels.
6. *Internal politization.* There has been an increase in the political structure and activity within the APA itself.
7. *Feminization.* There has been a substantial increase in the number of women in psychology and the roles they play.
8. *Diversification.* There has been an increase in representation and activity from members of diverse racial and ethnic groups.
9. *Internationalization.* There is increased recognition of the importance of psychology as it is developing outside of North America.
10. *Cognitivization.* The field has become more cognitively oriented.
11. *Expansion.* Psychologists have expanded their spheres of activity into areas not previously covered—for example, the increased conduct of therapy and the drive for prescription privileges.
12. *Legalization.* Both the practice and science of psychology have, like many functions in the United States, become more entwined with the courts, litigation, and lawyers.

The divisions have evolved in synchrony with these broader trends, both helping to effect the changes and being affected by them. The themes just elaborated should stand out as one reads the chapters of this volume. There are many problems for divisions created by the growth, specialization, and fractionation of psychology over the past 50 plus years. Most of these problems have affected all divisions to some degree, but some are more apparent in the histories of some divisions than in others. As will be apparent, these problems have led to conflict within divisions, among divisions, and with groups outside of psychology.

The shifting balance between science and practice can be seen in the dominance of practice orientations in the formation of many of the higher numbered divisions and in the evolution of some of the older divisions, such as Division 25 (Experimental Analysis of Behavior). The increased presence of psychologists in policy matters is especially apparent in the formation of the Divisions of Child, Youth, and Family Services (Division 37) and of Peace Psychology (Division 48). The expansion of psychology is especially apparent as the members of the Division of Psychoanalysis (Division 39) interact with physicians in defining appropriate spheres of activity.

AN OVERVIEW OF THE CHAPTERS

Chapter 1 concerns one of the most unusual of the APA Divisions, Division 9 (The Society for the Psychological Study of Social Issues; SPSSI). It is written by the division historian, Paul R. Kimmel. SPSSI was founded in 1936, well before the advent of APA divisions, but it became a charter APA division when the division structure was established during the 1940s. The overlap between the society and the division remains less than 100%. Although the division has functioned administratively, just as have other divisions in many respects, Kimmel focuses on the primary objective of SPSSI—the utilization of psychological knowledge in social action. He reviews SPSSI involvement in such areas as desegregation, peace efforts, poverty, diversity, and social responsibility. Kimmel shows how the accumulation of psychological information and social action can be combined in a single program.

Chapter 2, about the Division of Clinical Psychology (Division 12), is written by its president-elect, Donald K. Routh. Routh places the history of the division in the context of the broader history of clinical psychology and emphasizes the point that there was a clinical section of the APA beginning in 1919—well before the establishment of divisions in the 1940s. Indeed, one can trace a continuous history of what is now Division 12 beginning with the formation of the American Association of Clinical Psychologists in 1917. Division 12 has been a very active and complex unit; it currently has six sections. For much of the time period covered in this chapter, it was the largest of the APA divisions.

Chapter 3 recounts the history of Division 13 (Consulting Psychology) and is written by one of its past-presidents, Wilbur K. Rigby. As with the Division of Clinical Psychology, the roots of the Division of Consulting Psychology go back well before the APA reorganization of the 1940s. Rigby traces the title to 1924 and the antecedents of that event to a decade earlier. The earlier incarnation of the Division of Consulting Psychology died in 1927, however. An especially interesting feature of this chapter is a comparison of survey results from 1973 and 1989, showing the changes that occurred during that interval.

A noted historian of psychology, Ludy T. Benjamin, Jr., points out in his history of the Society for Industrial and Organizational Psychology (Division 14) in chapter 4 that there was an effort to organize a section on industrial psychology in the APA, parallel to those on clinical and consulting psychology, in 1922. In this case, the effort failed, however. The earliest organizations of industrial and organizations psychologists were within the Association of Consulting Psychologists and the AAAP during the 1930s. The organization itself has undergone three name changes since its birth as an APA division in the 1940s. Like many other APA divisions, Division 14 has one foot in science and one in practice, and this has created some difficulties.

The history of Division 26 (History of Psychology) is presented in chapter 5. It is written by one of the division's founding members, Ronald W. Mayer. Division 26 was not among the charter divisions created during the 1940s. The study of the history of psychology has always been a small, though important, part of the field. Among other topics, Mayer details the struggles of the division leadership to establish and maintain representation within the APA for this field and division. These efforts are culminating in the development of a new journal, *History of Psychology*, which is set to begin publication in 1998. Like some other divisions, the Division of the History of Psychology deals with a problem of multiple division membership for many of its members—many members have primary affiliations elsewhere.

Like Division 26, Division 28 (Psychopharmacology and Substance Abuse), discussed in chapter 6, was not among the charter divisions created during the 1940s. One of its most active officers, Herbert Barry III traces the story of the division from its founding in 1966 to the present. Unlike some proposed divisions, the proposal for a division of psychopharmacology met with little resistance from the existing divisions. Barry places the activities of the division within the broad context of interest in the relationships between drugs and behavior and shows how Division 28 has both facilitated broader trends and been affected by them.

A past-president of the division, Mathilda B. Canter, traces the origins of Division 29 (Psychotherapy) in chapter 7. Division 29 originated in a group called Psychologists Interested in the Advancement of Psychotherapy (PIAP) that was formed in 1960. Three years later it became a section of Division 12 and Division 29 in 1967. This pattern, wherein some of the newer divisions started as informal groups, became sections of other divisions, and finally emerged as separate divisions has been repeated in a number of cases in the history of APA divisions. Canter describes the many successes of the division and the manner in which administrative structures had to be changed to keep up with the growing complexity of the division.

In chapter 8, Nancy Felipe Russo, an active historian of the role of women in psychology, and Angela Dumont describe the history of Division 35 (Psychology of Women). They discuss the problems that the organizers had in gaining recognition of the new division and the barriers that had to be crossed in order to gain its acceptance. The rapid growth and remarkable diversity that have characterized this division as it was successfully organized are clear in this chapter.

Described in chapter 9 is a history of Division 38 (Health Psychology) written by one of its past officers, Kenneth A. Wallston. There are interesting parallels to the history of Division 29. Wallston traces the origins of the division to a 1969 *American Psychologist* article by William Schofield and a Task Force on Health Research established under the auspices of the APA Board of Scientific Affairs in 1973. These efforts led to the formation of a Section on Health Research, Section 2, in Division 18 (Psychologists in Public Service; see Volume I, *Unification Through Division*, Dewsbury, 1996). A petition to form Division 38, which emerged from the section, was approved in 1978. As was true of several other divisions, members of Division 38 struggled with the very definition and, in the process, helped it to coalesce as an identifiable subspecialty.

Carol L. Philpot, a former division president, traces the relatively brief, 12-year history of Division 43 (Family Psychology) in chapter 10. She shows how the division emerged from the family therapy movement and the Academy of Psychologists in Marriage Counseling, which was founded in 1959. She tells the story of the division's struggles to build membership, develop an effective administrative structure, ensure a sound financial framework, develop a publication program, and interface with other organizations. She shows how division activities have both affected and been affected by changing structures and organizations in the field both within and outside of the APA.

REFERENCES

Boring, E. G. (1967). Titchener's Experimentalists. *Journal of the History of the Behavioral Sciences, 3*, 315–325.

Dewsbury, D. A. (Ed.). (1996). *Unification Through Division: Histories of the Division of the American Psychological Association* (Vol. I). Washington, DC: American Psychological Association.

Doll, E. A. (1946). The divisional structure of the APA. *American Psychologist, 1*, 336–345.

Evans, R. B., Sexton, V. S., & Cadwallader, T. C. (Eds.) (1992). *100 years of the American Psychological Association*. Washington, DC: American Psychological Association.

Hilgard, E. R. (1945a). Psychologists' preferences for divisions under the proposed APA by-laws. *Psychological Bulletin, 42*, 20–26.

Hilgard, E. R. (1945b). Temporary chairmen and secretaries for proposed APA divisions. *Psychological Bulletin, 42*, 294–296.

Recommendations of the Intersociety Constitutional Convention of Psychologists: IV. (1943). Sample blank for survey of opinion on the proposed by-laws. *Psychological Bulletin, 40*, 646–647.

1

A HISTORY OF DIVISION 9 (SOCIETY FOR THE PSYCHOLOGICAL STUDY OF SOCIAL ISSUES)

PAUL R. KIMMEL

Because the history of Division 9 (Society for the Psychological Study of Social Issues) is so rich and diverse, I have chosen to provide some information on most of the contributions for which I could find records, rather than leave out some contributions in order to elaborate others. Even so, I would judge that I have only touched on about half of the activities of Division 9, and, therefore, even less of the activities of its parent organization, the Society for the Psychological Study of Social Issues (SPSSI). The amount of information provided on each contribution is primarily a function of the documentation available and its relevance to the APA. The interested reader is referred to the documents cited and to the SPSSI collection at the Archives of the History of American Psychology at the University of Akron, Ohio, for additional information.

THE EARLY YEARS

Division 9, one of the original divisions of the APA, as just mentioned, traces its roots to SPSSI, formed in September 1936 at the APA convention. SPSSI was later incorporated as a separate society, a status that it retains to this day. Although all Division 9 members must be SPSSI members, not all SPSSI members are Division 9 members. In addition to student members who are not eligible for APA membership, SPSSI also includes sociologists, anthropologists, political scientists, and members of the other social sciences. The society has always had a majority membership of psychologists, however (see Table 1). An initiative to change the name to the Society for the Study of Social Issues was soundly defeated in 1950 (*SPSSI Newsletter,* 1986b, 5).

The first SPSSI president (called *chairman* until 1945) was Goodwin Watson and the first secretary–treasurer was Isadore Krechevsky (a.k.a. David Krech). In August 1937, SPSSI was accepted as an affiliated organization of the APA at the annual meeting in Minneapolis. Between September 1936 and March 1945 when SPSSI received a formal invitation to become

TABLE 1
Division 9 Membership, Selected Years: 1948–1996

Years	Totals	Percentage of APA membership	Percentage of SPSSI membership*
1948	423	8%	
1950	485	6%	
1955	672	5%	
1960	804	4%	
1961	846		
1962	842		
1963	1062		75%
1964	1108		
1965	1307	5%	71%
1966	1401		
1968	1609		
1970	2068	7%	69%
1972	1881		
1973	2104		70%
1974	2146		
1975	2200	6%	
1980	2441	5%	80%
1985	2832	5%	
1986	2811		
1987	2790		
1988	2762		
1989	2785		
1990	2688	4%	
1991	2639		
1992	2610		
1993	2562		
1994	2486		75%
1995	2387	3%	68%
1996	2024		54%

1972 and 1996 had declines of more than 10% in Division 9 membership from the previous year.
*Percentages of Division 9 members in SPSSI are estimates It is impossible to tell whether the total membership figures include student members and/or delinquent members, who are not eligible for Division 9 membership (except for 1996, see last paragraph in text). Percentages for the APA are presented for the first year of membership and then at 5-year intervals beginning in 1950. Percentages for SPSSI are given for those years when the best figures were available.

one of the 19 proposed divisions of the newly organized APA, it was led by eight more presidents and two secretary–treasurers.[1]

There have been a number of articles published about SPSSI's founding and early history (Finison, 1976, 1977, 1978, 1979, 1984, 1986; Harris, 1980, 1986; Miller, 1986; Stagner, 1986), especially in the two 1986 issues of the Society's *Journal of Social Issues* (*JSI*, 1986, 1, 4) that commemorated its 50th anniversary. Because Division 9 of the APA—the focus of this chapter—began in 1945, I will not discuss this earlier information except to note that a key reason for the establishment and early popularity of the society was the lack of employment and public policy opportunities (especially for younger psychologists) in 1936. Seventeen percent of the APA membership joined SPSSI in its first year. It served as a support group for those who felt that the APA had "resisted all efforts to add functions such as a placement service, examination of the mental health impact of public issues, or pronouncements on fascism and other social movements" (Stagner, 1986, 35–36).

ADMINISTRATIVE STRUCTURE AND FUNCTION OF SPSSI AND DIVISION 9

SPSSI and Division 9 have an overlapping administrative structure. The officers include the president, president-elect, and secretary–treasurer. A council of 12 is elected by the membership. The Division 9 representative to the APA is elected by Division 9 members only. The SPSSI council exercises general supervision over the affairs of the society, including recommending actions based on members' suggestions, electing new members, approving the budget, maintaining liaison with committees, and appointing the general editor of the *JSI* and the editor of the *SPSSI Newsletter*. It is the only body authorized to issue statements in the name of the society. The president acts as the official representative of the society and Division 9, particularly with regard to policy matters.

Officers and Conventions

The interested reader is referred to Capshew (1986), who has presented a collective biography of the first 50 SPSSI/Division 9 presidents that includes their publications, presidential addresses, institutional locations, professional networks, and demographics. Table 2 provides a listing of SPSSI

---

[1] The SPSSI presidents through World War II were Gardner Murphy (1937), George Hartmann (1938), Edward Tolman (1939), Floyd Allport (1940), Kurt Lewin (1941), Otto Klineberg (1942), Gordon Allport (1943), and Ernest R. Hilgard (1944). Theodore Newcomb was the second secretary–treasurer (1941–1944), followed by Daniel Katz (1944–1947).

TABLE 2
Division 9 Presidents and Secretary–Treasurers

Date	Presidents
1946	Theodore M. Newcomb
1947	Rensis Likert
1948	Hadley Cantril
1949	Ronald O. Lippitt
1950	Daniel Katz
1951	David Krech
1952	Stuart W. Cook
1953	Dorwin Cartwright
1954	Eugene L. Hartley
1955	S. Stansfeld Sargent
1956	Marie Jahoda
1957	Alvin F. Zander
1958	R. Nevitt Sanford
1959	M. Brewster Smith
1960	Kenneth B. Clark
1961	Morton Deutsch
1962	Isidor Chein
1963	John R. P. French
1964	Jerome S. Bruner
1965	Herbert C. Kelman
1966	Jerome D. Frank
1967	Milton Rokeach
1968	Thomas F. Pettigrew
1969	Martin Deutsch
1970	Robert Chin
1971	Robert L. Kahn
1972	Marcia Guttentag
1973	Harold M. Proshansky
1974	Bertram H. Raven
1975	Albert Pepitone
1976	Harry C. Triandis
1977	Ezra Stotland
1978	Lawrence Wrightsman
1979	June Louin Tapp
1980	Cynthia P. Deutsch
1981	Leonard Bickman
1982	Clara Weiss Mayo
1983	Martha T. S. Mednick
1984	Lois Wladis Hoffman
1985	Marilynn B. Brewer
1986	Joseph E. McGrath
1987	Phyllis A. Katz
1988	Seymour Feshbach
1989	Jacqueline Goodchilds
1990	Stanley Sue
1991	Faye Crosby
1992	Sally Shumaker
1993	Stuart Oskamp
1994	Virginia E. O'Leary
1995	Michele Wittig
1996	Dalmas Taylor
1997	Barbara Gutek

Date	Secretary–Treasurers
1944–1947	Daniel Katz
1947–1950	Eugene L. Hartley
1950–1953	S. Stansfeld Sargent
1953–1955	Alvin Zander
1955–1958	Robert Kahn
1958–1961	Elizabeth Douvan
1961–1964	Margaret Luszki
1964–1970	Robert Hefner
1970–1976	John Kirscht
1976–1979	Lloyd Johnson
1979–1982	Robert Caplan
1982–1984	D. Wayne Osgood
1984–1986	Charlene Depner
1986–1989	Stanley E. Seashore
1989–1991	Martin Gold
1991–1992	Arnold Kahn
1992–1996	Barbara Gutek
1996–	Geoffrey Maruyama

presidents and secretary–treasurers from 1945 to date. Four of these presidents (and four of the earlier chairmen) also served as presidents of the APA. Eight presidents have received the APA Award for Distinguished Scientific Contributions, and nine others have received Awards of Distinguished Contributions to Psychology in the Public Interest.[2]

From 1946 until 1996, the annual meetings of Division 9 and the APA have coincided. SPSSI's decennial celebration was held during the first week of September 1946, at the University of Pennsylvania, preceding the APA meetings by a few days. The decennial program devoted 1 day to the council meetings, business meeting, and president's address; and 3 days to papers, speakers, and panels. There was a special exhibit of SPSSI activities and publications in the rooms reserved for the APA exhibits. In 1986, SPSSI's 50th anniversary celebration took place just before the APA meetings in Washington, DC. This was the second celebration featuring historical exhibits, speakers, panels, and presentations, and the first with a full-length musical satire on the division's history (Kimmel, 1986). Awards were presented to 37 of SPSSI's charter members. There have been several proposals over the years for SPSSI to sponsor its own annual convention, independent of the APA's annual meetings.[3] The 60th anniversary meeting in Ann Arbor, Michigan, in 1996 was the first such convention. Division 9 also

[2]Two out of every three of the APA Public Interest Awards have gone to Division 9 members.
[3]From 1953 to 1957, SPSSI sponsored annual joint meetings with the Society for the Study of Social Problems and the Society for Applied Anthropology. These 2-day conferences featured interdisciplinary panels and symposia.

participated in the APA meeting in 1996 and has plans to do so in coming years.

Central Office

Division 9 membership and activities grew rapidly after World War II. SPSSI's *Journal of Social Issues (JSI)* was launched in 1945. In 1946, the SPSSI council consulted their 400-plus members about setting up a secretariat. The membership endorsed seeking a full-time secretary to help promote the *JSI* and to assist the secretary–treasurer and various committees.

In November 1946, Jean Tiedke became the first paid officer of SPSSI and Division 9. Funds for her salary were raised by soliciting pledges from members. In 1951, Helen "Stevie" Service became the assistant secretary. The SPSSI/Division 9 secretariat moved to the University of Michigan's Institute for Social Research in 1953 and Service became co-editor of the *SPSSI Newsletter* (which had previously been part of the report of the SPSSI secretary–treasurer to the membership). The society was incorporated in Michigan in 1956 as a nonprofit organization.

In 1962, space limitations forced the central office to leave the Institute for Survey Research. Caroline Weichlein, the new administrative secretary, moved the division's files to her home, the Argus Building, and finally to the Municipal Court Building in downtown Ann Arbor. On the night of November 10, 1971, a fire that caused $500,000 worth of damage, started by a coffee maker in a neighboring office, destroyed the entire floor of the Municipal Court Building where the central office was located. Weichlein supervised the evacuation and restoration of most of the Division 9 documents from smoke and water damage. Early in 1972, the central office was moved to its present location in the Curtis Building on Main Street in Ann Arbor.

In 1983, the membership lists were computerized, and in 1984 the SPSSI council voted to sponsor an exhibit booth at the APA convention, the only division of the APA to do so. At eight of the next nine conventions, central office staff members Lynda Fuerstnau and Kathy Donahue staffed this exhibit booth with the assistance of the SPSSI council members. Book and journal orders were taken and new members were recruited. In 1986, a membership secretary was added to the central office, and Charlene Depner was appointed the first editor-in-chief of the newsletter. In 1987, an e-mail system enhanced central office's capacities. Members are encouraged to contact the central office by e-mail, fax, telephone, or mail.

In 1988, Michele Wittig took over from Depner as editor-in-chief of the newsletter, followed in 1991 by Susan Opotow, in 1994 by Linda Silka, and in 1996 by Amy Marcus-Newhall. In-house publishing of the publications catalog and the newsletter began in 1994, and two new half-time central office positions were created by the SPSSI council: an administrative associate to manage the office, especially its administrative and financial aspects; and a professional scientist in the public interest to carry out policy initiatives of the president and the SPSSI council, initiate funding searches, and facilitate the public interest activities of the membership. In January 1994, Ann Waldrop was hired as the first administrative associate. She created a new accounting system that expedites the division's fiscal reporting. In February 1995, Paula Skedsvold became the first SPSSI scientist in the public interest.

SPSSI as a Separate Organization

For more than 50 years, Division 9 has been an integral part of the APA and, as I will document, has "succeeded in pushing the APA toward socially responsible internal and public positions more rapidly" (Miller, 1986, 129). Over the years, there have also been varying degrees of separation between SPSSI and the APA. The *JSI* has always been an SPSSI, not an APA, journal. Division 9 does not make use of the APA's election, editorial, journal and book marketing services, journal subsidies, or liability insurance program. It was the first (and until 1983 the only) division to be part of a separately incorporated society.

In 1955, there was a proposal to combine Divisions 8 and 9 as part of a plan to simplify the divisional structure of the APA. The SPSSI council rejected this proposal in 1956, saying that such an amalgamation would destroy SPSSI. However, it voted to continue as a division of the APA to further the application of social science knowledge to action on social issues. In observance of the society's 20th anniversary, two of SPSSI's early members and presidents wrote, "In discussing the proposed reorganization of APA the Council of SPSSI believed that . . . SPSSI is unique among the divisions of the APA and that it is performing functions which should be preserved in any future organization of the APA" (Krech & Cartwright, 1956, 16).

In 1987, as the APA was considering a major restructuring (supported by Division 9), the SPSSI council formed a task force to consider separating from the APA. This task force concluded that such a separation was inadvisable, because there was much to be gained both by the association and the division in their continued affiliation (*SPSSI Newsletter*, 1987, 8).

When the American Psychological Society (APS) was established in 1989, SPSSI became a nonvoting organizational affiliate. Division 9 sent letters to both the APA and the APS stressing that each should promote human welfare, provide a home for public issues, take advocacy positions that promote the public good, and accord as many resources to public policy as to professional and research policy. SPSSI established a Society for Public Interest Psychology (which became the Coalition for Psychology in the

Public Interest) to guide the APS in the development of programs on social issues. This coalition disbanded in 1993. In 1996, SPSSI council voted to place the scientist in the public interest with the Government Relations Department of the APS on a full-time basis. The activities of this individual have shifted into the policy–advocacy area.

In 1992, the SPSSI council decided that should the society dissolve, its assets will go to a nonprofit organization to be determined by its directors. Before this time, the APA was designated to receive these assets.

SPSSI and the APA

In 1972, the SPSSI council voted to discontinue nominating Division 9 members for APA fellow status, a membership class that recognizes outstanding and unusual contributions to psychology. Earlier, they had decided to nominate primarily nontraditional, nonacademic, social issue-oriented persons as fellows. After polling the membership, it was decided to oppose irrelevant status distinctions such as that of APA fellow. Motions were made to encourage the APA to consider abolishing the status of fellow and to ask members who were already fellows to renounce that distinction. Both of these motions were defeated. In 1980, the SPSSI council voted to reinstate the fellow nomination process.

In 1976, the SPSSI council adopted a graduated dues structure (based on current income) that is still in operation. In 1979, Division 9 suggested to the APA that it adopt a similar dues structure. Although the APA did not embrace the idea of a sliding scale for dues, it did adopt the SPSSI idea of waiving dues for members with low incomes. SPSSI has a special-request option allowing members with financial hardship not to pay dues. In 1980, the APA decided to waive dues for up to 2 years for members making less than $7,500 the previous year. Today, the cutoff is $12,000 (for both the previous year and expected current dues year).

Also in 1976, the three Division 9 representatives to the APA council initiated a Public Interest Coalition (PIC) with representatives from other divisions who were concerned about the direction in which the APA council and board of directors was moving and who wanted to bring more social issues to the attention of the APA council. Over the years, PIC became adept in introducing and passing public policy proposals and resolutions, especially on national and international social issues, in APA council meetings.

SPSSI established its Court Watch Committee in 1978 in response to the *Bakke* case on reverse discrimination. This committee produced a position paper on affirmative action and developed the "Judicial Notebook" column that first appeared in the APA *Monitor* in 1979. This column, which has been picked up by other publications, has become a regular feature in the association's monthly newspaper, encouraging the involvement of psychologists in judicial decision making.

In 1984, Division 9 designated one of its APA council seats as a minority position. It urged the APA to adopt a similar approach to address the underrepresentation of minority group psychologists on the APA council, but the so-called Kiesler plan, named after Charles Kiesler, former APA executive officer, was voted down by the APA council. Division 9 continued to have a minority slate for its APA council representative until 1991.

Purposes

The purpose of the society and Division 9, as specified in Article II of the constitution and bylaws (1974), is, "to instruct the public on subjects useful to the individual and beneficial to the community (1) by obtaining and disseminating to the public factual data . . . through the promotion and encouragement of psychological research on significant and practical questions of social life and (2) by promoting and encouraging the application of the findings of such psychological research to the problems of society." And, "The Society's scientific research shall be carried on in and to serve the public interest."

As *JSI* editor Joseph McGrath noted, the members of Division 9 have long been interested in "the 3 Ps: prejudice, poverty, and peace" (1980a, 100). I will use these three "problems of society" to discuss many of the contributions that the division has made to the APA and psychology in general.

PREJUDICE

Following McGrath, I will use prejudice to include human rights, civil rights, and civil liberties. McGrath found that prejudice was "the single most frequently treated substantive topic" in the *JSI*, beginning with its first two issues (McGrath, 1980a, 101).

The Executive Secretary

At SPSSI's first midwinter meeting in 1949, the SPSSI council proposed hiring a professional executive secretary. In 1950, Otto Klineberg (SPSSI chairman in 1942–1943) accepted the council's offer to become executive secretary and set up the first central office. Klineberg worked for SPSSI and Division 9 on a half-time basis, generating research proposals, collaborating with other social science organizations, consulting with government bureaus and the United Nations, publicizing the organization, and taking care of administrative duties for the division. One of his first projects was to evaluate a curriculum for children on racial differences for UNESCO.

Klineberg established connections with other social science organizations through his work on race relations (*SPSSI Newsletter*, 1994), the evaluations he and Gerhart Saenger conducted for the UNESCO "Tensions Project," and his activities as SPSSI representative to the U.S. National Commission for UNESCO. Klineberg helped form the International Union of Scientific Psychology and the International Social Science Council. These and his many other collaborations increased the reputation and membership of SPSSI and Division 9. By 1955, Division 9 had nearly 700 members (see Table 1). In 1953, Klineberg resigned as executive secretary to work for UNESCO.

Brown v. Board of Education

Much of SPSSI's internationally known work on prejudice and the teaching of social science in the 1950s, including the development of a curriculum on racial differences, grew out of Klineberg's efforts. He was also responsible for Kenneth Clark's involvement in the National Association for the Advancement of Colored People's (NAACP) Legal Defense Fund's prosecution of the school desegregation cases (Klineberg, 1986). In 1950, Klineberg recommended that Clark synthesize the literature on the effects of race on childrens' personality development for the Mid-Century White House Conference on Children and Youth. When R. L. Carter, assistant attorney to Thurgood Marshall of the Legal Defense Fund, asked Klineberg about using social science material in their hearings, Otto told him about Clark's monograph (Clark, 1953) for the conference.

As a result of this recommendation, Clark served as general social science consultant to the NAACP legal staff from early 1951 through the final Supreme Court decision in 1954 (Kluger, 1976). He relied heavily on SPSSI for support in his work. At least 12 SPSSI members (including six past or future presidents of the division) were called as expert witnesses or submitted briefs in the four cases preceding *Brown v. Board of Education*.

Division 9 established the Committee on Intergroup Relations in 1949, chaired by Gerhart Saenger, to collect and analyze data on the psychological, social, and economic effects of segregation to challenge the contention that segregation does not constitute discrimination. The committee did not contemplate any immediate practical use of these materials (Clark, 1953, 5). However, as the court cases proceeded and the NAACP attorneys asked for more information, they realized that much of their work was relevant to the segregated school cases. A subcommittee drafted a preliminary summary of their findings for the Legal Defense Fund. The committee sponsored a symposium on the effects of segregation at the 1952 APA convention.

Stuart Cook, president of Division 9 in 1951–1952, joined the subcommittee and collaborated with Clark and Isadore Chein in rewriting their report. The resulting social science brief pulled together the essential points of the testimony of the expert witnesses at the hearings and Clark's White House conference memorandum (Evans, 1980, 67). It was signed by 32 prominent social scientists, including at least 23 SPSSI members, 15 of whom had been or became presidents of the society. The brief appeared as the appendix to the appellants' briefs in *Brown v. Board of Education*, which was accepted by the Supreme Court and considered in the first argument of the case in December 1952.

In preparation for the reargument, the Legal Defense Fund asked Clark about the impact of changing from segregated to desegregated public schools. With the assistance of the signers of the appendix and many other SPSSI members, Clark gathered data on racial desegregation in the United States. He made these data available to the Legal Defense Fund attorneys and published them in an entire *JSI* issue in 1953. SPSSI and the NAACP distributed free copies of this issue through trade unions, schools, corporations, and government and social work agencies. Favorable comments were received from a number of agencies about the utility of the *JSI* issue as a guide for implementing desegregation in education and housing.

Academic Freedom and Civil Liberties

In addition to working on school desegregation, race and psychological characteristics, and international issues, Division 9 was also involved with academic freedom and civil liberties in the early 1950s. In 1950, the SPSSI council unanimously adopted a set of resolutions condemning the University of California Board of Regents for its loyalty oath and discouraging members from filling vacated positions there.[4] In 1951, a standing academic freedom committee and an academic freedom fund were established "to make investigations . . . and to raise and disburse funds to aid victims of persecution" (Sargent & Harris, 1986, 60). Money for the fund came from voluntary contributions of members and was usually given to help defray legal expenses. Several SPSSI members who were adversely affected by investigations such as those of the Canwell Committee in Washington state, the Rapp–Coudert Committee in New York, and the University of California were supported by SPSSI both financially and through procedural advice and encouragement. Local committees, including at least one SPSSI council member when

---

[4]Professors in the University of California system were required to take an oath that they would not advocate or teach overthrow of the U.S. government by force or by illegal or unconstitutional methods. The faculties at Berkeley and UCLA got the regents to revise the requirement to a statement denying membership in the Communist Party. The oath requirement was part of the annual contract.

feasible, were set up to report on the cases being defended. (See Sargent & Harris, 1986, for a review of these cases.)

In some of these cases, Division 9 called on the American Civil Liberties Union, the American Association of University Professors and the APA for support. In 1950, the APA Council of Representatives passed a resolution initiated by Division 9 condemning the University of California for the dismissal of six professors who refused to sign the university's loyalty oath. The APA had committees on freedom of inquiry and on academic freedom and civil liberties but no funds to support their work. Although Division 9 members worked with the APA on a few of their cases and a SPSSI statement on academic freedom was published in the *American Psychologist* (SPSSI Statement on Academic Freedom, 1955), the APA was generally less direct than SPSSI in defending their members' academic and intellectual freedom of thought, speech, and scientific investigation. For example, in 1950, the APA board of directors, like the SPSSI council, recommended that APA members not accept positions as teachers or researchers in the California state university system and instructed the APA placement service to refuse assistance in filling vacancies (Smith, 1992). However, their recommendation focused on tenure conditions rather than the loyalty oath as the issue needing change. In 1954, the APA council passed a resolution asking the American Association for the Advancement of Science to study the impact of loyalty oaths on academic freedom.

The SPSSI Academic Freedom Committee disbanded in 1957 but was reinstated from 1970 to 1974 to deal with the blacklisting (for "security reasons") of members who were serving as consultants to government bureaus such as the Department of Health, Education and Welfare (Smith, 1986). The APA, again encouraged by Division 9 actions, was 1 of 11 scientific organizations that joined in a coordinated protest of Health, Education and Welfare's security clearance procedures. By the end of 1970, the *New York Times* noted that "few, if any, scientists have been barred from becoming advisors" (Lyons, 1970). From 1977 to 1987, task forces and ad hoc committees on academic freedom were set up by Division 9 to deal with specific problems brought to the SPSSI council by its members and colleagues (see *SPSSI Newsletter*, 1986a, 4–5).

Desegregation and Grants-in-Aid

From 1954 through the 1960s, Division 9 was actively involved in research and action on desegregation, especially in the South. The research on desegregation began with a small grants-in-aid program set up by the Committee on Program Emphasis in 1955. The amount of $1000 was initially allocated to this program from the society's funds, and four awards were made. In 1957, this amount was raised to $1500 "to attract proposals of greater promise." Most grants-in-aid applications came from social scientists in the South.

In 1956, the Committee on Desegregation and Integration was formed to serve as a clearinghouse for research and to facilitate communication among Southern social scientists. Many of these social scientists in responding to a questionnaire from this committee said it was dangerous to be identified as advocates of desegregation, although they approved of small regional meetings to discuss school desegregation. Thus the name of this committee was changed to the Committee on Desegregation and Integration of the Schools. It initiated regional round tables on school desegregation in New York City and Baltimore in 1957. It continued to survey on-going research and began to review books on desegregation. It was regionalized in 1960 and disbanded in 1962.

By 1958, the SPSSI grants-in-aid program was opened to a wider range of research proposals, but desegregation research was still the priority. There were no requests for grants-in-aid in 1959 and only a few in 1960. By 1961, SPSSI allocated $2200 for this program and more proposals came in. One principle for funding has been to make awards in new fields where money is scarce. For example, in 1962 the topics of prejudice and segregation, economic issues, international relations, education and attitudes toward change were suggested for the $8830 in available funds. In 1965, a three-person committee was established to review proposals and allocate funds. This committee structure is still in operation, and members are selected for 3-year terms. In every year since 1960 (except 1970 and 1974, when no funds were available), there have been more proposals than funds. The range of topics supported has greatly expanded. Abstracts of the supported research have been published in the *SPSSI Newsletter* since 1978.

Civil Rights Demonstrations and Martin Luther King, Jr.

In 1965, the SPSSI council authorized a fund of $1500 to support social scientists as official observers at civil rights demonstrations in the South. Notices appeared in the *SPSSI Newsletter* and *Trans-Action* and open letters were published to the presidents and members of the APA, American Economic Association, American Historical Association, American Anthropological Association, and American Orthopsychiatric Association. (The presidents of SPSSI, the Society for Applied Anthropology, and the Society for the Study of Social Problems had been working together for a year through SPSSI's Intersocietal Committee.) In 1967, Division 9 sponsored the Boston Conference on Observation, Research and Civil Rights Demonstrations. One function of this conference was to train social scientists as expert witnesses in civil rights cases. Funding for the conference came from SPSSI

($3000) and from Kenneth Clark's Metro Applied Research Center (MARC) ($3000) in New York City.

SPSSI and MARC established a national network of behavioral scientists able to furnish expert testimony as part of the NAACP's program against de facto segregation of the public schools. This network was coordinated from 1967 to 1970 by the Civil Rights Activities Committee with a budget of $1500. By the end of 1967, this network included 63 psychologists from 23 states and the District of Columbia. Planning sessions were held in the late 1960s in New York City to synchronize research, organization building, and legal action among members of Division 9, civil rights activists, members of the NAACP, King's Southern Christian Leadership Conference (SCLC), and other social science organizations. Robert Chin, chair of the SPSSI Committee on Civil Rights Activities and Movement, noted in the *SPSSI Newsletter* (1967, 7), "It is instructive to all of us to hear the specific disquietudes and mistrusts of the behavioral scientist by the civil rights activist."

In the interest of fighting de facto racial segregation, SPSSI made a grant of $5000 to SCLC in 1967 and also contributed to King himself to facilitate meaningful confrontations between SCLC, social scientists, and King's civil rights staff. King addressed more than 5000 psychologists at the APA's annual convention in 1967 as part of the Division 9 program. The Division 9 Committee on Travel Funds for Observation or Research on Civil Rights Events, also active from 1967 to 1970, facilitated quick responses to civil rights activities by covering travel expenses of social scientists. In 1968 to 1969, 15 grants totaling $2953.52 were made. Research reports from five grantees were published in the April 1968 edition of the *SPSSI Newsletter*.

The Civil Rights Activities Committee brought together research relevant to civil rights activists and collected reports on investigations of urban disturbances such as the Kerner Commission Report. At the 1970 midwinter meetings, the SPSSI council broadened the focus of this committee to include all minority groups and added voting rights, housing, and equal employment opportunities to the committee's agenda. A committee on racism was also set up that was subsumed by the Committee on Underrepresented Groups in 1974.

APA Conventions and Equal Opportunity

Another civil rights issue involving Division 9 and the APA was that of holding conventions in cities that had laws or policies violating the civil liberties of minority groups. In 1955, the APA council voted to hold their 1957 meetings in Miami Beach after obtaining guarantees from several hotels that their facilities would be open to all APA members, regardless of color.[5] Two SPSSI members went to Miami Beach in 1956 and found that some of these hotels *did* discriminate. A poll of SPSSI members following this test visit showed that 60% felt the APA should not meet in Miami. The results of this poll were reported to the APA council by the Division 9 representatives at their September 1956 meetings. The APA council voted against going to Miami Beach in 1957. Division 9 representatives to the APA council also argued against holding the 1969 meetings in Chicago, following the police actions at the Democratic National Convention in 1968, and against having the 1978 meetings in Atlanta, Georgia, a state that had not ratified the Equal Rights Amendment. The APA moved both conventions.

In 1963, Division 9 proposed that the APA form a committee on equal opportunity to ensure affirmative action in the training and employment opportunities of its members. The SPSSI council contributed $2000 to the APA for the establishment of this committee. In 1964, the APA established the Committee on Equal Opportunity in Psychology. The first two chairs of this committee were Division 9 members. Early subjects of interest to the committee were the conditions of education and teaching for psychologists in Appalachia and the South, but little was done because the APA did not fund this committee. Instead, the APA's Committee on Academic Freedom and Conditions of Employment (CAFCOE) became more active in reviewing cases of discrimination and writing reports, the first being on the employment testing of minority groups.

In 1968, at the request of Division 9, there was a census of African Americans on the APA staff. In 1969, Division 9 cosponsored a resolution prohibiting discriminatory practices by APA vendors that was passed by the APA council and monitored by CAFCOE. In 1972, regional and state associations were required to establish affirmative action programs for their governance positions by the APA council. In 1986, CAFCOE developed Guidelines for Conditions of Employment of Psychologists. CAFCOE was terminated by the APA in 1992, and its functions were taken over by the APA's boards of educational affairs and practice.

Race and Intelligence

Studies by psychologists on the intellectual potential of African Americans had been an issue for the society prior to its involvement in *Brown v. Board of Education* in 1953. In 1956, 1960, 1961, and 1969, the SPSSI

---

[5] In 1950, the APA council established a policy that meetings would only be held in establishments that did not discriminate on the basis of race or religion.

council issued public statements denouncing abuses of ability tests and questioning psychologists' findings and interpretations of racial differences in intelligence. In July 1964, the Division 9 Committee on the Uses and Abuses of Ability Testing published a guide to technical accuracy and social responsibility in the use of tests on children in minority groups (Guidelines, 1964). The APA central office issued a supportive press release on this guide.

President Chein wrote an article in the December 1961 *SPSSI Newsletter* criticizing APA past president Garrett's writings on the subject of racial differences in intelligence. Garrett responded to this article in the *SPSSI Newsletter* (May 1962a) and the *American Psychologist* (Garrett, 1962). Klineberg wrote two articles in the *American Psychologist* (1963, 1971) and chapters in *The Human Dimension in International Relations* (1964) and *Race, Science and Society* (1975), discounting research on IQ differences and race. The SPSSI-sponsored book, *Social Class, Race and Psychological Development* (Deutsch, Katz, & Jensen, 1968), also dealt with these issues. Co-editor Arthur Jensen's later negative comments on racial differences and the potential of compensatory education (1969) led to SPSSI council's 1969 public statement (sent to 5000 individuals, newspapers, and journals) that the available data did not support the attribution of differences in IQ measures between African Americans and White Americans to genetic differences. Other SPSSI commentaries on the lack of relationship between race and intelligence appeared in a SPSSI-sponsored book on the subject that came out in 1976 (*Genetic Destiny: Scientific Controversy and Social Conflict*, edited by Tobach & Proshansky).

There was a great deal of public controversy around SPSSI's 1969 statement and an alleged delay in publishing (in the *JSI*) a study by two of its members on the negative effects of busing. For example, Arthur Jensen threatened to sue SPSSI president (and former co-editor) Martin Deutsch about a comment he allegedly made in a talk about the Jensen article, and editorials in *Psychology Today* (Rice, 1973) and *The Wall Street Journal* (Otten, 1974) chastened the society and its journal for these activities. *JSI* editor Bert Raven responded to these editorials in the *SPSSI Newsletter* (1974), discussing the difficulties in dealing with their biases and innuendoes. Jensen did not sue, but these controversies may have had a negative impact on some of the membership. From 1970 to 1972, Division 9 lost 187 (nearly 10%) of its APA members. This was the first time since 1949 that the division had had a significant decrease in membership (refer to Table 1). (There has been a gradual decline in Division 9 membership since 1984.)

The recent book, *The Bell Curve* (Herrnstein & Murray, 1994), and article by Jensen (1993) indicate that the issue of race and intelligence has not disappeared from psychology nor has SPSSI's consistent critique, although no public statements have been issued in this area since 1969

(Klineberg, 1986). The Board of Scientific Affairs of the APA established a task force in 1994 to prepare a report on intelligence that appeared in the *American Psychologist* (Neisser et al., 1996). None of the SPSSI publications or statements mentioned here were cited in this article.

PEACE

The division's interest in war and peace, like its concerns about prejudice, goes back to its beginnings. A poll of SPSSI members in 1937 revealed that industrial conflict and war and peace were the two most important issues for the society. The third book that SPSSI sponsored was Gardner Murphy's *Human Nature and Enduring Peace* (1945). Its concluding chapter was a reprint of the psychologists' manifesto, a statement of ten principles about human nature vital to planning peace after World War II. This SPSSI-originated and circulated statement was signed by more than half the members of the APA.

International Understanding and UNESCO

After World War II and throughout the 1950s, much of Division 9's peace activity was related to its work with the U.N. and especially UNESCO. In 1947, the SPSSI council received a grant from the Department of Social Affairs of the U.N. to develop a proposal for an Institute of Human Sciences within the U.N. SPSSI members were also involved in the UNESCO study of tensions affecting international understanding mentioned previously. The first edition of an important SPSSI-sponsored book, *Research Methods in Social Relations* (Jahoda, Deutsch, & Cook, 1951), was partially supported by UNESCO (as well as by the Anti-Defamation League and the National Council of Christians and Jews). In 1954, Gordon Allport, SPSSI representative to the U.S. National Commission for UNESCO, called it "a productive research center, a vital agent of progress in our own profession and a worthy symbol of our own aspirations as citizens and as scientists" (*SPSSI Newsletter*, 1954, 3).

Committees were established on international studies (1947–1950), international relations (1949–1976), and international affairs (1961–1963). These committees were charged with maintaining active contact with public and private agencies in the United States and professional societies in other countries to create a network of organizations dedicated to using psychology for the preservation of peace. As mentioned, Division 9 played an important role in the establishment of the International Union of Scientific Psychology and the International Social Science Council. It also was instrumental in establishing the APA Committee on International Affairs in 1962 (*SPSSI Newsletter*, 1963).

Klineberg's departure for Paris, the congressional investigations of the peace movement and other "unamerican activities," and SPSSI's increased civil rights activities curtailed Division 9's U.N. and other peace initiatives somewhat from 1953 to 1960.

Vietnam and the Cold War

A shift from cooperative international peace efforts to opposition to national war efforts gradually took place within SPSSI in the early 1960s. The major impetus for this shift was the entry of the United States into the Vietnam conflict and increasing tension in the Cold War with the Soviet Union. In 1959, the SPSSI council formed an ad hoc committee on the role of psychologists in international affairs in response to an address by the executive secretary of the APA on the association's peace project. In 1961, an issue of the *JSI* was dedicated to psychology and policy in a nuclear age. In June 1962 (*SPSSI Newsletter*, 1962b), the only special issue of the *SPSSI Newsletter*, titled *Psychologists and Peace*, was prepared by the SPSSI Core Group on the Psychological Aspects of Arms Control and Disarmament. Nearly 22,000 copies of this newsletter, detailing what psychologists could do to promote peace, were mailed, including to the entire APA membership. In 1963, the SPSSI council authorized $3000 to bring young foreign scholars to Washington, DC, and to Philadelphia for an International Congress of Psychology and the APA convention. Also in 1963, the SPSSI council issued a public statement supporting the treaty banning nuclear weapons testing and formed the Subcommittee on Problems of Peace and War to encourage research on long-range threats to peace. A $1000 prize was awarded to the best essay on this topic.

Although the APA was either supportive of (e.g., the APA Committee on International Affairs cosponsored a symposium with Division 9 on the role of the social sciences in UNESCO at the 1963 annual meetings) or neutral toward most of the division's peace initiatives, there was less support for SPSSI's actions vis-à-vis U.S. foreign policy. During the 1964 APA meetings, the SPSSI council issued a press release regarding psychological aspects of foreign policy. Although the release was not published at that time, it caused APA executive officer Arthur Brayfield to inform the APA board of directors and the president of Division 9 that APA facilities could not be used in the release of the statement. Later that year, SPSSI central office did issue this news story, and in 1966 it sent out a four-page national press release from the SPSSI council commenting on American indifference to atrocities committed against the Vietnamese by the United States and its allies (*SPSSI Newsletter*, 1966a, 2).[6]

In 1967, the membership of SPSSI was polled on its attitudes toward the war in Vietnam. Finding that a majority of the membership favored either immediate or phased U.S. withdrawal, the SPSSI council issued a public statement advocating a phased withdrawal. In 1969, the SPSSI Committee on International Relations published in the *SPSSI Newsletter* (1969) an article on social science and U.S. foreign policy based on its meetings with U.S. government officials concerned with international affairs. In 1970, SPSSI published and distributed a manual titled *Canvassing for Peace: A Manual for Volunteers* (Abelson & Zimbardo, 1970). The purpose of this manual was to facilitate the work of student volunteers campaigning for peace candidates and promoting peace petitions concerning Vietnam. About 6500 copies were sold.

The APA governance was more circumspect than Division 9 with regard to the Vietnam conflict. In 1969, the APA council defeated a resolution calling for official APA participation in the October Vietnam moratorium, a nationwide protest against U.S. involvement in Vietnam. A resolution condemning the destruction of life in Indo-China was adopted by the board of directors in 1972. Responding to one of its members, the APA Council of Representatives authorized the newly formed Board of Social and Ethical Responsibility (BSERP) to investigate the possibility that American prisoners of war were being manipulated in the statement of their political opinions during their debriefings. After checking with the Department of Defense, BSERP reported in 1973 that it did not find any such cases. In 1974, the APA council passed a resolution calling for the establishment of registers of psychologists willing to counsel Vietnam veterans and their families gratis or at reduced rates. In 1975, a motion to support an amnesty resolution for Indochina war resisters was tabled by the APA council of representatives.

Committee on International Relations

In 1971, one of Division 9's longest standing committees, the Committee on International Relations, decided to focus on the roles played by decision makers and government agencies in ameliorating international conflicts. SPSSI sponsored a 2-day committee meeting at Columbia University with the director of the Arms Control and Disarmament Agency

---

[6]This was one of several SPSSI documents (including the 1946 statement by the international relations committee on psychology and atomic energy and the 1962 *SPSSI Newsletter* devoted to psychologists and peace) that are in the FBI's 24-page file on the society.

(ACDA) and members of his staff. The committee later assisted ACDA in its search for a behavioral scientist and provided the agency with a list of germane social science findings and hypotheses. Other meetings with government officials were held from 1972 to 1974 at Harvard, UCLA, and the Ohio State University. In 1976, meetings were held at New York University and at the U.N. with representatives of the U.N. Institute on Training and Research and of the International Studies Association. These meetings resulted in a proposal for a conference on cooperation between hostile parties to be held at Bellagio, Italy. The conference did not take place, and the committee was disbanded in 1977 (28 years after its establishment) when the SPSSI council decided that its focus was too narrow and its ambitions too high. (Other committees that were also dissolved at this time under criteria established by the SPSSI Committee on Committees were those on aging, coercive modes of therapy, and privacy.)

POVERTY

McGrath (1980a) used the term *poverty* to encompass class issues as well as problems of employment and poverty. SPSSI was originally organized to address employment problems of psychologists. The Johnson administration's war on poverty rekindled SPSSI interest in these issues.

Statements, Committees, and Volunteer Consultants

In 1963, near the beginning of the federal government's poverty programs, the SPSSI council issued a public statement at an APA press conference supporting national retraining and education programs for economically disadvantaged persons. They also established the Subcommittee on Poverty and Unemployment with a budget of $500. This subcommittee, and the Subcommittees on Peace and War and on Health and Mental Health, were set up to help SPSSI take more effective action. To quote President Jerome S. Bruner: "As an organization and as a conception, SPSSI is no longer an outgroup, a protest body. It is our task to crystalize the best thinking in the profession to cope with the widely ramified policy questions that affect the national well being and peace of the world" (*SPSSI Newsletter*, 1964, 5). The Subcommittee on Poverty and Unemployment was to encourage research through newsletter reports and grants-in-aid, to compile and organize findings through meetings and publications, and to communicate relevant information to policy makers through the mass media and testimony.

The subcommittee became the standing Committee on Problems of Poverty in 1964. In 1967, regional poverty committees were established. A major function of these regional committees was to monitor the costs, equitability, and effectiveness of government job training programs in their areas. SPSSI volunteers helped isolated and less affluent organizations and communities write proposals and applications for government programs, grants, and contracts. The committee compiled a roster of about 600 volunteer consultants by geographic area and substantive interest and distributed it to more than 1000 agencies in 1972. Only a few of these SPSSI volunteers were actually called on, however (*SPSSI Newsletter*, 1973, 10).

The standing committee set up subcommittees on program evaluation, values and attitudes, and communications. The subcommittee on program evaluation under Marcia Guttentag moved from its initial focus on poverty programs to assessment of a variety of social action programs. One result of their efforts was the influential *Handbook of Evaluation Research* (Guttentag & Struening, 1975) sponsored by SPSSI. The values and attitudes subcommittee contributed to a *JSI* issue on poverty dynamics and intervention (Kaplan, 1965). Two more *JSI* issues on poverty were published in 1970 (Guttentag, 1970a, 1970b).

The Social Science Information Service

A substantial number of the members on these three subcommittees were associated with federal government programs. Their work expanded under the "SPSSI as honest broker" program initiated by President Thomas F. Pettigrew in 1967. Pettigrew believed that behavioral science had "arrived" in Washington and that SPSSI was in a unique position to "maximize the service potential of the profession" (*SPSSI Newsletter*, 1967, 1). He called on the society to find new ways to serve as an honest broker between social scientists and policy makers. He suggested opening a small office in Washington to facilitate this activity. The APA was asked for assistance with funding and space for this initiative but was not able to collaborate. The SPSSI council expanded the agenda of the Poverty Committee and established a Social Science Information Service (SSIS) in Washington, DC, in 1971.

An early project of the SSIS was to provide a list of social scientists working on poverty-related topics to interested legislators and their staffs. A brochure was printed listing experts in the following areas: child development and education; crime, delinquency, and civil disorders; family relations; health and health care; poverty programs and social movements; racial and ethnic minorities; and training, employment, and economic behavior. Ruth Ray was hired as a part-time congressional liaison representative (CLR) to contact members of Congress and their committees in these areas. The brochure noted that SPSSI was not advocating or promoting any particular legislation but only informing legislators about the likely implications of various legislative proposals. The society offered to provide consultants, conduct literature reviews and original research, and identify likely implications of various bills. The experts recommended by the SSIS were to speak for themselves, not for SPSSI.

In 1972, Marjorie Hemmendinger succeeded Ruth Ray as CLR. She mailed letters to more than 80 professional social science organizations advising them of the SSIS and its activities. She later reported to SSIS and the Poverty Committee that "the whole concept of an honest broker is new enough to cause surprise and in some cases skepticism both on the Hill and in the professions" (Memo from Hemmendinger to Oliver Moles, chair of SPSSI, 1972). A disappointing response to a January 1973 mailing to all the new members of Congress was partially attributed to a change in the political climate after the Nixon reelection. An earlier mailing to heads of congressional committees and subcommittees had gotten more responses. In 1973, Lois Van Valkenburgh became the CLR, working 1 to 1 1/2 days per week, 10 1/2 months per year.

Highlights of SSIS's activities in 1973 included arrangement of oral testimony on a bill on runaway youths, collection of comments on pending national health insurance bills, and written testimony on programs for the aging. The Poverty Committee kept in touch with the APA, American Sociological Association (ASA), American Association for Public Opinion Research (AAPOR), and the newly established Association for the Advancement of Psychology (AAP). (SPSSI was a corporate member of AAP, the lobby group for the APA, and several Division 9 members served on its first board of directors.) In 1974, the SSIS became a separate committee of SPSSI and the Poverty Committee was phased out. This new committee was authorized to serve all other SPSSI committees (as needed), with Washington, DC, members of the other committees joining an SSIS steering committee whenever possible. The steering committee met quarterly and included representatives from the APA, ASA, and AAPOR.

In 1975, SSIS recruited experts in unemployment, education, family and child services, aging, health service delivery, privacy, prison standards, migrants, and the social impact of the energy crisis. Meetings were held with the General Accounting Office, Common Cause, the executive director of the ASA and their specialist for minorities and women, the administrator of the congressional fellows program for the AAAS, the head of the Science and Technology Division of the Library of Congress, the staff of the APA, and congressional staff aides. It was noted in the *SPSSI Newsletter* (1975) that over the previous 4 years the service had presented information to Congress on aging, nutrition, national health insurance, work satisfaction, juvenile delinquency, family and child services, coercive therapy in prisons, and runaway youths.

In 1976, there was an intensive effort by SSIS to locate and disseminate information on the social and psychological effects of unemployment and noneconomic effects of the national recession. This information was well received by Congress. The committee reported, however, that it could only have a marginal effect on the legislative process without greater resources. SPSSI sought $30,000 in foundation support for the SSIS to hire a half-time professional director and increase the CLR to full-time. A proposal drafted by the SSIS was sent to 11 foundations, but it was not successful. The SPSSI council decided that it was not productive to continue the SSIS without these additional resources. A subcommittee was appointed to develop SSIS services at the state and local levels, but by 1977, SPSSI's effort to serve as an honest broker had ended.

UNDERREPRESENTED GROUPS

About this time more women and minority group members were elected as SPSSI officers. Thirteen of the last 19 Division 9 presidents have been women (see Table 2) and two have come from ethnic minorities (Katz, 1991). This trend also applies to the gender and ethnic make up of the SPSSI council (Unger, 1986). As minority group members became more active in Division 9 governance, the division began to reach out to other minority groups of psychologists.

The Association of Black Psychologists and the Black Students Psychological Association

In 1969, SPSSI and the Association of Black Psychologists (ABP) worked with CAFCOE to ensure that more African American psychologists were placed on various APA committees and the APA Committee on Equality of Opportunity was formed. One of its early recommendations was that lecturers interested in social issues be invited to Black colleges as part of the APA's visiting scientist program. Division 9 wrote the APA board of directors supporting this recommendation as well as other ABP requests such as a conference on graduate education and the establishment of a committee to study the misuse of psychological tests with Black youths. The APA board of directors was unresponsive to these requests, although they did sponsor a conference on the recruitment of Black and other minority students and faculty (Smith, 1992).

SPSSI encouraged ABP members to join Division 9 and donated sets of SPSSI-sponsored books and *JSI* subscriptions to predominantly Black colleges. As mentioned earlier, regional and state associations were required by CAFCOE to establish affirmative action programs for their governance positions in 1972. SPSSI also wrote professional social science journals urging them to adopt affirmative action plans in their appointments of editors and editorial boards.

The Black Students Psychological Association (BSPA) was formed in 1969 in response to the negative manner in which psychology had presented itself in the Black community. With travel funds from SPSSI, Black students attended the Western Psychological Association meetings that year to present papers. In 1970, the BSPA, plus the Association of Women Psychologists and the Association of Psychologists for La Raza, were given program time by Division 9 at the APA convention in Miami Beach. In 1972, SPSSI helped fund the BSPA's national convention in New York and wrote letters to departments of psychology requesting that financial aid for the continued education of Black students who were in good academic standing be established.

The Association for Women in Psychology

The Association for Women in Psychology (AWP) was established to address the restricted roles of women in psychology. (Founders of the AWP had protested discrimination against women at the 1969 APA placement bureau.) The SPSSI council voted to support in principle about 50 resolutions submitted to the APA board of directors by the AWP. In 1970, the APA council passed AWP resolutions to delete full-time employment as a qualification for APA associate membership and to provide child care facilities at the 1971 APA meetings, paid for from registration fees. It defeated resolutions on discrimination in convention placement service, financial support, and office space for AWP, and more committee representation for women. Division 9 sponsored a resolution calling on the APA council to examine ways for disenfranchised members, students, and interest groups in psychology to be better represented. It also supported resolutions on abortion as a civil right (1969), discrimination by social class in educational and employment opportunities in psychology (1974), and the Equal Rights Amendment (1975).

SPSSI Committees on Underrepresented Groups

The SPSSI council formed committees on sex discrimination in psychology, Native American social action, and underrepresented groups, and recommended that special interest organizations like AWP and ABP be given special consideration in the society's elections, the filling of vacant SPSSI council positions, and attendance at council meetings as nonvoting participants with expenses paid by SPSSI. Representatives from under-represented groups attended the SPSSI council meetings from 1970 to 1974. SPSSI helped subsidize the activities of these underrepresented groups during their early years. For example, in 1970, the society's budget included $6600 in contributions to these groups. In 1972, the SPSSI council donated $1200 to La Junta de Sociologos Chicanos for the establishment of a national Chicano social science association. In 1974, $250 was given to the Association of Asian-American Psychologists to help with the circulation of their newsletter.

The Board on Social and Ethical Responsibility in Psychology

In 1971 and 1972, at the suggestion of Division 9's Committee on Social Responsibility and APA president Kenneth Clark, the APA established first the Committee and then the Board on Social and Ethical Responsibility in Psychology (BSERP). This board was charged with addressing the concerns of underrepresented groups such as African Americans, women, and gay men and lesbians. A full-time staff position was created at the APA headquarters to facilitate the activities of this board. Many of the people working on and with this board, including the APA staff officers, have been Division 9 members. Most of the resolutions on social issues that have come before the APA council of representatives in the past 20 years have been sponsored by this board (Smith, 1992). More recently, Committees on Ethnic Minority Affairs; Women in Psychology; Lesbian and Gay Concerns; Disability Issues in Psychology; and Children, Youth, and Families were established by the APA and then placed under their Public Interest Directorate formed in 1987. Full-time staff positions have been created to monitor women's programs and ethnic minority affairs.

Division 9 and Other APA Divisions and Boards

In 1973, a new division was added to the APA roster—Division 35, Psychology of Women (Mednick & Urbanski, 1991; see also chapter 8, this volume). This was the first of four divisions that have evolved from Division 9 activities and programs. In 1985, the Society for the Psychological Study of Lesbian and Gay Issues became Division 44 of the APA, and in 1987, the Society for the Psychological Study of Ethnic Minority Issues became Division 45. In 1979, at Division 9's recommendation to the APA council, the Board of Ethnic Minority Affairs (BEMA) was created from the APA's ad hoc Committee on Cultural and Ethnic Affairs (Smith, 1992). In 1990, BEMA and BSERP were united into the Board for the Advancement of the Public Interest in Psychology (so that the new Public Interest Directorate had a single board). Also in 1990, Division 48, Peace Psychology, another SPSSI off-spring, was established.

SPSSI'S MIDLIFE CRISIS

In a newsletter article (*SPSSI Newsletter*, 1977), President Lawrence Wrightsman wrote about SPSSI's midlife crisis. He was referring to financial problems that led to SPSSI's suspension of funding for the grants-in-aid program in 1970 and 1974, the skipping of the 1975 midwinter meeting, and the reduction in funding for SPSSI committees and interest groups. As causes of this crisis he mentioned the reductions in federal funding of social science research, fewer academic and research positions, inflation, and a general spirit of apathy and pessimism in the United States. In this crisis, as in 1956 when the SPSSI council set up a committee to ascertain "What has happened to SPSSI?," Division 9 leadership developed procedures to get more of the membership involved in the society.

Regional Groups and Self Surveys

In 1956, regional groups were formed in 11 cities; in 1977, they were established in 31.[7] A survey of the members' interests and concerns with regard to SPSSI and social issues was conducted in 1956; two more were done in 1977 to 1978. The 1956 (219 responses) and one of the 1977 to 1978 (608 responses) surveys found that about 90% of the respondents felt that SPSSI differs from the APA in its greater concern with "social action and social value orientation." The majority of the respondents did not want the organization to avoid controversy or to separate the conduct of science from the application of science. (In 1977, 80% said that SPSSI should be involved in making policy recommendations and lobbying.) Most respondents were inactive rather than active supporters of SPSSI activities. They said they would miss the publications most if the society were to dissolve. The social issues in which they were interested ranged over a variety of topics. The top ten topics listed in these two surveys are presented in Table 3 plus a similar list compiled in 1987 by central office from the answers to an open-ended question on a membership census (800 responses).

---

[7]The first local SPSSI groups began in 1949. None of these groups continued for very long (*SPSSI Newsletter*, 1977). Another effort was made by SPSSI council in 1984 to set up regional groups. Eleven groups were formed with the specific tasks of increasing SPSSI's impact, the number and commitment of its members, and revitalizing the organizational structure. A regional group coordinator was appointed to oversee this initiative. The New York City and Los Angeles groups continued to meet until 1994 (*SPSSI Newsletter*, 1989, 1990, 1993b).

TABLE 3
Significant Social Issues Mentioned in 1956, 1977, and 1986

1956–1959 (APA Meetings)	1977 (Membership Survey)
Juvenile delinquency	Freedom of speech
Education	Racism
Drugs	Energy conservation
Population control	Sexism
Leisure	Environmental protection
Mental health	Unemployment
The "Ugly American"	Crime prevention
Space exploration	Child abuse
Foundation grants and research	Health care
The "Cold War"	Arms race

1986 (Membership Survey)

International conflict
Civil rights and liberties
Health and safety
Children, youth and families
Human rights
Women's rights
Minority rights
Poverty and unemployment
Education
Aging

Work Groups, Core Groups, and Task Forces

Another strategy for involving the membership in SPSSI and Division 9 activities was to change and expand the structure and functioning of the society's committees. As a result of the 1956 self study, the SPSSI council voted in 1958 to support the activities of local, problem-centered work groups that would lay the ground work for sound, socially important research (*SPSSI Newsletter*, 1958). In some cases, standing SPSSI committees (like that on desegregation) functioned as local work groups, maintaining national contacts through correspondence. Members of the SPSSI council were designated to serve as liaisons to these work groups, and $1500 was allocated to the grants-in-aid fund to support work group projects.

In 1960, the SPSSI council decided to form core groups of members around specific social issues taken from the list of important social issues suggested by the members in 1956 (see Table 3). These core groups were added to the work groups already formed to address desegregation, international relations, man-in-space, psychological testing, cross-national research, and education. However, it was hard to find chairs for the core groups and the work groups did not increase the participation of the membership in the activities of the society as hoped. The SPSSI council decided that although these groups did well in facilitating SPSSI activities on an as-needed basis, they could not initiate such activities or maintain themselves without full-time staff support and budget.[8]

The SPSSI council discussions in 1963 led to the establishment of the three subcommittees on war and peace, poverty, and mental health. In 1976, during SPSSI's midlife crisis, the SPSSI council reorganized the descendants of these subcommittees. These subcommittees were either dissolved or reconstituted as task forces with specific goals and time frames. Members with ideas for new task forces were asked to send proposals stating their goals to the Committee on Committees. Ideas for goals were listed in the newsletter (*SPSSI Newsletter*, 1976, 3). From 1977 until the present, a wide range of task forces has been established by the SPSSI council and the membership (see Table 4 for a listing of most of these SPSSI subgroups).

Ties With Other Organizations

The division also established more and closer ties in the late 1970s with other policy organizations such as the Policy Studies Organization and the AAP, 7 of whose 22 board members, including the chair, were SPSSI members. Over the years, SPSSI learned that links with other organizations were most effective when made informally through members. More formal associations such as those with the Society for the Study of Social Problems in the 1950s (see Lee, 1986) and with the Evaluation Research Society (ERS) in the 1970s, have had problems. For example, without consultation, the ERS listed all the SPSSI council members as founders of their organization.

PUBLICATIONS

SPSSI has been involved in publishing books, articles, monographs, and journals since its early years. These publications provide an outlet for members' documents, a means of reaching the public, and a source of revenue for the society.

Books

SPSSI members have produced a variety of books for both students and professionals interested in social issues. These books have been published by different commercial and university publishers with all of the royalties

---

[8]Later efforts to do in-depth analyses of social issues leading to policy (1977), develop white papers on significant social issues (1982), and redefine SPSSI's mission (1982) also were aborted due to lack of volunteers and an unfamiliarity with the policy process.

TABLE 4
SPSSI Committees, Core Groups, Subcommittees, and Task Forces
1945 to 1996

Dates	Name
	Committees
1945–	Membership (Participation)
1945–	Program
1945–	Elections
1945–1953	Labor and Management
1945–1953	Editorial
1947–1950	International Studies
1948–1953	Intergroup Relations
1948–1950	Atomic Education
1949–1950	Teaching of Social Psychology
1949–1976	International Relations
1951–1953, 1974–1978	On the Function of SPSSI Committees
1951–1959	Program Emphasis
1960	Administrative
1949–1957, 1970–1974	Civil Liberties and Academic Freedom
1953–1959	Methods of Group Consultation
1954	New Members
1952–1954	Anti–Intellectualism
1954–1955	Use of Social Science Knowledge in Medicine
1954–1955	Use of Social Science in Social Work
1954–	Publications
1954–1955	Witness Performance Under Pressure
1955–1962	Cross National Research
1956–1962	Desegregation and Integration in Schools
1958–1962	Men in Space
1956–1957	APA Policy Revision
1956–1957	SPSSI Self–Study
1958–1960	Ethics
1958	Values
1958–1963	Education
1959–1964	Uses and Abuses of Ability Testing
1960–1969	Publications Negotiations
1963–1965	JSI Exchange List
1964–1965	Equal Opportunity
1964–1974, 1987	Poverty
1965–1968	Population Problems
1966–1967	Psychological Aspects of Long Range Planning
1966	Intersocietal
1967–1970	Civil Rights Activities (and Movement)
1967–1970	Travel Funds, Observation of Civil Rights Events
1968–1972, 1980–	Fellows (Nominating)
1969	Coordination of Social Policy
1969–1972	Population
1970–1975	Teaching of Social Issues
1970–1977	Invasion of Privacy
1970–1975	Sex Discrimination in Psychology
1970–1973	Social Responsibility
1970	Foundations

(continued)

TABLE 4
(continued)

Dates	Name
	Committees
1970	Educational Opportunity
1970	Graduate Education
1970–1990	Racism
1970–1972	Drugs
1970–1975	Police Community Relations
1970–1972	Public Organizations
1971–1975	Academic Renewal
1971–1975	Native American Action
1972	The New Assault on Equality
1972–1975	Socialization and the Law
1972–1977, 1986	Aging
1973–1977	Coercive Modes of Therapy
1973–1975	Rights of Children
1973–1974	Integration in Housing
1973–1974	Sino–American Exchange and Relations
1974	Underrepresented Groups
1974–1977	Social Science Information Service
1975	Courts
1978–	Courtwatch
1979	Social Policy Studies
1980–1981	Social Issues in Mental Health Policy
1981	Youth
1981–1982	Future
1981–1995	Continuing Education
1981–1989	The Media (Coverage of Social Issues)
1983–	Public Policy Fellow Oversight
1986–1987	Long Range Planning
1987–1988	Sexism
1987–1991	Children and Social Issues
1987	Women in Psychology
1987–1991	Gay and Lesbian Concerns
1987–	Continuing Education
1987–1989	Expert Bank
1988–1991	Speakers Bureau
1990–1992	James Marshall Investment Fund
1990	Social Action Intern
1990–1991	Organize a Mentoring Program
1993–	U.N. and International Interests
	Ad Hoc Committees
1954	Scientific Freedom
1959–1963	Role of Psychologists in International Affairs
1983–1987	Public Information
1984–1986	50th Anniversary
1985–1986	Public Policy Job Placement
1985–1986	Public Policy Networks
1986–1989	Social Issues Conference

Dates	Name
	Core Groups [Hard to Find Chairs, $100]
1961–1962	Social Science Research in Cultural Exchange
1961–1962	Social Aspects of Drug Addiction
1961–1964	Psychological Aspects of Arms Control and Disarmament
1961–1965	Psychological Implications of Increasing Population
1961–1965	Problems of Youth
1961–1963	Social Issues in Education
	Subcommittees [$500]
1963–1965	Poverty and Unemployment
1963–1966, 1984–1992	War and Peace
1963–1966	Health and Mental Health
	Task Forces
1977	Productivity in the Public Sector
1977	Code Authority National Association of Broadcasters
1977–1982	Academic Freedom
1978–1980	Social Psychology and Social Work
1978–1982	Sexual Orientation and Civil Liberties
1979–1980	Meaning of Social Issues
1983–1986	SPSSI History
1983–1984	Advocacy
1985–1986	Homeless
1987	Nuclear Winter
1987–1988	Separating from the APA
1987–1989	Social Issues and Health Technology
1987–1995	Organizational Structure of Central Office
1988–1991	International Issues and the U.N.
1989–1991	Health Policy
1991–1995	Grass Roots Initiatives
1991–1992	Scientific Concepts of Race
1992–1995	Medial Referral
1992–1995	Legislative Link
1992–1996	Electronic Communications
1993–1994	Activism, Education & Training, Research, Dissemination
1993–1995	Conflict of Interest
1993–	Major Gifts and Bequests
1993–	Electronic Journal Publications
1993–	Outstanding Service to SPSSI
1994–1995	Congressional Site Visit Planning
1994–1996	Theme Conference
1994–1996	Midyear Convention
1994–	Nonthematic Journal Publication
1994–	Scientist in the Public Interest Oversight
1994–	Federal Public Policy Liaison Oversight
1994–	Public Policy Task Force
1995	Rural Issues
1996	Investments
1996	JSI Contract Negotiation

Note. The core groups and subcommittees were allocated the money indicated to help them organize.

TABLE 5
A Listing of SPSSI-Sponsored Books

Date	Editors/Authors	Title
1939	Hartmann & Newcomb	*Industrial Conflict: A Psychological Interpretation*
1942	Watson	*Civilian Morale*
1945	Murphy	*Human Nature and Enduring Peace*
1947	Newcomb & Hartley	*Readings in Social Psychology*
1950	Kornhauser	*Psychology of Larbor-Management Relations*
1951	Jahoda, Deutsch, & Cook	*Research Methods in Social Relations*
1952	Swanson, Newcomb, & Hartley	*Readings in Social Psychology* (2nd ed.)
1954	Katz	*Public Opinion and Propaganda*
1954	Kornhauser, Dubin, & Ross	*Industrial Conflict*
1958	Maccoby, Newcomb, & Hartley	*Readings in Social Psychology* (3rd ed.)
1959	Selltiz, Jahoda, Deutsch, & Cook	*Research Methods in Social Relations* (2nd ed.)
1962	Sanford	*American College*
1963	Charters & Gage	*Readings in the Social Psychology of Education*
1965	Kelman	*International Behavior*
1965	Proshansky & Seidenberg	*Basic Studies in Social Psychology*
1965	Steiner & Fishbein	*Current Studies in Social Psychology*
1968	Deutsch, Katz, & Jensen	*Social Class, Race and Psychological Development*
1970	Abelson & Zimbardo	*Canvassing for Peace: A Manual for Volunteers*
1970	Wechsler, Solomon, & Kramer	*Social Psychology and Mental Health*
1972	McClintock	*Experimental Social Psychology*
1975	Mednick, Tangri, & Hoffman	*Women and Achievement*
1975	Struening & Guttentag	*Handbook of Evaluation Research*
1976	Katz	*Towards the Elimination of Racism*
1976	Koocher	*Children's Rights and the Mental Health Professions*
1976	Selltiz, Wrightsman, & Cook	*Research Methods in Social Relations* (3rd ed.)
1976	Tobach & Proshansky	*Genetic Destiny: Race as a Scientific and Social Controversy*
1977	Tapp & Levine	*Law, Justice and the Individual in Society*
1978	Wispe	*Altruism, Sympathy and Helping Behavior*
1979	Frieze, Bar-tal, & Carroll	*New Approaches to Social Problems: Applications of Attribution Theory*
1980	Levinger & Moles	*Divorce and Separation*
1980	Bickman (1980–1983) Oskamp (1984–1988)	*Applied Social Psychology Annual* (Vols. 1–8)
1981	Kidder	*Research Methods in Social Relations* (4th ed.)
1981	Rubin	*The Dynamics of Third Party Intervention: Kissinger in the Middle East*
1982	Paul, Weinrich, Gonsiorek, & Hofvedt	*Homosexuality: Social, Psychological and Biological Issues*

Date	Editors/Authors	Title
1983	Evans	*Environmental Stress*
1983	Friedman & DiMatteo	*Interpersonal Issues in Health Care*
1983	Perlman & Cozby	*Social Psychology*
1983	Struening & Brewer	*Handbook of Evaluation Research* (university ed.)
1984	Miller & Brewer	*Groups in Contact: The Psychology of Desegregation*
1985	Gilbert	*Men in Dual-Career Families*
1985	Safir, Mednick, Izraeli, & Bernard	*Women's World: The New Scholarship*
1986	Kidder & Judd	*Research Methods in Social Relations* (5th ed.)
1986	Seidman & Rappoport	*Redefining Social Problems*
1986	White	*Psychology and the Prevention of Nuclear War*
1987	Zanna & Darley	*The Compleat Academic: A Practical Guide for the Beginning Social Scientist*
1988	Kellerman & Rubin	*Leadership and Negotiation in the Middle East*
1988	Fine & Asch	*Women With Disabilities: Essays in Psychology, Culture, and Politics*
1989	Katz & Taylor	*Eliminating Racism: Profiles in Controversy*
1989	Unger	*Representations: Social Constructions of Gender*
1989	Blanchard & Crosby	*Affirmative Action in Perspective*
1990	Edwards, Tindale, Heath, & Posavac	*Social Influence Processes and Prevention*
1990	Murphy	*Gardner Murphy: Integrating, Expanding, and Humanizing Psychology*
1991	Robinson, Shaver, & Wrightsman	*Measures of Personality and Social Psychological Attitudes*
1991	Judd, Smith, & Kidder	*Research Methods in Social Relations* (6th ed.)
1991	Gonsoriek & Weinrich	*Homosexuality: Research Implications for Public Policy*
1991	Barron & Graziano	*Social Psychology*
1992	Bercovitch & Rubin	*Mediation in International Relations: Multiple Approaches to Conflict Management*
1992	Bryant, Edwards, Tindale, Posavac, Heath, Henderson, & Suarez-Balcazar	*Methodological Issues in Applied Social Psychology*
1992	Clayton & Crosby	*Justice, Gender, and Affirmative Action*
1992	Fine	*Disruptive Voices: The Possibilities of Feminist Research*
1993	Stroebe, Stroebe, & Hanson	*Handbook of Bereavement*
1993	Oskamp	*Gender Issues in Contemporary Society*
1994	Heath, Tindale, Edwards, Posavac, Bryant, Henderson-King, Suarez-Balcazar, & Myers	*Applications of Heuristics and Biases to Social Issues*
1995	Bunker & Rubin	*Conflict, Cooperation, and Justice: Essays Inspired by the Work of Morton Deutsch*
1996	Kagawa-Singer, Katz, Taylor, & Vanderryn	*Health Issues for Minority Adolescents*

going to the society. SPSSI has sponsored 76 books, including 63 new books, 9 revisions of existing books, 3 study guides, and a three-volume work in Spanish. More than half of these books have been published since 1980 (see Table 5).

The largest number of these books (22) have been oriented toward students. It has been said that SPSSI "helped define as well as legitimate social psychology" in the United States through these publications (Perlman, 1986, 110). The second major topic has been war and peace and international relations with ten volumes. Eight volumes have focused on women, six on racial issues, and four on industrial relations. To date more than 100 members have served as editors or authors. Most of the books are edited volumes. Perlman (1986) estimated that the cumulative book royalties from the late 1940s to the end of 1986 (in current dollars) were more than $2.8 million, more than half of which came from the first five editions of *Research Methods in Social Relations*. He noted that "SPSSI has been able to engage in many activities not practical for other APA Divisions primarily because of these royalties" (Perlman, 1986, 111).

The Journal of Social Issues

In his overview of SPSSI's publication history, Perlman (1986) pointed out that SPSSI has been involved in publishing books and journals focused on politically and socially sensitive topics since 1939. SPSSI's early hopes of influencing the general public through its publications have not been fulfilled, however, with the possible exception of a few issues of the *JSI* such as the 1953 volume on desegregation (Clark, 1953). Nevertheless, a citation analysis of the *JSI* shows that the society's journal publications have clearly had an impact on social scientists. The *Social Science Citation Index* ranked the *JSI* sixth of 31 social issues journals and eighth of 26 social psychology journals in terms of citation impact in 1990.

In 1994, the *JSI* generated 55% of the society's income. The *JSI* is an important part of SPSSI's identity, an outlet for publication, and a seminal source of information, helping social scientists to better understand social issues. McGrath (1980b) provided a historical perspective of the journal's first 36 years that was brought up to date by Perlman (1986, 1995) on SPSSI's 50th and again on the *JSI*'s 50th anniversary. A listing of the *JSI* editors appears at Table 6.

GIVING SPSSI AWAY

In 1969, President George Miller exhorted the members of the APA to "give psychology away" (Miller, 1969). SPSSI took his message to heart.

TABLE 6
Editors of the Journal of Social Issues

Year	Editor
1945–1950	Ronald Lippitt
1949	Harold H. Kelley[a]
1951–1955	M. Brewster Smith
1955–1959	John Harding
1960–1965	Robert Chin
1963	Leonard Solomon[a]
1966–1969	Joshua Fishman
1970–1974	Bertram H. Raven
1974–1978	Jacqueline D. Goodchilds
1979–1983	Joseph E. McGrath
1983–1987	George Levinger
1988–1992	Stuart Oskamp
1992–1997	Daniel Perlman
1997–2000	Phyllis A. Katz

[a] Acting editor.

Over the past 25 years, the society has established several programs offering no-cost consultation to organizations and groups in need of such services.

SPEAKER'S BUREAU AND EXPERT BANK

The first formal pro bono effort was the Volunteer Consultants Program established by the Poverty Committee in 1972. As noted previously, a roster of 600 volunteers was compiled and sent to 100 agencies, but there was little demand for their services. In 1979, the SPSSI council set up a speaker's bureau with 129 volunteers willing to speak to groups on important social issues. Speakers agreed to travel up to 200 miles and to give any honoraria they received to SPSSI. There were 80 requests for speakers that year. In 1980, there were 155 volunteers (categorized by region and topics) and 366 requests. By 1982, it was reported in the newsletter that "requests for speakers have been light" and there were few new volunteers (*SPSSI Newsletter*, 1982, 4). In 1984, it was noted that more than 200 SPSSI members had been on the roster and a total of more than 500 requests for speakers had been received, most of which came from colleges (*SPSSI Newsletter*, 1984). In 1986, fewer than a dozen requests for speakers were received (*SPSSI Newsletter*, 1987b, 10), but in 1988 (*SPSSI Newsletter*, 1988, 18), there were 56 requests and a Speakers Bureau Committee was formed.

There was an effort to establish an expert roster to assist with AAP programs in 1979, but few SPSSI members volunteered. In 1987, the speaker's bureau was converted into an expert bank that was to serve the needs of the media and the Public Interest Office of the APA. The expert bank was abandoned in 1989, due to a lack of requests for experts. The speaker's bureau and its committee ended in 1991. A media referral task force was created in 1992 to identify SPSSI researchers who might serve as commentators to the media.

A U.N. Nongovernmental Organization

Since 1992, Division 9 members wishing to volunteer information or services domestically have been directed by the media referral task force to the APA's media referral service. On the international side, in 1993, Division 9's Committee on the U.N. and International Issues, chaired by Hedwin Niemark, compiled and distributed a roster of 93 SPSSI volunteers with skills in international issues to all the U.N. missions and 300 of the U.N.'s departments and agencies. Interviews with U.N. personnel about this roster indicate that, as with SPSSI's domestic volunteer efforts, there has been little demand for the pro bono services of SPSSI's experts.

Since 1987, SPSSI has, however, been successful in influencing the U.N. as a nongovernmental organization (NGO) with consultative status. As a result of materials prepared by SPSSI's U.N. representatives, language in a number of official documents has been changed or supplemented. In 1989, the APA council approved a resolution on children's rights drafted by one of SPSSI's NGO representatives. A SPSSI-organized coalition of NGOs provided support for the Seville Statement on Violence, which set the stage for the formation of the UNESCO Culture of Peace Programmme, of which Division 9 member, David Adams, is senior programme specialist (*SPSSI Newsletter*, 1996, 16).[9]

Since 1987, SPSSI has had from one to five NGO representatives at the U.N. All but one APA convention since 1989 has had a Division 9-sponsored U.N. program, featuring eminent international figures. U.N. ambassadors and officials have met and collaborated with APA members and officers through these Division 9 activities. (The APA does not have NGO status at the U.N.)

Public Policy Fellows

In the April 1982 newsletter, SPSSI advertised for a public policy fellow (PPF) to work with the APA, AAP, and other professional associations in Washington, DC, on policy analysis and legislative activities. I was selected

---

[9] See the *SPSSI Newsletter* (1987a) for a comparison of the Seville Statement and the psychologists' manifesto from 1945.

TABLE 7
Public Policy Fellows

Years	Name	Policy Issues
1983–1986	Paul Kimmel	U.S. Institute of Peace
1987–1989	Gregory Wilmoth	Teen pregnancy, invasion of privacy
1989–1990	Melissa Warren	Homelessness
1990–1991	Allison Rosenberg	Homeless children
1991–1992	Lisa Goodman	Violence against women
1992–1994	Susan Limber	Child maltreatment
1994–1995	Tammy Mann	Rights of the child
1995–1996	Marisa Reddy	Psychology and the law

as the first PPF and began working full-time in the Office of Public Affairs at the APA in January 1983. Working with an oversight committee from Division 9, we established an association that allowed the PPFs to work on SPSSI issues, APA policy work, and their own legislative programs. My personal interest was in the establishment of the U.S. Institute of Peace (USIP), which had been endorsed by SPSSI and then the APA council in 1980. Working with SPSSI, the APA, the AAP, the ASA, and other professional associations, we generated a grassroots and expert testimony campaign that assisted with the passage of the USIP legislation in 1984.

The APA board of directors was concerned that the association's sponsorship of a fellow for only one division was inequitable, so SPSSI moved the position to the AAP in 1985. I remained as PPF until March 1986, working on implementation of the USIP legislation, providing press releases for SPSSI programs and publications, speaking at meetings, writing a newsletter column and professional articles, and supporting some AAP legislative initiatives. The second PPF, Gregory Wilmoth, found a home in the Public Interest Directorate established by the APA in 1987. There he worked with the APA legislative office on his own, SPSSI's, and APA's social issues. The eight Division 9 PPFs are listed in Table 7 with their major legislative interests and dates of tenure. This program is currently funded by the James Marshall Foundation through Division 9, with space and fringe benefits provided by the APA.

Public Policy Interns and SAGES

In 1987, SPSSI's Public Policy Internship Committee selected the first interns to receive grants of $1500 to help local advocacy organizations accomplish their goals. These three young scholars engaged in research and evaluations that contributed to the intervention programs of their sponsor–supervisors, participated in APA convention programs, and shared

TABLE 8
SPSSI/Division 9 Awards and Grants

Dates	Name
1947–1954	Edward L. Bernays
1948–[a]	Kurt Lewin Memorial
1956–[b]	Grants-in-Aid
1968–	Gordon Allport Intergroup Relations
1983–	Clara Mayo Memorial
1990–	Otto Klineberg Memorial
1991–	Applied Social Issues Internship
1993–	Social Issues Dissertation
1993–	Robert Chin Memorial
1994–	SAGES Program
1994–	Outstanding Service
1995–	Louise Kidder Early Career

[a] Except 1955
[b] Except 1970 and 1974.

their experiences with other interns and SPSSI members. Since 1987, 25 interns have fostered community-based public interest advocacy and activism with the help of SPSSI Applied Social Issues Intern Awards.

In 1994, the first SPSSI Action Grant for Experienced Scholars (SAGES) was awarded. These grants of as much as $2000 encourage intervention, nonpartisan advocacy, and public policy implementation projects by retired social scientists over the age of 60. Their projects are undertaken in cooperation with organizations at any level—local to federal—with universities and colleges worldwide or with the U.N. To date, four action grants have been given to senior researchers.

Other Awards

In addition to these applied social issues activities, Division 9 also sponsors a variety of competitive awards, most in the memory of past members (see Table 8).

In 1947, the Edward L. Bernays' Atomic Energy Award was offered by SPSSI for the best research on the social implications of atomic energy. A SPSSI committee issued a public statement on atomic energy at the request of several groups of atomic scientists. This first Division 9 award was continued until 1954 (no awards were given in 1950 and 1953) to stimulate research on a series of different topics proposed by Bernays.[10] In 1948, the first Kurt Lewin Memorial Award was presented. Named after

---

[10] The Bernays' Foundation later provided a $1000 award for a book published in 1973–1974 that most effectively applied in-depth psychological analyses to an important social issue.

one of the founders and chairmen of SPSSI, this prestigious award has been presented annually (with the exception of 1955) for "outstanding contributions to the development and integration of psychological research and social action."

The Gordon Allport Intergroup Relations Prize was established in 1968 to honor the division's eighth chairman. Currently supported by the David and Carol Myers' Foundation and a Memorial Fund at Harvard University, $1000 is awarded annually to the best paper or article on intergroup relations. In 1976, SPSSI supervised a social issues dissertation award offered by *Psychology Today*. In 1980, student dissertations on social issues were added to the types of research supported by grants-in-aid. In 1983, a special grants-in-aid program on racism, sexism, and nonverbal communication was established in memory of President Clara Mayo. The funds for this program were increased to $60,000 by her parents' estate in 1995.

The Otto Klineberg Intercultural and International Relations Award honors the society's executive secretary and chairman by awarding $1000 each year to the best paper or article on Klineberg's favorite topics. It was established in 1990. In 1993, a fund was established by John Cheney to honor Robert Chin, Division 9's 34th president. This $1000 award supports research and scholarship on child abuse. Also in 1993, SPSSI established the Social Issues Dissertation Award for doctoral dissertations in psychology that display scientific excellence and potential application to social problems. A first and second prize are awarded annually.

The Louise Kidder Early Career Award, begun in 1995, is named for one of SPSSI's recent awardees for Outstanding Service to the Society. Five hundred dollars is given annually to a social issues researcher who has made a substantial contribution to the field within 5 years of receiving his or her graduate degree. None of the SPSSI monetary awards require the nominees to be current members of the society. However, the nonmonetary, Outstanding Service to SPSSI awards, established in 1993, obviously go only to society members.

Theme Conferences

In 1986, SPSSI put on its first national theme conference (television as a social issue) in New York City. The second social issues conference (computers and social issues) was held in Chattanooga, Tennessee, in 1989. The third (health technology and public policy) took place in Washington, DC, in 1992. These conferences bring together scholars and policy makers involved with a common social issue for formal and informal discussions. Since 1994, Division 9 has been offering $10,000 awards for the development, implementation, and formal evaluation of national-level, SPSSI-sponsored theme conferences consistent with the society's goals and objectives. These theme conferences are to expand the dissemination of research findings on critical social issues. In 1995, two research workshops (psychological thriving and the changing role of people at work) were sponsored by SPSSI to support social science researchers on policy issues in the discussion of their current needs. Awards of $2000 to $4000 are available to support such workshops.

DIVISION 9 TODAY

With more resources than ever before, SPSSI and Division 9 are consolidating their past activities through the addition of an official historian and looking to the future through a series of new initiatives.

Continuing Education, Clearinghouses, and Liaisons

In 1987, Division 9 was granted full APA approval to sponsor continuing education programs. Two SPSSI-sponsored programs in applied psychology held at Claremont College in California in 1993 and 1994 granted continuing education credit. In 1991 and 1992, the SPSSI council again reorganized its committee structure. Former task forces in the areas of children, youth, and families; lesbian and gay issues; racism; sexism; and AIDS/HIV issues were transformed into clearinghouses with topic coordinators to facilitate the flow of information to and from the society. A grassroots task force (1991–1995) was formed to enhance communication on social issues among social scientists and people involved in grassroots organizing. A public policy task force (1994) arranges activities to provide information to policy makers about psychological research with policy implications, and a federal public policy liaison task force (1994) plans meetings between SPSSI volunteer retirees and the federal policy community. A number of liaisons to associated organizations were established, including APA Divisions 27 (Society for Community Research and Action), 41 (American Psychology–Law Society), and 48 (Peace Psychology), plus several APA boards and committees, the APS, the InterAmerican Society of Psychology, and the American Association of Applied and Preventative Psychology.

Electronic Communications, Archives, and International Conferences

Task forces on electronic communications (1992) and nonthematic journal publications (1994) are facilitating communications among members and organizing an electronic journal.

Four task forces were established at the 1993 midwinter SPSSI council meeting to examine current society procedures and develop new programs within activism, education and training, research, and dissemination (*SPSSI Newsletter*, 1993a). An official SPSSI historian was added in 1993, and all of the division's historical documents were taken from the central office to the Archives of History of American Psychology in Akron, Ohio, in 1994. The Division 9 bylaws and administrative handbook were updated in 1994. During the summer of 1994, SPSSI members took part in symposia and publicized the society at three international conferences in Europe.

CONCLUSION

Today, SPSSI has more than 3700 members, about evenly divided by gender. Fifteen percent of those whose ethnicity is known are members of minority groups; 28% are students; 54% belong to Division 9. We have a budget of more than $300,000 and net assets of more than $740,000. With a rich heritage and a dedicated membership, Division 9 continues to be a vital force within the APA. As SPSSI's 1996 Kurt Lewin Award winner and 48th president Marilynn Brewer wrote, "SPSSI represents sufficient membership 'clout' to have appreciable influence on the [APA's] commitment to socially responsible behavior, advocacy in the public interest, and support for policy relevant research. (In serving on various APA boards, I have seen numerous occasions on which concerns over what 'SPSSI-types' would think have influenced the direction of recommended actions.)" (*SPSSI Newsletter*, 1984, 1)

REFERENCES

Abelson, R. P., & Zimbardo, P. (Eds.). (1970). *Canvassing for peace: A manual for volunteers*. Ann Arbor, MI: SPSSI.

Brown v. Board of Education. (1954). 347 U.S. 483.

Capshew, J. H. (1986). Networks on leadership: Quantitative study of SPSSI Presidents, 1936–1986. *Journal of Social Issues, 42*(1), 75–106.

Clark, K. B. (Ed.). (1953). Desegregation: An appraisal of the evidence. *Journal of Social Issues, IX*, Whole No. 4.

Constitution and By-laws of the Society for the Psychological Study of Social Issues. (September, 1974). Ann Arbor, MI: SPSSI.

Deutsch, M., Katz, I., & Jensen, A. (Eds.). (1968). *Social class, race, and psychological development*. New York: Holt, Rinehart & Winston.

Evans, R. I. (1980). *The making of social psychology: Discussions with creative contributors*. New York: Gardner Press.

Finison, L. J. (1976). Unemployment, politics, and the history of organized psychology. *American Psychologist, 31*, 747–755.

Finison, L. J. (1977). Psychologists and Spain: A historical note. *American Psychologist, 32,* 1980–1984.

Finison, L. J. (1978). Unemployment, politics, and the history of organized psychology, II: The Psychologists League, the WPA, and the National Health Program. *American Psychologist, 33,* 471–477.

Finison, L. J. (1979). The early history of the Society for the Psychological Study of Social Issues: Psychologists and labor. *Journal of the History of the Behavioral Sciences, 15,* 29–37.

Finison, L. J. (1984). The Society for the Psychological Study of Social Issues, peace action and theories of conflict. *American Psychologist, 38,* 1250–1252.

Finison, L. J. (1986). The psychological insurgency: 1936–1945. *Journal of Social Issues, 42,* 21–33.

Garrett, H. E. (1962). The SPSSI and racial differences. *American Psychologist, 17,* 260–263.

Guidelines for testing minority group children. (1964). Supplement, *Journal of Social Issues,* XX (Suppl. 2), 127–145.

Guttentag, M. (Ed.). (1970a). The poor: Impact on research and theory. *Journal of Social Issues, 26,* Whole No. 2.

Guttentag, M. (Ed.). (1970b). Professionals and the poor. *Journal of Social Issues, 26,* Whole No. 3.

Guttentag, M., & Struening, E. (Eds.). (1975). *Handbook of evaluation research.* New York: Sage.

Harris, B. (1980). The FBI's files on APA and SPSSI: Description and implications. *American Psychologist, 35,* 1141–1144.

Harris, B. (1986). Reviewing 50 years of the psychology of social issues. *Journal of Social Issues, 42*(1), 1–20.

Herrnstein, R. T., & Murray, C. (1994). *The bell curve: Intelligence and class structure in American life.* New York: Free Press.

Jahoda, M., Deutsch, M., & Cook, S. W. (1951). *Research methods in social relations.* New York: Holt, Rinehart & Winston.

Jensen, A. R. (1969). How much can we boost IQ and scholastic achievement? *Harvard Educational Review, 39,* 1–123.

Jensen, A. R. (1993). Test validity: g vs. "tacit knowledge." *Current Directions in Psychological Science, 2,* 9–10.

Journal of Social Issues. (1986). Vol. 42, 1, 4.

Kaplan, B. H. (Ed.). (1965). Poverty dynamics and interventions. *Journal of Social Issues,* XXI, Whole No. 1.

Katz, P. (1991). Women, psychology and social issues research. *Psychology of Women Quarterly, 15,* 665–676.

Kimmel, P. R. (1986). The SPSSI investigation, or Special Prosecutors for Stopping Soviet Infiltration. *Journal of Social Issues, 42*(4), 115–143.

Klineberg, O. (1963). Negro–white differences in intelligence test performance. *American Psychologist, 18*, 198–203.

Klineberg, O. (1964). *The human dimension in international relations*. New York: Holt, Rinehart & Winston.

Klineberg, O. (1971). Black and white in international perspective. *American Psychologist, 26*, 119–128.

Klineberg, O. (1975). Race and psychology. In L. Kuper (Ed.), *Race, science and society*. Paris: UNESCO Press.

Klineberg, O. (1986). SPSSI and race relations in the 1950s and after. *Journal of Social Issues, 42*(4), 53–60.

Kluger, R. (1976). *Simple justice: The history of* Brown vs. the Board of Education *and Black America's struggle for equality*. New York: Knopf.

Krech, D., & Cartwright, D. (1956). On SPSSI's first twenty years. *American Psychologist, 11*, 470–473.

Lyons, R. D. (1970, October 3). H. E. W. relaxes rules for consultants. *New York Times*, 1, 10.

McGrath, J. E. (1980a). What are the social issues? Timeliness and treatment of topics in the Journal of Social Issues. *Journal of Social Issues, 36*(4), 98–108.

McGrath, J. E. (1980b). Social science, social action, and the Journal of Social Issues. *Journal of Social Issues, 36*, 109–124.

Mednick, M. T., & Urbanski, L. (1991). The origins and activities of APA's Division of the Psychology of Women. *Psychology of Women Quarterly, 15*, 651–663.

Miller, D. K. (1986). Screening people in, not out: Comment on Morawski. *Journal of Social Issues, 42*(1), 127–132.

Miller, G. A. (1969). Psychology as a means of promoting human welfare. *American Psychologist, 24*, 1063–1075.

Murphy, G. (1945). *Human nature and enduring peace*. Boston: Houghton Mifflin.

Neisser, U., Boodoo, G., Bouchard, T. J., Boykin, A. W., Brody, N., Ceci, S. J., Halpern, D. F., Loehlin, J. C., Perloff, R., Sternberg, R. J., & Urbina, S. (1986). Intelligence: Knowns and unknowns. *American Psychologist, 51*, 77–101.

Otten, A. L. (1974, March 7). Racial wrangling. *Wall Street Journal*, 14.

Perlman, D. (1986). SPSSI's publication history: Some facts and reflections. *Journal of Social Issues, 42(4)*, 89–114.

Perlman, D. (1995, August). *Journal of Social Issues at fifty: Reflections on the journal's history*. Poster session presented at the American Psychological Association meeting, New York.

Regents of University of California v. Bakke. (1978). 438 U.S. 265.

Rice, B. (1973, December). Race, intelligence, and genetics: The high cost of thinking the unthinkable. *Psychology Today, 7*, 89–95.

Sargent, S. S., & Harris, B. (1986). Academic freedom, civil liberties, and SPSSI. *Journal of Social Issues, 42*, 43–68.

Smith, M. B. (1986). McCarthyism: A personal account. *Journal of Social Issues, 42*, 71–80.

Smith, M. B. (1992). The American Psychological Association and social responsibility. In R. B. Evans, V. S. Sexton, & T. C. Cadwallader (Eds.), *100 Years: The American Psychological Association a historical perspective* (pp. 327–345). Washington, DC: American Psychological Association.

SPSSI Newsletter. (1954, October).

SPSSI Newsletter. (1958, November).

SPSSI Newsletter. (1961, December).

SPSSI Newsletter. (1962a, May).

SPSSI Newsletter. (1962b, June).

SPSSI Newsletter. (1963, April). No. 102.

SPSSI Newsletter. (1964, January). No. 105.

SPSSI Newsletter. (1965). No. 21.

SPSSI Newsletter. (1966a, April). No. 112.

SPSSI Newsletter. (1967, November). No. 117.

SPSSI Newsletter. (1968, April). No. 118.

SPSSI Newsletter. (1969, April). No. 121.

SPSSI Newsletter. (1972, November). No. 132.

SPSSI Newsletter. (1973, November). No. 135.

SPSSI Newsletter. (1974, May). No. 136.

SPSSI Newsletter. (1975, July). No. 139.

SPSSI Newsletter. (1976, November). No. 142.

SPSSI Newsletter. (1977, November). No. 145.

SPSSI Newsletter. (1982, April). No. 158.

SPSSI Newsletter. (1984, November). No. 166.

SPSSI Newsletter. (1986a, July). No. 171.

SPSSI Newsletter. (1986b, November). No. 172.

SPSSI Newsletter. (1987a, April). No. 173.

SPSSI Newsletter. (1987b, November). No. 175.

SPSSI Newsletter. (1988, July). No. 177.

SPSSI Newsletter. (1989, November). No. 180.

SPSSI Newsletter. (1990, April). No. 181.

SPSSI Newsletter. (1993a, April). No. 190.

SPSSI Newsletter. (1993b, July). No. 191.

SPSSI Newsletter. (1994, July). No. 194.

SPSSI Newsletter. (1996, March). No. 199.

SPSSI Statement on Academic Freedom. (1955). *American Psychologist, 10*, 35.

Stagner, R. (1986). Reminiscences about the founding of SPSSI. *Journal of Social Issues, 42*(1), 35–42.

Tobach, E., & Proshansky, H. M. (Eds.). (1976). *Genetic destiny: Scientific controversy and social conflict.* New York: AMS Press.

Unger, R. K. (1986). SPSSI council: A collective biography. *Journal of Social Issues, 42,* 81–88.

2

A HISTORY OF DIVISION 12 (CLINICAL PSYCHOLOGY): FOURSCORE YEARS

DONALD K. ROUTH

The field of clinical psychology is now more than 100 years old (Routh, 1996). Lightner Witmer (1867–1956) founded the first psychology clinic at the University of Pennsylvania in 1896 (Witmer, 1896, 1897) and somewhat more than a decade later (Witmer, 1907) attempted to define the nature of the emerging field of clinical psychology. Arguably the most innovative notion behind Witmer's work was the idea that psychologists should try to help people and not just study them (McReynolds, 1996). In modern times, clinical psychology has become perhaps the most common psychology specialty in the world (Sexton & Hogan, 1992) and has evolved into a field of general practice subsuming many more specialized areas such as clinical child psychology, clinical geropsychology, research, the clinical psychology of women, child (as well as adult) health psychology, and the clinical psychology of ethnic minority individuals.

Key source materials concerning the predecessors of Division 12 (from 1917 to 1945) are located in two places: the American Psychological Association files of the Manuscript Division, U.S. Library of Congress, and the papers of various named individuals at the Archives of the History of American Psychology, University of Akron. An almost complete file of the division's newsletters from 1947 to the present is in the author's possession.

EARLY HISTORY OF CLINICAL PSYCHOLOGY

The roots of clinical psychology, as conceptualized by Witmer (1907), can be found as far back as the eighteenth century in the work of J. Rodriguez Pereira (1715–1780), who taught deaf persons to speak (Routh, del Barrio, & Carpintero, 1996). Other forerunners included J. M. G. Itard (1774–1838), who attempted to rehabilitate the wild boy of Aveyron, and Edouard Seguin (1812–1880), a pioneer on the education of children with mental retardation. Other important roots of clinical psychology lay in psychometric testing as developed by Francis Galton (1822–1911), James McKeen Cattell (1860–1944), and Alfred Binet (1857–1911). In his clinic, Witmer not only engaged in the assessment and remediation of human problems, especially those of children with academic difficulties, but also trained doctoral psychology students in the same types of activities. In 1907, Witmer founded a journal, *The Psychological Clinic*, devoted mostly to case histories of children seen in his clinic. Within a year after this time, in 1908, what is now regarded as the first clinical psychology internship training program was founded by Henry H. Goddard (1866–1957) at the Vineland Training School in New Jersey (Doll, 1946). Many of the early interns at Vineland had been graduate students at the University of Pennsylvania.

Since the time of Galton's book, *Hereditary Genius* in 1869, a certain subgroup of psychologists have had a strong interest in individual differences. Galton himself tried to measure the presumed basis of higher mental functions in terms of simple sensory or motor measures such as auditory acuity and strength of grip. Galton's disciple Cattell (1890) originated the term "mental test," but like Galton focused on the measurement of relatively simple sensory and motor skills. It is probably no accident that Cattell was in turn one of the mentors of Witmer, the founder of clinical psychology. Of course, it was Binet in France rather than any of these British or American psychologists who developed the first workable "intelligence" test (Binet & Simon, 1905). Goddard at the Vineland Training School quickly had Binet's scale translated into English and began to try it in the diagnosis of mental retardation. Goddard's findings agreed with those of many others at the time that the Binet test was very effective for this purpose. If there is any practical skill that all of the early clinical psychologists had in common, it was the use and interpretation of the Binet test. The success of the Binet scale even turned aside the emphasis on intervention so prominent in Witmer's case studies. The Binet test made early (pre-World War II) clinical psychology more of a psychometric discipline rather than one focused on therapy.

After World War II, the emphasis of clinical psychology on therapeutic intervention was reinstated, and its linkages to such movements as psychoanalysis were thus strengthened. Sigmund Freud (1856–1939) published his first book on psychological intervention, *Studies in Hysteria* (with Breuer), in 1895, very close to the time that Witmer's clinic was founded. Freud arguably had more influence on clinical psychology than any other individual. The influence of behavior therapy on clinical psychology did not begin much before the 1960s.

THE AMERICAN ASSOCIATION OF CLINICAL
PSYCHOLOGISTS: 1917–1919

Although the field of clinical psychology is more than 100 years old, its first organization was not founded until about 80 years ago (hence the subtitle of this chapter, "Fourscore Years"). The present Division 12 (Clinical Psychology) is a direct descendent of an independent organization, the American Association of Clinical Psychologists (AACP) founded on December 28, 1917, at the meeting of the APA in Pittsburgh. As detailed in the discussion that follows, this organization lasted only 2 years.

The "founder" of the AACP was J. E. Wallace Wallin (1876–1969). Wallin obtained his PhD in psychology from Yale University in 1901. He gained some of his knowledge of clinical psychology by visiting Witmer at the University of Pennsylvania in 1907. Later, he spent a summer at the Training School in Vineland, New Jersey (Wallin, 1968). As a historical figure, he is probably better known as a special educator than as a clinical psychologist. According to Wallin's (1955) autobiography, his motive in founding the AACP was the need to ensure the professional competence of individuals who were doing psychological evaluations, in particular the Binet test. He had invested much time and effort in acquiring experience giving and interpreting Binet tests and was concerned about the fact that persons such as school teachers or academic experimental psychologists with no supervised clinical experience were attempting to give and interpret these tests. Though Wallin denied this, some of the impetus for founding the AACP may also have come from the upsurge in applied psychology generally associated with World War I (Routh, 1994). In any case, the bylaws of the AACP stated,

> The objects of the Association are to promote an *esprit de corps* among psychologists who have entered the practical field, to provide media for the communication of ideas, to aid in establishing definite standards of professional fitness for the practice of psychology, and to encourage research in problems relating to mental hygiene and corrective education. (Routh, 1994, p. 169)

Wallin and seven other "founders" of the AACP such as Leta S. Hollingworth (1886–1939) chose 48 individuals as potential members of the organization, 46 of whom subsequently joined it (Hollingworth, 1917, 1919). See Table 9 for a list of these individuals.

TABLE 9
Members of the American Association of Clinical Psychologists:
1917–1919

Bird T. Baldwin	William Healy	H. C. Stevens
Gardner C. Bassett	Samuel B. Heckman	Arthur H. Sutherland
Charles S. Berry	David S. Hill	Reuel H. Sylvester
Augusta F. Bronner	Leta S. Hollingworth	L. M. Terman
Frank G. Bruner	Buford J. Johnson	Clara H. Town
Harry W. Crane	Frederic Kuhlmann	J. E. Wallace Wallin
Josephine Curtis	Florence E. Mateer	Jean Weidensall
Walter F. Dearborn	Francis N. Maxfield	F. L. Wells
Grace M. Fernald	James B. Miner	Guy M. Whipple
Mabel R. Fernald	David Mitchell	S. Harold Williams
S. I. Franz	George Ordahl	Elizabeth Woods
Robert H. Gault	Rudolf Pintner	Helen T. Woolley
Arnold L. Gesell	W. H. Pyle	Robert M. Yerkes
Henry H. Goddard	Clara Schmitt	Herman H. Young
Thomas H. Haines	Stevenson Smith	
Mary Hayes	Lori Stecher [Weeber]	

Source: D. K. Routh (1994), *Clinical psychology since 1917: Science, practice, and organization* (New York: Plenum Press), p 14.

Looking over this membership list, one recognizes the names of several who have continued to be identified with the history of clinical psychology, for example David Mitchell (1884–1956), a PhD graduate of the University of Pennsylvania who may have been the first to earn his living in the private practice of psychology (Meltzer, 1966; Mitchell, 1919, 1931). Others on the list would now be identified more with other areas of psychology. For example, Robert M. Yerkes (1876–1956) is far better known as a comparative psychologist than as a clinician (Dewsbury, 1996). The AACP retained its 46 members until it disbanded. To put this number in perspective, it might be recalled that the original APA when it formed in 1892 had only 31 members.

During its brief 2-year life, the AACP met only once, at the APA convention in 1918 in Baltimore, when it sponsored a symposium. According to Wallin (1961), so many people tried to come to this symposium, and the discussion was so heated, that the speakers were unable to make their presentations. They did publish their papers the next year in the *Journal of Applied Psychology*, however (e.g., Gesell, 1919).

THE CLINICAL SECTION OF THE AMERICAN PSYCHOLOGICAL ASSOCIATION: 1919–1937

Many members of the APA regarded the new, independent organization of clinical psychologists (the AACP) as unduly divisive to psychology.

Thus, the president of the APA, Yerkes, acted quickly to have a compromise negotiated under which the AACP disbanded itself in 1919 and was reconstituted as the "Clinical Section" of the APA. This was the first organized subgroup of the APA and in this sense can be regarded as a prototype of the various divisions the APA formed after World War II. The psychologist who carried out these negotiations on behalf of the APA was Bird T. Baldwin (1875–1928), who was already well known as the first director of the University of Iowa's Child Welfare Research Station, the first such child development institute in the United States. Arnold L. Gesell (1880–1961), another early well-known child development researcher (who was a physician as well as a psychologist) negotiated on behalf of the AACP. The purposes of the Section of Clinical Psychology as agreed on by the conference committee were

> (a) To promote a mutual understanding and an *esprit de corps* among those working in the field of clinical psychology, and a cooperative relationship with those engaged in allied fields.
> (b) To encourage and advance professional standards in this field in cooperation with such committees on certification as may be appointed by the A.P.A. as a whole.
> (c) To encourage research and the suitable publication of scientific results in the field of clinical psychology. (Routh, 1994, p. 170)

The same 46 persons who had been members of the AACP became the original members of the APA Clinical Section. The section had 62 members in 1924 and 291 members by 1935 (Routh, 1994). As an independent organization, the AACP had been free to set its own dues. However, its successor, the Clinical Section of the APA, was restricted by its bylaws and its agreement with the APA from charging dues. The Clinical Section could impose "assessments" on its members for special purposes but was not allowed to ask them for more than $1 per year (Routh, 1994). This restriction naturally limited the scope of the section's activities, which consisted almost entirely of annual meetings of the membership.

As it had agreed to do as part of the negotiations mentioned previously, the APA for a few years did set up a procedure for certifying "consulting psychologists"—psychologists who were professionally qualified to offer their services to the public. Frederick L. Wells (1884–1964) served as the executive officer of the APA Standing Committee on the Certification of Consulting Psychologists. Before it was discontinued in 1927, this committee certified 25 "consulting psychologists," 17 of whom (including Wells himself) had been members of the original AACP. However, this "certification" procedure was considered ineffective as a mechanism for regulating the professional practice of psychology and was terminated for this reason. State and provincial licensing laws for psychologists, the principal way of regulating practice today, did not come along until after World War II.

The Clinical Section of the APA sponsored one or more symposia or paper sessions at most of the APA annual meetings during its 18 years of existence. It failed to plan such sessions only in 1928 and 1929 because of the illness of its chair Herman H. Young (1887–1931) of Indiana University. At the APA meeting in Cambridge, Massachusetts, in 1922, most of the sessions were held relatively early in the week in Emerson Hall at Harvard University. However, the Clinical Section had its sessions at the Boston Psychopathic Hospital on the afternoon of the last day. This was done in order to make it possible for theoretical/experimental psychologists to leave early and the clinical psychologists to come later, if they wished (Routh, 1994).

In 1927 the APA Clinical Section approved some new, more professionally oriented bylaws (Routh, 1994), perhaps in reaction to the demise of the APA's procedure for certifying "consulting psychologists." However, these bylaws were apparently not shared with the APA leadership until 1935. Article 2.1 ("to encourage and advance professional standards," Routh, 1994, p. 171) was then found to be objectionable by the APA and was deleted, leaving the Clinical Section with only the ability to provide a forum for research presentations. The members of the Clinical Section in turn found this limitation unacceptable. Thus, in 1937 they disbanded themselves to form a section in a new organization, the American Association of Applied Psychologists (AAAP). At this time the APA as a whole seemed to be moving in the opposite direction from its Clinical Section. For example, in 1927, the APA passed a bylaws amendment requiring published research beyond the dissertation as a membership requirement (Fernberger, 1932).

THE CLINICAL SECTION OF THE AMERICAN ASSOCIATION OF APPLIED PSYCHOLOGISTS: 1937–1945

During the 1930s in the United States, psychology practitioners actively began to organize themselves at the state level. A representative example might be an organization that called itself at first the Pennsylvania Association of Clinical Psychologists. It was the forerunner of the present Pennsylvania Psychological Association (Knapp, Levin, & French, 1993). By 1937, these various state associations coalesced into the AAAP. The AAAP made room for "sections" representing different applied interest groups, including clinical psychology. Thus, when the Clinical Section of the APA disbanded, it formally transferred its goodwill and assets to the

Clinical Section of the AAAP (English, 1938), which had 229 members on its founding. Its other sections included educational, and industrial and business psychology. This "section" structure provided the template for the "divisions" of the post-World War II APA, which was created by a merger of the AAAP, the APA, and some other organizations.

The Clinical Section of the AAAP sponsored various programs at its annual meetings. Although the AAAP was a separate organization, most of its members also belonged to the APA, and the two groups generally met at the same time and place. The AAAP and its sections' convention programs, not surprisingly, focused on professional issues and used presentation formats such as symposia or roundtable discussions rather than paper sessions. The AAAP met in 1939 in Washington, DC, for the first time completely separately from that year's APA convention. On that occasion, the AAAP discovered that it did not have a well-developed mechanism for reviewing research papers submitted for presentation at its meeting—it has always depended on the APA to do that. Thus, it became clear that there were disadvantages to a purely guild organization of psychologists (Routh, 1994).

The AAAP Clinical Section was prohibited by its bylaws from collecting dues but could by a two-thirds vote impose special assessments on its members, the amount of which was not explicitly constrained.

DIVISION 12 OF THE AMERICAN PSYCHOLOGICAL ASSOCIATION

During the period 1945 to 1947, Division 12 became one of the original divisions of the reorganized APA, the divisions that began their 50th or Golden Anniversary celebration at the 1996 APA convention. Reasonably enough, the plan for numbering these divisions was that Division 1 was concerned with General Psychology, Division 2 the Teaching of Psychology, and so on. According to this plan, Division 11 was to have included the domain of abnormal psychology and psychotherapy and Division 12 that of clinical psychology. The members who were to have been a part of these two groups thought they had too much in common to have separate divisions, so Division 11 ceased to exist, and the members all joined Division 12, designated as the Division of Clinical and Abnormal Psychology (Shaffer, 1945). Later, in 1954, its name was shortened to the Division of Clinical Psychology. This is one of the few times in the history of the APA in which two divisions merged (usually divisions engage in fission, not fusion). See Table 10 for an outline of the chronology of significant events related to Division 12 and its predecessor organizations.

TABLE 10
Chronology of Significant Events in the History of Clinical Psychology and of Division 12 and Its Predecessors

Date	Event
1896	Founding of the first psychology clinic by Lightner Witmer, at the University of Pennsylvania in Philadelphia
1907	First publication of the journal, *The Psychological Clinic*, by Witmer
1908	Founding of the first clinical psychology internship program, by Henry Goddard, Vineland Training School, New Jersey
1917	Founding of the American Association of Clinical Psychologists (AACP) in Pittsburgh
1919	Incorporation of the AACP as the Clinical Section of the APA
1937	Founding of the Clinical Section of the American Association of Applied Psychologists (AAAP)
1945	Founding of Division 12, the Division of Clinical and Abnormal Psychology, part of the new APA
1954	Division 12's name changed to the Division of Clinical Psychology
1963	Founding of Section 1 of Division 12 (Clinical Child Psychology), by Alan O. Ross
1963	Affiliation of Psychologists Interested in the Advancement of Psychotherapy (PIAP) as Section 2 of Division 12
1966	Founding of Section 3, Division 12 (now known as the Society for a Science of Clinical Psychology) by Leonard Krasner and others
1971	Founding of the Section on Continuing Professional Education, also known as Section 2, by C. Eugene Walker and others
1980	Founding of the Section on the Clinical Psychology of Women, Section 4, by Bonnie Strickland
1980	Affiliation of the Society of Pediatric Psychology as Section 5 (originally founded in 1968 by Dorothea Ross, Lee Salk, and Logan Wright)
1986	Founding of Section 6 on Ethnic Minority Clinical Psychology
1988	Founding of Section 7 on the Theory and Practice of Group Psychotherapy by Arthur Teicher
1993	Founding of the Section on Clinical Geropsychology, the present Section 2

PHILOSOPHY AND APPROACH OF THE DIVISION IN RELATION TO THOSE OF THE APA

The purpose of the original APA (founded in 1892) had been to advance psychology as a science (Fernberger, 1932). Clinical psychology organizations, in contrast, have always tried to include among their objectives the advancement of psychology not only as a science but also as a profession in the sense of the delivery of services by practitioners. The APA's bylaws now state that the overall organization exists in order to advance psychology as a science, as a profession, and as a means of promoting human welfare. Division 12 as an organization continues to emphasize both science and practice.

MEMBERSHIP GROWTH

Immediately after its founding in the post-World War II era, Division 12 had a much more impressive growth in membership than had any of its predecessors. The first executive committee meeting of the new division found itself with "about a thousand applications for membership and an additional 500 requests for application blanks" (Executive Committee Meeting, 1947, p. 2). The division already officially had 482 members by 1948. In that year, the division executive committee had enough to do that it began to meet regularly in midyear, at the time of the meeting of the American Orthopsychiatric Association (Mid-Year Meeting of Executive Committee, 1948). By 1949, the division had more than 1000 members (Editorial, 1949); by 1960 Division 12 had 2376 members; by 1970 the total was 3662; by 1981 it was 4579; and by 1992 it was 6417.

The reason for the growth of membership in Division 12 was principally the burgeoning growth of the field of clinical psychology, especially in the postwar era. The U.S. government was hard pressed to cope with the rising tide of mental health problems in the country at that time and especially with the mental health needs of the huge number of veterans returning from World War II (e.g., Carter, 1950). The new National Institute of Mental Health (NIMH) and the U.S. Veterans Administration (VA) both began to provide generous funding for training in clinical psychology. The VA provided a large number of positions for clinical psychologists as well. The NIMH and the VA provided the impetus for the APA to accredit graduate training in clinical psychology for the first time. Before this, there was never an official consensus about standards of training in the field. The Boulder conference in 1949 implemented the well-known scientist–practitioner model of clinical training (Raimy, 1950) suggested by an APA committee headed by David Shakow (1901–1981). As George A. Kelly noted in his retrospective comments on this era,

> Much, perhaps too much, has hinged on the Veterans Administration's far-sighted clinical psychology program blue-printed by James G. Miller and the many-sided support given to the projects of the American Psychological Association by the National Institute of Mental Health. Indeed, psychologists should be careful not to lose sight of the fact that it was Robert Felix and Daniel Blain, both psychiatrists, who, through their respective agencies, first invited psychology to play a major role in the mental health effort. (1956, p. 2)

Many years later, in the 1970s and 1980s, with government training funds decreasing, there were demands for more streamlined training in professional psychology. This trend led to a "practitioner" model of training without such a demanding research component. At that time, schools of professional psychology swelled the ranks of doctoral graduates (including those in clinical psychology) and increased Division 12 membership still more.

At present, however, Division 42 (Psychologists in Independent Practice), not Division 12, is the largest one in the APA, no doubt in part because it is less restrictive than is Division 12 in terms of the kind of training required for membership. Perhaps the biggest controversy within Division 12 during its history concerned the question of whether the division was an "interest group" (the position more often favored by researchers and academics) or whether it should require prospective members to be fully trained for clinical practice (the position more often favored by practitioners). Already at the beginning of Division 12's existence after World War II, "the feeling expressed was: somehow it seems too easy to get into this Division" (Business Meeting, 1947, p. 4). After considerable debate on the issue during the 1970s, Nicholas Cummings (1979) as president sent out a referendum ballot inquiring whether members preferred the division to be a credentialling group, an interest group, or a combination of the two. Subsequently, the division officially voted 1266 to 679 (i.e., by a 65% majority) for the credentialling option (Kovacs, 1980). Current bylaws therefore limit its membership to individuals "with training appropriate to the conduct of such clinical activities as defined by the Council of Representatives of the American Psychological Association" (Bylaws, 1981, p. 27). The division does, however, extend membership to persons who have made significant scientific contributions to clinical psychology, regardless of whether they were clinically trained.

CHARACTERISTICS OF PROGRAM PRESENTATIONS AT ANNUAL CONVENTIONS

When Division 12 was formed after World War II and became the largest APA division, it therefore commanded many hours of program time at each annual convention. From that time until the present, the division has been able to offer a full range of programs at each convention, including scientific paper sessions (and later poster sessions as well), symposia, invited addresses, discussion hours, social hours, and so on. There is an address by the president of the division and by the president of each of its sections, and many award presentations as well. Each year there is a program committee with a standardized set of procedures for reviewing the papers submitted to ensure their scientific and professional quality. Carl R. Rogers (1902–1987) noted in his 1949 presentation to the division what a transformation had occurred during the 1930s and 1940s:

At the beginning of that period, the lonely clinician often wondered if he belonged in the psychological profession. When he looked at APA programs, he was sure he did not belong. It would have been hard at that time to convince him that by 1949 there would be about twelve hundred members of a Clinical Division, that it would be the largest of any of the Divisions, and that it would be spearheading the development of psychology in many significant ways. (1949, p. 1)

One successful innovation introduced by Division 12 to the APA conventions was the postdoctoral institute (PDI). The idea for PDIs came from a committee headed by Anne Roe (1904–1991) soon after the founding of the new division (Roe, 1948). The first such institute was offered at the 1950 APA convention on the campus of Penn State University (Advanced Training Institute in Clinical Psychology, 1950) and was considered successful both professionally and financially. Offering these institutes immediately became an annual event. PDI speakers are paid to conduct workshops lasting several hours or even a day or two to help practitioners update themselves on developments on topics of interest to them. In 1966 the division presented a special award to Joseph Zubin (1900–1990), a clinical psychology researcher and faculty member at Columbia University and the New York State Psychiatric Institute because he had presented so many successful PDI workshops at APA conventions. The PDI workshops at their best present the latest scientific information of direct relevance to the everyday work of the clinical practitioner. The persons who pay to attend them are often clinical psychologists, but need not be. In addition to other advantages, the PDI program often has provided the division with substantial financial profits to use in support of some of its other activities.

INTERACTIONS WITH OTHER DIVISIONS

Clinical psychology today regards itself as a general practice field involving the provision of psychological health services, and it is linked closely with many narrower or overlapping specialties. Over the years psychology as a whole has spun off a large number of areas of professional endeavor. One of these, industrial/organizational psychology, the clientele of which consists largely of commercial organizations, has relatively little overlap with the clinical area. Other specialties, especially those involving human service delivery, necessarily overlap to a greater or lesser extent with clinical psychology. Many persons who identify with these specialties still consider themselves to be clinical psychologists. For example, Arthur Benton, a prominent neuropsychologist, once stated, "I believe that clinical neuropsychology is, or should be, an integral part of general clinical psychology. To think of the two as separate disciplines operates to impoverish both fields of activity" (1975, p. 7).

Table 11 illustrates some of the linkages just mentioned by listing more than 20 different APA divisions and for each one naming some prominent psychologists associated with them who also had major ties to clinical psychology and thus to Division 12.

The developmental psychologists in Table 11 would generally be regarded today as just that—and not very "clinical." The field of child develop-

TABLE 11
Interactions With Other Divisions

APA Division Number	Present Name	Prominent Psychologists Associated with Both Clinical Psychology Organizations and Others
6	Comparative and Physiological	Robert M. Yerkes
		S. I. Franz
7	Developmental	John E. Anderson
		Bird T. Baldwin
8	Personality and Social	Gardner Lindzey
		Walter Mischel
		Henry A. Murray
16	School	Arnold Gesell
17	Counseling	Carl R. Rogers
20	Adult and Aging	David Wechsler
22	Rehabilitation	S. I. Franz
27	Community	Seymour Sarason
29	Psychotherapy	George A. Kelly
		Hans Strupp
32	Humanistic	Rollo R. May
33	Mental Retardation	Edgar A. Doll
35	Women	Janet T. Spence
37	Child, Youth and Family Services	Nicholas Hobbs
38	Health	Joseph D. Matarazzo
39	Psychoanalysis	Bruno Bettelheim
		Erik Erikson
		Robert R. Holt
		David Rapaport
40	Neuropsychology	Arthur Benton
		Oscar A. Parsons
42	Independent Practice	David Mitchell
43	Family	John Elderkin Bell
		K. Daniel O'Leary
45	Ethnic Minority	Guillermo Bernal
		Gail Wyatt
49	Group	Jules Barron
50	Addictions	Peter Nathan
		G. Terence Wilson

ment research has long since proved itself as an independent, nonclinical research area.

The personality/social psychologists in Table 11, in the same sense, are for the most part persons who have made major contributions in that area who just happened to be clinically trained as well. An exception would be Henry A. Murray (1893–1988), whose interests were inherently more clinical. Originally trained as a physician, Murray later got a PhD in biochemistry but was so fascinated by the work of Carl Jung (and subsequently, by that of Freud) that he decided to devote the remainder of his career to psychology. Despite his lack of formal training in this field, he was hired by Morton Prince (1854–1929) as a faculty member at the Harvard Psychological Clinic. Murray's major 1938 book (written with C. Morgan), *Explorations in Personality*, was a milestone in the development of "personology" as an area of research involving personality, social, and clinical psychology. As a Harvard faculty member, Murray personally trained a distinguished group of clinical researchers.

It would be tedious to discuss every name in Table 11. Two of them that should not be neglected are George A. Kelly (1905–1967) and Carl R. Rogers (1902–1987). Kelly developed his own original methods (involving the "repertory grid") of assessing clients and their personal constructs, as well as an approach to treatment known as *personal construct therapy*. Rogers also developed his own brand of therapy, ultimately known as *person-centered therapy* and pioneered in the empirical study of psychotherapy process and outcome, and he was bold enough to begin the tape recording of actual therapy sessions. Both Kelly and Rogers have significant posthumous influence in Europe as well as the United States (Routh, 1994). It would be difficult to say whether their contributions were greater in the area of "clinical psychology" than they were in various overlapping fields, including personality, counseling, or in Rogers's case, humanistic psychology.

FINANCES

As of 1947 the bylaws of Division 12 specified minimum dues of $1 and allowed additional dues to be assessed by a majority vote of the membership (Routh, 1994). During the 1946 to 1947 year, the division's budget was $690 (Business Meeting, 1947). The present budget of Division 12 of approximately $300,000 could hardly have been imagined in those days. The largest single source of income for the division continues to be dues and assessments from the membership (now more than $25 per year per member). Its largest single expense is for publications, which presently include a news bulletin (*The Clinical Psychologist*) and a journal (*Clinical Psychology: Science and*

Practice). The second largest expense of the division is travel costs for meetings of its board of directors, attended by about 20 persons counting elected officers, committee chairs, and liaisons to other organizations.

PUBLICATIONS

Division 12 began publishing its newsletter in 1947 and has done so continuously (in one form or another) since that time. Since 1957, the newsletter has had an editor apart from elected officials of the division (G. A. Kelly, 1957). In the fall of 1958 the newsletter (Volume 11, No. 4) began to be printed rather than mimeographed. In 1966, under the editorship of Donald K. Freedheim, the newsletter took on its present official name of *The Clinical Psychologist* and in addition to the news began to publish brief, professionally oriented articles that were submitted to it for review (A New Policy for the Division Newsletter, 1966). In 1968 the APA journal *Professional Psychology* began as a spinoff of the Division 12 newsletter, which in 1969 resumed publication under its original name of *The Clinical Psychologist*. The newsletter editors of Division 12 have thus far included Elizabeth B. Wolf, D. Craig Affleck (1928–1970), Leonard Haber, Freedheim, Norman Milgram, Jerome H. Resnick, Sandra Harris, Samuel Turner, Lawrence Cohen, Gerald Koocher, Ronald Blount, and Lawrence Siegel. The most famous "spoof" in the history of the newsletter may have been its printing of a group photograph of the executive committee in which Julian Rotter appeared twice, once standing and once sitting (Barclay, 1974, p. 22).

There were suggestions almost from its beginning that Division 12 should publish its own scholarly journal (e.g. Holt, 1948). The most prestigious journals in the field in the view of Division 12 members were those published by the APA, namely the *Journal of Abnormal and Social Psychology* and the *Journal of Consulting Psychology* (Chotlos, Scheerer, & Holt, 1952). It was not until 1988 that Division 12 sponsored a peer-reviewed scholarly journal, the *Clinical Psychology Review*, co-edited by Alan Bellack and Michel Hersen and published by Pergamon Press (1988 Brings Major Changes for *The Clinical Psychologist*, 1987). When this sponsorship began, the Division 12 membership finally approved by almost a 2-to-1 vote a dues increase that it had rejected more than once before that time.

During 1989 to 1992, the division also published an additional separate newsletter, *The Clinical Psychology Bulletin*, twice a year to handle time-sensitive material (Schroeder, 1990). Gerald Koocher and Ronald Blount took this on as an additional duty, using desktop publishing technology. The division's arrangement with Pergamon Press terminated in 1992.

In 1994 Division 12 began its own journal, *Clinical Psychology: Science and Practice,* published for it by Oxford University Press, and edited by Alan E. Kazdin. In this case, unlike that of the *Clinical Psychology Review,* the division itself owns the journal and names the editor.

ADMINISTRATION AND AWARDS

As in any such organization, election to leadership in Division 12 and its predecessors served the dual purpose of providing service to the organization and honoring the person elected. See Tables 12 and 13 for a chronological listing of the presiding officers and the secretaries and treasurers of the organizations. In 1957 it was recommended that Division 12 begin a separate program of awards to honor various individuals who had made distinguished contributions to the field (Hunt, MacKinnon, Rodnick, Shaffer, & Tolman, 1957). The awards began in 1958 (see Table 14). It is beyond the scope of this chapter to provide much information about these individuals and their many contributions to the field of clinical psychology. So far, the division has chosen to name only one of its awards after someone. Its early career award, first given in 1994, was named after David Shakow (1901–1981), the originator of the scientist–professional model of training that emerged after World War II. The interested reader is referred to the book by Routh (1994) for further details concerning officers and awardees.

An important change in the way Division 12 operated came when it decided, effective as of March 1989, to establish a central office in Oklahoma City and to hire Judy Wilson as its administrative officer (Schroeder, 1989). Wilson (who is not a psychologist) previously had served as the administrative assistant to Russell L. Adams, an elected secretary of Division 12. The subsequent officers of the division, including the author of this chapter, find it difficult to understand how the organization was able to get along before it took this step. Wilson has continued in this role up to the present.

SECTIONS

Division 12 is unusual among APA divisions in the existence and strength of its sections, of which there are now six. Section 1 deals with clinical child psychology, Section 2 with clinical geropsychology, Section 3 with the science of clinical psychology, Section 4 with the clinical psychology of women, Section 5 with pediatric psychology (i.e., child health psychology), and Section 6 with ethnic minority psychology. Unlike the division, the sections are simply interest groups, and most of them therefore have members who do not belong to Division 12. Section members elect their

TABLE 12
Presiding Officers of Division 12 and Its Predecessors

American Association of Clinical Psychologists

1917–1918	J. E. Wallace Wallin
1918–1919	J. E. Wallace Wallin

Clinical Section of the American Psychological Association

1919–1920	Francis N. Maxfield
1920–1921	Francis N. Maxfield/David Mitchell
1921–1922	Francis N. Maxfield
1922–1923	Frederick L. Wells
1923–1924	David Mitchell
1924–1925	David Mitchell/Arnold L. Gesell
1925–1926	David Mitchell/Helen T. Woolley
1926–1927	Augusta F. Bronner
1927–1928	Augusta F. Bronner/David Mitchell
1928–1929	Herman H. Young
1929–1930	Herman H. Young/S. I. Franz
1930–1931	S. I. Franz/Frederick Kuhlmann
1931–1932	Frederick Kuhlmann/James B. Miner
1932–1933	Frederick Kuhlmann/Edgar A. Doll
1933–1934	Edgar A. Doll
1934–1935	Clara H. Town
1935–1936	Martin L. Reymert
1936–1937	Gertrude H. Hildreth

Clinical Section American Associaiton of Applied Psychologists

1937–1938	Francis N. Maxfield/Andrew W. Brown
1938–1939	Edgar A. Doll
1939–1940	Edgar A. Doll
1940–1941	Frederick Kuhlmann
1941–1942	Frederick Kuhlmann/Francis N. Maxfield/Carl R. Rogers
1942–1943	Carl R. Rogers
1943–1944	Carl R. Rogers
1944–1945	Carl R. Rogers/Bertha M. Luckey
1945–1946	Robert A. Brotemarkle

Division of Clinical and Abnormal Psychology (Division 12), American Psychological Association

1945–1946	Edgar A. Doll
1946–1947	Laurance F. Shaffer
1947–1948	David Shakow
1948–1949	David Wechsler
1949–1950	Carl R. Rogers
1950–1951	Norman A. Cameron
1951–1952	Samuel J. Beck
1952–1953	O. Hobart Mowrer
1953–1954	William A. Hunt
1954–1955	Harold M. Hildreth

Division of Clinical Psychology (Division 12)
American Psychological Association

1955–1956	Jean W. Macfarlane
1956–1957	George A. Kelly
1957–1958	Anne Roe
1958–1959	James Grier Miller
1959–1960	E. Lowell Kelly
1960–1961	Nicholas Hobbs
1961–1962	Robert R. Holt
1962–1963	Victor C. Raimy
1963–1964	Starke R. Hathaway
1964–1965	Sol L. Garfield
1965–1966	Ivan N. Mensh
1966–1967	George W. Albee
1967–1968	Florence C. Halpern
1968–1969	Joseph McVicker Hunt
1969–1970	Alan O. Ross
1970–1971	Julian B. Rotter
1971–1972	Norman L. Farberow
1972–1973	Edwin S. Shneidman
1973–1974	Theodore H. Blau
1974–1975	Hans H. Strupp
1975–1976	Gordon Derner
1976–1977	Max Siegel
1977–1978	Norman Garmezy
1978–1979	Nicholas A. Cummings
1979–1980	Seymour B. Sarason
1980–1981	Allan G. Barclay
1981–1982	Logan Wright
1982–1983	Bonnie R. Strickland
1983–1984	Peter Nathan
1985	Lee B. Sechrest
1986	Jules Barron
1987	Patrick H. DeLeon
1988	Rogers H. Wright
1989	Charles D. Spielberger
1990	Norman Abeles
1991	Jerome H. Resnick
1992	George Stricker
1993	David H. Barlow
1994	Martin E. P. Seligman
1995	Gerald P. Koocher
1996	Nathan Perry
1997	Lynn P. Rehm
1998	Donald K. Routh

own officers, but only Division 12 members within a section can vote for the representative of the section to the Division 12 board.

The sectional organization of the division was originally suggested by E. Lowell Kelly because of what he described as its increasing size and diversity (E. L. Kelly, 1960). In 1962 the bylaws change making sections

TABLE 13
Secretaries and Treasurers of Division 12 and
Its Predecessor Organizations

	American Association of Clinical Psychologists
	Secretary
1917–1918	Leta S. Hollingworth
1918–1919	Leta S. Hollingworth

	Clinical Section, American Psychological Association
	Secretary
1919–1920	Leta S. Hollingworth
1920–1921	Augusta F. Bronner
1921–1922	Augusta F. Bronner/Clara H. Town
1922–1923	Clara H. Town
1923–1924	Edgar A. Doll
1924–1925	Edgar A. Doll
1925–1926	Charles S. Berry
1926–1927	Charles S. Berry/Mabel R. Fernald
1927–1928	Augusta F. Bronner
1928–1929	Charles S. Berry
1929–1930	—
1930–1931	James B. Miner/Luton Ackerson
1931–1932	Luton Ackerson
1932–1933	Luton Ackerson
1933–1934	Luton Ackerson
1934–1935	Edward B. Greene
1935–1936	—
1936–1937	—

	Clinical Section, American Association of Applied Psychologists
	Secretary
1937–1938	C. M. "Mac" Louttit
1938–1939	Elaine F. Kinder
1939–1940	Elaine F. Kinder
1940–1941	Elaine F. Kinder
	Secretary-Treasurer
1941–1942	Elaine F. Kinder
1942–1943	Gertrude F. Hildreth
1943–1944	Gertrude F. Hildreth
1944–1945	Frank P. Bakes
	Secretary
1945–1946	Frank P. Bakes

	Division of Clinical and Abnormal Psychology (Division 12) American Psychological Association
	Secretary
1945–1946	Frank P. Bakes
1946–1947	David Rapaport
1947–1948	David Rapaport
1948–1949	David Rapaport
1949–1950	Anne Roe
1950–1951	Anne Roe/Harry V. McNeill

Division of Clinical and Abnormal Psychology (Division 12)
American Psychological Association

	Secretary-Treasurer
1951–1952	Ann Magaret
1952–1953	Ann Magaret
1953–1954	Ann Magaret Garner
1954–1955	Helen D. Sargent

Division of Clinical Psychology (Division 12)
American Psychological Association

	Secretary-Treasurer
1955–1956	Helen D. Sargent
1956–1957	Helen D. Sargent/Ivan N. Mensh
1957–1958	Ivan N. Mensh
1958–1959	Ivan N. Mensh
1959–1960	Ivan N. Mensh
1960–1961	Sol L. Garfield
1961–1962	Sol L. Garfield
1962–1963	Sol L. Garfield
1963–1964	Florence C. Halpern
1964–1965	Florence C. Halpern
1965–1966	Florence C. Halpern
1966–1967	Norman L. Farberow
1967–1968	Norman L. Farberow
1968–1969	Norman L. Farberow
1969–1970	William Schofield
1970–1971	William Schofield
1972–1973	Allan G. Barclay
1973–1974	Allan G. Barclay
1974–1975	Allan G. Barclay
1975–1976	Allan G. Barclay
1976–1977	Allan G. Barclay
1977–1978	Allan G. Barclay
1978–1979	Allan G. Barclay
1979–1980	Lee B. Sechrest

	Secretary	Treasurer
1981–1982	Lee B. Sechrest	Laura C. Toomey
1982–1983	Jeanne S. Phillips	Laura C. Toomey
1983–1984	Jeanne S. Phillips	Laura C. Toomey
1985	Russell L. Adams	Laura C. Toomey
1986	Russell L. Adams	Laura C. Toomey
1987	Russell L. Adams	Laura C. Toomey
1988	Carolyn S. Schroeder	Laura C. Toomey
1989	Carolyn S. Schroeder	Laura C. Toomey
1990	June M. Tuma	Laura C. Toomey
1991	June M. Tuma	Gerald P. Koocher
1992	June M. Tuma	Gerald P. Koocher
1993	Donald K. Routh	Gerald P. Koocher
1994	Donald K. Routh	Edward Craighead
1995	Donald K. Routh	Edward Craighead
1996	Janet Matthews	Edward Craighead
1997	Janet Matthews	Edward Craighead
1998	Janet Matthews	Edward Craighead

Note. — indicates that there was no secretary for that year

TABLE 14
Recipients of Awards of the Division of Clinical Psychology
American Psychological Association

Year	Name	Type of Contribution Honored
1958	John G. Darley	Scientific and Professional
	Frederic Lyman Wells	Scientific and Professional
1959	Starke R. Hathaway	Scientific and Professional
	David Shakow	Scientific and Professional
1960	David Rapaport	Scientific and Professional
	David Wechsler	Scientific and Professional
1961	Samuel J. Beck	Scientific and Professional
	Henry A. Murray	Scientific and Professional
1962	Stanley D. Porteus	Scientific and Professional
	Carl R. Rogers	Scientific and Professional
1963	Edgar A. Doll	Scientific and Professional
	Jean W. Macfarlane	Scientific and Professional
1964	Norman A. Cameron	Scientific and Professional
	Robert W. White	Scientific and Professional
1965	George A. Kelly	Scientific and Professional
	Bruno Klopfer	Scientific and Professional
1966	Harold M. Hildreth*	Scientific and Professional
	Nicholas Hobbs	Scientific and Professional
	Joseph Zubin	Continuing Education (PDIs)
1967	William A. Hunt	Scientific and Professional
	Paul E. Meehl	Scientific and Professional
1968	Jerry W. Carter, Jr.	Scientific and Professional
	Julian B. Rotter	Scientific and Professional
1969	Noble H. Kelley	Scientific and Professional
	Seymour B. Sarason	Scientific and Professional
1970	John Elderkin Bell	Scientific and Professional
	R. Nevitt Sanford	Scientific and Professional
1971	Rollo R. May	Scientific and Professional
	Silvan S. Tomkins	Scientific and Professional
1972	E. Lowell Kelly	Scientific and Professional
	Anne Roe	Scientific and Professional
1973	Florence C. Halpern	Scientific and Professional
	Joseph McVicker Hunt	Scientific and Professional
1974	Robert R. Holt	Scientific and Professional
	Evelyn Hooker	Scientific and Professional
1975	Gardner Lindzey	Scientific and Professional
	O. Hobart Mowrer	Scientific and Professional
1976	Sol L. Garfield	Scientific and Professional
	Eliot H. Rodnick	Scientific and Professional
1977	Norman L. Farberow	Scientific and Professional
	Edwin S. Shneidman	Scientific and Professional
1978	Erich Fromm	Scientific and Professional
	Bernard Kalinkowitz	Scientific and Professional
	Sheldon Korchin	Scientific and Professional
	Benjamin B. Wolman	Scientific and Professional
1979	Bruno Bettelheim	Scientific and Professional
	Erik Erikson	Scientific and Professional
1980	Molly Harrower	Scientific and Professional
	Karen Machover	Scientific and Professional
1981	Hans H. Strupp	Scientific and Professional
	Carl N. Zimet	Scientific and Professional

Year	Name	Type of Contribution Honored
1982	Alan O. Ross	Scientific and Professional
	Janet T. Spence	Scientific and Professional
1983	Joseph D. Matarazzo	Scientific
	Stanley F. Schneider	Training
	Jack Wiggins, Jr.	Professional
1984	Mary D. S. Ainsworth	Scientific
	Louis Cohen	Professional
1985	Harold L. Rausch	Professional
	Saul Rosenzweig	Scientific
1986	Lester Luborsky	Scientific
	Jeanne S. Phillips	Professional
1987	Robert A. Harper	Professional
	Morris B. Parloff	Scientific
	Oscar A. Parsons	Scientific
	Robert D. Weitz	Professional
1988	Ronald E. Fox	Professional
	Norman Garmezy	Scientific
	Frank J. Sullivan	Public Service
1989	Patrick H. DeLeon	Scientific and Professional
	Charles D. Spielberger	Scientific and Professional
1990	Herman Feifel	Scientific
	Rogers H. Wright	Professional
1991	(no awards given)	
1992	Jules Barron*	Special
	Alan E. Kazdin	Scientific
	Donald K. Routh	Professional
1993	K. Daniel O'Leary	Scientific
	Robert J. Resnick	Professional
1994	Susan Nolen-Hoeksema	Shakow Award (Early Career)
	Kenneth Pope	Professional
	G. Terence Wilson	Scientific
1995	Allan G. Barclay	Professional
	Judy Garber	Shakow Award (Early Career)
	Jonathan Kellerman	Media
	Herbert C. Quay	Scientific
1996	Thomas N. Bradbury	Shakow Award (Early Career)
	Hans J. Eysenck	Centennial Award
	Edna B. Foa	Scientific
	Paul E. Meehl	Centennial Award
	Diane J. Willis	Professional
1997	Thomas E. Joiner	Shakow Award (Early Career)
	Arnold A. Lazarus	Professional
	Lizette Peterson	Scientific

*Awarded posthumously

possible passed by a margin of more than 4 to 1 (Members Approve Reorganization Plan, 1962). As noted in Table 10, the first of the sections, Clinical Psychology, was founded by Alan O. Ross (1921–1993), shortly after the division had voted for a bylaw change permitting sections to form. It was approved in 1963 (Executive Committee Meets, 1963). Section 1 had special historical significance to clinical psychology in that it restored the original emphasis in the field on work with children. After World War II, because of all the funding from the Veterans Administration, the field had veered very far in the direction of work exclusively with adults. Section 1 supports a peer-reviewed scientific publication, the *Journal of Clinical Child Psychology*. A history of Section 1 was previously published by the author of this chapter (Routh, 1991).

The original Section 2 of Division 12 was formed when Psychologists Interested in the Advancement of Psychotherapy (PIAP), an interest group originally founded in the late 1940s, affiliated with the division in 1963 (Executive Committee Meets, 1963). Before very many years, this section broke off and became APA Division 29 (Psychotherapy), a sizable practitioner-oriented group. The subsequent comments of Max Siegel (1918–1988) when he was president of Division 12 perhaps provide some insight into the attitude of those who broke away: "It is quite clear to me that if Division 12 had not been the conservative, reactionary, and anti-practitioner Division that it was over a decade ago, there would have been no need for a Division of Psychotherapy (29)" (Siegel, 1977, p. 1).

Another group, known as the Section on Continuing Professional Development, grew out of a young turks organization known as the Corresponding Committee of Fifty (which functioned from 1961 to 1973). After the 1973 transition, it was a section of Division 12 until 1986, when it disbanded. During these latter years it was known as Section 2.

Section 3, which formed in 1966, was originally called the Section for the Development of Clinical Psychology as an Experimental–Behavioral Science. Its founders were academics (as are most of its present members). Many of them were part of the behavior therapy movement that burgeoned in the 1960s. Most have by now broadened their interests to include cognitive as well as behavioral approaches. Many of the leaders of Section 3 previously held office in an organization outside the APA, the Association for the Advancement of Behavior Therapy (AABT). One notable statement of what at least some members of Section 3 think was McFall's (1991) manifesto. This document stated, in part:

> Psychological services should not be administered to the public (except under strict experimental control) until they have satisfied these four minimal criteria:
>
> 1. The exact nature of the service must be described clearly.
> 2. The claimed benefits of the service must be stated explicitly.
> 3. These claimed benefits must be validated scientifically.
> 4. Possible negative side effects that might outweigh any benefits must be ruled out empirically. (McFall, 1991, p. 80)

In 1991, Section 3 voted to change its name to the Society for a Science of Clinical Psychology (Oltmanns & Krasner, 1993). One of Section 3's most visible activities at present is the electronic mail (e-mail) network it maintains, which is largely devoted to the discussion of research issues.

In the most recent era, division leaders coming up through Section 3 such as David Barlow and Martin E. P. Seligman have emphasized the importance of an interdependency of science and practice. Barlow appointed a task force led by Dianne Chambless, whose report (Chambless, 1995) emphasized the desirability that practitioners use "empirically supported" treatments. The task force tried to spell out criteria by which these might be identified and listed some examples. This task force report has drawn praise from the community of academic and research clinical psychologists but has proven to be controversial among some practitioners, who already feel themselves under new pressure for accountability from the managed health care system.

Section 4, concerned with the clinical psychology of women, emerged from an equal opportunity affirmative action committee originally headed by Bonnie R. Strickland, appointed in 1975 (Barclay, 1975). This section was approved in 1980. Its charter members included 116 women and 32 men (Rayburn, 1993).

The Society of Pediatric Psychology, originally founded in 1968 by a committee consisting of Dorothea Ross, Lee Salk (1926–1992), and Logan Wright, operated for many years as a sort of special interest group attached to Section 1 (Pediatric Psychology, 1968). In 1980, this group became Section 5 of the division. It publishes the *Journal of Pediatric Psychology*, perhaps the leading journal of its kind.

Section 6, concerned with Ethnic Minority Clinical Psychology, was formed in 1986, and like Section 4 emerged out of the division's concerns for promoting equal opportunity and affirmative action in the field of clinical psychology (Jones, 1992).

Briefly, from 1988 to 1992, the division had another section (designated with the number 7) devoted to group psychotherapy. However, this section disbanded on the formation of a new APA division devoted to group psychology and group psychotherapy.

The division's newest section, Clinical Geropsychology, was founded in 1993 by Barry A. Edelstein and his colleagues (Members Sought for New Section II, 1993). This group decided to take over the vacant designation of Section 2 and thus became the third group to do so. To the chapter author, it seems to have better prospects for becoming a permanent section of the division than did the others with this "unlucky" number. An interest in clinical psychology and the older person had been expressed much earlier in division publications (e.g., Pressey, 1968).

CENTENNIAL CELEBRATIONS

In 1993, Division 12 officers were already beginning to think about the centennial of their field (e.g., Barlow, 1993). In 1996, Division 12 joined with other clinical psychology organizations all over the world, as well as with the APA and the University of Pennsylvania, in celebrating the founding of the first psychology clinic by Lightner Witmer at the University of Pennsylvania in 1896. A variety of special programs related to this theme was planned for the 1996 APA convention in Toronto, including a gala at the National Hockey Hall of Fame there. Any APA division wishing to designate items in its convention program as part of this centennial was invited to do so. As indicated in Table 14, Division 12 selected two clinical psychologists, Hans J. Eysenck and Paul E. Meehl, for its 1996 centennial awards. As Meehl commented to me, it is interesting that one of these awardees is associated with a dimensional and the other one with a categorical approach to psychopathology. One of them is also associated with behavior therapy and the other with psychodynamic psychotherapy, thus representing the continued pluralism of the field as well as some of the best research and rationales for practice it has to offer. A separate centennial celebration was held at the University of Pennsylvania in October 1996.

CONCLUSION

Division 12 has built well on the foundations of its predecessors stretching back to the AACP, founded 80 years ago. It was for a long time the largest APA division and continues to be quite a successful one. It provides for its members a unique combination of the "learned society" and the "professional guild." Although it has many advantages, this mixed type of organization also has built in communication problems, as noted by Routh (1994). Thus, Division 12 needs to continue searching for ways to facilitate a continuing dialogue between those clinical psychologists who are primarily academics and researchers and those who devote most of their energies to professional practice in the field.

REFERENCES

A New Policy for the Division Newsletter. (1966, Fall). *The Clinical Psychologist, 20,* 5.

Advanced Training Institute in Clinical Psychology. (1950, March). *Newsletter, Division of Clinical and Abnormal Psychology, 3,* 1–3.

Barclay, A. (1974, Spring). Highlights from the minutes of the executive committee midwinter meeting, Holiday Inn, Palm Beach, Florida, 14–16 February, 1974. *The Clinical Psychologist, 27,* 22–23.

Barclay, A. (1975, Fall). Minutes, Executive Committee, Division of Clinical Psychology, Palmer House, Chicago, 28 August 1975. *The Clinical Psychologist, 29,* 25–26.

Barlow, D. H. (1993, Winter). Presidential column. *The Clinical Psychologist, 46,* 2.

Benton, A. (1975, Winter). Introduction: Interface of clinical psychology and clinical human neuropsychology. *The Clinical Psychologist, 29,* 7.

Binet, A., & Simon, T. (1905). [A new method for the diagnosis of intellectual level of abnormal persons.] *Année Psychologique, 11,* 191–244.

Breuer, J., & Freud, S. (1986). Studies in hysteria. In *The standard edition of the complete psychological works of Sigmund Freud* (Vol. 2, 1–306). London: Hogarth Press and the Institute of Psycho-Analysis. (Original published 1895)

Business Meeting. (1947, November). *Newsletter, Division of Clinical and Abnormal Psychology, 1,* 3–7.

Bylaws. (1981, Fall). *The Clinical Psychologist, 34,* 27–31.

Carter, J. W., Jr. (1950). The community health service program of the National Institute of Mental Health, U.S. Public Health Service. *Journal of Clinical Psychology, 6,* 112–117.

Cattell, J. M. (1890). Mental tests and measurements. *Mind, 15,* 373–381.

Chambless, D. L. (1995, Winter). Task Force on Dissemination of Empirically-Validated Psychological Treatments: Report and recommendations. *The Clinical Psychologist, 48,* 3–24.

Chotlos, J. W., Scheerer, M., & Holt, R. (1952, June). Report of the Committee on Publication Outlets in Clinical Psychology. *Newsletter, Division of Clinical and Abnormal Psychology, 5,* 7–9.

Cummings, N. (1979, Winter). President's message: Should Division 12 be a credentialling group, an interest group, or a combination of both: A referendum. *The Clinical Psychologist, 32,* 1, 27.

Dewsbury, D. A. (1996). Robert M. Yerkes: A psychobiologist with a plan. In G. A. Kimble, C. A. Boneau, & M. Wertheimer (Eds.), *Portraits of pioneers in psychology* (Vol. II, pp. 87–105). Washington, DC: American Psychological Association.

Doll, E. A. (1946). Internship program at the Vineland laboratory. *Journal of Consulting Psychology, 10,* 184–190.

Editorial. (1949, February). *Newsletter, Division of Clinical and Abnormal Psychology, 2,* 1–2.

English, H. B. (1938). Organization of the American Association of Applied Psychologists. *Journal of Consulting Psychology, 2,* 7–16.

Executive Committee Meeting. (1947, November). *Newsletter, Division of Clinical and Abnormal Psychology, 1,* 2–3.

Executive Committee Meets. (1963, Spring). *Newsletter, Division of Clinical Psychology, 16,* 1.

Fernberger, S. W. (1932). The American Psychological Association: A historical summary, 1892–1930. *Psychological Bulletin, 29,* 1–89.

Galton, F. (1978). *Hereditary genius.* New York: St. Martin's Press. (Originally published 1869)

Gesell, A. (1919). The field of clinical psychology as an applied science: A symposium. *Journal of Applied Psychology, 3,* 81–84.

Hollingworth, L. S. (1917, December 28). Minutes of the American Association of Clinical Psychologists. American Psychological Association Papers, Manuscript Division, U.S. Library of Congress, Washington, DC.

Hollingworth, L. S. (1919, October 27). Letter to J.E.W. Wallin. Wallin papers, Archives of the History of American Psychology, University of Akron, Ohio.

Holt, R. R. (1948, August). Letter to the editor. *Newsletter, Division of Clinical and Abnormal Psychology, 1,* 20–21.

Hunt, J. McV., MacKinnon, D. W., Rodnick, E. H., Shaffer, L. F., & Tolman, R. S. (1957, August). Awards. *Newsletter, Division of Clinical Psychology, 10,* 6–8.

Jones, R. T. (1992). Section VI: Racial/ethnic and cultural issues. *The Clinical Psychologist, 45,* 53–56.

Kelly, E. L. (1960, Winter). A few words from the president. *Newsletter, Division of Clinical Psychology, 13,* 1.

Kelly, G. A. (1956, October). President's message. *Newsletter, Division of Clinical Psychology, 10,* 1–3

Kelly, G. A. (1957, August). A letter to the division membership [announcing the appointment of Elizabeth B. Wolf as newsletter editor]. *Newsletter, Division of Clinical Psychology, 10,* 1.

Knapp, S., Levin, Z., & French, J. (1993). *A history of the Pennsylvania Psychological Association.* Harrisburg: Pennsylvania Psychological Association.

Kovacs, A. L. (1980, Winter). Results of bylaw ballot. *The Clinical Psychologist, 33,* 1.

McFall, R. M. (1991, November). Manifesto for a science of clinical psychology. *The Clinical Psychologist, 44,* 75–88. (Presidential address delivered to Section 3, Division 12 in 1990)

McReynolds, P. (1996). Lightner Witmer: A centennial tribute. *American Psychologist, 51,* 237–240.

Meltzer, H. (1966). Psychology of the scientist: XVII. Research has a place in private practice. *Psychological Reports, 19,* 463–472.

Members approve reorganization plan. (1962, Fall). *Newsletter, Division of Clinical Psychology, 15,* 5.

Members sought for new Section II, Clinical Geropsychology. (1993, Spring). *The Clinical Psychologist, 46,* 93.

Mid-Year Meeting of Executive Committee. (1948, June). *Newsletter, Division of Clinical and Abnormal Psychology, 1,* 1–2.

Mitchell, D. (1919). The clinical psychologist. *Journal of Abnormal Psychology*, *14*, 325–332.

Mitchell, D. (1931). Private practice. In R. A. Brotemarkle (Ed.), *Clinical psychology: Studies in honor of Lightner Witmer* (pp. 177–190). Philadelphia: University of Pennsylvania Press.

Murray, H., & Morgan, C. (1938). *Explorations in personality*. New York: Oxford University Press.

1988 Brings Major Changes for *The Clinical Psychologist*: New Format and New Editor. (1987, Fall). *The Clinical Psychologist*, *40*, 84.

Oltmanns, T. F., & Krasner, L. (1993, Winter). A voice for science in clinical psychology: The history of Section III of Division 12. *The Clinical Psychologist*, *46*, 25–32.

Pediatric psychology. (1968, Fall). *The Clinical Psychologist*, *22*, 62.

Pressey, S. L. (1968, Summer). Clinical psychology and the older person. *The Clinical Psychologist*, *21*, 180, 205.

Raimy, V. C. (Ed.). (1950). *Training in clinical psychology*. New York: Prentice-Hall.

Rayburn, C. A. (1993, Winter). Section IV, the Clinical Psychology of Women: The first 12 years (1980–1992). *The Clinical Psychologist*, *46*, 33–37.

Roe, A. (1948, April). Preliminary announcement of the Committee on Post-Graduate Education. *Newsletter, Division of Clinical and Abnormal Psychology*, *1*, 3–5.

Rogers, C. R. (1949, September). A message from the new president. *Newsletter, Division of Clinical and Abnormal Psychology*, *3*, 1.

Routh, D. K. (1991, May). The Section on Clinical Child Psychology: A 30-year retrospect and prospect. *The Clinical Psychologist*, *44*, 33–36.

Routh, D. K. (1994). *Clinical psychology since 1917: Science, practice, and organization*. New York: Plenum Press.

Routh, D. K. (1996). Lightner Witmer and the first 100 years of clinical psychology. *American Psychologist*, *51*, 244–247.

Routh, D. K., del Barrio, V., & Carpintero, H. (1996). European roots of the first psychology clinic in North America. *European Psychologist*, *1*, 44–50.

Schroeder, C. S. (1989, November). Summary minutes, Division 12 Board of Directors' meeting, December 8–9, 1988, Orlando, Florida. *The Clinical Psychologist*, *42*, 92–100.

Schroeder, C. S. (1990, November). Archival minutes of the Board of Directors October 1989 meeting. *The Clinical Psychologist*, *43*.

Sexton, V. S., & Hogan, J. D. (1992). Epilogue. In V. S. Sexton & J. D. Hogan (Eds.), *International psychology: Views from around the world* (pp. 467–477). Lincoln: University of Nebraska Press.

Shaffer, L. F. (1945). Letter to David Rapaport. American Psychological Association Papers, Division of Clinical Psychology Section, Manuscript Division, U.S. Library of Congress, Washington, DC.

Siegel, M. (1977, Winter). Contemporary issues in professional psychology. *The Clinical Psychologist, 30*, 1, 10.

Wallin J. E. W. (1955). *The odyssey of a psychologist.* Wilmington, DE: Author.

Wallin, J. E. W. (1961). A note on the origin of the APA clinical section. *American Psychologist, 16*, 256–258.

Wallin, J. E. W. (1968, Winter). Pioneer institutional psychologists and some early APA developments: A historical note. *The Clinical Psychologist, 21*, 82–84.

Witmer, L. (1896). Practical work in psychology. *Pediatrics, 2*, 462–471.

Witmer, L. (1897). The organization of practical work in psychology. *Psychological Review, 4*, 116.

Witmer, L. (1907). Clinical psychology. *The Psychological Clinic, 1*, 1–9.

3

A HISTORY OF DIVISION 13 (CONSULTING PSYCHOLOGY)

WILBUR RIGBY

This chapter reviews the vicissitudes of the evolution of the Division of Consulting Psychology from the early antecedents in 1915 through 1995. The material reviews a limited and short-lived existence of a division of consulting psychology in the American Psychological Association (APA) in the 1920s, a nearly 20-year period when there was no group called "consulting psychologists" within the APA, and developments since the restructuring of the APA and the establishment of divisions in 1946. Uncertainty and lack of agreement about the definition of consultation is noted, as is the ability of the membership and executive board to tolerate ambiguity in that matter. A provisional definition that probably would be accepted by a majority of the membership is as follows:

> A consulting psychologist is one who has received recognition as an
> expert in one or more areas and who provides assistance to individuals

Some of the material in this chapter was taken from an earlier history of the division by the author that was printed in the division's journal (Rigby, 1992) and described much earlier in the division's newsletter (Rigby, 1973a, 1973b, 1973c). Other information was obtained from division newsletters, correspondence, and other archival materials. Some contributions came from other APA journals and from books, as noted in the references and the text.

Appreciation is expressed to Sarah Jordan of the APA Division Services Office, Dr. Leonard Allen, and Dr. Paul J. Lloyd for assistance in collecting background information. Appreciation also is expressed to Dr. Bernard Lubin and Dr. John R. Barry for their review of a draft of this material.

or organizations in regard to psychological aspects of their activities. Consultation involves a broad range of techniques and styles of functioning and is offered by a specialist to others who want assistance in the management of psychological and human relations problems.

EVENTS PRIOR TO APA DIVISION FORMATION

The title Division of Consulting Psychology was first adopted by the APA in 1924 and antecedents of that development go back some 10 years prior (Fernberger, 1932; Ives, 1967). The following account of the early history of Consulting Psychology is taken from Fernberger's 1932 paper. An initiating event occurred in 1915 when the APA passed a resolution, proposed by Guy Whipple, "That the Association discourages the use of mental tests for practical psychological diagnosis by individuals psychologically unqualified for this work" (Fernberger, 1932, p. 46). Noting the absence of a mechanism to enforce that admirable but not notably effective resolution, the APA appointed a committee in 1917 to develop a statement of "qualifications for psychological examiners and other psychological experts" (Fernberger, 1932, p. 46). The committee presented a preliminary report in 1918, and in 1919 the APA established a committee to give attention to ways of developing certification procedures. The initial report of that committee in 1920 recommended establishment of "a Standing Committee on Certification of Consulting Psychologists" (Fernberger, 1932, p. 47).

Birth of the Division

The standing committee appears to have gone to work promptly and in 1921 indicated that the sole area they believed "certification of consulting psychologists is now practicable is limited to that concerned with the measurement of various types of intelligence and special abilities therein" (Fernberger, 1932, p. 47). They recommended that a Section of Consulting Psychologists be established within the APA and that certification be designated by election to membership in that section, with an application deadline of January 1, 1923. The primary qualification for membership was to be "a doctoral degree in psychology, education, or medicine or equivalent qualifications" (Fernberger, 1932, p. 47).

The standing committee's report included a statement that "the term Clinical Psychology is not properly applicable to this Section and should not be used" (Fernberger, 1932, p. 47). However, there was already in existence a section of clinical psychology within the APA, established in 1919, and the committee recommended that all members of that section should be eligible to join the proposed section. No definition of consultation was given, and it seems there may have been considerable uncertainty about the meaning of the terms consulting psychology and consulting psychologist. It appears that the words were used in those days to refer to applied psychologists in general (Ives, 1967), although the focus of this committee was on members of the clinical section.

The standing committee's recommendations were accepted by the APA and a committee of five persons was appointed to develop the details and administer the program of certification via election to membership in the new section. Efforts to develop the new group appeared to be proceeding well, but at the time of the deadline for receipt of applications only 25 persons had applied, and only 13 of those were elected to membership. The committee then recommended development of sections of educational and industrial psychology, which would provide certification in those areas. The APA rejected that recommendation and, instead, approved a motion that "the Committee be continued for the ensuing year under its old instructions and that it confine its certification to members of the Section of Clinical Psychology" (Fernberger, 1932, p. 49). In 1924 the title was changed from "section" to "division" and, on incorporation of the APA in 1925, Article XI of the bylaws established the Division of Consulting Psychology, to be composed of members of the APA to whom certificates had been awarded.

Death and Rebirth

During the years after 1923 a few more persons were admitted to membership, with the number certified reaching the grand total of 25. The total was low partially because very high membership standards were established and most persons doing clinical work at that time did not meet those standards and thus were not eligible for certification. A number of suggestions were made to use titles such as psychometrist, psychometrician, or psychometric assistant for such persons and for those said to be engaged in "routine mental testing" (Fernberger, 1932, p. 50). However, no procedures for certification at a lower level were developed. In addition, problems were encountered in terms of devising mechanisms for dealing with unprofessional conduct. The entire effort to certify consulting psychologists, and thereby to control the clinical (and other applied) work of that time, appears to have bogged down rather quickly, and in 1927 it was abandoned entirely. That result was officially recognized by deletion from the APA bylaws of the article that had established a division of consulting psychology.

The testing movement in psychology had received great impetus during World War I when psychologists contributed to the development and use of tests of general intelligence and other measures of special abilities. That carried over into the post-war years and testing was extended to additional areas. The efforts of the APA in the 1920s to certify consulting psychologists appear to have risen out of concern that such activities were being carried out by people who were marginally qualified and by a desire to increase the qualifications and skills of persons doing such work. After those efforts were discontinued in 1927 there was no group called "consulting psychologists" within the APA for a period of almost 20 years.

During that period a group known as the Association of Consulting Psychologists was organized outside the APA (Fryer & Henry, 1950). In 1937, that group and the clinical section of the APA joined to bring about the creation of the American Association of Applied Psychology (AAAP; Fryer & Henry, 1950). In those days most members of the clinical section felt strongly that the APA was unwilling to give sufficient recognition and support to applied psychology, and they opted to form a separate organization. During World War II applications of psychological knowledge and principles became firmly established in the military services and, by the time the war ended, had broadened to a quite varied array of activities. In 1945, AAAP and the APA were reunited in order to establish a single national organization representing all of psychology. Division status for both consulting and clinical groups was offered partly to bring AAAP members back within the fold. In 1946 Division 13 (Consulting Psychology) was established as one of the 19 charter divisions of the restructured APA. The division did not really get organized and functioning, however, until 1948 (Jane Hildreth, personal communication, 1973) apparently due to factors such as soliciting and processing applications for membership, developing plans for annual meetings and programs, and related matters.

MEMBERSHIP

The division had a modest beginning with a total membership of less than 200. Leadership was strong and membership increased over the years, although the increase was somewhat sporadic. (Information about membership characteristics was obtained from surveys in 1973 and in 1989.)

Numerical Factors

It should be noted that until 1958, the APA organization provided only for fellows and associates—there was no group called members—and that, if one had a doctoral degree, fellow status was relatively easy to obtain (Daniel & Loutitt, 1953). The 1958 APA bylaws revision provided for the category of members and required that elevation to fellow status depended on more than ordinary accomplishments and contributions. Thus, the group called fellows prior to 1958 corresponds to the group called members since that year. Nevertheless, the claim of the newly established Division 13 that it continued the earlier emphasis on high standards seems defensible. It was composed only of fellows (pre-1958 definition), did not have associate members, and persons had to hold associate status in the APA for 5 years before they were eligible to join the division. Steps to change membership standards were not taken hastily. It was not until 1963, 5 years after the APA bylaws revision, that the division admitted members, and it did not have associate members until 1987. Membership trends since 1948 are indicated in Table 15.

In 1963, when the category of member was introduced, the division more than doubled in size (Rigby, 1992). There was also a noteworthy increase in the number of fellows, with that category increasing by 56 persons to a total of 288. The fellow group has shown a gradual decline since that year, whereas the number of members has increased but in a fluctuating manner with some years showing a decrease from the previous year. As early as 1965 there were more members than fellows, and that relationship has remained since that time. Total membership reached its peak thus far—959—in 1993, with a small decline since that year.

A development in the early to middle 1960s that is not clearly evident in Table 15 had an interesting effect on membership numbers (Harper, 1992). A group called Psychologists in Private Practice (PPP) had developed outside the APA organization and wanted to join some division of the APA. The leadership of Division 13 was interested in increasing the total membership of the division. Decisions were made to amend the division's bylaws so that a member category was added to the existing fellow category and to send a special invitation to join Division 13 to all members of PPP. Many of the members did apply and became members of Division 13. It appears that this group accounted for most of the 265 additions to the division's rolls in 1963. The goals of each group seemed to have been accomplished. The practice-oriented group had become part of an APA division, and Division 13 had doubled its total membership. It soon became clear, however, that the longer range perspectives and goals of the two groups were not completely harmonious. The practice-oriented group proposed that the name of the division be changed to the Division of Private Practice and that activities be modified accordingly. There was spirited debate at several of the business meetings in regard to those proposals. That debate culminated in a vote in 1965 to retain the traditional name and, by implication at least, to reject any significant alteration of the division's activities. A number of the persons who joined Division 13 during those years retained their membership, but most of the practice-oriented persons continued their efforts and eventually developed Division 42, Psychologists in Independent Practice.

TABLE 15
Membership Trends in Division 13 Since 1948

Year	Fellows	Members	Associates	Total
1948	189	—	—	189
1950	184	—	—	184
1955	233	—	—	233
1960	232	—	—	232
1963	288	209	—	497
1964	285	249	—	534
1965	277	296	—	573
1966	275	310	—	585
1968	262	333	—	595
1970	247	337	—	584
1972	224	347	—	571
1973	227	336	—	563
1974	221	438	—	659
1975	211	478	—	689
1976	209	491	—	700
1977	198	491	—	689
1978	200	487	—	687
1979	193	487	—	680
1980	193	479	—	672
1981	184	543	—	727
1982	174	614	—	788
1983	191	688	—	879
1984	184	737	—	921
1985	178	759	—	937
1986	172	753	—	925
1987	174	748	14	936
1988	165	730	27	922
1989	154	716	39	909
1990	148	721	40	909
1991	153	739	38	930
1992	148	736	33	917
1993	148	778	33	959
1994	146	779	27	952
1995	137	750	28	915

Source. 1948–1972 Yearbooks and Directories of APA. The "Registers" for 1967, 1969, and 1971 do not provide division membership data; 1973–1994 APA Directory/Register Publications, 1995 Figures from February 1995 End of Month Report from Management Information Service.
Note. — indicates there was no member or associate category that year. The member category was established in 1963, the associate category in 1987.

Membership Characteristics

In 1971, in an effort to obtain current information about the membership and their desires in terms of division activities and goals, a questionnaire devised by Doris R. Kraemer and Norman Kaplan was printed in the fall newsletter. As is often the case with newsletter questionnaires, the return was minimal—less than 10% in this instance. At its winter meeting in

February 1973, the executive board accepted a recommendation by W. K. Rigby, who was then chair of the Public Information Committee, to send a special mailing of the questionnaire to each member of the division—and assigned the task to the Public Information Committee.

The special mailing, with a modified format of the questionnaire and a catchy cover letter, obtained a sizeable response. A total of 332 persons—58% of the membership—provided the requested information. Tabulation of the responses (Rigby, 1973) showed that 85% of the respondents were males and 91% held the PhD degree. Five percent had the EdD degree and 1% were at the MA level. The remainder did not mark this item. The respondents were a chronologically mature group with the median age being 53 and the median years since obtaining the highest degree being 19. Cumulative percentages for age groups showed that 26% were more than 60 years of age, 56% were more than 50, and 93% were more than 40 years of age. Only 7% were 40 or younger and only 1% were 30 years of age or younger.

Approximately 97% of the respondents indicated they were either licensed or certified in one or more states. Forty-eight percent reported they held the ABPP diploma, 4% indicated their applications were in process, and 4% stated they planned to apply. Almost all belonged to one or more other divisions and primary areas of interest, as indicated by those memberships, included (in declining order) clinical, psychotherapy, counseling, state association affairs, personality and social psychology, and industrial/organizational psychology. Numerous other interest areas were represented by smaller numbers of the respondents.

Consultation practice was predominantly solo, part-time, with 43% of the respondents checking that category. Next in frequency was solo, full-time at 26%. Running a rather distant third and fourth were members of a consultation firm, full-time at just over 9% and group practice, full-time at just under 9%. All other categories were 5% or less. It is interesting that approximately 44% of the respondents indicated that in 1973 they were engaged in full-time consultative work. These figures should be interpreted with caution, however, because lack of a clear distinction between direct service and consultative activities obscured the results. Some persons included direct service work as consultation, whereas others excluded such activities.

A later survey (Hellkamp & Morgan, 1990), somewhat similar to the one completed in 1973, was conducted in 1989 and provided a more current profile of membership characteristics. Response rate was similar to that of the 1973 survey—approximately 58%. Comparison of data from the two surveys (Hellkamp, 1993) indicated that the membership characteristics were essentially unchanged for age, gender, ethnicity, and highest degree. Membership in other divisions and in state psychological associations also remained much the same. There was a decrease in the proportion reporting solo consulting practices and an increase in those reporting full-time work with consulting firms. Still, much consultation is provided on a part-time basis by persons in academia, various governmental agencies, and in clinical or counseling practices. The survey data indicate that consultation services were provided over a greater range of work settings in 1989 than in 1973. Consultation to the media, religious groups, sports organizations, forensic settings, psychological rehabilitation, and mental retardation agencies was reported either initially or with more frequency in the 1989 survey. It appears the greatest shift was from consultation in clinical areas (48% in 1973) to consultation in the business/industrial area (63% in 1989).

The division welcomes women and members of minority groups and has made a number of efforts to attract such persons to membership. Still, the percentages for members who responded to the two survey requests—in 1973 and 1989—remained much the same. Ethnicity data are not included in the APA directories and cannot be reliably determined by examination of names. The directories do indicate that the percentage of women members of the division has increased from 15.9% in 1985 to 20.5% in 1990, and to 21.3% in 1995. These modest gains appear to be a result of limited interest on the part of potential applicants rather than of exclusionary efforts by the division.

DEFINING CONSULTATION

As noted, the efforts in the 1920s to develop a division of consulting psychology offered no definitions and indicated there may have been considerable uncertainty and lack of agreement about the meaning of the terms *consultation* and *consulting psychology*. Responses to a request for definitions in the 1973 survey indicated quite clearly a continuing uncertainty and lack of agreement in regard to the definition of *consultation*, especially in terms of whether direct service activities should or should not be considered consultation. In an effort to clarify the situation, a special request was made by Gordon Derner, then president of the division, to a variety of persons to provide additional carefully considered material. Based on all the information received, a draft of a definition developed by the Public Information Committee and modeled after a definition of mental health consultation devised by MacLennen, Quinn, and Schroeder (1971) received lively discussion by the executive board and eventually culminated in the following definition:

> A consulting psychologist is one who has received recognition as an expert in one or more areas of functioning and who provides specialized technical assistance to individuals or organizations in regard to the

psychological aspects of their work. Such assistance is advisory in nature, and the consultant has no direct responsibility for its acceptance and implementation. There is ordinarily a contractual relationship between the consultant and client, usually involving a fee for service, but a psychologist employed on a salary basis may serve as a consultant within and/or outside the employing organization. Consultation involves a broad range of techniques and styles of functioning and is offered by a specialist either to other psychologists less knowledgeable in some aspect of their work or to other specialists in other fields who need assistance in the management of psychological and human relations problems. (Division 13 Executive Board, 1973)

A final outcome of the early survey questionnaire was the development of the division's first brochure, which included the previous definition of a consulting psychologist. That definition with minor modifications has been included in several subsequent revisions of the brochure.

A 1979 revision of the division's bylaws included the following new paragraph:

3. Consulting Psychology, for the purposes of these Bylaws, shall be defined as the function of applying and extending the special knowledge of a psychologist, through the process of consultation, to problems involving human behavior in various areas. A consulting psychologist shall be defined as a psychologist who either accepts direct responsibility for helping clients by analyzing problem situations, or who provides counsel to an individual or organization who has responsibility for using or not using what is offered. Consulting psychologists may have as clients individuals, institutions, agencies, corporations or other kinds of organizations. (Division 13 Executive Board, 1979)

That paragraph remained in a further revision of the bylaws in 1988. In a recent journal article (Leonard, 1992), seven currently prominent consultants gave their definitions of consultation, which varied considerably. Some included direct service as consultation but others were silent on that matter.

Arriving at specific definitions of consulting psychology and consulting psychologists does not appear to have been a burning issue for division members. The topic has been given attention only sporadically and it has seldom been referred to in minutes of business and executive board meetings. The membership appears to acknowledge that definitions may vary and that reasonable diversity is acceptable. In the 1920s the term *consulting psychologist* appears to have referred to psychologists—with a focus on the clinical group—who were applying psychological knowledge outside the universities. In more recent years the term appears to emphasize the development of expertise and skills that may be useful in dealing with problems in a wide variety of situations.

ACTIVITIES AND DEVELOPMENTS

From what initially was a limited range of activities, the division gradually increased and expanded its APA convention program offerings, improved its newsletter and journal publications, and developed several awards programs. Consultation first increased in established areas and later expanded into new areas, a trend that appears to be continuing.

Officers

The list of presidents and secretary–treasurers in Table 16 contains a number of well-known people who have made and are continuing to make important contributions to various areas of psychology. A wide variety of interest and content areas are represented. Most members of Division 13 have a primary content area in which they have considerable experience and have developed expertise that is recognized by others. Their interest in the Division of Consulting Psychology is either to improve their skills and opportunities in consultation or to assist others in so doing. Both academic and nonacademic backgrounds are represented. In the past 20 years, ten presidents have been from academic settings and ten have been from other backgrounds ranging from solo consulting or clinical practices to government agencies to consulting firms. Since the early 1970s an effort has been made to keep a balance in the appointive offices between people with academic and nonacademic assignments and to obtain a good representation of the various interest areas in psychology. During that period, members of the executive board were able to work together very amicably even during the time leading up to the formation of the American Psychological Society in 1988. A number of members of the executive board have commented that this group has been more pleasant, informal, and collegial than boards of other divisions on which they have served. That benign pattern may be related to the chronological maturity of the members and also to a general orientation toward finding solutions for difficulties and problems.

From 1946 through 1962 the division had two representatives to the Council of Representatives, and from 1963 through 1971 there were three representatives. From 1956 through 1971 the division secretary–treasurer was always one of those representatives. Beginning in 1972, when the Albee Commission's formula for regulating the size of council became effective, the division has had only one representative. A listing of those who have served as the division's representatives to the council is presented in Table 17. Although the total membership of the division has increased by approximately 60% since 1972, the vote for council representation has not approached the level needed for a second representative. In 1981, the division

TABLE 16
Presidents and Secretary–Treasurers of Division 13: 1946–1995

Year	President	Secretary–Treasurer
1946–1947	Jack W. Dunlap	Gilbert J. Rich
1947–1948	Donald E. Super	Emily T. Burr
1948–1949	Morris S. Viteles	Helen L. Koch
1949–1950	Emily T. Burr	Helen L. Koch
1950–1951	Harold M. Hildreth	Helen L. Koch
1951–1952	Bertha M. Luckey	Emily L. Stogdill
1952–1953	Morton A. Seidenfeld	Emily L. Stogdill
1953–1954	E. Lowell Kelly	Katharine B. Greene
1954–1955	George A. Kelly	Katharine B. Greene
1955–1956	Rose G. Anderson	Katharine B. Greene
1956–1957	Jay L. Otis	Katharine B. Greene
1957–1958	Thomas W. Richards	Ruth M. Hubbard
1958–1959	Harold Edgerton	Ruth M. Hubbard
1959–1960	Edwin R. Henry	Ruth M. Hubbard
1960–1961	Marie P. Skodak	Ruth Bishop Heiser
1961–1962	Albert Ellis	Ruth Bishop Heiser
1962–1963	Orlo L. Crissey	Ruth Bishop Heiser
1963–1964	Edward M. Glaser	Margaret Ives
1964–1965	John R. Barry	Margaret Ives
1965–1966	Theodore H. Blau	Margaret Ives
1966–1967	Noble H. Kelly	Reuben S. Horlick
1967–1968	Margaret Ives	Reuben S. Horlick
1968–1969	John J. Brownfain	Reuben S. Horlick
1969–1970	Max Siegel	Melvin A. Gravitz
1970–1971	Karl F. Heiser	Melvin A. Gravitz
1971–1972	Hyman Meltzer	Melvin A. Gravitz
1972–1973	Gordon F. Derner	Doris R. Kraemer
1973–1974	Fred E. Spaner	Doris R. Kraemer
1974–1975	Malcolm L. Meltzer	Doris R. Kraemer
1975–1976	Reuben S. Horlick	Norman Kaplan
1976–1977	Clifford Swenson	W. K. Rigby
1977–1978	Norman Kaplan	W. K. Rigby
1978–1979	Raymond D. Fowler	W. K. Rigby
1979–1980	Doris Kraemer	W. K. Rigby
1980–1981	Robert A. Harper	Leonard Allen
1981–1982	W. K. Rigby	Leonard Allen
1982–1983	Thomas Backer	Clyde A. Crego
1983–1984	Leonard Allen	Clyde A. Crego
1984–1985	Allen S. Penman	Clyde A. Crego
1985–1986	Mack T. Henderson	Clyde A. Crego
1986–1987	Vytautas J. Bieliauskas	David J. Lutz
1987–1988	W. K. Rigby	David J. Lutz
1988–1989	Clyde A. Crego	David J. Lutz
1989–1990	Paul J. Lloyd	David J. Lutz
1990–1991	Sharon E. Robinson	David J. Lutz
1991–1992	Kenneth Bradt	David J. Lutz
1992–1993	Allan G. Barclay	John E. Deleray
1993–1994	David J. Lutz	Richard Weigel, Secretary; John E. Deleray, Treasurer
1994–1995	David Hellkamp	John E. Deleray
1995–1996	John E. Deleray	Richard Weigel

Source. American Psychologist

TABLE 17
Division 13 APA Council Representatives

Year	Representatives
1946	Robert A. Brotemarkle and Arthur T. Jersild
1947	Jack W. Dunlap and Douglas H. Fryer
1948	Alice I. Bryan (one to be elected)
1949	Bertha M. Luckey and Morris S. Viteles
1950	Bertha M. Luckey and Emily T. Burr
1951–1952	Emily T. Burr and Rose G. Anderson
1953	Rose G. Anderson and Edward A. Rundquist
1954–1955	Edward A. Rundquist and Marie P. Skodak
1956	Marie P. Skodak and Katherine B. Greene
1957–1959	Ruth M. Hubbard and George K. Bennett
1960–1962	Ruth Bishop Heiser and Jay L. Otis
1963	Margaret Ives, Noble H. Kelley, and Albert Ellis
1964	Margaret Ives, Noble H. Kelley, and Orlo L. Crissey
1965	Margaret Ives, Orlo L. Crissey, and Edward M. Glaser
1966	Orlo L. Crissey, Edward M. Glaser, and Reuben S. Horlick
1967	Edward M. Glaser, Reuben S. Horlick, and Theodore H. Blau
1968	Reuben S. Horlick, Theodore H. Blau, and Noble H. Kelley
1969	Noble H. Kelley, Hyman Meltzer, and Melvin A. Gravitz
1970	Noble H. Kelley, Melvin A. Gravitz, and Margaret Ives
1971	Melvin A. Gravitz, Margaret Ives, and Joseph B. Margolin
1972	Margaret Ives
1973–1974	Joseph B. Margolin
1975–1977	Doris R. Kraemer
1978–1980	Fred E. Spaner
1981	No Representative
1982–1983	Vytautas J. Bieliauskas
1984–1986	W. K. Rigby
1987–1989	John R. Barry
1990–1995	Robert A. Harper

Source. *American Psychologist.*

did not have council representation having failed to garner sufficient votes for even one representative.

A very unusual development occurred in the middle 1970s (Rigby, 1980) when Reuben S. Horlick served as president for 3 consecutive years. In 1974 Malcolm L. Meltzer was the elected president but was unable to serve because of health problems. Horlick, as president-elect, served as the acting president. In 1975 Horlick served as the duly elected president. In 1976 Clifford Swenson was the elected president but spent most of the year in Sweden on a Fulbright scholarship. Horlick, because of his experience and his location in the Washington area, again served as the acting president, although Swenson participated as distance and time allowed.

A number of other noteworthy developments occurred during the 1970s and 1980s. Norman Kaplan was recognized and lauded for his successful efforts in reorganizing and rejuvenating the membership committee. Leonard Allen, in private practice in the District of Columbia, proved so useful in communicating with the APA headquarters staff and in arranging meetings, luncheons, and dinners that he became known as the division's "all purpose utility infielder." David J. Lutz established a record for service as secretary–treasurer, holding that assignment for 6 consecutive years. Robert Harper recruited some of the best-known names in the APA membership for a series of symposia at the annual conventions. Those attracted sufficiently large audiences so that they ordinarily were scheduled for a large ballroom in one of the convention hotels. Members of the consulting firm Rohrer, Hibler, & Replogle International staff presented a series of symposia during the annual conventions titled "A Day in the Life of a Consultant" (with a variety of subtitles) that drew standing-room-only audiences and were scheduled for progressively larger rooms as the series advanced. Edward M. Glaser, founder and previous president of the Human Interaction Research Institute (HIRI) in Los Angeles, in collaboration with Howard Davis of the National Institute of Mental Health (NIMH), authored a number of publications and papers on the transfer, via consultation, of research findings to the applied world. Thomas Backer, current president of HIRI, established contacts with a variety of other organizations ranging from the performing arts to national advocacy groups. Those included the Entertainment Industries Council, the Entertainment Industry Workplace AIDS Task Force, the International Arts–Medicine Association, the National Alliance for the Mentally Ill, and the Hispanic Initiative on Drug Abuse and AIDS Research. Backer also worked with NIMH and the National Institute on Drug Abuse (NIDA). A goodly number of symposia, workshops, and publications grew out of those efforts. Many others made important contributions, including those who absorbed part of the expense of attending the midwinter meetings of the executive board during years when the division experienced financial limitations but the board did not want to increase the special assessment for all members.

Publications

Since the early years of its "rebirth," the division has published a newsletter with a variety of persons serving as editor. In 1981, under the editorship of Paul Lloyd, it became an expanded newsletter that carried additional substantive articles and was titled *Consulting Psychologist*. That title had to be discontinued because it was already in use by the National Psychological Consultants to Management for their publication, and beginning in 1982 it was published as the *Consulting Psychology Bulletin*. In 1992, under the editorship of Skipton Leonard, the publication further evolved into a journal titled *Consulting Psychology Journal: Practice and Research*.

CONVENTION ACTIVITIES AND
RECENT ANNUAL CONFERENCES

For many years the division has sponsored an active program during the annual convention of the APA. Individual paper sessions have been included, but in recent years there has been an emphasis on symposia and panel discussions, many of which have been cosponsored by one or more other divisions. The program usually has included a presidential address and conversation hours, and both preconvention and in-convention workshops have been offered.

Beginning in 1993 the division has sponsored an annual conference on Consultation to Corporations and Business that met in February or March in the Colorado Rockies (John Deleray, personal communication, 1996). The first conference was located in Vail, Colorado, and subsequent meetings have been in Keystone, which provided more suitable facilities. The concept grew out of informal discussions by several persons in division leadership positions during the APA convention in 1992. No formal committee structure has evolved and, thus far, responsibility for developing and conducting the meetings has been on a voluntary basis. What that bodes for the future remains to be seen. Excellent program leaders have been available and attendance has increased from about 20 in 1993 when severe winter weather in the eastern United States interfered with travel plans, to about 60 in 1994 and nearly 70 in 1995. The conferences have taken on something of an international flavor, including participants from England, Europe, and the Orient. Enthusiasm is high among the organizing group, and it is anticipated that the conferences will be continued in the future.

AWARDS

The Consulting Psychology Research Awards were first given in 1967 as a James McKeen Cattell Fund Award (Barry, 1975). The program was initiated by Hyman Meltzer and further developed by Robert Jones who was then chair of the Research and Scientific Affairs Committee. During the second year, questions were raised by Robert Thorndike, representing the Cattell Fund, about the adequacy of the study of the self-fulfilling prophecy phenomenon that had been awarded first prize in the initial year. Following correspondence with Clifford Swensen, who followed Robert Jones as chair of the Research and Scientific Affairs Committee, the Cattell Fund discontinued its support and no awards were given in 1969 (Meltzer, 1980). (See Table 18 for a list of award recipients.)

As a result of resourceful efforts by Swensen, the awards were sponsored, beginning in 1970, by the National Psychological Consultants to Manage-

TABLE 18
The Consulting Psychology Research Award

Year	Cattell Fund Award
1967	First Prize: Robert Rosenthal and Lenore Jacobson Second Prize: James Alsobrook Honorable Mention: Tommy T. Stigall
1968	First Prize: Thomas N. Ewing and William M. Gilbert Second Prize: Arnold Shapiro Honorable Mention: H. Stephen Leff, Rudy V. Nydegger, and Mildred Buck

Source. Division 13 newsletters.

ment (NPCM). That organization continued to sponsor the awards through 1992, with a 3-year hiatus in 1981, 1982, and 1983. The break came about after NPCM expressed dissatisfaction that some awards were given for studies not in the industrial/organizational area. The division did not wish to limit the awards to the industrial/organizational area and the two groups were not able to work out a mutually satisfactory solution, with NPCM sponsorship ending—temporarily, it turned out—in 1980. By 1984, satisfactory agreements were redeveloped and NPCM continued to support the research award through 1992. The division has been most appreciative of NPCM's lengthy support. The recipients of the awards during that era are listed in Table 19. It will be noted that through 1979 first prize, second prize, and honorable mention awards were offered and beginning in 1984 only one award was offered.

In 1981, Hyman Meltzer, who was active in division affairs for many years, generously offered to fund the research award. The winners for that year are listed in Table 20. Although he planned to continue his support, the Meltzer Award ended after 1 year because of Meltzer's death in 1982.

In recent years the division has been privileged to present two additional awards. One is the Perry L. Rohrer Award, retitled in 1993 as the RHR International Award, for excellence in career achievement in psychological consultation. That award is funded by Rohrer, Hibler & Replogle International, and was initiated in 1983. The second is the Harry Levinson Award, initiated in 1992, for integration of a wide range of psychological theory and concepts into consultation leading to more effective and humane organizations. That award is funded by earnings of a trust fund established by Levinson and administered by the American Psychological Foundation. The winners of these two award programs are listed in Tables 21 and 22.

The division has given two Special Divisional Awards. In 1982, an award for achievement in psychological consultation was presented to John Stuart Currie, Allen Carter, and George Greaves for their work during the "missing children" episode in Atlanta, Georgia, during which a number of

TABLE 19
The Consulting Psychology Research Award[a]

Year	Winners
1970	First Prize: Ralph M. Stogdill, Nicholas P. Coady and Adele Zimmer
	Second Prize: Merle B. Karnes, Audrey S. Hodgins and James Teska
	Honorable Mention: Richard I. Evans, Richard M. Rozelle, Thomas M. Lasater, Theodore M. Dembroski, and Ben P. Allen
1971	No listing of winners found in the *Newsletter*
1972	First Prize: Edward M. Glaser and Samuel N. Taylor
	Second Prize: Edward L. Levine
	Honorable Mention: Edward M. Glaser and Harvey L. Ross
1973	First Prize: Richard I. Evans, Richard M. Rozelle, Robert Noblitt, and Don L. Williams
	No other winners listed in the *Newsletter*
1974	First Prize: Stephen W. Larsen, John E. Lochman, Howard V. Selinger, Jack M. Chinsky, and George J. Allen
	Second Prize: Roy M. Hamlin, Paul R. Haskin, Connie J. F. Daye, Nancy J. Wilder, and Martha E. Wilzbach
	Honorable Mention: Donald Meichenbaum
1975	No listing of winners found in the *Newsletter*
1976	First Prize: Edward Seidman, Julian Rappaport and William Davidson
	Second Prize: Charles L. Slem
1977	First Prize: Ronald M. Roesch
	Second Prize: Richard I. Evans, Richard M. Rozelle, Maurice Mittlemark, William Hansen, Alice Bare, and Janet Harris
	Honorable Mention: Marilyn Machlowitz
1978	First Prize; Edward L. Levine, Leila Bennett, and R. A. Ash
	Second Prize: Leonard Jason
	Honorable Mention: Robert E. Kelley
1979	First Prize: Marilyn Machlowitz
	Second Prize: Edward M. Glaser
	Honorable Mention: Luciano L'Abate
1980	No award
1984	Eric Gopland, Steven Walfish and Anthony Broskowski
1985	No award
1986	Nancy Norvell
1987	Thomas Backer and Irene Shifren Levine
1988	Jo-Anne Normandin
1989	Jeffrey Fisher, Jack Chensky, and Roxane Silver
1990	Maurice J. Elias and John F. Clabby
1991	Lester Tobias
1992	Joyce L. Shields

Source. Division 13 newsletters.
[a] Sponsored by The National Psychological Consultants to Management.

young black children were missing and some were murdered, and there was much anxiety and fear throughout the community.

In 1986, an award for distinguished service was presented to Margaret Ives in recognition of her many valuable contributions to the division over the years.

TABLE 20
The Meltzer Research Award

Year	Winners
1981	First Prize: George J. Allen, Laurie Heatherington, Michal Lah, Jack Thaw, and Vivian Lesh Second Prize: Steven Penrod

Source. Division 13 newsletters.

TABLE 21
The Perry L. Rorher/RHR International Award

Year	Winner
1983	Warren Benis
1984	Harry Levinson
1985	Edward M. Glaser
1986	Douglas Bray
1987	Chris Argyris
1988	Edgar H. Schein
1989	Sylvia Hertz
1990	Vytautas J. Bieliauskas
1991	DeWayne Kurpius
1992	Henry Janzen
1993	W. Brenden Reddy
1994	Arthur M. Freedman
1995	Warren A. Ketcham

Source: Division 13 Newsletters and Journals

TABLE 22
The Harry Levinson Award

Year	Winner
1992	Frederick I. Herzberg
1993	Laurence J. Gould
1994	Michael A. Diamond
1995	Terry L. Maple

Source· Division 13 journals.

CONCLUSION

In the middle 1990s the Division of Consulting Psychology represents a good balance of academic and applied psychologists, both in the general membership and on the executive board. A very broad range of interest areas is represented. The division is a mid-sized one with a total membership of nearly 1000 persons who have an interest in the advancement and extension of consultation. Opportunities for consultation continue to expand both in established areas and in new areas, and it appears that the division will continue to grow at a moderate rate.

REFERENCES

Barry, J. (1975). The what, how and why of the Division 13 Consulting Psychology Research Award. *Newsletter, 27*(1).

Daniel, R. S., & Loutitt, C. M. (1953). *Professional problems in psychology.* New York: Prentice Hall.

Division 13 Executive Board. (1973). Brochure of the Division of Consulting Psychology.

Division 13 Executive Board. (1979). Proposed by-laws of the Division of Consulting Psychology. *Newsletter, 31*(1).

Fernberger, S. W. (1932). The American Psychological Association: A historical summary, 1892–1930. *Psychological Bulletin, 29,* 1–89.

Fryer, D. A., & Henry, E. R. (Eds.). (1950). *Handbook of applied psychology* (Vol. 1). New York: Holt, Rinehart & Winston.

Harper, R. A. (1992). Division 13's history: Impressions from within. *Consulting Psychology Journal, 44*(2), 9–10.

Hellkamp, D. (1993). History of the Division of Consulting Psychology: 1972–1992. *Consulting Psychology Journal, 45*(1), 1–8.

Hellkamp, D., & Morgan, L. (1990). A 1989 profile of consulting psychologists: Survey of APA Division 13. *Consulting Psychology Bulletin, 42,* 4–9.

Ives, M. (1967, Fall). Whither consulting psychology? The future in the light of past and present developments. *Newsletter, 21*(1).

Kraemer, D., & Kaplan, N. (1971). Public information questionnaire: Who and what is a consulting psychologist? *Newsletter, 25*(1).

Leonard, S. (1992). What is consultation? That's an interesting question! *Consulting Psychology Journal, 44*(2), 18–23.

MacLennen, B., Quinn, R., & Schroeder, D. (1971). *The scope of community mental health consultation and education.* PHS Publication No. 2169. Rockville, MD: Public Health Service.

Meltzer, H. (1980). The story of the Division 13 Consulting Psychology Research Award. *Newsletter, 32*(1).

Rigby, W. K. (1973a). History and present status of the Division of Consulting Psychology—Initial report. *Newsletter, 25*(1).

Rigby, W. K. (1973b). History and present status of the Division of Consulting Psychology—Intermediate report. *Newsletter, 25*(2).

Rigby, W. K. (1973c). History and present status of the Division of Consulting Psychology—Final report. *Newsletter, 25*(3).

Rigby, W. K. (1980). Minutes—Midwinter Executive Board meeting, February 16, 1980. *Newsletter, 32*(1).

Rigby, W. K. (1992). History, 1924 to 1972, of the Division of Consulting Psychology. *Consulting Psychology Journal, 44*(2), 2–8.

4

A HISTORY OF DIVISION 14 (THE SOCIETY FOR INDUSTRIAL AND ORGANIZATIONAL PSYCHOLOGY)

LUDY T. BENJAMIN, JR.

Division 14 of the American Psychological Association (APA) is currently designated The Society for Industrial and Organizational Psychology (SIOP). It began three name changes ago in 1945 as the Division of Industrial and Business Psychology, one of the 19 original divisions of the APA. In its first half-century, this special interest group has witnessed significant changes in the nature of the field and its practitioners. In that 50 years industrial psychology developed from its roots in testing and personnel issues to involvement with human factors to an emphasis on such topics as management, motivation, leadership, organizational design, and group processes, emphases that changed industrial psychology to industrial/organizational psychology, and in that transformation, joined psychology with theoretical influences from sociology, political science, economics, and management. The prototypical industrial psychologist changed from being an academically based consultant/applied researcher who dabbled occasionally

Appreciation is expressed to Winfred Arthur, Jr., James T. Austin, William Howell, Raymond Katzell, Laura Koppes, and especially to Paul Thayer for their very helpful comments on earlier versions of this chapter.

in the problems of industry to a modern industrial/organizational practitioner employed full-time outside the academy.

This chapter is not a history of industrial/organizational psychology. That subject is the stuff of books, not chapters (although a very fine treatment can be found in an article by Katzell & Austin, 1992). Like the other chapters in this volume, this one is a divisional history—and a selective one at that. It simply is not possible to cover adequately the 50-year history of a division in the space allotted. The strategy adopted here is one of breadth rather than depth, providing brief mentions of the principal events and issues in the division's history, with a somewhat greater coverage of certain topics. A principal focus of the chapter is on the first decade of the division, because much of what happened there defined its course into the 1990s. Discussions of the founding of the division, its early membership, bylaws, convention programs, and committee structure are followed by sections on membership; publications; principal activities in practice, science, and education; and the founding of SIOP.

This history begins, however, with a treatment of the origins of applied psychology in America, particularly the early applications to business. That section is followed by a description of the direct precursors of Division 14—for example, the Association of Consulting Psychologists and the American Association for Applied Psychology. These antecedents are important for an understanding of the historical context in which the APA division originated and developed.

THE BEGINNINGS OF APPLIED PSYCHOLOGY

The "new psychology" in America had yet to reach the age of consent when it ventured beyond the boundaries of the laboratory and into the world of American business. The purists railed against such premature ventures and warned these purveyors of suspect psychological knowledge to stay home and perfect their science. Yet these psychologists, steeped in American pragmatism and Yankee know-how (and, perhaps, in need of money), would not be restrained. The new science of the mind was arguably the most applicable of all sciences, and these pioneering psychologists wasted little time trying to prove it.

America in the late nineteenth century was undergoing a social metamorphosis brought on by increased industrialization, new waves of immigration, growth of the cities, and reform movements in education. There were, of course, numerous problems inherent in such social upheaval. What was needed was an applied science to solve those problems. G. Stanley Hall led the way for an applied psychology by offering psychology's services to the field of education, "the one chief and immediate field of application for all this work [psychology]" (1894, p. 718).

The business world beckoned as well. With "the formation of large industrial empires . . . came new management problems and a growing preoccupation with efficiency" (Napoli, 1981, p. 28). And psychologists, equipped with the battery of mental tests developed by James McKeen Cattell and others, were poised to answer the questions that American business had about advertising, selling, personnel selection, job analysis, efficiency, and management styles. "Applied psychologists, with their widening variety of psychological tests, provided a timely management tool that attracted attention among the leaders of some of America's largest corporations" (Napoli, 1981, p. 28).

By the turn of the twentieth century, American businesses were seeking the services of psychologists to solve their problems in much the same way that some had sought the services of phrenologists in the previous century. Thus Walter Dill Scott began his work on advertising at the encouragement of advertising executives in Chicago in late 1901, leading to his first book on the subject, *The Theory of Advertising* (1903). He published a second book on advertising in 1908 (*The Psychology of Advertising*) and two other books in 1911: *Increasing Human Efficiency in Business* and *Influencing Men in Business*.

Harry Hollingworth, a student of Cattell, began his applied psychology career in 1909, the year he received his doctorate, with a series of lectures to the Men's Advertising League of New York City (Benjamin, 1996). Two years later he achieved some measure of fame in America's corporate community for his very successful work for the Coca-Cola Company studying the effects of caffeine on human behavior and mental processes (Benjamin, Rogers, & Rosenbaum, 1991; Hollingworth, 1912).

Harvard University's Hugo Münsterberg also began his career in business in 1909 with an article on psychology in the marketplace. His most influential book appeared 4 years later: *Psychology and Industrial Efficiency* (1913). As noted in the quotation from Napoli, American business, at the turn of the century, was concerned with efficiency. And it was thus no accident that both Scott and Münsterberg published books on that subject. Efficiency meant more effective advertising, better training of workers, more scientific management, improved employee selection procedures, better accounting methods, and better ways to control the performance of workers and the quality of their output.

Münsterberg's 1913 book was exceptionally popular and, for a short time, it even appeared on the best-seller lists for nonfiction (Hale, 1980). His strong advocacy for the value of applied psychology, especially to the problems of the workplace, is evident in the following passage:

We stand before the surprising fact that all the manifold results of the new science have remained book knowledge, detached from any practical interests. Only in the last ten years do we find systematic efforts to apply the experimental results of psychology to the needs of society. . . . The knowledge of nature and the mastery of nature have always belonged together. . . . If the psychologists were to refrain from practical application until the theoretical results of their laboratories need no supplement, the time for applied psychology would never come. (Münsterberg, 1913, pp. 5–7)

It should be clear that applied psychology, including industrial and organizational psychology (which was typically called business or economic psychology in its earliest years), was alive and well prior to World War I (see Landy, 1993, for broader coverage). The success of the war work for psychologists provided a host of opportunities in industry and the military in the 1920s. Walter Dill Scott and colleagues, fresh from their successes on the Committee on the Classification of Personnel in the Army, founded the Scott Company in 1919 to offer consulting services to businesses. John B. Watson, exiled from academia in 1920, found considerable success in the New York City business community, making a name for himself and for a behavioristic approach to advertising (Buckley, 1982, 1989). James McKeen Cattell and colleagues founded The Psychological Corporation in 1921 to offer applied research to clients, largely from the business community (Sokal, 1981). Even a popular magazine for business executives, titled *Industrial Psychology Monthly*, appeared in 1926 under the editorship of Colgate University psychologist Donald A. Laird (Benjamin & Bryant, 1996).

Whereas most industrial psychologists remained in university positions, doing their consulting from an academic base, by the 1920s some psychologists were finding full-time employment in industry or as freelance consultants, for example Marion Bills, Elsie Bregman, Lillian Gilbreth, Harry Hepner, Beardsley Ruml, and Daniel Starch. These individuals labeled themselves *consulting psychologists, business psychologists, economic psychologists,* or *industrial psychologists*. As their numbers grew they joined with their applied colleagues in the universities in efforts to influence the APA to recognize this expanding field of psychology. They asked for program time at the annual meeting and for recognition as a section of the APA. The leadership of the APA, however, denied such requests, reminding their colleagues of the APA's sole objective as a society to advance psychology as a science. When it became obvious that the APA would not recognize the application of psychology, these business psychologists looked elsewhere for their needs.

ORGANIZATIONAL BEGINNINGS

The APA reluctantly established a section on clinical psychology in 1919 when it appeared that a rival national organization was about to be founded. And in 1921 the APA created a separate section on consulting psychology. The following year the APA's Committee on the Certification of Consulting Psychologists asked the association to create two new sections on educational psychology and industrial psychology. It was presumed that membership in such sections would be seen as establishing an individual's qualifications for consulting in those areas. The APA committees set up to study the proposal found that "industrial psychologists were generally but unenthusiastically favorable to a special section" (Napoli, 1981, p. 58). Perceiving no strong support from either the educational or industrial psychologists, further action on the proposal was dropped.

Efforts to organize in industrial psychology languished until the early 1930s. Opportunities for industrial psychologists continued to expand as they reminded the business community that

> the stability of the business enterprise depends no less upon the soundness of its psychological foundation than upon the solidity of its economic and technical supports. . . . The failure to study . . . the effectiveness of human behavior in industry can only result in serious waste in the form of individual maladjustment and of industrial inefficiency. (Viteles, 1932, p. 4)

As pressures in industry for psychological services grew, so did the number of individuals offering to provide those services. Thus part of the organizational motivation was to provide a means to distinguish between legitimate industrial psychologists and those unqualified to practice (see Brotemarkle, 1940, on psychological charlatans). A significant opportunity arose in 1930 when New York's Association of Consulting Psychologists (ACP) reorganized. This organization had begun in 1921 as a state-wide group of mostly clinical and educational psychologists but with a small core of industrial psychologists. In 1930 it was decided to expand the organization more broadly in the Northeast, to better publicize the benefits of applied psychology, and to pursue a code of ethics for psychologists in applied work (which it adopted in 1933).

The APA voiced its displeasure with the ACP for its designs on a national role and noted that APA's own clinical section represented those issues nationally. However, fully cognizant of the comatose state of the APA's clinical section, ACP continued its efforts, even establishing a national journal for professional psychologists in 1937, the *Journal of Consulting Psychology*.

The debates over a national organization took a new turn at the 1936 APA meeting when New York University's Douglas Fryer was nominated by applied colleagues to head a committee to create a new national organization for applied psychologists (see National Committee, 1937). Fryer moved quickly and by the following year had worked out a constitution for the new organization that would be called the American Association for Applied Psychology (AAAP). Both the clinical section of the APA and the ACP disbanded to make way for the new association. And ACP's journal would become the official organ of the AAAP.

The AAAP held its first meeting in 1937 in Minneapolis in conjunction with the annual meeting of the APA. Most of the members of AAAP were also members of the APA and that substantial overlap continued throughout the brief life of the former. Initially the AAAP membership was divided into four sections: clinical, consulting, educational, and industrial. The Industrial and Business Section of AAAP (Section D), under the leadership of Harold E. Burtt and Walter Van Dyke Bingham, established committees that began work immediately on a constitution (chaired by Morris Viteles) and a code of ethical standards (chaired by Carroll L. Shartle) that were specific to the division.

The constitution, adopted in 1939, limited membership in the section to AAAP fellows or associates who "at the time of application for membership, are actively engaged in the application of psychology in business, industry, public service or allied fields" (American Association for Applied Psychology, 1940, p. 1). The purposes of the section were

(a) to promote high standards of practice in the application of psychology to business, industry, public service, and allied vocational fields;
(b) to promote research and publications in these fields; (c) to facilitate the exchange of information and experience among its members; (d) to promote the development of new professional opportunities, and (e) to contribute in general to the advancement of applied psychology. (AAAP, 1940, p. 1)

From 1938 until 1945, industrial psychologists had their organizational home in AAAP. Section D was never large, reaching approximately 85 members by 1945. The membership, however, was inclusive of the most visible individuals in the field, particularly those in university positions. However, the membership, and even the leadership, also included some psychologists whose full-time employment was in industry. (See Table 23 for a listing of the officers of Section D of the AAAP.)

As World War II ended in 1945, the AAAP merged with the newly reorganized APA. By approving the new APA constitution, the AAAP effectively voted itself out of existence. The story of that merger and the reorganization of the APA is told in a number of sources, but nowhere

TABLE 23
Presidents of the American Association for Applied Psychology (AAAP)
and Officers of the Industrial and Business Section: 1938–1945

| Year | AAAP President | Industrial and Business Section | |
		President	Secretary
1938	Douglas H. Fryer	Harold E. Burtt	Marion A. Bills
1939	Donald Paterson	Walter V. Bingham	Marion A. Bills
1940	Horace B. English	Morris S. Viteles	Marion A. Bills
1941	Edgar A. Doll	Arthur Kornhauser	Millicent Pond
1942	Walter V. Bingham	Arthur Kornhauser	Kinsley R. Smith
1943	Chauncey Louttit	Arthur Kornhauser	George K. Bennett
1944	A. T. Poffenberger	Paul S. Achilles	George K. Bennett
1945	Carl R. Rogers	Carroll L. Shartle	Rensis Likert[a]
			Beatrice Dvorak[a]
			Floyd L. Ruch

[a] Resigned because of new wartime assignment

better than Capshew and Hilgard (1992). For our purposes in this chapter it is sufficient to say that the five sections of the AAAP (military psychology became a fifth section) continued as sections of the new APA as part of the 19 divisions begun in 1945. Bruce V. Moore of Pennsylvania State College (now University) was elected the first president of Division 14. In the next 8 years, he would be followed by eight more presidents who had also been members of Section D in the AAAP.

THE FOUNDING OF DIVISION 14

At the 1944 meetings of the APA and AAAP, temporary organizing committees were formed for each of the proposed 19 divisions. Carroll Shartle was appointed to chair the organizing committee for Division 14 (Hilgard, 1945). These groups met at the 1945 APA meeting in Evanston, Illinois, and drafted ballots for the election of the initial officers of the divisions and their representatives to the newly formed APA Council of Representatives. For Division 14, in addition to Moore as the first president, Floyd L. Ruch was elected secretary for a 3-year term, and Paul S. Achilles and John G. Jenkins were elected to the APA Council of Representatives. These four officers constituted the initial executive committee for the division and, as such, handled the charter appointments for the business of the division.

There were three initial problems to solve in the transition from Section D to Division 14: (a) development of criteria for membership that were consistent with the APA membership standards, (b) development of the division bylaws that also needed to be consistent with the APA bylaws, and (c) planning the first division program for the 1946 APA meeting in Philadelphia. The first of these assignments was handled by a membership committee comprised of Ruch, Achilles, and Harold Burtt as chair.

When the merger of the AAAP and the APA occurred, the APA had two classes of membership, fellow and associate, which has been discussed already in an earlier chapter in this volume. Divisions were given the option of having both categories of membership or limiting themselves to the fellow category only. Division 14 selected the two-category plan. As in the days of Section D, all members had to be "actively engaged in the application or study of psychology in business, industry, public service or allied vocational fields and whose activities are in conformity with the standards [meaning the ethical standards for practice] adopted by the Division" (Burtt, 1947). Fellows had to (a) have a doctoral degree based on a psychological dissertation, (b) have prior membership in the APA or the AAAP (grandparenting for AAAP members was discontinued after August 1946), and (c) have 4 years of postdoctoral professional experience, two of which must be in the application of psychology to business, industry, and so on, or a record of significant published research "of direct value to the application of psychology in business." Associates could have a doctoral degree with a psychology-based dissertation, or 2 years of graduate work in psychology, or 1 year of graduate work in psychology and 1 year of experience in the application of psychology to business, industry, and so on (Burtt, 1947).

The membership committee of the division was responsible for evaluating applicants, and such evaluations were not always easy, especially for some candidates in industry applying to become associates. The final arbiter of such cases was, however, the APA Membership Committee, which had to approve all recommendations for new division members who were not already members of the APA. The first official division membership rosters were established in 1947 at the APA meeting in Detroit, and the count for Division 14 was 80 fellows and 50 associates as charter members (Ruch, 1947).

The bylaws revision was handled rather easily. Moore chaired the revision committee with Marion Bills, Arthur W. Kornhauser, and Carroll Shartle as members. It was decided that the objectives from the Section D bylaws had served the group well and so those were retained, with only one addition. The fifth objective, which read, "to contribute in general to the advancement of applied psychology" was amended by adding the words "as a means of promoting human welfare" to the end of the statement (Bylaws, 1946, p. 1). That added phrase was consistent with a change in the APA bylaws that was fostered largely by psychologists who promoted a social agenda for psychological research (the membership of the Society for the Psychological Study of Social Issues, SPSSI).

The only items of real debate in the bylaws were the categories of membership. Other than that, there were minor changes required to bring the document into compliance with the APA bylaws. The revised bylaws were sent to the division membership in June 1946 and approved at the business meeting that September. Earlier, in April, Moore had sent a draft of the bylaws to Dael Wolfle, the executive secretary of the APA. Wolfle wrote to Moore that Division 14 was the first of the divisions to complete the bylaws task and that with his permission he would like to send the draft to the other divisions as a model (Moore, 1946).

The initial program committee was composed of Ruch, Bills, and Rensis Likert, with John Jenkins as chair. Moore indicated that he appointed Bills because of her ties to the American Management Association; it was his wish to schedule some joint programming with that association at future APA meetings (Moore, 1946), and this indeed came to pass. It is not clear how program hours were apportioned to divisions for 1946. Certainly the number of hours differed across divisions. In addition to its business meeting and the presidential address by Bruce Moore, which was delivered at an evening banquet, Division 14 scheduled three events: two paper sessions and a roundtable discussion on internship opportunities in industry. After the second meeting in 1947, when the major part of the division program was once again scheduled for Saturday morning, one member suggested changing to a weekday for future meetings: "It is a fallacy that industrial representatives want Saturday meetings; they much prefer to attend on company time" (Ruch, 1947, p. 4).

THE EARLY ORGANIZATIONAL STRUCTURE OF DIVISION 14

The 1945 APA bylaws specified very little about divisional structures. They required divisions to have a president and a secretary (see Table 24 for a listing of key officers), and such other officers and committees as the division deemed necessary. Division representatives to the APA council were also defined. In its initial year, Division 14 began with approved bylaws before the 1946 meeting. Those bylaws specified those committees necessary to handle the ongoing responsibilities such as membership and program. An executive committee was also mandated, consisting of the two APA council representatives, the two officers, and three members to be elected at large. An election committee, chaired by M. W. Richardson, was also part of the bylaws, and Moore appointed one even though the APA Central Office agreed to handle the elections for the division.

The only other committee in existence in the first year of the division was the Committee on Standards and Code of Ethics, which was a direct holdover from a Section D committee that Shartle had chaired at the AAAP

TABLE 24
Presidents and Secretary–Treasurers of Division 14

Year	President	Secretary/Treasurer[a]
1945–1946	Bruce V. Moore	Floyd L. Ruch
1946–1947	John G. Jenkins	Floyd L. Ruch
1947–1948	George K. Bennett	Floyd L. Ruch
1948–1949	Floyd L. Ruch	Harold Seashore
1949–1950	Carroll L. Shartle	Harold Seashore
1950–1951	Jack W. Dunlap	Harold Seashore
1951–1952	Marion A. Bills	Leonard W. Ferguson
1952–1953	Jay L. Otis	Leonard W. Ferguson
1953–1954	Harold A. Edgerton	Leonard W. Ferguson
1954–1955	Edwin E. Ghiselli	Erwin K. Taylor
1955–1956	Leonard W. Ferguson	Erwin K. Taylor
1956–1957	Edwin R. Henry	Erwin K. Taylor
1957–1958	C. H. Lawshe	Erwin K. Taylor
1958–1959	Joseph Tiffin	Orlo L. Crissey
1959–1960	Erwin K. Taylor	Orlo L. Crissey
1960–1961	Raymond A. Katzell	Orlo L. Crissey
1961–1962	Orlo L. Crissey	Brent N. Baxter
1962–1963	William McGehee	Brent N. Baxter
1963–1964	S. Rains Wallace	Brent N. Baxter
1964–1965	Brent N. Baxter	Philip Ash
1965–1966	Ross Stagner	Philip Ash
1966–1967	Marvin D. Dunnette	Philip Ash
1967–1968	Philip Ash	Herbert H. Meyer
1968–1969	Stanley E. Seashore	Herbert H. Meyer
1969–1970	William A. Owens	Herbert H. Meyer
1970–1971	Herbert H. Meyer	Donald L. Grant
1971–1972	Douglas W. Bray	Donald L. Grant
1972–1973	Robert M. Guion	Donald L. Grant
1973–1974	Edwin A. Fleishman	Paul W. Thayer
1974–1975	Donald L. Grant	Paul W. Thayer
1975–1976	Lyman W. Porter	Paul W. Thayer
1976–1977	Paul W. Thayer	Mary L. Tenopyr
1977–1978	John P. Campbell	Mary L. Tenopyr
1978–1979	C. Paul Sparks	Mary L. Tenopyr
1979–1980	Mary L. Tenopyr	Lewis E. Albright
1980–1981	Victor H. Vroom	Lewis E. Albright
1981–1982	Arthur C. MacKinney	Lewis E. Albright
1982–1983	Richard J. Campbell	Virginia R. Boehm
1983–1984	Milton D. Hakel	Virginia R. Boehm
1984–1985	Benjamin Schneider	Virginia R. Boehm
1985–1986	Irwin L. Goldstein	Ann Howard
1986–1987	Sheldon Zedeck	Ann Howard
1987–1988	Daniel R. Ilgen	Ann Howard
1988–1989	Ann Howard	Marilyn K. Quaintance[b] John Hinrichs
1989–1990	Neal W. Schmitt	Marilyn K. Quaintance Manuel London
1990–1991	Frank J. Landy	Marilyn K. Gowing Manuel London
1991–1992	Richard J. Klimoski	Elaine Pulakos Manuel London

Year	President	Secretary/Treasurer[a]
1992–1993	Wayne F. Cascio	Elaine Pulakos
		Ralph A. Alexander
1993–1994	Paul R. Sackett	Nancy T. Tippins
		Ralph A. Alexander
1994–1995	Walter C. Borman	Nancy T. Tippins
		Ronald D. Johnson
1995–1996	Michael A. Campion	Nancy T. Tippins
		Ronald D. Johnson
1996–1997	James L. Farr	William H. Macey
		Ronald D. Johnson

[a] Initially the position was titled *secretary* but it was changed to *secretary–treasurer* in 1947.
[b] In 1988–1989 the secretary/treasurer position was divided between a secretary and a financial officer. In the listings since 1988, the first name in the secretary/treasurer column is the secretary, the second name is the financial officer.

and continued to chair for the division. That committee filed its report with the division in March 1946 and it was mailed to members of the executive committee for comment. It is not clear what happened to that report, but apparently it was not acted on at the 1946 business meeting at the APA. The committee was continued but never developed a code of ethics approved by the division. Instead the project was preempted by the APA, which published its *Ethical Standards of Psychologists* in 1953. Harold Edgerton and Leonard Ferguson (both of whom would soon be presidents of Division 14) were members of the eight-person APA Committee on Ethical Standards for Psychology and a number of other industrial psychologists served on the subcommittees (e.g., Brent Baxter, Edwin Ghiselli, Harold Seashore). It is likely that the division canceled its efforts on drafting ethical standards because standards for the practice of industrial psychology were to be part of the broader APA document.

In 1947 a committee on policy and planning was established to make recommendations about the operations of the division and how it might accomplish the goals stated in its bylaws. Marion Bills chaired that committee. By 1949 the committee was abolished. Its recommendations became part of the agenda of the executive committee in shaping the division's structure over the next several years, particularly in developing committees to deal with public relations and professional practice.

A committee on training, chaired by Alexander Wesman, was added in 1948. It began by surveying the membership about recruitment of students, graduate course work, training opportunities, and future job opportunities (Wesman, Husband, & Mold, 1949). But like the policy and planning committee, it too disappeared by 1953. It would surface later in several forms, such as the Task Force on Internships, the Committee on Professional Education Policy, and finally as the Education and Training Committee.

In 1949, a committee on professional relations was added, with Harold Taylor as chair. Noting the importance of this committee, Carroll Shartle wrote,

> During the coming months our Division has an opportunity to make considerable progress in the professional development of Business and Industrial Psychology. Clinical psychology has moved ahead significantly in training, internships, professional practice and relations with other professions. It is now time for *us* to get going. We are one of three areas in which the American Board of Examiners in Professional Psychology [ABEPP] awards the diploma; yet we have perhaps done the least of any of the three in moving forward. (Shartle, 1949, p. 1)

One of the first items of business for this committee was a proposal from Roger Bellows that was sent originally to the APA in 1949 but forwarded to the division for its comment. Bellows (1949, August 10), a director in a psychological consulting firm, asked the APA to form a board for control and certification of psychological consulting firms. The Professional Relations Committee noted that no such boards existed to govern the practices of groups of lawyers or physicians and felt that certification of individuals (via ABEPP) offered sufficient control of psychological practice. Their recommendation was forwarded to the APA board of directors, which agreed with the committee.

The Committee on Training recommended in 1951 that the division consider adding a workshop as part of the annual program and that the workshop be focused on providing postdoctoral education and training for all industrial psychologists, especially those working full-time in industry. The first workshop was offered at the 1953 APA meeting in Boston and was a considerable success. Enrollment was limited to 30, although 31 actually attended, 25 of those from industry. Some division members objected to the division's sponsoring an activity that charged members a fee and that, because of the enrollment limit, was closed to some members who might want to attend. But the program continued under the supervision of a new continuing committee, the Workshop Committee. Soon the division was offering workshops at not only APA meetings but meetings of the Midwestern Psychological Association as well. The workshop offerings grew from one in 1953 to four offerings by 1956; the income from the 1956 workshops generated a profit of $560, which was added to the division treasury. This program continued to be one of the most successful activities of the division, both financially and in terms of its training benefits. (In the 1970s the Workshop Committee was merged with the Continuing Education Committee shortly before the division became an approved sponsor of continuing education programs in 1979 under the auspices of the APA Continuing Education Sponsor Approval System.)

The committees did not always make the progress expected. At the 1953 business meeting there was discussion about abolishing the Professional Relations Committee because of its inactivity. Yet the executive committee recommended its continuance and appointed Bernard Bass as the new chair and Ernest J. McCormick as a new member of the committee. The newsletter committee also had suffered from inactivity and it was abolished in 1953.

Although several committees were established as continuing committees, only two were added to the list of standing committees in the division's bylaws revision of 1955: Public Relations and Professional Practices (a separation of the functions of the Professional Relations Committee). Both of those committees would play significant roles in the division's development. Public Relations was designed to promote the division's interests in business and industry, with other relevant professional groups, and with the public. Toward those ends this committee would develop a speakers bureau for industry and public groups, encourage the writing of articles for publication in popular magazines, and prepare pamphlets for distribution to prospective students, businesses, and the general public.

The Professional Practices Committee, initially chaired by Raymond Katzell, was to concern itself with issues of licensure, certification, ethics, and state and national legislation. In its initial years it dealt with California's licensure law that recognized clinical psychology only, with clinical psychologists working in industry, with requests from industrial psychologists in several states for advice on legislation. In the 1950s, state psychological associations were variously engaged in seeking licensure for the practice of psychology, principally clinical psychology, and one of the immediate functions of this committee was to ensure that the practices of industrial psychologists were not hindered in any way. Sometimes this committee suggested the formation of special committees such as the Committee on Relations with ABEPP that was formed in 1958 to keep the division informed about ABEPP's practices relative to industrial psychology, and in 1976 the Committee on Legal Issues that generated a number of court briefs.

In the ensuing years a number of other special committees were formed. Most of those grew out of the work of three committees: Public Relations, Professional Practices, and the Education and Training Committee. They dealt with proposals for and concerns about graduate education in industrial/organizational psychology including internships, publications, awards, professional schools, Doctor of Psychology degrees, APA reorganization, psychological testing, sponsored conferences, and specialty guidelines for the practice of industrial/organizational psychology. Several of these special committees eventually became standing committees as the division expanded its services for members and its purview of industrial/organizational psychology. Some of the outcomes of that expansion will be evident later in this chapter.

MEMBERSHIP

As noted earlier, Division 14 began with a charter membership of 130 in an APA of approximately 4000 members. The membership was divided between fellows and associates as defined in the bylaws cited earlier. That bifurcation existed until 1958 when the APA changed its membership designation to add the category of *member* and to redefine *fellow* as an individual who had made an unusual or outstanding contribution to psychology. Previous fellows were grandparented into the new fellow status if they wished. In 1957 Division 14 had a total of 236 fellows and 357 associates. It voted to do away with the "associate" category of membership for the following year and reported its 1958 membership as 250 fellows and 409 members. The associate category was restored by the division in 1963 (see Table 25 for membership totals in 5-year intervals for the APA and the division).

Although there have been debates in the division throughout its history concerning membership criteria, the basic definitions for the three classes have not changed in any significant way. Concerns were expressed about the psychological qualifications of some associates, and ways were debated about narrowing the eligibility criteria for that category. But mostly the definitions were left vague to include graduate students, practitioners with master's degrees, psychologists in other fields who had interests in industrial/organizational psychology, and nonpsychologists in industry who were involved in psychological work. In truth the associate category has never been very large. It reached its peak of 329 in 1985 and has declined since to a figure of 262 in 1996.

TABLE 25
APA and Division 14 Membership Totals: 1945–1995

Year	APA Membership	Fellows	Division 14 Members	Associates	Total
1945	4086	80		50	130
1950	7273	165		123	288
1955	13,475	213		301	514
1960	18,215	254	480		734
1965	23,561	252	609	73	934
1970	30,839	243	711	155	1109
1975	39,411	238	948	184	1370
1980	50,933	236	1436	281	1953
1985	60,131	234	1936	329	2499
1990	70,266	240	2017	288	2545
1995	79,098	209	2096	253	2558

Note. For 1960 there was no listing that separated associates and members. It was during that time that the associate category disappeared.

Since the new designation of fellow in 1958, the division has maintained the size of its fellow category at around 240, although it has declined by about 15% since 1990. The largest figure for that category was 257 in 1962, and the lowest is the 1996 figure of 208. Although the fellow and associate categories have remained rather small, the member category has grown considerably since its initiation. It reached 1046 by 1976 and 2010 by 1987 and has remained virtually the same through 1996. When the member category began in 1958, the ratio of fellow to member was 1 to 1.64; in 1996 that ratio was 1 to 10. (For a profile of Division 14 members as of 1993, see Balzer & Howard, 1994.)

The division has always been dominated by university-based psychologists; however, a significant number of psychologists from industry have served in leaderships positions, including the division's presidency. This melding of the academy and industry began in the days of the AAAP; academic psychologists sought to involve those psychologists located in industry, the government, and private consulting firms. There was an early recognition by the academic psychologists that good relations with those in the business world were critically important for a variety of reasons, such as access to field research, consulting opportunities, training opportunities for graduate students, public relations in the business world and, arguably of greatest importance, progress in the science due to a better integration with practice.

These continued efforts on the part of the academicians have had some success. Still, the industry-based psychologists have found other organizational venues for themselves. One group of 14 psychologists involved in personnel research in companies such as General Motors, U.S. Rubber, Eli Lilly, and the Chesapeake & Ohio Railroad met at Antioch College in May of 1951 to discuss shared interests. Five months later this same group met in Dearborn, Michigan. From that meeting the group drew its name, The Dearborn Conference, and it has been meeting twice each year since that time (Meyer, 1997).

As early as 1952 Marion Bills was listed in the division business meeting minutes as being secretary of a group called Industrial Psychologists Employed in Private Industry. It is not clear if that was a subset of Division 14 members; it appears that it was a small, informal organization independent of the division. When it began meeting is unknown. It bears no apparent relationship to another group, The No-Name Group, that began meeting in May 1955.

The No-Name Group held its first meeting in Hartford, Connecticut, hosted by Robert Finkle, who then worked for the Metropolitan Insurance Company. Attendance at that first meeting included industrial psychologists from U.S. Steel, Standard Oil, DuPont, General Electric, Owens-Illinois, and Detroit Edison. The group never had more than 30 members at any one time. Seven of that group served as Division 14 presidents: Brent Baxter, Douglas Bray, Richard Campbell, Orlo Crissey, Marvin Dunnette, Edwin Henry, and Herbert Meyer (Carlson, 1991; Crissey, 1980). The No-Name Group apparently did not meet after 1991.

It is not known if any women were part of The No-Name Group; none are listed in any of the documents collected on this organization (in the Orlo Crissey Papers at the Archives of the History of American Psychology). As already noted, female industrial psychologists were not often in positions of leadership within Division 14, at least not in the first 20 years. There were at least a handful of female psychologists working in industry in the 1920s whose work is now being rediscovered as a result of the research of Laura Koppes (see Koppes, Landy, & Perkins, 1993). But their numbers were almost nonexistent in universities at the time the division began. This absence was not shared by other applied fields. For example, in 1952 there were 1088 ABEPP diplomates in psychology. Among the clinical group there were 337 women and 367 men. For the counseling and guidance group the figures were 59 women to 164 men. And for the industrial diplomates the numbers were 6 women and 155 men. In the 1950s, and much later, management often was reluctant to use women as business consultants. Consider a 1947 job advertisement for staff psychologists prepared by Rohrer, Hibler, & Replogle, a consulting firm of psychologists:

> *Essential requirements for staff psychologists:*
> 1.) A mature personality. 2.) A broadly humane and realistic social philosophy. 3.) A deep and abiding interest in people per se. 4.) a Ph.D. in Psychology from a reputable graduate school. 5.) Male—between 30 and 45 years of age. (Janney, 1947)

Women were mentioned in the advertisement. Under the section that read "Qualifications which are preferable, but not essential, for staff psychologists," it read: "2. Wife and children" (Janney, 1947).

The report of the APA Task Force on the Status of Women in Psychology published in 1973 called the division to task for its poor record of recruiting women into careers in industrial/organizational psychology.

> The outstanding fact about women psychologists in nonclinical applied areas such as industry and engineering is that there are so few of them. Women make up roughly one-fourth of APA's total membership, but they account for 5% or less of the membership in two divisions: . . . Division 14 and the Society of Engineering Psychology (Division 21). . . . The APA members who work in applied areas, and particularly those in Divisions 14 and 21, are the gatekeepers of such areas and should assume the responsibility for changing and improving the status of women psychologists in these fields. (Task Force, 1973, p. 614)

Nancy Felipe Russo identified part of the problem when she notified Division 14 president Edwin Fleishman about her concerns with one of the division's brochures describing industrial/organizational psychologists as potential clients in industry (Russo, 1974). The Division 14 brochure, titled "The Industrial Organizational Psychologist," included sections labeled "To Evaluate His Experience" and "What Support Will He Need From You?" Under the heading "What to Look for in an Industrial Psychologist" the answers were, "He should be able to grasp the major problems of the organization; He can propose research and action commensurate with the problem; His expectations are realistic; He has persuasive communication skills" (The Industrial Organizational Psychologist, no date, p. 3). In response, the sexist language was removed and the brochures were reprinted.

Although industrial/organizational psychology was late in being part of the changing gender composition of psychology, the change has occurred. Women now account for more than 25% of the membership of the division and well over 50% of the enrollment in doctoral programs in industrial/organizational psychology. Data comparing doctorates awarded in industrial/organizational psychology in 1971, 1981, and 1991 show that for men the numbers have remained constant: 64, 67, 66. For women those figures are 4, 20, and 76. Thus, between 1971 and 1991, industrial/organizational psychology doctorates awarded annually have increased by 109%, and women account for all of that increase (Pion et al., 1996). One could argue that women are still underrepresented in the division leadership positions, at least at the top level. There have been only three women presidents of the division through 1996. From 1945 to 1975 there were ten men who served as secretary–treasurer. Only one of those, Harold Seashore, was not subsequently elected to the presidency. Since 1975, of the seven people who have served as secretary, six have been women, and only two of them have served as president.

PUBLICATIONS

When asked about publications of Division 14, individuals familiar with the division would most likely think of TIP, the quarterly newsletter that is more like a journal in terms of its size and some of its content. The acronym stands for The Industrial Psychologist, its original name when it began in 1963. When the division's name changed in 1973, the journal name changed to reflect that: The Industrial/Organizational Psychologist. Yet it remained TIP not TIOP. The newsletter history actually begins much earlier.

Section D of the AAAP had a newsletter and shortly after the founding of Division 14 there were members calling for such a publication. At its

1948 meeting, the division's policy and planning committee explored that possibility. The editors of the journal, *Personnel Psychology*, which had begun publication that year, offered some of its pages for division news. No record could be located to determine what happened to that proposal, but the journal did not publish any division news. A trial newsletter was first issued in January 1949 in Floyd Ruch's presidency. Ruch's editorial on the front page concerned the fiasco of public opinion polling in the 1948 presidential election and what psychologists could do to restore confidence in polling techniques (Ruch, 1949; see also Katz, 1949). The newsletter was published twice that year and continued to be published on an irregular basis thereafter. It was mimeographed, usually four to six pages in length, and consisted mostly of minutes of the annual business meeting and abbreviated committee reports. Then in 1963 the division began publication of *TIP*, albeit irregularly, with Robert Perloff as its first editor. In its early years *TIP* focused mostly on division business: minutes of meetings, committee reports, lists of new members and associates, an occasional obituary, surveys of industrial/ organizational programs, and editorials on issues germane to industrial/organizational psychologists and their students. Over time the coverage of Division 14 decreased and more space was devoted to brief articles, typically on such issues as training, licensure, and public relations.

One of the earliest publications of the division was a directory of members. Perhaps the first printed version appeared in 1951. It was intended not only for the membership but also to be given to business people as an advertisement of consultant services. Each member was allowed to list up to two occupational affiliations, with the second one typically being a consulting position. The directory also indicated which members were fellows, which ones were diplomates, and which ones were willing to offer their services as consultants (designated by a small letter "c" by their names).

A brochure on the nature of industrial psychology, to be used to encourage businesses to use the services of psychologists, appeared as early as 1953, and went through several revisions. A later brochure titled "A Career in Industrial/Organizational Psychology" was written for prospective graduate students, and a still later version, "The Science and Practice of Industrial and Organizational Psychology," was published in 1986 to reach students, clients, and the general public.

In 1980 the division was responsible for a landmark publication: *Principles for Validation and Use of Personnel Selection Procedures* (1980). Its recognition by the courts in several significant legal decisions changed the nature of employee selection by companies and altered the interpretation of Equal Employment Opportunity Commission guidelines.

In addition, a number of reports from the division were published as journal articles, typically in the *American Psychologist* (see, for example,

Division 14 Committee on Professional Education Policy, 1959; Division of Industrial Psychology Education and Training Committee, 1965).

Currently the division publishes two book series, one with greater emphasis on research and the other on practice. The first series is titled "Frontiers of Industrial and Organizational Psychology." Raymond Katzell was the initial series editor and the first volume published was *Career Development in Organizations* (1986), edited by Douglas T. Hall. The second series is titled the "Professional Practice Series." Douglas Bray was the inaugural series editor and edited the first volume in 1991, titled *Working with Organizations and Their People: A Guide to Human Resources Practice*.

PRACTICE, SCIENCE, AND, OH YES, EDUCATION

When the division began in 1945 it specified five goals. The first was to ensure high standards of practice and the second was to promote research and publication in the field. The third and fourth goals were for the clear benefit of Division 14 members: Provide a forum for exchange of information and experience, and develop new professional opportunities for industrial/organizational psychologists. And the last was a generic call to advance applied psychology. Education was not an explicit part of the division's natal objectives, yet it would be added as the field of industrial/organizational psychology grew and diverse models of training proliferated.

The division experienced great difficulty in gaining agreement on education and training issues. In 1957, division president C. H. Lawshe established a committee chaired by Robert Guion to develop guidelines for the *professional* education of industrial psychologists and the committee published its seven recommendations in 1959 (Division 14 Committee on Professional Education Policy, 1959). Yet it would be another six years before this committee (under a new name) would be able to agree on curriculum requirements for the doctorate in industrial psychology (see Division of Industrial Psychology Education and Training Committee, 1965). Over the years the Education and Training Committee debated some critical issues such as the accreditation of industrial/organizational programs by the APA, alternative training models (e.g., professional schools, business schools), alternative degrees (the PsyD), the role of continuing education, the core curriculum, and internships. The division sought to find ways to recruit better students, to reward students for their achievements, and to have students better identify with the division. Thus, although education may be an afterthought in the bylaws it has not been ignored. Still there is no denying that the focus of the division's life has been on enhancing practice and science.

Professional practice concerns, as previously noted, began with the early interest in a code of ethics and the certification of quality provided by the diploma from the ABEPP. It continued through actions on licensure (see Howard & Lowman, 1982), the workshop program, a number of legal briefs, public information campaigns to promote industrial/organizational practice, and a variety of published books (for example, the professional practice series) and articles including guidelines for selecting test validation consultants and the "Specialty Guidelines for the Delivery of Services by Industrial/Organizational Psychologists" (1981).

For industrial/organizational psychologists, practice and science were inseparable. The original 19 divisions were conceived as constituting two groups: the content areas, meaning the various scientific subfields of psychology (Divisions 1–11), and the applied fields (Divisions 12–19), which included both researchers and practitioners, the latter group being suspect by the association members at large in terms of its commitment to the science of psychology. For the founders of Division 14, this dichotomy was a false one. They were scientists whose laboratories happened to be the workplace.

In the course of its history the division has maintained an emphasis on science as the basis for its profession. Its initial goal, as stated in its bylaws, was to "promote high standards of practice." That meant more than just ethics; it meant the scientific skills required to provide clients in business and industry with the expertise that they were buying. It meant ensuring that students trained in industrial/organizational psychology were good scientists (which was one of the reasons the division continued to reject doctoral training models that minimized science training; see MacKinney, 1969; Stagner, no date). In promoting science the division sponsored occasional research conferences in addition to its annual APA programs. It sponsored publications like the frontier series, which grew out of a proposal by the Committee on Scientific Affairs in 1982. It was especially active in fostering research innovations. In addition to conferences on that topic, it founded the James McKeen Cattell Award in 1964 to recognize excellence in research designs for solving human behavior problems in organizations (renamed for Edwin Ghiselli in 1984).

A SEMI-AUTONOMOUS SOCIETY

Eighty years after the founding of a scientific APA the success of professional psychologists was evident in the governance of the association. Long denied a role of authority in APA affairs, applied psychologists who in the 1960s and 1970s had successfully battled psychiatry, insurance companies, and state legislatures on practice issues, used their organizational and political skills to take control of their destiny within the APA. The red flag for much of the scientific community occurred in 1976 when clinical psychologist Theodore Blau was elected to the presidency of the APA, the first private practitioner to hold an office that had been perceived as the exclusive domain of academic psychologists, particularly those whose research was in traditional experimental areas. New divisions were being added at what some considered an alarming rate and these were viewed principally as divisions related to the clinical practice of psychology. The policy-making body of the APA, the Council of Representatives, was now in the control of individuals largely identified with practice issues, chiefly in the health care area. The scientists complained about this reversal of power and called for a reorganization of the APA. Responding to those concerns the first of several blue-ribbon reorganization committees was created by the Council of Representatives in 1979. The practitioners, however, had fought too long and too hard to relinquish voluntarily their new-found power. And so reorganization attempts failed, resulting in an exodus of some of the APA's scientists and the founding of the rival American Psychological Society (APS) in 1988.

Division 14 members were not idle spectators in this power struggle. Division members had long considered themselves part of the APA's scientific community. Still, their involvement in practice and consulting led them to be supportive of clinical psychology's gains in the marketplace. However, when the APA began to exert greater control over division activities and when it was clear that the health care practice group was working to define practice in its own image, industrial/organizational psychologists grew increasingly concerned about such possibilities as the APA accreditation of industrial/organizational graduate programs, required licensure of industrial/organizational psychologists, and continuing education requirements (Howell, 1986; Thayer & Hirsch, 1986). The result was to incorporate Division 14 independently of the APA, which led to the creation of the Society for Industrial and Organizational Psychology (SIOP).

This incorporation was a watershed for the involvement of industrial/ organizational psychologists within the APA. In 1984 the percentage of Division 14 members participating in the APA convention was the highest of any of APA's divisions (Sackett, 1986). Yet as disillusionment grew with an APA that seemed most concerned with guild issues, industrial/ organizational psychology began to create an existence outside of the APA. In April of 1986, SIOP held its first meeting independent of the APA convention. These meetings continued as an annual event. Eventually the very successful workshop programs were moved from the APA meetings to the SIOP meetings. SIOP changed its election procedures to fit its own calendar year and not that of the APA, and it took control of its treasury. Not surprisingly in the ensuing years participation of industrial/organizational psychologists at the APA meetings has declined significantly.

CONCLUSION

This brief history has focused on the disciplinary and organizational antecedents of Division 14/SIOP and on the division's initial decade (see Table 26 for a chronology of significant events in the division's history). The objectives listed in its 1946 bylaws are still largely intact in the most recent version. But its organizational structure is much more complex. Today its committee structure is very much a mirror of the central office of the APA. The division's current bylaws list a number of standing committees, including scientific affairs, professional affairs, and education and training, matching three of the four principal program directorates of the APA (the fourth match, the division's public policy and social issues committee, was abolished in the 1980s). In addition there is a public relations committee,

TABLE 26
Significant Events in the History of Division 14: 1945–1995

Year	Event
1945	Division 14 founded; Bruce V. Moore was first president
1947	George K. Bennett was first non–university-based president
1949	Published first newsletter
1951	Marion A. Bills was first woman president
1953	Workshop program initiated; first one led by Edwin R. Henry and Stephen Habbe
1962	Name changed to Division of Industrial Psychology
1963	*The Industrial Psychologist (TIP)* began publication
1964	James McKeen Cattell Award for Research Design established
1965	Published model curriculum for doctoral training in industrial psychology
1970	S. Rains Wallace Dissertation Research Award established
1973	Name changed to Division of Industrial and Organizational Psychology
1977	Distinguished Professional Contributions Award established
1980	National Conference of Graduate Students in Industrial/Organizational Psychology held first annual meeting at Ohio State University
1981	Published "Specialty Guidelines for the Delivery of Services by Industrial/Organizational Psychologists"
1983	Incorporation—Name changed to Society for Industrial and Organizational Psychology (SIOP)—a Division of the APA
1983	Distinguished Scientific Contributions Award established
1984	Cattell Award is renamed the Edwin E. Ghiselli Award for Research Design
1986	First volume published in the series, *Frontiers of Industrial and Organizational Psychology*
1986	First annual Industrial/Organizational–Organizational Behavior Doctoral Student Consortium was held in Washington, DC
1989	Distinguished Service Contributions Award established
1991	First volume published in the Professional Practice series
1992	Ernest J. McCormick Award for Distinguished Early Career Contributions established

an awards committee, a state affairs committee, a continuing education and workshop committee, and three committees that oversee publications, again reflecting most of the primary activities of the APA. In short, although only 2500 members strong, Division 14 has created much of the same structure that defines the much larger APA.

Whereas other applied specialties have fragmented within the APA, clinical psychology (Division 12) being the prime example (spawning large divisions for psychotherapy and independent practice and a number of smaller ones), Division 14 has mostly held on to the science and practice of industrial/organizational psychology. There have been some defections, beginning in the 1950s when human factors went its own way with the founding of APA's Division 21, Engineering Psychology, in 1956, and the founding of the Human Factors Society in 1957. And in 1960 those psychologists with a special interest in consumer behavior founded Division 23 (Consumer Psychology), a new division proposal that the Division 14 leadership opposed. But those special interest groups within the APA started small and have remained so. Today Divisions 21 and 23 have fewer than 800 members combined, and of the 48 APA divisions, only three are smaller than Division 21 and only one smaller than Division 23.

Although industrial/organizational psychology has changed considerably since 1945, especially on the organizational side where organizational development and organizational behavior are principal emphases in research and practice today, the goals of Division 14/SIOP have remained virtually unchanged, serving industrial/organizational psychologists and their constituency well. SIOP retains its commitment to a membership of psychologists requiring either membership in the APA or the APS for membership in SIOP.

In one sense the division began in the ACP and AAAP with a group of psychologists who believed, like Münsterberg, that knowledge of nature and the mastery of nature belonged together. And their work has continued in an organization that has never lost sight of the importance of a real integration of science and practice.

REFERENCES

American Association for Applied Psychology. (1940, January). Bulletin No. 3. Walter Van Dyke Bingham Papers, Carnegie Mellon University Library.

American Psychological Association. (1953). *Ethical standards of psychologists*. Washington, DC: Author.

American Psychological Association, Division 14. (1980). *Principles for the validation and use of personnel selection procedures*. Berkeley, CA: Author.

Balzer, W. K., & Howard, A. (1994). 1993 profile of Division 14 members: Note-worthy trends. *The Industrial-Organizational Psychologist, 31(3)*, 95–97.

Bellows, R. W. (1949, August 10). Letter to Dael Wolfle. American Psychological Association Archives, Library of Congress Manuscript Division.

Benjamin, L. T., Jr. (1996). Harry Hollingworth: Portrait of a generalist. In G. A. Kimble, C. A. Boneau, & M. Wertheimer (Eds.), *Portraits of pioneers in psychology* (Vol. 2, pp. 119–135). Mahwah, NJ: Erlbaum.

Benjamin, L. T., Jr., & Bryant, W. H. M. (1996). A history of popular psychology magazines in America. In W. Bringmann, H. E. Luck, R. Miller, & C. E. Early (Eds.), *A pictorial history of psychology* (pp. 585–593). Munich: Quintessenz.

Benjamin, L. T., Jr., Rogers, A. M., & Rosenbaum, A. (1991). Coca-Cola, caffeine, and mental deficiency: Harry Hollingworth and the Chattanooga trial of 1911. *Journal of the History of the Behavioral Sciences, 27*, 42–55.

Bray, D. W. (Ed.). (1991). *Working with organizations and their people: A guide to human resources practice.* New York: Guilford Press.

Brotemarkle, R. A. (1940). The challenge to consulting psychology: The psychological consultant and the psychological charlatan. *Journal of Applied Psychology, 24*, 10–19.

Buckley, K. W. (1982). The selling of a psychologist: John Broadus Watson and the application of behavioral techniques to advertising. *Journal of the History of the Behavioral Sciences, 18*, 207–221.

Buckley, K. W. (1989). *Mechanical man: John Broadus Watson and the beginnings of behaviorism.* New York: Guilford Press.

Burtt, H. E. (1947, December 15). Letter to Floyd L. Ruch. American Psychological Association Archives, Library of Congress Manuscript Division.

Bylaws, Division of Industrial & Business Psychology. (1946). American Psychological Association Archives, Library of Congress Manuscript Division.

Carlson, H. C. (1991, August 13). *The No-Name Group: History treading on the heels of the future.* Paper presented at the annual meeting of the Academy of Management, Miami Beach, FL.

Capshew, J. H., & Hilgard, E. R. (1992). The power of service: World War II and professional reform in the American Psychological Association. In R. W. Evans, V. S. Sexton, & T. C. Cadwallader (Eds.), *The American Psychological Association: A historical perspective* (pp. 149–175). Washington, DC: American Psychological Association.

Crissey, O. L. (1980). *The No-Name Group.* Orlo Crissey Papers, Archives of the History of American Psychology, University of Akron, OH.

Division 14 Committee on Professional Education Policy. (1959). Professional education in industrial psychology: A statement of policy. *American Psychologist, 14*, 233–235.

Division of Industrial Psychology Education and Training Committee. (1965). Guidelines for doctoral education in industrial psychology. *American Psychologist, 20*, 822–831.

Hale, M., Jr. (1980). *Human science and social order: Hugo Münsterberg and the origins of applied psychology*. Philadelphia: Temple University Press.

Hall, D. T. (Ed.). (1986). *Career development in organizations*. San Francisco: Jossey-Bass.

Hall, G. S. (1894, August). The new psychology as a basis of education. *Forum*, 710–720.

Hilgard, E. R. (1945). Temporary chairmen and secretaries for proposed APA divisions. *Psychological Bulletin, 42*, 294–296.

Hollingworth, H. L. (1912). The influence of caffeine on mental and motor efficiency. *Archives of Psychology*, Whole No. 22.

Howard, A., & Lowman, R. L. (1982, January). *Licensing and industrial/organizational psychology: Background and issues*. American Psychological Association Archives, Library of Congress Manuscript Division.

Howell, W. C. (1986). Industrial/organizational psychology issues on credentialing: Licensure and state board relations. *Professional Practice of Psychology, 7*, 37–48.

Janney, J. E. (1947). *Qualifications for staff psychologists of Rohrer, Hibler, & Replogle: Psychological Counsel to Management*. American Psychological Association Archives, Library of Congress Manuscript Division.

Katz, D. (1949). An analysis of the 1948 polling predictions. *Journal of Applied Psychology, 33*, 15–28.

Katzell, R. A., & Austin, J. T. (1992). From then to now: The development of industrial-organizational psychology in the United States. *Journal of Applied Psychology, 77*, 803–835.

Koppes, L. L., Landy, F. J., & Perkins, K. N. (1993). First American female applied psychologists. *The Industrial Organizational Psychologist, 31(1)*, 31–33.

Landy, F. J. (1993). Early influences on the development of industrial/organizational psychology. In T. K. Fagan & G. R. VandenBos (Eds.), *Exploring applied psychology: Origins and critical analyses* (pp. 83–118). Washington, DC: American Psychological Association.

MacKinney, A. C. (1969, January 3). *The professional doctorate degree in industrial-organizational psychology*. Division 14 Archives, Archives of the History of American Psychology, University of Akron, OH.

Meyer, H. (1997). An early stimulus to psychology in industry: A history of the Dearborn Conference Group. *The Industrial-Organizational Psychologist, 34(3)*, 24–27.

Moore, B. V. (1946, April 25). Letter to the Division 14 Executive Committee. American Psychological Association Archives, Library of Congress Manuscript Division.

Münsterberg, H. (1913). *Psychology and industrial efficiency*. Boston: Houghton Mifflin.

Napoli, D. S. (1981). *Architects of adjustment: The history of the psychological profession in the United States*. Port Washington, NY: Kennikat Press.

National Committee for Affiliation and Association of Applied and Professional Psychology. (1937). The proposed American Association for Applied and Professional Psychologists. *Journal of Consulting Psychology, 1,* 14–16.

Pion, G. M., Mednick, M. T., Astin, H. S., Hall, C. C. I., Kenkel, M. B., Keita, G. P., Kohout, J., & Kelleher, J. C. (1996). The shifting gender composition of psychology: Trends and implications for the discipline. *American Psychologist, 51,* 509–528.

Ruch, F. L. (1947, September 9). Minutes of the annual meeting. Industrial and Business Section, APA. American Psychological Association Archives, Library of Congress Manuscript Division.

Ruch, F. L. (1949, January). *Newsletter.* American Psychological Association Archives, Library of Congress Manuscript Division.

Russo, N. F. (1974, October 30). Letter to Edwin Fleishman. American Psychological Association Archives, Library of Congress Manuscript Division.

Sackett, P. R. (1986). I/O psychology: The state of the practice. *Professional Practice of Psychology, 7,* 15–26.

Scott, W. D. (1903). *The theory of advertising.* Boston: Small, Maynard.

Scott, W. D. (1908). *The psychology of advertising.* Boston: Small, Maynard.

Scott, W. D. (1911a). *Increasing human efficiency in business.* New York: Macmillan.

Scott, W. D. (1911b). *Influencing men in business.* New York: Ronald Press.

Shartle, C. L. (1949, December). *Newsletter: A message from the president.* American Psychological Association Archives, Library of Congress Manuscript Division.

Sokal, M. M. (1981). The origins of The Psychological Corporation. *Journal of the History of the Behavioral Sciences, 17,* 54–67.

Specialty Guidelines for the Delivery of Services by Industrial/Organizational Psychologists. (1981). *American Psychologist, 36,* 664–669.

Stagner, R. (no date). *A Psy.D. degree for industrial psychology?* Division 14 Archives, Archives of the History of American Psychology, University of Akron, OH.

Task Force on the Status of Women. (1973). Report. *American Psychologist, 28,* 611–616.

Thayer, P. W., & Hirsch, H. R. (1986). Industrial/organizational psychology issues and credentialing. *Professional Practice of Psychology, 7,* 27–36.

The Industrial-Organizational Psychologist. (no date). Brochure in American Psychological Association Archives, Library of Congress Manuscript Division.

Viteles, M. (1932). *Industrial psychology.* New York: W. W. Norton.

Wesman, A. G., Husband, R. W., & Mold, H. P. (1949, July). Report of the Committee on Training. Division 14 Archives, Archives of the History of American Psychology, University of Akron, OH.

5

A HISTORY OF DIVISION 26
(HISTORY OF PSYCHOLOGY)

RONALD W. MAYER

A division of the history of psychology emerged late in the APA's history. Psychology's past, though long, has been of minor interest to most psychologists. There are several reasons. First, the past, through philosophy, represented the very discipline from which psychology, during its formative years, was trying to escape. Most psychologists during psychology's first 100 years sought independence from departments of philosophy or education. Studying the philosophical past from which psychology emerged was like incorporating the past from which one was trying to flee.

Second, the development of psychology as a modern science at the turn of the twentieth century was too close for objective review. The long past relied heavily on parent philosophy. The short history was still too personal to be scientifically respectable. Until midcentury, the history of psychology as a discipline subsisted somewhere between the history and philosophy of science and a collection of personal reminiscences about psychological mentors and colleagues, or both.

Leaders of the new science were still alive—too close in time for the first and second generation of psychologists to permit a really independent field of study. Objective investigation demands respectable distance. Too close examination of oneself negates the very dictum by which psychology

The author wishes to thank Michael Werthheimer for his very detailed corrections and helpful suggestions. Thanks also to Donald Dewsbury for his guidance in producing this chapter.

won its birthright—rejection of introspective methods and obeisance to objective observation.

Early historical scholars during the first half of this century were, after all, only third-generation psychologists. Modern psychology, commencing as it did with the work of Wilhelm Wundt in Leipzig in 1879, was only 20 years young at the century's end. James McKeen Cattell, one of psychology's earliest and most articulate spokespersons and vice president of the American Association for the Advancement of Science, spoke at that association's 50th anniversary in 1898 and said, "The history of psychology here prior to 1880 could be set forth as briefly as the alleged chapter on snakes, in a natural history of Iceland—'There are no snakes in Iceland.'" But during the next two decades and the last of the nineteenth century he rightfully noted, "There was then trained a second generation of psychologists, and we ourselves now have our students, a third generation" (Cattell, 1947, p. 110).

One of those third-generation students was Edwin G. Boring who wrote in 1929 and then revised in 1951 the classic A *History of Experimental Psychology*. It was this book, perhaps more than any other single event, that made the history of psychology not only a serious scholarly field of study but propaedeutic to any meaningful discussion of the scientific findings accumulating in this new field.

Hilgard, Leary, and McGuire (1991) thoroughly documented the major events in the history of psychology in the United States. Their careful review discusses both the persons and the ideas that emerged as useful in the study of psychology's history. E. G. Boring and Robert I. Watson are identified both for their personal and theoretical contributions to the field.

Gardner Lindzey, who became president-elect of the APA the same year the division was founded, noted a certain reluctance for self-examination by psychologists:

> Psychologists, as befits their position midway between the natural sciences and the humanities, typically have been ambivalent about examining their own past. One might speculate that the formation of a Division of the History of Psychology of the American Psychological Association suggests some amelioration in the characteristic reluctance of psychologists to be concerned with their origins. (Lindzey, 1980, pp. xv–xvi)

Psychology majors in many undergraduate departments were frequently required to complete a history and systems course. And graduate departments frequently required students aspiring to the PhD degree to have a knowledge of the history of their field. But students typically lacked interest in pursuing history further. The history of organizations seems to generate even less interest, as Pate (1990) suggested when discussing the writing of organizational histories.

THE HISTORY OF PSYCHOLOGY GROUP

Division 26, History of Psychology, was founded in 1965 out of what was then known as the History of Psychology Group. This informal group met at the American Psychological Association conventions and formed the nucleus of what later became Division 26. Robert I. Watson was the chief organizer and inspirational leader of this group. Ernest R. Hilgard (1982), at a symposium commemorating Watson's life and work, documented Watson's leadership.

Watson, David Bakan, and John Burnham served as a committee to convene these informal sessions at the APA meetings. The purpose was to exchange ideas and provide opportunity to meet like-minded psychologists also interested in the background of their field. Burnham was a professional historian and Bakan was not much interested in the minutiae of organizational details. It therefore fell on Watson to play host, moderator, and recorder. He argued early for the advisability of keeping the group informal. Spontaneity, collegiality, and cooperative sharing could be throttled by too much organizational structure, he argued.

The group first met at the Chicago APA meetings in 1960. An announcement placed in the convention program invited any persons interested in the history of psychology to attend a discussion group. Watson chaired the session and asked those attending to suggest topics of primary interest. An agenda was thus formed on the spot. Twenty-six persons attended the first meeting. Fifteen others sent their regrets. Almost 25% (or 9) of the original 41 interested persons later became presidents of the division.

Those attending were James Barclay, Michael Wertheimer, Robert B. MacLeod, Alexander Mintz, Edgar O. Wood, Paul Mountjoy, Ronald Walker, Paul Singer, Keith Davis, (Rev.) Walter Farrell, Faye Karpf, Abraham S. Luchins, F. Theodore Perkins, Abram M. Barch, Carolyn Hardin, Gabriel Ofiesh, Cedric A. Larson, Ronald W. Mayer, Kenneth Kunert, Saul Rosenzweig, W. Edgar Gregory, Harold Grant, Virginia Staudt, Nicholas Hobbs, Robert I. Watson, and John C. Burnham. Four of those later became presidents of Division 26: Watson, Wertheimer, MacLeod, and Staudt.

The fifteen persons sending regrets were David Bakan, Frank Freeman, Karl M. Dallenbach, Leonard Ferguson, Gardner Murphy, David Shakow, George Levinger, Ernest R. Hilgard, Erwin A. Esper, R. J. Herrnstein, S. L. Crawley, Frederick Wyatt, J. A. Cardno, Edwin G. Boring, and Jerome Schneck. Six of this group later became presidents of the division. Four of them (Dallenbach, Murphy, Hilgard, and Boring) were past presidents of the APA itself.

The History of Psychology Group identified three areas of particular interest and concern. First was the lack of publication outlets for historical papers. Second, it was recognized that no university department provided opportunity, let alone encouragement, for doctoral work in the history of psychology. And third, several persons expressed concern and even dismay that historical documents at the APA (as well as papers owned by private psychologists) were being destroyed—or at least not systematically preserved.

Concern about the availability of publishing outlets for historical papers was clearly evident. The group identified about a dozen journals in which historical articles might possibly be published. Most agreed that the APA did not encourage historical articles. A proposal was made that "the board of editors be petitioned to make definite provision for historical articles" and that the availability of other outlets for historical articles should be communicated to members of the APA.

How to reverse the reluctance of doctoral programs to permit historical dissertations yielded few suggestions. Such dissertations were widely considered to be more suitable for a teaching rather than a research doctorate. Departments of education and sociology, it was argued, were more likely to accept historical research.

On the third issue, the group resolved to take some action. Official APA records were in need of preservation. Papers of individual psychologists were no less important. A letter addressed to the executive director of the APA was to make several requests: (a) appoint an official APA archivist to collect materials and encourage others to preserve their papers, and (b) reserve some space at the APA headquarters for an official library and archives.

The first meeting of the history group thus seemed a success. Watson, several weeks after the convention, mailed out a four-page summary of the meeting, stating that the group agreed to "constitute itself as a special interest group within the APA. Next year at the APA meetings in New York it will either meet again or sponsor a symposium or both. Meantime the possibility of being sponsored by some division will be investigated" (R. Watson, personal communication, fall 1960).

In March of the following year, Watson wrote a letter to the History of Psychology Group and attached a mailing list of 91 interested persons. These names came from all those in the APA directory who mentioned an interest in history. Names of others were also added. This formed the basis for a mailing. In this second "newsletter," Watson relayed various suggestions for the second meeting in New York. He also reported that the APA would soon take action on the petition requesting an archivist. No word was forthcoming, however, from the board of editors regarding the APA outlets for the publication of historical papers. This state of affairs, unfortunately, continued for some 35 years.

The second meeting of the History of Psychology Group was held in New York in 1961. About twenty persons attended. The November "newsletter" following the meeting reported favorably on action being taken on the earlier archival recommendation. "The Board of Directors of the APA has now appointed an *Ad Hoc* Committee on Psychological Archives. Members are Leonard Carmichael, W. Clark Trow, and Robert I. Watson, Chairman." One ad hoc committee meeting had already been held, and plans were being made to recommend how to handle the association's records and to give advice concerning the preservation of documents by individual psychologists.

The need for publication outlets had also received some attention. Numerous journals over the years had carried book reviews. Chief among these were the APA journals—*The Psychological Review* founded in 1894 and *The Psychological Bulletin,* founded in 1904. The newsletter reported that Watson had received a letter from Clifford T. Morgan, chair of the publications board, stating that the Council of Editors (and more specifically the editors of *Psychological Bulletin* and *Psychological Review)* had considered the group's concern and that there was no policy prohibiting historical articles and that they would be glad to accept articles if they were "contributions to knowledge."

During subsequent years, several division members served on the advisory board for *Contemporary Psychology,* the book review journal of the APA, first edited by Edwin G. Boring. Michael Wertheimer and Donald Dewsbury both served for many years as advisory editors, as did Benjamin Harris, beginning in 1991, to help make arrangements for reviewing books in the history of psychology. Another member, Ludy T. Benjamin, Jr., was made associate editor of the *American Psychologist* in 1979 to handle historical articles and obituaries in that journal.

The third meeting of the History of Psychology Group was held in St. Louis in 1962. A symposium on the teaching of the history of psychology had been organized by Michael Wertheimer. It included papers by Boring, Watson, Robert MacLeod, and O. J. Harvey. Boring reviewed his nearly four decades of teaching the history of psychology. Afterward, he dropped in to visit the History of Psychology Group during their third business meeting. That naturally caused quite a stir; it was a pleasant surprise for everyone. Recollection has it that he made some typically humorous comments but did not even sit down; at least any remarks he might have made were not recorded in reports of the meeting. As the most visible historian of psychology at the time, he no doubt was aware that his presence, not to mention his participation, would have influenced the group's deliberations.

In a March 1963 newsletter, the last one sent out by Watson, he briefly summarized the papers delivered by Boring and Watson at the symposium, and he provided more extensive abstracts of the papers by MacLeod and Harvey. Attached to the newsletter were the names and addresses of group members. The list had now grown to 111 persons.

Watson had been open and eager from the very beginning to involve others in the leadership of the group. At the first meeting he had asked for volunteers to chair the second meeting. At the second meeting he humorously announced that there would be a new chair and said nominations would be accepted. At the third meeting, having gotten no one to serve as chair, he asked if a committee would volunteer to take charge of the newsletter. This was the vehicle that kept the group together and provided continuity from one year to the next. Leonard Ferguson volunteered to help, if others would assist. Cedric Larson and Ronald Mayer also volunteered.

The fourth meeting was held in Philadelphia in 1963 and was followed by a sixth newsletter. Ferguson then wrote (personal correspondence of January 29, 1963) to announce his appointment as editor of *The Journal Press* and asked to be excused from any further work on the newsletter committee. Larson and Mayer subsequently managed to edit the next ten or so issues until after the group officially received division recognition and a new newsletter was started.

Nothing had been planned for a fifth meeting at the 1964 Los Angeles convention, but Mayer managed to secure a room and a time at the last minute and arranged to have it appear in the convention program.

Formation of a New Division

At the close of the fifth meeting, a decision was made to seek division status. Division organization, a perennial topic at these group meetings, had always been quickly shelved; other topics of greater interest demanded more attention. Besides, Watson had argued that formal groups frequently interfered with creative activity and he expressed on several occasions a reluctance to become too overly organized. And because the persons attending the meetings never exceeded more than 20 to 30 in number, formal organization seemed somewhat premature.

After the Los Angeles History of Psychology Group business meeting ended, David Bakan ventured aloud to several of us, "I think it's time to start a division. Why don't we talk to Bob now and see if he doesn't agree." Watson displayed little initial enthusiasm for the idea; but he did not actively oppose it. Watson himself confessed that,

> Quite deliberately the group was without officers, dues, or even an official name. Many of us found this state of affairs congenial. When the possibility of a formal division within the APA was first broached,

I demurred. The argument that convinced me that such a step was necessary was the comment of one young psychologist to the effect that the division of the history of psychology would give a stamp of authenticity to work in this area—that it would help bring recognition that the history of psychology is a form of specialization. (Watson, 1972, p. 288)

Bakan suggested that I write to the APA and inquire about the requirements for starting a new division; then just go out and do it. In less than a year, the new division was approved—but it was a year filled with frantic activity that was not lessened at all by the rather sudden change in the rules of council.

After the convention was over, Bakan wrote to Mayer (personal correspondence, September 29, 1964) and forwarded a current volume of the APA reports. He called attention to item IV-A-I, the formation of the Division of the Experimental Analysis of Behavior. This might "give you some idea of what is involved in connection with the formation of our Division of the History of Psychology." In a second letter, he said,

> I just want to write to you to underline the importance of our decision to form a division of the history of psychology. Although I have a natural aversion to the multiplication of bureaucracy, I am old enough to know that sometimes it is desirable and necessary. I think that the formation of a division will do a great deal to encourage research in the field and this is something to give some visibility to the field so that, for example, a young person might feel that a topic in the history of psychology would be suitable for an MA or PhD thesis.

A few days later (October 4), Mayer wrote to Arthur Brayfield, executive officer of the APA, describing the history of the History of Psychology Group, the debate regarding the advisability of seeking division status, and requesting information regarding the "one percent rule" (whereby petitions for new divisions must be signed by at least 1% of the APA membership) and the forms necessary for division petitioning. A week later Mayer sought Bakan's advice about whether more member support might be forthcoming if newsletter readers were consulted regarding the pros and cons of forming a division. On October 22, Bakan replied by saying,

> In my own mind I don't think that the issue is a 'pro or con' one, only whether there are enough people who are sufficiently interested. But by all means put something on it in the Newsletter and get some concern with the question. The big problem is whether there are enough people interested to make it. Perhaps you might ask your readers in the Newsletter for suggestions of other people who should be getting the Newsletter, and who might be interested in being charter members of the new division. (D. Bakan, personal communication, October 22, 1964)

On October 27, Arthur Brayfield's administrative associate, Jane Hildreth, finally responded. Her delay had been prompted only by her interest in increasing the probability of a successful division bid. Nobody had seriously thought about the mechanics of organization; and surely no one had imagined a time line to successfully complete the task prior to the next convention. But Hildreth wrote with some detail regarding the tasks and timing necessary to achieve division status during the coming year.

The major stumbling block to the development of a history division was the increasing number of new divisions. The APA's board of directors and council were growing increasingly concerned about the proliferation of divisions. Division 26 was one of the first to face such organizational reservations, though today there are 49 separate divisions.

Most of the areas of psychology at that time were well represented by division status. But new interest groups, not readily identifiable with traditional areas in psychology, were requesting recognition and some representation. The increasing momentum toward fragmentation needed to be moderated. Part of the plan to decrease the impetus toward fragmentation had begun in that summer of 1964. Council had voted to add four more rules to the Rules of Council. These additional steps spelled out in considerable detail were further encumbrances to the petition for division status. Hildreth of course had been more than a chance onlooker to the debate. Nothing had yet been published. But as soon as the new rules were en route to the publisher she simultaneously mailed a copy of the galley proofs to us.

But aside from the question of proliferation, should there be yet another "general" division of psychology? After all, Division 1 (General Psychology) could encompass history. The division bylaws clearly stated the division's "concern . . . with . . . such problems as: (1) historical, systematic, and methodological aspects of psychology as a whole" (Wertheimer & King, 1996). Indeed, members of the executive committee of Division 1, at its September 6 meeting the next summer, argued that "the history of psychology should find a home in the Division of General Psychology." Nevertheless, they went ahead without formal complaint and endorsed the new petition (Wertheimer & King, 1996).

It was perhaps fortuitous that Jane Hildreth had served earlier as Boring's secretary and was, no doubt, familiar with and sympathetic to the goals of the potential petitioners. Her letter spelled out in some detail the steps we would have to go through. A petition endorsed by 200 signatories would thus be necessary, because the APA 1964 directory listed 18,328 members and fellows (associate members were not counted). B. F. Skinner had recently submitted a petition approved for a division of the experimental analysis of behavior. She included a copy and said, "it seems to meet the new criteria, in case you would like to use it as a guide" (J. Hildreth, personal communication, October 27, 1964).

The petition needed to include a purpose, evidence of a functioning group, names and addresses of petitioners, minutes of meetings, bylaws, provisional officers, approval by the board of directors, division presidents, and representatives to council. It was a daunting task.

Watson offered to draw up a petition statement and suggested that the mailing lists of the History of Psychology Group and the *History of Behavioral Sciences Newsletter* be used as a source for petitioners. This list of 800 names was divided geographically and the three of us (Watson, Mayer, and Larson) sent petitions to persons whose names appeared in each of our parts of the country. To increase the pool of potential petitioners, letters were also sent to department chairs explaining our plans and asking for names of persons who might have a special interest in the history of psychology. A total of 222 petitioners was finally obtained (personal communication, Charles Gersoni, Associate Executive Secretary, July 10, 1965).

In retrospect, the manner in which the division was formed reflected the changing times. There was no great groundswell demanding a history division. Less than a dozen persons seemed particularly motivated. It appears that a few activists managed to marshal support from a wide array of friends and colleagues. Most of the signatories were either sympathetic colleagues or dedicated scholars whose major commitments were to other more traditional fields of psychology.

In less than two months prior to the convention, numerous other documents were needed. Watson, Bakan, Richard Littman, Larson, and Mayer served as an organizing committee preparing the necessary materials. As the end of the school year and summer vacations approached, Hildreth seemed the only one interested in and convinced that a deadline could be met.

In addition to meeting the quota of petition signers, a set of division bylaws needed to be written. Time was running out. Hildreth sent copies of the most recently approved bylaws, those of Division 25 (Experimental Analysis and Behavior). And Joseph Lyons, secretary–treasurer of Division 24 (Theoretical and Philosophical Psychology) had recently worked on that division's petition process and offered to help. I asked him to draft some bylaws and they were adopted essentially as he wrote them. They borrowed heavily on those of Division 24 and were modified after discussion on several points. One was the advisability of including associate members who were, in those days, non–doctoral-level members.

The bylaws have been changed several times over the years. The 1967 elections contained a ballot proposition requesting a vote on "affiliate" membership status within the division. In 1971, John Popplestone recommended some substantive changes. In 1991 President Elizabeth Scarborough argued that at minimum editorial changes needed to be made to the bylaws.

Toward that end she suggested myriad changes that were not substantive but necessary to clarify the meaning of the bylaws. These were passed without debate.

Ten days before Jane Hildreth needed to distribute 150 copies of application materials to council members and others, we still did not have a "purpose" for the division. Richard Littman was asked to draft a statement of purpose. He did so and, after much editing and without retyping, forwarded a rough copy that stood, with minor changes, as the purpose for the division (Personal communication, August 13, 1965). Joseph Lyons suggested that the tripartite aims of the APA (science, professional, and human welfare) be worked in. The original statement of purpose was then as follows:

> The purpose of this organization shall be (a) to encourage and facilitate original scholarship in the history of psychology; and (b) to extend the awareness and appreciation of the history of psychology as an aid to the understanding of (1) contemporary psychology in its aims as a science, profession and means of promoting human welfare, (2) its relation to other scientific and scholarly fields, and (3) its role in society. (Mimeographed copy presented to council)

Aside from Boring, Watson was clearly the most active and prominent member of the group. Mayer asked him to be the contact person for the group and to represent the petitioners, if needed, at the council meeting on September 7.

EARLY MEETINGS

The History of Psychology Group met for the sixth and last time during the 1965 APA convention weekend at the Chicago Palmer House. Council was to vote on the history petition the next day.

Bakan agreed to chair the meeting. Nineteen persons attended. A 1-hour, 15-minute program by Josef Brozek included his paper on "Histories of Psychology," with a panel of commentators. That was followed by a 35-minute business meeting. Watson reported that no serious obstacles had surfaced prior to the vote by council the next day. Littman presented the bylaws for the group's approval. Cedric Larson took minutes of the meeting, which were published in the fall.

Those attending the Chicago meeting sat around a table and added their names to a sign-up sheet. Those attending were David Bakan, Josef Brozek, Ilse Bry, Robert Davis, Joseph Franklin, Margaret Gorman, Philip Gray, W. Edgar Gregory, Joe Hazel, Cedric Larson, Richard Littman, Ronald Mayer, John Popplestone, Wallace Russell, Virginia S. Sexton, John Sullivan, Robert Watson, Michael Wertheimer, and Theta Wolf.

The next day the council approved the new division with little discussion. Before leaving the convention, work began on how to handle certain housekeeping chores prior to a formal election the next spring. Watson and Bakan suggested and concurred in potential committee chairs. Mayer followed up on their suggestions and obtained a working interim committee. A program chair was needed for the following year as well as for 1967, the 75th anniversary of the founding of the APA. Josef Brozek, who had earlier made suggestions about future program topics, agreed to handle the first formal meeting in 1966. Watson and Bakan volunteered to assist on the committee. It was hoped that Littman would handle the 75th anniversary meeting but his plan to be abroad precluded participation. At Watson's suggestion, David Krantz at Yale was asked to serve. John Popplestone agreed to serve as election chair and Robert Davis as membership chair. Others were cooperative about volunteering where help was needed.

The fall newsletter announced approval of the division, contained notes on the organizing meeting, and published a review of interim plans and provisional committees. It also contained a final list of charter members and an analysis of their membership affiliation with other divisions.

The first formal planning discussion was to be held at the 1966 APA convention in New York City. But because the first set of officers would not be elected until shortly before the meetings, the provisional committee of Watson, Bakan, and Mayer had to plan for it, with Watson presuming, but not knowing, that he would chair the business meeting. We requested 10 hours of program time—three symposia, three paper sessions, an invited address, business meeting, and a social hour.

The program included two paper sessions and three symposia: A symposium titled, "Current Developments in Psychology"; a panel on "Russian and Soviet Psychology" chaired by Gregory Razran; and a symposium on "The Role of Psychology in the Curriculum," featuring Robert Harper, Krantz, Wertheimer, and Brozek with MacLeod as chair and commentator. There were two invited addresses—one by Eric Carlson and one by Robert Watson on "Prescriptive Science."

The election of officers was announced at the business meeting. Edwin G. Boring, by pre-arrangement, was honorary president. (Hilgard (1982) recounted how this came about to solve the dilemma that existed between the wish to honor Boring on the one hand and his desire not to be elected president of the division on the other hand.) Robert Watson was elected president, Gardner Murphy, president-elect, and John Popplestone, secretary–treasurer.

The second division meeting, held in September 1967 at the APA's 75th anniversary, was anticipated with some excitement. The 50th anniversary, coming as it did during the middle of World War II, was not only a noncelebration, there was not even a convention in that year. But on the occasion of the 75th celebration, the Archives of the History of American Psychology generated an impressive exhibit. The archives had developed a special relationship to the division. John Popplestone, founder of the archives, was the first secretary–treasurer of Division 26 and actively recruited division leaders and members to support the archives. The division celebrated the occasion by mounting a special program. David Krantz prepared a program for the APA's diamond jubilee.

Membership

The original classes of members were fellows, members, and foreign affiliates. Of the 222 charter members, 140, or 63% were APA members and 82 (37%) were fellows. At the time of division organization, those who were fellows in other divisions were permitted to become charter fellows of the division without any additional eligibility review. Later, the division required that the status of fellows be reserved for those making significant contributions to the history of psychology. In 1990 newly elected fellows of the division were required to present a lecture at the next annual meeting.

The addition of an associate class of members in the division occurred early. In part to avert criticism that the history of psychology was not really a scholarly field, and in part to bolster prestige, the division recognized only those with PhDs as eligible members. Unfortunately, this meant excluding some competent and conscientious historians who were associates of the APA. From the beginning, associates did not have high status. There was some concern also, in preparing the bylaws, that including an associate category would merely encourage those who were not serious psychologists. At that time only those with the PhD degree were allowed to be full, voting members of the APA. The issue continued to be particularly troubling. One original organizing committee member did not possess a PhD and would thus not be eligible for membership. The APA, still struggling to maintain an academic image, was trying to achieve parity with other disciplines.

Another subject of early discussion was the role of historians from other countries who were interested in exchanging ideas with division members. Josef Brozek was most vocal in encouraging a class of foreign affiliates. He provided names of psychologists, through his extensive connections to Europe, who were interested in creating contacts with American psychologists interested in the history of psychology.

By the second year of existence of the division, it became apparent that persons in disciplines related to psychology and residing within the United States would also provide stimulation to division members; and a domestic affiliate class of membership was suggested. A proposal to change the bylaws to include an "affiliate" class thus appeared on the 1967 ballot. The vote passed overwhelmingly, 112 to 8. The only objections to adding an affiliate class was the fear that some psychologists eligible for APA membership might avoid the APA dues by becoming affiliates of the division; or, that those in related fields might pass themselves off as psychologists. Because there was no mechanism for collecting dues from affiliates, the problem of additional expense in mailing the newsletter, especially to foreign lands, was not taken lightly, especially if the number of affiliates were to become substantial. It was generally agreed that the expense involved in collecting money from foreign affiliates outweighed any financial gain, and no dues were imposed.

Any new field needs fresh blood to remain viable. But this posed a special problem for Division 26. By its very nature, the study of the past frequently attracts older scholars. The study of the history of any field (not least of all psychology) has not, in recent years, attracted large numbers of students in psychology. And though the future of the organization and field requires younger members, no academic programs existed to provide a steady supply of new talent. Student affiliate status applied originally to graduate students in psychology who were endorsed by a division member. There were few such candidates during the early years. An undergraduate student affiliate membership class was finally formalized in 1976. At that time the executive committee unanimously recommended that any APA "student in psychology" would be automatically eligible for "student affiliate" membership in Division 26.

Gender differences among Division 26 members have been remarkably more pronounced than in most other APA divisions. Of Division 26 members in 1995, 82% were men and 18% women. Out of 48 divisions, History of Psychology ranked 45th in percentage of women members, lower than all other divisions except Military (15%) and Applied Experimental (16%) and the same proportion as Theoretical and Philosophical (18%).

It is interesting to note that, when compared to other academic disciplines in the humanities and social sciences, the proportion of women in the division matches that of the percentage of doctorates (20%) awarded to women in philosophy (Thurgood & Weinman, 1991)—the lowest represented field of female doctorates except for economics (9%) and quantitative psychology (20%). Scarborough and Furumoto suggested that historians have emphasized ideas and theory rather than the applications of psychology, "Ignoring the . . . applied aspects eliminates most women psychologists for women were more prominent in the applied areas" (1987, p. 185).

The geographical distribution of division members is not diverse. Terrell (1983) reported that more than a third (197) of division members reside in just four states—New York, California, Illinois, and Massachusetts. No members were found in Alaska, Hawaii, Wyoming, or the U.S. territories. This geographical distribution parallels that of APA membership in general in which the same four states have the largest number of members. One difference, however, was that persons from foreign countries constituted 3.5% of APA members, whereas there was almost twice that percentage (7.2%) of Division 26 members from foreign countries (including Canada). The data further reveal that more than a third of division members reside in the Northeast. The remainder are equally distributed (20%) among the South, Midwest, and West Coast.

The original charter members represented all other divisions within the APA. Members from all 23 divisions had signed the petition. Perhaps they portrayed a group of "joiners." Of the 222 petitioners, only 17% belonged to no other division within the APA. More than half (51%) belonged to at least one or two divisions. About a third belonged to three or more divisions. The largest number of petitioners belonged to the divisions of Teaching of Psychology (Division 2; 15%), and Personality and Social Psychology (Division 8; 13%). General Psychology (Division 1), Experimental Psychology (Division 3), and Clinical Psychology (Division 12) members each constituted 10% of the signatories.

Membership in the division grew steadily. But it was always an effort. From the beginning, a natural wellspring for new members never existed. Probably unique among the divisions, with the possible exception of Division 24 (Theoretical and Philosophical Psychology), which was organized a year earlier, no subspecialty or professional identification existed—only the theories, the great psychologists, and the anecdotal stories surrounding them. Soliciting widely among those departments known to have a history of psychology requirement yielded many charter members. Prominent psychologists, already guaranteed a place in the history books, were another source of easy persuasion. The division can boast that its membership includes twelve past presidents of the APA. Of the presidents, six are fellows and six are members of the division. The 1996 chief executive officer of the APA, Raymond D. Fowler, is also a member.

But the relative size of the division has long been a problem, bordering as it often did on the minimal percentage necessary to retain a seat on the Council of Representatives. Of the then 20 APA divisions established by petition, Division 26 placed third from the bottom in 1980 in membership size. When compared with the original 18 divisions operating according to 1945 bylaws, Division 26 was larger than only one other (Hilgard, 1987, pp. 760–761).

A major source for names of potential members was "division interest slips" included with the APA dues statement each year. But in 1981, the APA membership office reported that no other division save one had fewer requests for membership applications than did Division 26. It was clear that history was not high on anyone's agenda. There have been five membership chairs (Robert C. Davis, Mayer, William Wilsoncroft, Randall Wight, and

TABLE 27
Membership in Division 26 and the APA as a Whole

Year	Division 26 N	APA N	Division 26 as percentage of the APA
1966	234	24,923	0.94
1967	293	28,070	1.04
1968	312	30,345	1.03
1969	367	34,279	1.07
1970	409	37,001	1.11
1971	437	38,862	1.12
1972	452	40,609	1.11
1973	477	42,658	1.12
1974	463	44,229	1.05
1975	493	43,812	1.13
1976	504	48,841	1.03
1977	482	49,649	0.97
1978	488	52,048	0.94
1979	473	53,875	0.88
1980	470	56,175	0.84
1981	473	58,825	0.80
1982	468	63,149	0.74
1983	503	65,863	0.76
1984	550	68,845	0.80
1985	622	71,093	0.87
1986	728	73,663	0.99
1987	825	76,259	1.08
1988	823	76,601	1.07
1989	840	74,341	1.13
1990	869	74,441	1.17
1991	936	81,197	1.15
1992	1048	86,377	1.21
1993	1066	87,134	1.22
1994	1049	90,491	1.16
1995	1022	95,979	1.06
1996	1003	93,949	1.07

Source. Year-end APA divisional membership totals report.

Edward Haupt) since the division started. Each has conducted membership drives, the first occurring in 1974. Wilsoncroft in 1984 and Wight in 1991 aggressively solicited potential new members by conducting extensive letter-writing campaigns. As a result, the division grew in numbers. But the APA also grew. As Table 27 shows, the fourfold division membership increase since its inception has barely enabled it to hold its own proportionately to the larger association. When looking at division membership as a proportion of the total APA membership, Division 26 has fairly consistently held at around 1% of the total (Figure 1).

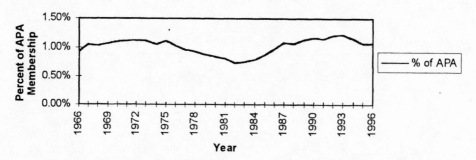

Figure 1. Membership in Division 26 as Percentage of APA as a Whole.

Officers

History of psychology is not a one-issue specialty, so leadership within the division has come from many quarters. Presidents of the division (Table 28) have represented a variety of fields and have generally been scholars recognized for their work in the history of psychology. They have represented areas as diverse as psychology itself—experimental, developmental, personality, clinical, and perception, for example. About a third of the presidents were experimentalists, a third personality/social psychologists, and a third applied. Very few were professionally trained as historians of psychology. And there have been gender differences. During the first 15 years, only two of the division presidents were female, but during the past 15 years, a third of the presidents have been women.

The original bylaws called for all officers to serve a 1-year term. In 1969 it was argued that some continuity in division governance could be achieved if the secretary–treasurer would continue for 3 years and be eligible for a second term. A bylaw change was made to permit that. There have been seven secretary–treasurers, each serving for 3 or 6 years.

The division has always been represented on the APA Council of Representatives. There have been ten division representatives to the APA council; of these, seven have also been presidents of the division.

Because council representation is based on proportional votes representing at least .50% of the APA's members, securing enough endorsements to maintain a representative has always been a challenge to the division. Most division members have loyalties to their subject-matter fields; allocating token points to Division 26 has frequently been a secondary, charitable act. Finally, in 1995, the division lacked sufficient support and lost its full seat on the council. An alliance with Division 24 (Theoretical and Philosophical Psychology) permitted the forming of a coalition to maintain representation on the council. In 1996, Division 26 regained its full seat.

TABLE 28
Officers of Division 26

Year	President	Secretary–Treasurer	Council representative
1966	Edwin G. Boring (Honorary President)		
1967	Robert I. Watson	John A. Popplestone	Benjamin Wolman/ Michael Wertheimer
1968	Gardner Murphy	John A. Popplestone	Benjamin Wolman/ Michael Wertheimer
1969	Robert B. MacLeod	John A. Popplestone	Michael Wertheimer/ Robert Watson
1970	Karl M. Dallenbach	John A. Popplestone	Robert Watson/Wallace Russell
1971	David Bakan	John A. Popplestone	Robert Watson/Wallace Russell
1972	Mary Henle	John A. Popplestone	Wallace Russell/ Robert C. Davis
1973	Solomon Diamond	Virginia Staudt Sexton	Robert C. Davis
1974	Josef M. Brozek	Virginia Staudt Sexton	Robert C. Davis
1975	Nicholas Pastore	Virginia Staudt Sexton	John A. Popplestone
1976	John J. Sullivan	Virginia Staudt Sexton	John A. Popplestone
1977	David L. Krantz	Virginia Staudt Sexton	John A. Popplestone
1978	Michael Wertheimer	Virginia Staudt Sexton	Barbara C. Ross
1979	John A. Popplestone	Eileen Gavin	Barbara C. Ross
1980	Virginia Staudt Sexton	Eileen Gavin	Barbara C. Ross
1981	Ernest R. Hilgard	Eileen Gavin	John A. Popplestone
1982	Barbara C. Ross	Elizabeth S. Goodman	John A. Popplestone
1983	Ludy T. Benjamin	Elizabeth S. Goodman	John A. Popplestone
1984	David E. Leary	Elizabeth S. Goodman	Laurel Furumoto
1985	Daniel N. Robinson	Hendrika Vande Kemp	Laurel Furumoto
1986	Thomas C. Cadwallader	Hendrika Vande Kemp	Laurel Furumoto
1987	Rand B. Evans	Hendrika Vande Kemp	John A. Popplestone
1988	Wolfgang G. Bringmann	Ronald W. Mayer	John A. Popplestone
1989	Wilse B. Webb	Ronald W. Mayer	John A. Popplestone
1990	Marion White McPherson	Ronald W. Mayer	Thomas C. Cadwallader
1991	Elizabeth Scarborough	Ronald W. Mayer	John A. Popplestone
1992	Joseph D. Matarazzo	Ronald W. Mayer	John A. Popplestone
1993	Neil R. Bartlett	Ronald W. Mayer	John A. Popplestone
1994	Jill G. Morawski	Alvin H. Smith	Michael Wertheimer
1995	Henry Minton	Alvin H. Smith	Michael Wertheimer
1996	Laurel Furumoto	Alvin H. Smith	Michael Wertheimer
1997	Donald A. Dewsbury	Alvin H. Smith	Michael Wertheimer

Publications

A newsletter was issued shortly after the first formal 1966 New York meeting. Following official establishment of the division, Watson was unsure whether the division could afford a newsletter and asked that one more issue of the "History of Psychology Group" newsletter be issued. The word

"Group" was dropped from its masthead. It contained the election results for the new officers, the names of participants in the 1966 program and the titles of their papers, a call for papers for the 1967 convention, and an announcement of the establishment of the American Archives of the History of Psychology. It also contained current and anticipated research activities of division members as compiled by Josef Brozek for the 1966 program.

The division finally decided to issue a regular newsletter. The first issue came out in the spring of 1968. Marion White McPherson and John Popplestone were its editors. It contained remarks made at the "Happenings in the History of Psychology" session by Gardner Murphy as president-elect, an "Archives Corner" by John Popplestone, a report by Josef Brozek on the National Science Foundation summer institute for college teachers in the history of psychology, the division bylaws, and a list of division members. The second newsletter was a memorial to Edwin G. Boring, containing a charcoal sketch reproduction, several tributes, and a twelve-page spread of letters Boring had written to several division members.

Popplestone and McPherson continued to edit the newsletters until 1978, when Ludy T. Benjamin, Jr., took over—for 5 years. Wolfgang Bringmann and Charles Early, alternatively, were editors until 1993, when James L. Pate started editing the issues. Continuing features in the newsletter were listings of bibliographies, an information exchange, short articles, minutes and other matters pertaining to the division's business.

Should the division attempt to sponsor a journal, providing a publication outlet for its members? The paucity of outlets for historical articles had been a serious concern of division members since the first History of Psychology Group meeting in 1960 and one of the major reasons for forming a new organization—an opportunity to communicate with other scholars. Discussion of inaugurating a history of psychology journal, sponsored by either the division or by the APA, occurred informally on and off for three decades. Whereas members in other divisions rely on laboratories for new research or clinics for professional practice, historians of psychology, essentially scholars, need libraries with books and journals and archives with documents. Without publishing outlets, the historian is essentially out of business.

In 1963, Robert I. Watson was able to obtain financial backing for founding the *Journal of the History of the Behavioral Sciences* (*JHBS*), which provided interdisciplinary coverage and wide-ranging articles on the history of psychology. Another division president, Barbara Ross, soon took over the editorship. But some division members thought that publication opportunities were still too limited.

Some 25 years later, Charles Early, then the division newsletter editor, conducted a survey of division members to assess reactions to the newsletter and to determine potential support for and advisability of converting the newsletter to a full-fledged journal. The findings, reported to the division in 1990, indicated that most members responded favorably to the newsletter's length, format, and content. Most wanted more and longer articles and a newsletter that was published at least four times per year. In response to the question, "Should the newsletter be expanded into a journal?" 42% answered with an unequivocal "yes" and 73% said they would be willing to support a journal through increased dues.

Finally, an ad hoc committee chaired by Ludy Benjamin, Jr., was appointed in 1992 to examine the feasibility of creating a new journal. The committee reported that an audience did exist. It argued that both the JHBS and the APA journals had published only a few historical articles each year. The APA seemed prepared to endorse either the idea of a new journal or a historical section in an existing APA journal. There was some disagreement over whether enough material existed to support both JHBS and an APA history journal. In 1995 the journal committee reported to the division that, pending approval by council, a quarterly journal would be published jointly with the APA. After 5 years the journal would be eligible to become a full APA journal, but the editorial control of the journal would be maintained by division members. In February 1996, the APA Council of Representatives voted to approve a plan for a new journal on the history of psychology.

Finances

The division has never had much of a problem with finances. From the beginning, financial issues attracted little attention. Occasionally, proposals were made to pay large honoraria to invite prospective prominent speakers, of which there were many. It was also hoped that financial support for student papers would encourage participation by the younger generation at the convention. Sponsoring social hours, sometimes elaborate, to attract new members or indulge old ones, was an on and off again temptation.

Division expenses were never a burden; most members had academic appointments. Many officers and committee chairs were able to use university facilities, postage, and student assistants for division mailings and committee projects. In 1964, for example, total newsletter costs to the division, including postage for mailing was $6.94. In 1966, after division status was achieved and the number of members doubled, the newsletter cost the division $12.05 to print and mail. By 1979 with increased membership and cost of printing and postage, the cost to the division rose to $918.32. Even at that, the editor reported that much of the cost (including typing the masters, postage for foreign members, etc.) was not borne by the division. Universities today can no longer afford to be quite so generous. But the advantages of reduced costs due to university affiliation was, however, sometimes offset by reduced income from a disproportionately large number of dues-exempt older APA members.

Finally, in 1975, the executive committee proposed and the members adopted a division assessment of $2.00 per year. The assessment was to be temporary. But each year the division approved continuation of the assessment. It was later increased to $5.00 per year when additional expenses relating to the APA centennial celebration were anticipated. Additional income, however, was unexpectedly received by the generous allocation of royalties from an APA centennial publication.

The original attempt to avoid bureaucratic complexity did place constraints on program planning. Newsletter editors tried hard to keep costs down. Program chairs did not offer honoraria to attract colleagues with historiographic skills from other disciplines, a practice that might otherwise have stimulated member research. And membership chairs were sometimes limited in the extent to which they could conduct effective membership drives.

Following the economy of the times, division finances increased. The division began with an annual income of about $600 in the 1960s growing to $846 in 1975 and to $4692 in 1979. During the 1990s the annual income had increased to $6000. Expenses, however, rarely exceeded income.

DIVISION PROJECTS AND PROGRAMS

The service commitment of the division has been two pronged. One initiative arose from the recognition that members could, or indeed should, serve as a conscience to APA activities around matters historical. The preservation of association archival materials, ceremonial events like the sesquicentennial and centennial celebrations, participation by the APA in international activities—all these begged for attention from historians.

However, the division recognizes the need to lead in historical scholarship. Teaching history was often haphazard at best—frequently falling to those with broader general experimental backgrounds or those old enough to have a wider perspective on the discipline. Unlike most other divisions, the program and newsletter were major sources of intellectual stimulation— and outlets for creative energies.

The original bylaws called for a program committee of three appointed by the executive committee. The program at the annual convention, however, has typically been the responsibility of the program chair, with little direction from the executive committee. Eleven of the persons who served as program chairs had been or became presidents of the division. In 1975 a dispute arose over who appoints program chairs and invited addresses. Later bylaws specify that the president appoints, for 1 year. But the need for long-range planning meant more careful coordination and better continuity. And in 1974 the APA made a specific request that divisions provide for more explicit continuity in the appointment of program committees.

The hours allotted to programming at the annual convention have varied from 10 to more than 20. One meeting reached 43 hours, if one counts programs shared with other divisions and additional hours allocated for centennial celebrations. Program topics have been wide ranging. There were sessions on historiography and on research techniques in the history of psychology. There were sessions on the teaching of psychology. Biographical studies and the history of various theories and subdisciplines have always been popular. Papers on women in psychology, psychology and religion, and foreign developments in psychology have been frequent. Prominent speakers have included, for example, James Gibson and B. F. Skinner in 1975.

A number of program chairs complained that the number of good papers submitted was low. Several chairs reported that they accepted virtually every paper that was proposed, in order to fill up the program. Often authors of papers and other program participants were nonmembers of the division. A cursory check of several division programs revealed that program participants were frequently not members. One program had fewer than 30% of the papers authored by Division 26 members. And less than 50% of all participants were division members. Another check of a program 10 years earlier revealed similar data; only 42% of the papers were by division members.

There are several reasons for the paucity of papers from division members. Because the study of history concerns all of the divisions of the association, one would expect that a wide range of persons with primary commitments to other areas within psychology would be interested in preparing historical papers. Because most members of the division are specialized in fields other than history, and because many are older, their scholarly contributions may already have been made in other substantive fields and thus they are less likely to contribute to a history division.

There is also competition for papers from other scholarly organizations. The International Society for the History of the Behavioral and Social Sciences (Cheiron) attracts a large number of historical papers. This may have contributed significantly to a decrease in presentations at division meetings. One cursory check of a Cheiron program revealed that about a fourth of the paper participants were by members of Division 26. Of the total of 68 participants listed, almost a fifth were division members; 12% were fellows in Division 26.

Program activities have been stimulated by several major anniversaries for psychology that were of special interest to division members. The centennial of Wundt's laboratory founding, the 75th and, of course, the centennial celebrations of the APA, in which the division had particular interest, were sources of division pride.

During the 1979 centennial of the founding of Wundt's laboratory in Leipzig, the APA arranged for special programming. The division worked hard to help make the celebration a success. The Council of Representatives authorized a budget of $2000 and asked the division to arrange ten invited addresses. This proved impractical, and a total of seven lectures was arranged. Wertheimer, Sexton, and Popplestone (as chair) were the committee members. The invited addresses were given by Peter Behrens, Arthur Blumenthal, Wolfgang Bringmann, Carl Graumann, Marilyn Marshall, Michael M. Sokal, and Thom Verhave. In 1980, the concluding year of the celebration, ten additional program hours (beyond the two ordinarily allowed for lectures) were granted the division for ten special centennial lectures in Montreal. The lectures were by Ruben Ardila, John Burnham, Fairfid Caudle, Raine Daston, Donald O. Hebb, Mary Henle, Mildred Mitchell, Daniel Robinson, Michael Sokal, and Michael Wertheimer.

On the occasion of the APA's own centennial celebration, division members provided prominent leadership in the overall planning. The APA early established a task force to plan for the occasion. The chair and all but one of the eight task force members were members of Division 26. Various divisions planned programming relevant to their specialties. But for Division 26, it was a special challenge to contribute in a unique way. Each division formed a centennial committee. Division 26 was no exception and had eleven members serving on it, including a liaison between the committee and the APA task force.

It was perhaps no accident that members elected a prominent APA leader to serve as division president for the 1992 centennial year. Joseph Matarazzo, past president of the APA in 1990, was elected that year to serve as president-elect of Division 26, and thus as division president during the 1992 centennial celebration. A centennial calendar was prepared and was mailed with the fall 1989 newsletter; it contained the names, birth, and death dates of prominent psychologists.

The division has also sought to build bridges with other professional groups. Division liaisons have served with groups like the Committee on Women and various international associations. Such interchange has been fruitful for both groups. The division has periodically made financial contributions to other groups, including applied, academic, and social action groups.

Several workshops have drawn the attention of members: workshops on history, convention programs, historiography, regional meetings, the APA accreditation, and oral history projects. A History of Psychology Workshop was arranged in 1980 for the purpose of assisting members and interested others in honing skills in the writing of history.

Another workshop titled "Discovering Your Roots in Psychology" was planned in connection with the 1989 convention. The workshop was organized by Wolfgang Bringmann to assist those interested in writing a "personal" history of psychology for the 1991–1992 centennial celebration. Sample ideas were histories of universities, hospitals, societies, and individuals.

The division also was active in encouraging historical exhibits and providing an opportunity for an outreach to other APA groups. An ad hoc APA museum committee reported in 1971 on the purchase by the APA of two glass cases and an exhibit table. The division voted to provide some financial support to help in these exhibits. The History of Division 1 (General Psychology), which also actively supported these exhibits, provides more detail (Wertheimer & King, 1996). The new APA building had space for exhibits on its first floor. Rand Evans recommended in 1981 that the division help prepare or at least support historical exhibits in the main lobby. Such exhibits could ideally educate both the lay public and the psychologists visiting the building giving a better appreciation for the background of the science and the practice of psychology.

Preservation of the APA archival material was a continuing concern of the division and a focus for division action. Archival materials have always served as the main source of data for the historian. Psychologists, as scientists, recognize the importance of maintaining accurate records for later analysis and replication. But saving records relating to professional activities of psychologists has been haphazard at best; often they are not saved at all. Recognizing the need for a systematic procedure for maintaining records relating to the American Psychological Association in particular, and psychologists in general, led to an early interest in and controversy over the placement and care of archival materials. Preserving archival materials was of primary interest since the first meeting of the History of Psychology Group, because the APA had not always systematically and adequately preserved materials a historian would later find useful.

During the very first year of the division, two groups were in competition for the preservation of archival materials. A committee had been created by the APA to investigate the appropriate placement of the association's materials. During the same period of time, John Popplestone and Marion White McPherson at the University of Akron, Ohio, were negotiating with the university to establish an archive of American psychology. This effort culminated in the founding of the Archives of the History of American Psychology in November of 1965. Prominent psychologists, including many division leaders, agreed to serve on a board of advisors.

Some of the "old-timers" (Saul Rosenzweig and Edwin G. Boring) supported the idea of working with the Library of Congress. Younger psychologists, such as Robert I. Watson, wanted to encourage the efforts of the Akron group; a sure place was better than the prospects of an uncertain future location. A resolution to "endorse, encourage, support" the Akron archives was placed on the division's 1967 elections ballot and passed overwhelmingly.

More recent interest in archival preservation stemmed from the need to put one's own house in order. Popplestone reported to the division executive committee in 1975 that the ad hoc committee on APA archives no longer existed and that Jane Hildreth directed APA archival activity as the need arose. This led the division in 1988 to appoint a division archivist and to create bylaw changes formalizing the arrangement. The division also asked that the APA review its holdings at the Library of Congress. It had come to the division's attention that materials at the library had been haphazardly collected and were virtually unavailable, being stored in unsorted and uncataloged boxes.

The division worked with the APA to develop a plan whereby a committee of division members would advise the association on archival matters. Wilse Webb had the idea and Joseph Matarazzo and Neil Bartlett helped to implement it. The APA Council of Representatives in 1989 approved a procedure whereby the division nominates a committee with staggered terms of members, to assist the APA in working with the Library of Congress. At the 1990 meeting, Wilse Webb reported that the availability of the APA archival materials at the Library of Congress had improved.

The first History Oversight Committee was established in June 1993 and included Donald Dewsbury (chair) with Rand Evans, Elizabeth Scarborough and later Deborah Johnson as members. The committee charge is,

> To serve as an advisory committee concerning the status of historical matters relevant to the Association and to the psychological community at large, and will make an annual report with recommendations to the Board of Directors. (D. Dewsbury, personal communication)

CONCLUSION

How can the division remain viable? It is currently working on a new journal; it may need to resolve the conflict of dual loyalties with Cheiron; younger members need to be brought in, notwithstanding the current cultural shift away from classical academic pursuits. Interaction with other disciplines (history, philosophy, literature, applied fields) needs to be cultivated.

Since the founding of the division, a number of important developments have emerged in the field. Some doctoral programs in the history of psychology (the University of New Hampshire and Carlton and York

Universities in Canada) were inaugurated, as were Cheiron and *The Journal of the History of the Behavioral Sciences,* both founded during this period. History of psychology became a requirement in some accreditation programs. And an active review of the preservation of archival materials at the APA was initiated.

As psychology's short history becomes longer, as the twenty-first century approaches, and as electronic tools improve, the depth and breadth of scholarly work in the history of psychology will, it is to be hoped, not only continue but expand. Cattell's third-generation students spawned a fourth and then a fifth. Psychology's past remains constant; but its history continues to grow.

REFERENCES

Boring, E. G. (1950). A history of experimental psychology. New York: Appleton-Century-Crofts.

Cattell, J. McK. (1947). *James McKeen Cattell: Man of science* (Vol. II). Lancaster: The Science Press.

Hilgard, E. R. (1982). Robert I. Watson and the founding of Division 26 of the American Psychological Association. *Journal of the History of the Behavioral Sciences,* 18, 308–311.

Hilgard, E. R. (1987). *Psychology in America: A historical survey.* San Diego, CA: Harcourt Brace Jovanovich.

Hilgard, E. R., Leary, D. E., & McGuire, G. R. (1991). The history of psychology: A survey and critical assessment. *Annual Review of Psychology,* 42, 79–107.

Lindzey, G. (Ed.). (1980). A history of psychology in autobiography (Vol. 7). San Francisco: Freeman.

Pate, J. L. (1990, Spring). The why and how of organizational histories. *History of Psychology Newsletter* 22(½).

Scarborough, E., & Furumoto, L. (1987). *Untold lives: The first generation of American women psychologists.* New York: Columbia University Press.

Terrell, D. J. (1983, February). Three continents and light planets to go. *History of Psychology Newsletter,* 5, 37–38.

Thurgood, D. H., & Weinman, J. M. (1991). *Summary report 1990: Doctorate recipients from U.S. universities.* Washington, DC: National Academy Press.

Watson, R. I. (1972). "Working paper." In T. S. Krawiec (Ed.), *The psychologists* (Vol. 1, pp. 275–298). New York: Oxford University Press.

Wertheimer, M., & King, D. B. (1996). A history of Division 1 (General Psychology). In D. A. Dewsbury (Ed.), *Unification Through Division: Histories of the Divisions of the American Psychological Association* (Vol. I, pp. 9–40). Washington, DC: American Psychological Association.

6

A HISTORY OF DIVISION 28 (PSYCHOPHARMACOLOGY AND SUBSTANCE ABUSE)

HERBERT BARRY, III

The formation of Division 28 in 1966 established a group of APA members who were interested in research on drugs that alter behavior. Division 28 sponsors or cosponsors most of the psychopharmacology programs at the annual conventions and also influences APA policies. Advocacy by Division 28 has resulted in the APA journal *Experimental and Clinical Psychopharmacology* and educational programs that train psychologists to qualify for the privilege of prescribing psychotherapeutic drugs.

Division 28 also has strengthened behavioral research in the field of pharmacology. Members of Division 28 have contributed to psychopharmacology outside the APA, as members of pharmacological societies and as editors, reviewers, and authors of articles in psychology, pharmacology, and psychopharmacology journals.

APA members may belong to multiple divisions. An APA division therefore does not segregate its members into an exclusive group. Many

Helpful information and suggestions for improvements were kindly contributed by Robert L. Balster, Larry D. Byrd, Donald A. Dewsbury, Suzette M. Evans, Stephen C. Fowler, Victor G. Laties, M. Marlyne Kilbey, David M. Penetar, Antonio E. Puente, and Bernard Weiss.

153

members of Division 28 are active in Divisions 25 (Experimental Analysis of Behavior), 6 (Physiological and Comparative Psychology), 12 (Clinical Psychology), 50 (Addictions), and others.

GROWTH OF PSYCHOPHARMACOLOGY

The broad field of psychology includes studies of drug effects on behavior. The physiological functions of the human body are affected by endogenous pharmacological substances, such as epinephrine, acetylcholine, dopamine, and serotonin, and by intake of diverse drugs, including morphine, cocaine, phenobarbital, diazepam, caffeine, and alcohol. Physiological psychologists have generally used laboratory animals to study drug effects. Psychopharmacology research was a distinctive specialty for many APA members several years before Division 28 was founded.

Early Research

Division 6 (Physiological and Comparative Psychology) was one of the original 19 APA divisions, established in 1944. The APA journal in that field, *Journal of Comparative Psychology*, published occasional articles on drug effects several decades before Division 28 was founded. Notable early reports were on the effects of caffeine (Miller & Miles, 1935) and alcohol (Miller & Miles, 1936) on behavior of rats.

Psychopharmacology research was accelerated dramatically in the United States in 1954 by the U.S. Food and Drug Administration (FDA) approval of chlorpromazine hydrochloride (Thorazine) as an antipsychotic drug. This psychotherapeutic agent alleviated symptoms of many chronically hospitalized schizophrenics. The populations of mental hospitals decreased drastically within a few years. The success of treatment with chlorpromazine encouraged pharmaceutical companies to expand their search for better antipsychotic drugs and for other psychotherapeutic agents. In 1955 the FDA approved meprobamate (Miltown and Equanil) as a muscle relaxant and antianxiety medication. In 1960 the FDA approved a benzodiazepine, chlordiazepoxide (Librium), as a new type of antianxiety agent. In 1963 the FDA approved another benzodiazepine, diazepam (Valium).

These were the most prominent of the new psychotherapeutic drugs introduced before Division 28 was founded. Many large pharmaceutical companies hired psychologists to direct behavioral pharmacology laboratories, using mice, rats, primates, and other species of laboratory animals to develop and test new psychoactive drugs. Concurrently, the National Institute of Mental Health (NIMH) rapidly increased the funding of research grants for psychopharmacology research. A growing number of experimental psychologists at universities and research corporations obtained these grants.

The founding of Division 28 in 1966 expressed and also accelerated recognition of psychopharmacology as an important specialized field. The word "psychopharmacology" was used with increasing frequency by psychologists and pharmacologists. The first of many textbooks on psychopharmacology was published in 1968 (Thompson & Schuster).

Psychopharmacologists in the APA

The Division of the Experimental Analysis of Behavior (Division 25) was founded in 1964. Studies of drug effects constituted a minority of the programs of Division 25, but they were the principal topics of the research by several of the original members. The psychopharmacology researchers included Joseph V. Brady, Bernard Weiss, Victor G. Laties, John Boren, Carl L. Scheckel, Leonard Cook, George A. Heise, and Albert Weissman. Some of these members directed psychopharmacology research laboratories at pharmaceutical companies using behavioral tests of laboratory animals to develop and test new psychotherapeutic drugs.

Several APA members doing psychopharmacology research were affiliated with Division 6 (Physiological and Comparative Psychology). These APA members studying effects of drugs on behavior of laboratory animals included Murray E. Jarvik, Neal E. Miller, Conan Kornetsky, and Larry Stein.

Although Division 6 was one of the original group of APA divisions, founded in 1944, that division had no program at the annual conventions from 1948 to 1964. The psychopharmacology papers during that span of years were generally sponsored by Division 3 (Experimental Psychology). Psychopharmacology was a small portion of the programs of that large, diverse division.

The psychopharmacologists active in Divisions 25 and 6 shared important affiliations outside of the APA. The most closely related group was the Behavioral Pharmacology Society, which originated as a small discussion group at the annual spring meetings of the Eastern Psychological Association. Some of the psychopharmacologists in the APA were also members of the American Society for Pharmacology and Experimental Therapeutics (ASPET).

Two types of research on the psychological effects of drugs may be distinguished: preclinical and clinical psychopharmacology. The psychopharmacologists active in the APA were predominantly interested in preclinical psychopharmacology. They were experimenters and behaviorists who used laboratory animals as models for studying effects of drugs in humans.

Clinical psychopharmacology assesses the therapeutic effectiveness of drugs to counteract emotional distress, such as depression or anxiety. Clinical psychopharmacologists were predominantly psychiatrists rather than psychologists. Many clinicians in the APA disapproved of drugs as agents for psychotherapy.

FOUNDING OF DIVISION 28

The Division of Psychopharmacology began in 1966 with some unusual attributes. It represented a specialized aspect of psychology with strong links to other disciplines, notably pharmacology, neuroscience, physiology, and chemistry. Many of the original leaders of Division 28 were active members of Division 25, which began 2 years earlier. Several pharmaceutical corporations contributed financially as corporate sponsors.

Approval of the New Division

In 1965, Harley Hanson and Carl L. Scheckel initiated an effort to establish a new APA division. The provisional name was Division of Behavioral Pharmacology. The organizing committee collected 2080 petitions from members of the APA by May 1966. The unusually large number of petitions for the proposed division compensated for the lack of prior organizing meetings.

The leaders of the existing divisions did not object to the new division. It was approved by the APA Council of Representatives at its September 1966 meeting. Some members of the council believed there were too many divisions, but most of the members agreed with the organizing committee that none of the existing divisions adequately represented the topic of behavioral pharmacology.

The executive committee of Division 28, in a meeting on October 14, 1966, at Albert Einstein Medical College, chose the name Psychopharmacology instead of Behavioral Pharmacology. It was not a unanimous decision because some members objected to "Psycho" and preferred a closer correspondence to the name of Division 25 (Experimental Analysis of Behavior).

First Program

The 1967 APA convention in Washington, DC, was the first that contained a Division 28 program. The new division was allotted 11 hours. The scientific presentations consisted of three symposia and two paper sessions. There was a 1-hour business meeting but no presidential address. Table 29 lists the authors and titles of the talks in the three symposia. Several of the speakers were pharmacologists and not members of the APA.

The symposium on drugs as reinforcers was an early report on the subsequently prominent and successful effort to develop laboratory animal models for addictive drug self-administration by humans. Charles R. Schuster and several of his students and colleagues became leaders in this field. The symposium on brain acetylcholine reported on a neurotransmitter that has continued to be an important topic in psychopharmacology. The symposium on brain amines described neurotransmitters that have become increasingly important in subsequent psychopharmacology research. One of the speakers, Julius Axelrod, won the 1977 Nobel Prize in Physiology or Medicine for his research on catecholamines. The level of serotonin has subsequently been shown to have a very important role in human behavior.

TABLE 29
Symposia at the First Division 28 Program: 1967

Addiction and Drugs as Reinforcers Chair: Conan Kornetsky	
Presenter	Title of Symposia
J. R. Weeks	"Self-maintained morphine addiction and relapse in rats"
C. R. Schuster	"Pharmacological and psychological variables affecting self-administration"
J. R. Nichols	"Opiates as reinforcing agents, some variables which influence drug-seeking in animals" J. H. Jaffe: Discussant
Brain Acetylcholine and Behavior Chair: P. L. Carlton	
G. A. Heise	"Anticholinergics and behavior"
S. P. Grossman	"Behavioral responses to central cholinergic stimulation"
N. Weiner	"Relations between brain acetylcholine and memory"
R. W. Russell	"Cholinergic mechanisms in the extinction of acquired responses" R. A. Levitt, P. Glow, E. E. Coons: Discussants
Brain Amines and Behavior Chair: J. V. Brady	
J. Axelrod	"Fate of norepinephrine in the CNS and effect of psychoactive drugs"
L. Stein	"Norepinephrine and positive reinforcement"
C. L. Scheckel and E. Boff	"Catecholamines and avoidance behavior"
A. Weissman	"Behavioral effects of blocking serotonin biosynthesis" S. S. Kety, P. B. Dews: Discussants

The 1967 Division 28 program included two sessions for presentation of a total of 12 papers. They included a wide range of experimental techniques and drugs. Several were early reports of subsequently productive research topics. Carlson (1967) and Berger, Margules, and Stein (1967) reported on interference with learning caused by anticholinergic drugs. Moskowitz and DePry (1967) tested effects in humans rather than laboratory animals of an ancient instead of recent drug. Barry and Kubena (1967), who studied the recent topic of discriminative drug effects, reported on an initial application of the technique to the operant procedure of pressing a lever for food reinforcement.

Initial Officers

Table 30 identifies the nine officers in 1968, showing their corporate or university affiliations. Seven of them worked in one of three northeastern states, New York, New Jersey, or Pennsylvania. Only two, Peter Carlton and George A. Heise, were faculty members in a psychology department. Three, including the president, were faculty members in a medical school. The other four were employed by a pharmaceutical company. Carlton and Heise also had been employed by a pharmaceutical company in New Jersey until a few years before Division 28 was founded.

The first president of Division 28, Murray E. Jarvik, had credentials that differed from most of his psychopharmacology colleagues. He had earned an MD degree preceding his PhD. He was a member of both the psychiatry and psychology departments at Albert Einstein School of Medicine, Yeshiva University. A few years later he joined the psychiatry department at the University of California at Los Angeles.

TABLE 30
Initial Officers of Division 28 in 1966–1968

Office	Officer	Institutional or Psychopharmacological Affiliation
President	Murray E. Jarvik	Albert Einstein College of Medicine
President-Elect	Victor G. Laties	University of Rochester School of Medicine
Secretary	Carl L. Scheckel	Smith Kline and French
Treasurer	Peter L. Carlton	Rutgers University
Council Representative	Larry Stein	Wyeth Labs
	Harley Hanson	Merck Institute
Executive Committee	John Boren	Merck Institute
	George Heise	Indiana University
	Conan Kornetsky	Boston University School of Medicine

Two Scientific Orientations

Most of the initial members of Division 28 were experimental psychologists with a background of studying drug effects in laboratory animals. Their primary vocational interests were in scientific research rather than in therapy. Two different behaviorist traditions were represented, behavioral pharmacological control and psychopharmacological statistical inference. Sometimes the proponents of one tradition attacked the other, but more often they cooperated. Inclusion of both behaviorist traditions in Division 28 helped the members to integrate diverse psychopharmacological techniques.

The proponents of behavioral pharmacological control were interested in the experimental analysis of behavior. They included the majority of the initial officers of Division 28. Most of them had participated in the formation of Division 25 with B. F. Skinner as their leading exemplar. Joseph V. Brady, the first president of Division 25, was among the early Division 28 officers. Their scientific technique was to establish sufficient control over behavior so that drug effects could be demonstrated with a small number of animals. They chose objective terminology, such as *reinforcement* instead of *reward* and *percentage of free-feeding body weight* instead of *intensity of hunger drive*. Their conclusions were limited to the observed behavior without theoretical inferences about motivations or cognitions. These points of view were expressed in a methodological book (Sidman, 1960).

The proponents of behavioral pharmacological control generally tested a wide range of drug doses in a small number of animals. Drug effects were attractive experimental manipulations because psychoactive drugs are powerful agents for changing behavior. Many of these psychopharmacologists were employed by pharmaceutical companies and became active in pharmacology societies. Pharmacologists are well aware that different doses of a drug can induce complex differential effects.

The proponents of testing psychopharmacological theories were interested in psychobiology. They made theoretical inferences about behavioral and physiological responses under a complex combination of conditions. They advocated experimental variation of multiple conditions, including physiological variables. The typical experiment measured the effect of a single dose of a drug under different experimentally varied conditions. The effects of drugs were assessed on behavior and on biological functions with the help of tests of statistical significance. The experiments required a large number of animals because behavior was influenced by multiple conditions in addition to the drug treatment.

The proponents of testing psychopharmacological theories were dominant among APA researchers and in most PhD programs in psychology. Most of them were members of Division 6 (Physiological and Comparative

Psychology). Neal E. Miller was a leading advocate of the theoretical, inferential emphasis. Murray E. Jarvik and Larry Stein were the initial Division 28 officers who shared this tradition. They were outnumbered among the leaders of Division 28, but they induced many proponents of behavioral pharmacological control to use larger numbers of animals, to test statistical significance of the drug effects, and to measure physiological functions in addition to behavior.

SUCCESSION OF LEADERS

Division 28 gradually increased the scope of its activities and the number of officers. Two officers deserve special attention because of their unique roles: the program chair and the president.

Expansion of Psychopharmacological Functions

Table 31 lists the 26 members of the executive committee, 1996 to 1997. The past president, president, president-elect, and program chair are listed in Table 32.

The large number of functions in 1996 to 1997 indicates a great increase in the variety of activities by Division 28 after the first group of nine officers in 1968. The numerous officers in 1996–1997 do not signify a costly bureaucracy because they were not paid for their many hours of service.

Program Chairs

The Division 28 program at the annual convention is the most laborious and important function of the division. The program chair is appointed by the executive committee, usually the year before the important responsibility of organizing and selecting the program at the annual convention.

The 32 program chairs for the annual meetings from 1967 through 1998 are listed on the left-hand side of Table 32. They include ten people who subsequently served as president. One program chair, Larry D. Byrd, had previously served as president. Marian Fischman in 1977, the 11th program chair, was the first women to hold the position. Beginning with Fischman, 12 of the 22 most recent program chairs were women. The first woman president, Linda Dykstra in 1989, was more than 10 years later and was preceded by 19 consecutive male presidents. Beginning with Dykstra, four of the ten most recent presidents were women.

TABLE 31
Executive Committee of Division 28: 1996–1997

Elected Officers

President	M. Marlyne Kilbey
Past President	Stephen C. Fowler
President-Elect	Nancy A. Ator
Council Representative	Alice M. Young
Members-at-Large	Harriet de Wit
	Richard Meisch
	Carolyn M. Mazure

Appointed Officers

Program Chair	Charles France
Newsletter Editor	Craig Rush
ASPET/Neuroscience Liaison	Nancy A. Ator
APA Public Affairs Liaison	George E. Bigelow
Adult Development and Aging Liaison	Stephen Daniel
American Psychological Society Liaison	Donald A. Overton
Board of Scientific Affairs	Ronald W. Wood
Oral History Project	Herbert Barry, III
CPDD Liaison	Dorothy Hatsukami
Committee on Continuing Education	Maxine L. Stitzer
Committee on Awards	William L. Woolverton
Committee on Prescription Privileges	M. Marlyne Kilbey
Corporate Liaison	James E. Barrett
Drug Enforcement Agency Liaison	Christine A. Sannerud
Membership Chair	Ralph Spiga
New Fellows Chair	Marilyn Carroll
Neurobehavior Toxicology Committee	Deborah Cory-Slechta
Public Information	James P. Zacny
Secretary	David M. Penetar
Treasurer	Jane B. Acri
Women's Network Representative	Carolyn M. Mazure

Presidents

The president serves 3 years on the executive committee as president-elect, president, and past president. The year listed in the table for each president is the end of the term, when he or she presided over the Division 28 program and gave the presidential address at the annual convention.

The first president, Jarvik, took office at the end of the 1966 APA meeting and presided over the Division 28 activities in 1967 and also 1968. The subsequent presidents served for 1 year except two presidents, Carlton and Schuster. Their terms were 2 years in accordance with a change in the Division 28 bylaws in 1975. New bylaws in 1979 changed the term to 1 year, which is prevalent in the other APA divisions.

TABLE 32
Program Chairs and Presidents of Division 28

Year	Program Chair	President
1967	Carl Scheckel	Murray E. Jarvik
1968	George A. Heise	Murray E. Jarvik
1969	Larry Stein	Victor G. Laties
1970	Peter L. Carlton	John J. Boren
1971	Travis Thompson	Larry Stein
1972	Bernard Beer	Bernard Weiss
1973	Jerry Sepinwall	Leonard Cook
1974	Irving Geller	George A. Heise
1975	Russell Leaf	Travis Thompson
1976	Donald A. Overton	Peter L. Carlton
1977	Marian W. Fischman	Peter L. Carlton
1978	Chris E. Johanson	Charles R. Schuster
1979	George E. Bigelow	Charles R. Schuster
1980	Robert L. Balster	Joseph V. Brady
1981	Klaus A. Miczek	Herbert Barry, III
1982	Alice M. Young	John L. Falk
1983	James L. Howard	Larry D. Byrd
1984	Elkan Gamzu	James H. Woods
1985	Sharon Hall	John A. Harvey
1986	M. Marlyne Kilbey	Conan Kornetsky
1987	Hugh Evans	Donald A. Overton
1988	Larry D. Byrd	George E. Bigelow
1989	Barbara L. Slifer	Linda A. Dykstra
1990	Warren Bickel	Robert L. Balster
1991	David Penetar	Klaus A. Miczek
1992	Nancy A. Ator	Ronald W. Wood
1993	Harriet de Wit	Maxine Stitzer
1994	Marilyn E. Carroll	Lewis S. Seiden
1995	Suzette M. Evans	John Grabowski
1996	Kimberly Kirby	Stephen C. Fowler
1997	Charles P. France	M. Marlyne Kilbey
1998	Nancy Piotrowski	Nancy A. Ator

All except two of the presidents were primarily active in preclinical rather than clinical psychopharmacology research, testing effects of drugs on the behavior of laboratory animals rather than humans. The two exceptions, George E. Bigelow and Maxine L. Stitzer, began their careers in research on laboratory animals. Three of the early presidents, Boren, Stein, and Cook, were employees of pharmaceutical companies. The other presidents were faculty members of universities, some in the psychology department, others in the school of medicine, one in the school of pharmacy.

In accordance with APA policy, the members of Division 28 had a choice between at least two nominees for president-elect. The ballot contained three nominees in 1990 and two in the other years. Beginning in 1980, the winner of the election was usually the defeated nominee the year before. This is probably an unusual practice. The strong network of professional and personal affiliation among the active members has contributed to a choice between two acceptable nominees each year, maximizing the occurrence of eventual election of both nominees.

DIVISION 28 PROGRAMS AT THE APA CONVENTIONS

The Division 28 program gradually expanded in the APA conventions after 1967. The allotted number of hours more than doubled. Many sessions were sponsored jointly by Division 28 and one or more other divisions. The cosponsors include clinical divisions, such as 12 and 50, in addition to Divisions 25 and 6.

Invited Addresses

The programs have featured several types of invited addresses. Some of the speakers were leading members of Division 28. Others were pharmacologists or psychiatrists who were not APA members. An early example was an invited address in 1968 by Leonard Cook, a pharmacologist employed by a pharmaceutical company. He was subsequently president of the division, in 1973.

The programs have included memorials for important psychopharmacologists who have died. In 1973 George A. Heise gave the first of several Carl L. Scheckel Memorial Lectures in honor of the first secretary of Division 28, Carl L. Scheckel. In 1977 Larry Stein gave a James Olds Memorial Lecture.

In subsequent years, new fellows of Division 28 gave invited addresses. Awards for members were also the occasions for invited addresses. In 1981 Norman A. Krasnegor received a Distinguished Service Award. The title of his address, "Perspectives of Behavioral Pharmacology and Substance Abuse," was a precursor of the change in the name of Division 28. Annual invited addresses were given by the winners of the Young Psychopharmacologist Award. Irwin Lucki was the first to receive the award in 1984. Annual invited addresses were also given by the recipients of the Solvay Duphar Award for outstanding research on affective disorders by senior investigators. James E. Barrett was the first to receive the award in 1992.

Poster Sessions

The introduction of poster sessions in 1979 greatly increased the number of reports that could be presented. Several dozen posters are feasible in a large room in a single session. This type of presentation has become increasingly popular at the APA conventions and other large scientific meetings.

One 50-minute poster session in 1979 was followed by two sessions in 1980. An appropriate schedule for posters is a longer time span in a space that accommodates a larger number of posters. Accordingly, there was a poster session of three hours in 1987 and of four hours in 1988.

Hospitality Suite

In addition to the sessions listed in the program of the APA meeting, a Division 28 hospitality suite is a regular focus for social contacts at the annual meetings. In the first few years, it was also sponsored by Division 25. Subsequently, it was in a separate hotel suite, but there was much intermingling between the two groups. Free snacks and drinks were available. In some years, an informal program of papers was scheduled there.

PROMINENT TOPICS IN DIVISION 28 PROGRAMS

Psychopharmacology has a broad scope. Topics include therapeutic agents for diverse psychopathological conditions, neurotransmitters in the brain, toxic chemicals in the food and environment, and drugs that are taken for pleasurable effects. Diverse behavioral techniques have been applied to several species of laboratory animals and to humans. The scope of psychopharmacology becomes progressively enlarged because of the introduction of new drugs and the development of new research techniques.

Therapeutic Agents

Introduction of chlorpromazine and other drugs to treat psychopathological conditions led to a rapid expansion of psychopharmacological activity, which included the founding of Division 28. Most of the research reported at the meetings was preclinical, using laboratory animals as models for the drug effects, rather than clinical.

In the first Division 28 program in 1967, a paper by Latz, Bain, and Kornetsky reported on chlorpromazine. Effects of the same drug and other antipsychotic agents were reported in subsequent meetings. Larger numbers of papers in subsequent programs were on drugs to relieve anxiety or depression. In the 1967 program, a paper by Berger, Margules, and Stein included oxazepam, a benzodiazepine that counteracts anxiety.

Drug therapy for other psychopathological conditions includes a stimulant, methylphenidate (Ritalin), which paradoxically counteracts hyperactivity in children. The 1978 meeting included a symposium, "Direct Measurements of the Hyperactive Child's Response to Stimulant Drugs."

Brain Neurotransmitters

Therapeutic effects of drugs may be attributed to effects on neurotransmitters in the brain. Table 29 includes two symposia on that topic, brain acetylcholine and behavior and brain amines and behavior. A symposium in 1968 was on chemical brain stimulation, hunger, and thirst. Much early interest in effects of the psychedelic drug LSD focused on the effect of the drug on serotonin (5-hydroxytryptamine) in the brain.

Pharmacological and physiological research has revealed a large number of neurotransmitters. A prominent example is the discovery of endogenous enkephalins, which reproduce the analgesic effects of morphine and other opiates. The discovery of opiate receptor subtypes has stimulated reports on various types of opiate receptors and antagonists. These and other types of neurotransmitters have been the topic of many research reports in Division 28 programs.

Behavioral Toxicology

In addition to drugs that are therapeutic at small doses, some chemical agents are toxic at small doses. Behavioral tests are sensitive measures of damaging effects of many pharmacological substances in the environment and in food, such as lead and methyl mercury.

The first conference on behavioral toxicology in the United States was in 1972 (Weiss & Laties, 1975). The organizers, Bernard Weiss and Victor G. Laties, were early presidents of Division 28. The 1977 Division 28 program included a symposium titled "Lead-Induced CNS Changes and Patterning of Behavior." In 1980 Division 28 established the Neurobehavioral Toxicity Test Standards Committee, chaired by Ronald W. Wood.

Drug Self-Administration

Table 29 shows that the first Division 28 program included a symposium titled "Addiction and Drugs as Reinforcers." The 1975 program included a symposium titled "Self-Administration of Drugs." Preclinical research on drug self-administration by laboratory animals has emphasized intravenous self-administration by rats or primates. The rapid onset of the drug effect by the intravenous route appears to maximize the reinforcing effect.

Several types of drugs have reinforcing effects. Many studies of drug self-administration have used cocaine, which appears to be an especially strong reinforcer for laboratory animals and for human victims of its dangerous effects. A symposium in 1988 was titled "Progress in Understanding the Behavioral and Neurobiological Effects of Cocaine."

Nicotine has attracted special interest because of the strong reinforcing effect and health hazard of cigarettes in humans. Murray E. Jarvik, first president of Division 28, was a leader in the early psychopharmacological studies of nicotine self-administration by laboratory animals.

Division 28 programs have included sessions on smoking and the effort to quit smoking by humans. A symposium in 1978 was titled "Research on Smoking Behavior: Deprivation Effects and the Successful Quitter." The 1982 meeting contained a symposium titled "Nicotine as a Reinforcer in Humans and Experimental Animals" and a paper session titled "Experimental Studies of Cigarette Smoking." The 1986 meeting contained a symposium titled "Nicotine Replacement Treatments in Smoking Cessation" and "Gender Differences in Smoking Cessation."

Other self-administered drugs that have attracted much interest include marijuana and alcohol. The second Scheckel Memorial Lecture, presented in 1974, was titled "The Behavioral Pharmacology of Marijuana" by Herbert Barry, III. This drug has not shown dependable reinforcing effects in laboratory animals. A symposium in the 1977 meeting was titled "Animal Models of Alcohol Intake." Clinical applications were emphasized in a symposium in the 1982 meeting, "Alcohol Problems: How to Treat and Prevent Them."

Drugs as Discriminative Stimuli

The study of discriminative stimulus attributes of drugs originated from psychobiology and behavioral neuroscience. A drug effect is transformed from an unconditional stimulus to a conditional stimulus that guides a choice response. The first publications on this technique were by Donald A. Overton (1964, 1966). He regarded the drug effect as a distinctive state that can support state-dependent learning.

A more limited theoretical assumption is that in addition to different sensory experiences, differential drug conditions can be discriminative stimuli. Animals are trained to make differential responses, depending on whether they have been injected with a drug or the placebo.

The first program of Division 28 included a paper by Barry and Kubena (1967) on this technique. The discriminative response differentiates well among the established categories of psychoactive drugs. Many pharmaceutical companies and pharmacologists use this technique for the purpose of identifying similarities and differences among drugs. The technique has also been applied to humans, indicated in a symposium in the 1990 Division 28 program, "The Current Status of Human Drug Discrimination Research."

Classically Conditioned Drug Effects

Classical conditioning is an important mechanism for learning and therefore an important topic for studying behavior. A rapid technique for learning an avoidance response is to associate the consumption of a sweet fluid with an aversive pharmacological effect that causes nausea, such as lithium. A symposium in the 1975 Division 28 program was titled "Psychopharmacology and Learned Taste Aversions."

A more specifically psychopharmacological application of classical conditioning is a conditional compensatory response to a behaviorally toxic drug effect. This is one of the mechanisms for tolerance to a drug. An article by Siegel (1975) reported this response to morphine in rats. A symposium in the 1977 Division 28 program was titled "Conditioned Tolerance and Opponent Process." This effect was described in a subsequent review article by Solomon (1980).

PUBLICATIONS AND COMMUNICATIONS

The majority of the members of Division 28 do not regularly attend the APA conventions. The Division 28 newsletter provides a service for all the members. Division 28 also communicates with members and others by other methods. A rapid, inexpensive method is the Division 28 discussion group on the Internet.

Newsletter

One of the early activities of Division 28 was the production of a newsletter. The first editor, Harley Hanson, produced four issues in 1967. The name was "The Needle," and the first page featured a large drawing of a syringe and needle. The issue preceding the annual meeting summarized the Division 28 program in 1967 and 1968. Russell C. Leaf produced one issue of the Division 28 newsletter in 1969 or 1970. The newsletter lapsed for several years and resumed in 1973, with Travis Thompson as editor. One issue each year contained a summary of the program at the annual meeting. Several new features were continued by his successors. Invited articles described research by members at various universities. Other occasional items of information included news of psychopharmacology funding and references to recent books on psychopharmacology. Beginning in 1981, the president of Division 28 usually contributed an article.

Larry Byrd became the editor in 1976 and continued until he became president-elect in 1981. Subsequent editors were Nancy Leith, 1981 to 1982 and 1986 to 1987, Don R. Cherek, 1983 to 1985, Cynthia S. Pomerleau, 1988 to 1993, James P. Zacny, 1994 to 1996, and Craig R. Rush, beginning in 1997.

Psychopharmacology Publications

Leaders of Division 28 organized psychopharmacology symposia at annual meetings of ASPET, a pharmacological society. The papers presented at these meetings were published in book form.

Two psychopharmacology symposia organized by Division 28 members were included in the 1974 ASPET meeting. The papers were published in the form of a special issue of *Federation Proceedings,* the journal of the Federation of American Societies in Experimental Biology (FASEB; Weiss, 1975) and a book (Weiss & Laties 1976). Ten years later, in 1984, Seiden and Balster organized psychopharmacology sessions at an ASPET meeting. The papers were published in the form of a book (Seiden & Balster, 1985).

The APA established the *Journal of Experimental and Clinical Psychopharmacology* in 1993. This journal publishes articles on preclinical and clinical psychopharmacology. The first editor, Charles R. Schuster, is a former president of Division 28. Schuster previously was the first nonphysician to be director of the National Institute on Drug Abuse.

Electronic Mail

Ronald W. Wood, while he was president of Division 28 in 1992, initiated electronic communication via the Internet. He established the Division 28 discussion list, which grew within a few years to more than 400 members.

An important participant in the discussion list is the APA Science Directorate. The discussion list, in addition to providing an inexpensive outlet for members to communicate, also gives news of federal government actions, such as budget proposals and appropriations for the National Institutes of Health and National Science Foundation.

Oral History of Psychopharmacology

An oral history project, begun in 1991, was part of the preparation for the APA centennial in 1992. The project, directed by Herbert Barry, III, has continued after that celebration and after preparation of the present printed history of Division 28.

Interviews have been conducted with several early leaders of Division 28. The transcripts will be deposited in the Archives of the History of

Psychology at Akron, Ohio. In addition, there is a plan to publish selected portions of the transcripts.

EXECUTIVE COMMITTEE

Most of the activities of a division are initiated and coordinated by its executive committee. The policies and actions are governed by the bylaws. Functions of special importance are the finances, controlled by the treasurer, and membership, controlled by the membership chair. Other officers with special responsibilities are the secretary and the Division 28 member of the APA Council of Representatives.

Bylaws

A small group of people conducted the business for Division 28 in its first few years. Table 30 lists the nine officers in 1967. The organization of the division was in accordance with standard APA policies for divisions.

In accordance with the prevalent APA custom, the presidents served for a single year after the 2 years for the first president, Murray E. Jarvik. There was a 3-year term for presidents of Division 25. New bylaws in 1975 specified a 2-year term for presidents Carlton and Schuster.

The new bylaws also increased the 1-year terms of other officers. The new terms were 3 years for the secretary and 2 years for the treasurer and APA council representative. The executive committee was obliged to appoint a membership chair and newsletter editor. A student member status was also created.

Another revision of the bylaws, in 1979, changed the term of the president to 1 year. The secretary's term continued to be 3 years, but it became an appointed instead of an elected position. Voting membership of the executive committee was limited to those elected by the Division 28 members in the annual ballot. They are the past president, president, president-elect, council representative, and the three members at large of the executive committee.

Appointed members, who perform designated tasks, have no vote. In practice, most of the decisions are made by consensus in the meetings of the expanded executive committee without a formal vote limited to the subgroup of members eligible to vote. A change in the name of Division 28 in 1991 expressed a desire to broaden the scope beyond the initial emphasis on the scientific study of drug effects in laboratory animals. The name was expanded by adding ". . . and Substance Abuse" so that it became the Division of Psychopharmacology and Substance Abuse. The name was changed because a substantial number of Division 28 members were doing research on abusive intake of drugs, including alcohol and tobacco.

Division 28 retained a scientific focus, but the name change increased the topical overlap with Division 12 (Clinical Psychology) and with Division 50 (Addiction). Future rivalry with these other divisions is likely if Division 28 continues to become more interested in the clinical and social issues of drug abuse.

Finances

At the time Division 28 was founded, the financial resources of most divisions depended on the number of members. The annual APA dues included a fee for each division membership after the first. The APA in return transferred to each division a subsidy determined by the number of members.

Division 28 at the outset had an additional source of income in the form of corporate affiliates. President Jarvik stated at the initial business meeting in 1967, "Division 28 was born with a silver spoon in its mouth." This referred to several corporate affiliates, which contributed annual dues of $100 or more.

This technique for affiliation and financial support by pharmaceutical companies was imitated from the pharmacology society, ASPET. Some Division 28 members objected to the corporate subsidy, but the benefactors did not restrict the uses of the funds. The initial list of eight corporate affiliates in 1968 expanded in subsequent years. There were 17 in 1988. In more recent years, Division 28 has been supported by a smaller number of companies, generally in the form of sponsorship of specific programs. The contributions financed the hospitality suite at the annual meetings and enabled a program of invited speakers and awards.

For 10 years, beginning in 1984, Burroughs Wellcome Pharmaceutical Company gave a larger annual amount for the expenses of the Young Psychopharmacologist Award. This was for the best research achievements within 5 years after the PhD. The same award was continued by Division 28 after termination of the support by the company. A subsequent annual grant was initiated by the Solvay Duphar Pharmaceutical Company in 1992.

An endowment by members of Division 28, Robert A. and Phyllis Levitt, established the Levitt Award for the best psychopharmacology dissertation research. The first recipient was Carol A. Paronis in 1995.

For many years, Division 28 was one of very few APA divisions that did not charge an assessment to its members. This may have contributed to its relatively large membership. A modest assessment was begun in 1988.

A subsequent source of substantial income for Division 28 was from continuing education courses on psychopharmacology for psychologists who attended the APA convention. Their clinical practice or research caused them to seek current knowledge about psychoactive drugs. A potential function of the courses was to prepare psychologists for the prospective prescription privileges that are advocated by the APA.

Members and Fellows

In 1967 there were 328 members of Division 28. Within a few years afterward, letters were sent to members of selected other divisions, inviting them to join Division 28. The recipients included members of Divisions 6 (Physiological and Comparative Psychology) and 25 (Experimental Analysis and Behavior) but also of clinically oriented divisions, such as 12 (Clinical Psychology). This initiative induced a large increase in membership to 1600 in 1971. The membership subsequently decreased gradually to slightly fewer than 1000 in 1996. The majority of the members of Division 28 have a primary interest in another division but substantial interest in psychopharmacology.

The initial membership chair was Conan Kornetsky in 1967. Bernard Beer was membership chair in 1974. The next membership chair, Norman Krasnegor, sent invitational postcards in 1976 to about 7000 APA members, including all new associates and members in addition to members of Divisions 6, 12, and 25. This resulted in more than 250 new members in 1977.

Donald A. Overton became membership chair in 1978. He introduced a technique that contributes to the evaluation of candidates for fellow. He used lists in *Current Contents: Life Sciences* to count the number of publications of the nominees and also the number of publications that cited their publications. This provided an objective measure of the prospective fellow's scientific productivity and impact.

Overton continued as membership chair until he became president-elect in 1986. Subsequent membership chairs, who continued his technique for evaluating candidates for fellow, included Jim Smith, Stephen C. Fowler, and Warren K. Bickel. Beginning in 1995, Marilyn Carroll continued this important function in the position of new fellows chair. The concurrent membership chairs were Jed E. Rose and Ralph Spiga.

Another category of members consists of distinguished affiliates. The first three, elected in 1978, were Peter B. Dews, Pierre Renault, and Hannah Steinberg. Subsequent distinguished affiliates, in 1995, were Louis Harris and Barends Olivier.

There is also a category of student affiliates. It has been a rather inactive category, although many PhD candidates have participated in the programs at the annual meetings.

Additional Functions

One of the most active founders of Division 28 was the first secretary, Carl L. Scheckel, who was employed by a pharmaceutical company, Smith Kline & French. He died prematurely but contributed greatly to the early activities of the division. Subsequent secretaries were Roy Pickens, Jerry Sepinwall, Herbert Barry, III, James W. McKearney, Stephen T. Higgins, and David M. Penetar.

The annual ballot for the members of Division 28 includes at least two nominees for election of one member at large of the executive committee, who serves for 3 years. Three members at large therefore serve concurrently.

The 1979 revision of the bylaws specified that the voting members of the executive committee are those elected in the annual mail ballot of the Division 28 members. These included the three members at large and only four others: the president elect, president, past president, and APA council representative. The members at large therefore have substantial voting power. They usually represent diverse points of view and seldom unite against other officers on the infrequent controversial issues.

Division 28 initially had four members on the Council of Representatives. Shortly afterward, the APA allocated the number of council representatives by an annual apportionment ballot. Division 28 has continuously qualified for one representative, although sometimes by a very small margin. Its apportionment vote has generally been less than 1% of the total but more than the 0.50% minimum.

Murray E. Jarvik was an initial member of the Council of Representatives in addition to being president of Division 28. The two initial elected representatives are identified in Table 30. They were followed by Victor G. Laties, Nancy K. Mello, Herbert Barry, III, Charles R. Schuster, Norman Krasnegor, George E. Bigelow, James L. Howard, John Grabowski, M. Marlyne Kilbey, Stephen C. Fowler, and Alice M. Young.

INTERACTIONS WITH OTHER ORGANIZATIONS

Some of the APA programs and policies have been initiated by members of Division 28 on behalf of their special needs for psychopharmacology. Division 28 also has interests in common with other APA divisions, resulting in cooperation or competition. The field of psychopharmacology is related to pharmacology, and Division 28 accordingly has liaisons with some pharmacology organizations. In accordance with the other scientifically oriented divisions of the APA, the American Psychological Society (APS) has some common interests, which give rise to both cooperation and competition.

INFLUENCES OF DIVISION 28 ON APA POLICIES

In 1982, while John L. Falk was president of Division 28, the APA issued an *amicus curiae* brief. This brief advocated minimal use of drugs in the treatment of mental illness, arguing that drugs were ineffective. Division 28 had not been consulted. President Falk led a protest, which induced the APA to retract the general statement.

In a subsequent reversal of policy, the APA supported the addition of prescription privilege to the practice of psychology. Division 28 had long advocated the improvement of psychopharmacology training of psychologists and had provided expertise to the APA on curriculum development.

Division 28 members were key members of the APA psychopharmacology task force, which developed the concept of three levels of training. Division 28 strongly supported the principle that all psychologists doing service delivery need some training in psychopharmacology. Division 28 has a strong interest in ensuring that psychologists who move into increased decision-making roles regarding medications should have sufficient high-quality training to do this safely and effectively.

OTHER APA DIVISIONS

When Division 28 was founded, many of its members were also members of Divisions 25 (Experimental Analysis of Behavior), 6 (Physiological and Comparative Psychology), 3 (Experimental Psychology), or 12 (Clinical Psychology). The preclinical psychopharmacology orientation of Division 28 differentiated its programs at the annual APA conventions from the clinical psychopharmacology programs of Division 12. In subsequent years an increasing number of Division 28 sessions were on toxic effects of drugs in humans and on therapy for problems due to drug consumption. Division 12 cosponsored many of these sessions.

In 1977, Division 28 opposed a proposal for a new APA division representing psychologists interested in substance abuse. The Society of Psychologists Interested in Substance Abuse had several sessions in the same city at the same time as the APA convention in 1979. Similar interests were subsequently represented by Division 50 (Addiction), founded in 1995. Its interests overlap with those of Division 28 and also of Division 12 and other clinically oriented divisions.

The founders of Division 50 had a primary interest in service delivery. Division 28 was more focused on research on drug abuse. Division 28 supported the establishment of Division 50 and subsequently worked cooperatively with Division 50 on several issues. Divisions 28 and 50 cosponsored many sessions at APA conventions. Members of both divisions worked together with other components of the APA to craft the specialty examination to be used by the National College of Professional Psychologists to certify addiction psychologists.

Rivalry between Division 28 and Division 50 is a potential outcome of their overlapping interests. A more probable development is that Division 28 might recreate its original role as a scientifically oriented division of preclinical psychopharmacology, studying drug effects on laboratory animals.

Pharmacology Societies

Other societies representing psychopharmacologists include the Behavioral Pharmacology Society, Behavioral Toxicology Society, International Study Group Investigating Drugs as Reinforcers, and the Society for Stimulus Properties of Drugs. Larger organizations containing psychopharmacologists include the Society for Neuroscience, ASPET, American College of Neuropsychopharmacology, Committee on Problems of Drug Dependence (CPDD), and Research Society on Alcoholism. Many members of Division 28 are also active in one or more of these related societies.

A few years after Division 28 was founded, it established liaisons with organizations in pharmacology. In 1974, Bernard Weiss was the liaison with ASPET. In subsequent years, several leaders of Division 28 became leaders of the CPDD. The Division 28 executive committee includes a member who provides liaison with the CPDD. An additional liaison with the CPDD is by an APA staff member.

Many members of Division 28 are also members of the Behavioral Pharmacology Society, a small organization founded in 1953. It has a 2-day meeting in May, usually in the northeastern United States. The executive committee of Division 28 meets twice each year. One meeting is usually at the Behavioral Pharmacology Society in the spring. This interim meeting is a useful addition to the executive committee meeting at the beginning of the APA convention in August. Both annual meetings of the executive committee are usually very lengthy, especially the one at the APA convention.

American Psychological Society

In 1988, some of the scientifically and academically oriented APA members founded the APS because they were dissatisfied with the perceived clinical emphasis of the APA. Many of the members of the APS terminated their membership in the APA.

Although Division 28 is scientifically oriented, it has not been greatly affected by the APS. Division 28 established a liaison with the APS, but very few members of Division 28 dropped APA membership because of joining the APS. The annual meeting of the APS has attracted few members of Division 28.

Psychopharmacology is an interdisciplinary specialty, with a network of scientists both in and outside the APA. Most members of Division 28 are affiliated with other societies outside the APA, such as in pharmacology and neuroscience, rather than with the APS. The lack of special interest divisions in the APS deters most psychopharmacologists from participating in the annual meetings of the APS. In addition, the annual meeting of the APS in June conflicts with other meetings, such as CPDD and Research Society on Alcoholism, attended by some Division 28 members.

CONCLUSION

Psychopharmacology is a distinctive special interest topic in the APA. Drugs alter behavior, and the behavior of many people includes consumption of drugs for therapy or for pleasure. Abusive intake of drugs is an important component of psychopathology. The increasing problems of pathological drug intake and increasing interest in therapeutic interventions have resulted in a change in the name of Division 28 from Psychopharmacology to Psychopharmacology and Substance Abuse.

The prospect of psychologists becoming licensed to prescribe psychotherapeutic drugs will probably stimulate greater clinical interest and activity in Division 28. Leaders of Division 28 are already conducting courses to help make psychologists qualified to prescribe psychotherapeutic drugs.

The formation of the APS has increased the importance of Division 28 as a component of the APA. Division 28 is a scientifically oriented special interest that is weakly represented in APS. The desire of the APA to retain and encourage its scientifically oriented members has been indicated by the Science Directorate, the activities of which include advocacy for increased federal support of psychopharmacological and other scientific research, and the founding of the *Journal of Experimental and Clinical Psychopharmacology*. Division 28 is in a position to strengthen the position of the APA as the largest and most inclusive psychological organization, integrating clinical with scientific components. The scientifically oriented members of Division 28 can benefit from cooperation with clinically oriented divisions, such as 12 and 50.

REFERENCES

Barry, H., III, & Kubena, R. K. (1967, August). *An operant technique for training discrimination between drug and nondrug state*. Paper presented at the annual meeting of the American Psychological Association, Washington, DC.

Berger, B. D., Margules, D. L., & Stein, L. (1967, August). *Prevention of learning of a fear response by oxazepam and scopolamine*. Paper presented at the annual meeting of the American Psychological Association, Washington, DC.

Carlson, N. J. (1967, August). *Effects of scopolamine on learning, reversal, and re-reversal in the T-maze*. Paper presented at the annual meeting of the American Psychological Association, Washington, DC.

Latz, A., Bain, G. T., & Kornetsky, C. (1967, August). *Attenuated effect of chlorpromazine on conditioned avoidance as a function of rapid acquisition*. Paper presented at the annual meeting of the American Psychological Association, Washington, DC.

Miller, N. E., & Miles, W. R. (1935). Effect of caffeine on the running speed of hungry, satiated, and frustrated rats. *Journal of Comparative Psychology, 20,* 397–412.

Miller, N. E., & Miles, W. R. (1936). Alcohol and removal of reward. An analytical study of rodent maze behavior. *Journal of Comparative Psychology, 21,* 179–221.

Moskowitz, H., & DePry, D. (1967, August). *Effect of alcohol upon two types of attention*. Paper presented at the annual meeting of the American Psychological Association, Washington, DC.

Overton, D. A. (1964). State-dependent or "dissociated" learning produced with pentobarbital. *Journal of Comparative and Physiological Psychology, 57,* 3–12.

Overton, D. A. (1966). State-dependent learning produced by depressant and atropine-like drugs. *Psychopharmacologia (Berl.), 10,* 6–31.

Seiden, L. S., & Balster, R. L. (Eds.). (1985). *Behavioral pharmacology: The current status*. New York: Liss.

Sidman, M. (1960). Tactics of Scientific Research: Evaluating Experimental Data in Psychology. New York: Basic Books.

Siegel, S. (1975). Evidence from rats that morphine tolerance is a learned response. *Journal of Comparative and Physiological Psychology, 89,* 209–220.

Solomon, R. L. (1980). The opponent-process theory of acquired motivation: The costs of pleasure and the benefits of pain. *American Psychologist 8,* 691–712.

Thompson, T., & Schuster, C. R. (1968). *Behavioral pharmacology*. Englewood Cliffs, NJ: Prentice-Hall.

Weiss, B., & Laties, V. G. (Eds.). (1975a). *Behavioral toxicology*. New York: Plenum Press.

Weiss, B., & Laties, V. G. (Eds.). (1975b, August). Current status of behavioral pharmacology. *Federation Proceedings, 34,* 1754–1903.

Weiss, B., & Laties, V. G. (Eds.). (1976). *Behavioral pharmacology: The current status*. New York: Plenum Press.

7

A HISTORY OF DIVISION 29 (PSYCHOTHERAPY): THE MANY FACES OF PSYCHOTHERAPY

MATHILDA B. CANTER

The history—the story of Division 29—began about 35 years ago. Although this is not a very long time by historical standards, it is, unfortunately, a long enough time in which to lose records, reports, and people—the stuff of which such histories are made. So I have become a detective, trying to piece together from available data the material that belongs in this chapter. Let me assure you, however, that what I don't have evidence for, I do not include. This may be taken as a somewhat less than complete, perhaps, but—it is hoped—never less than accurate account of the Division of Psychotherapy of the American Psychological Association (APA).

BEGINNINGS

The development of psychotherapy as a practice area for psychologists was largely a post-World War II phenomenon. This aspect of clinical

This chapter is an abbreviated, reorganized, and updated version of A History of the Division of Psychotherapy American Psychological Association, commissioned by the division on the occasion of the APA centennial, written by this author and printed by the Division in 1992. I would like to thank Jack G. Wiggins, who read this manuscript and made helpful comments.

psychology became a strong interest for a growing number of psychologists whose needs for affiliation were more and more strongly felt.

Psychologists Interested in the Advancement of Psychotherapy

The first issue of the *PIAP Bulletin* (July 1961) was a real find and provided the kinds of background information I was seeking: It was during the 1960 APA convention that a group of psychologists sharing interests in psychotherapy banded together to form Psychologists Interested in the Advancement of Psychotherapy (PIAP), an organization dedicated to the advancement of the teaching and practice of psychotherapy, the training of psychotherapists, and the conduct of research in psychotherapy. This action was based on their perception that the APA and its divisions were not representing them adequately in terms of the particular scientific and professional interests they felt needed to be addressed.

An active and ambitious group, chaired by Arthur H. Davison, PIAP presented workshops and institutes in major areas of the United States, led by professionals who had made recognized contributions in the field of psychotherapy. They presented programs at APA conventions. And they started plans for publishing a journal. Plans to organize a new division of the APA were discussed, with considerable heat generated, apparently, but the final decision was to defer action and see how responsive the APA and particularly Division 12 (Clinical Psychology) would be to their needs.

PIAP: A Section of Division 12

In February of 1963, the Division of Clinical Psychology unanimously approved PIAP as a section of their division. This seemed a natural and appropriate affiliation, and according to a PIAP report dated April 1963 and found in the APA's membership files, for the first time psychotherapy as a field was explicitly represented in the APA. PIAP developed its own bylaws, elected its own officers and executive board, assessed membership dues, and published a bulletin for its membership. A search of the Library of Congress yielded two more issues of that bulletin.

In the *PIAP Bulletin* (June 1963) the treasurer reported sending out bills to more than 600 members (dues were $5 per year then) and quickly the membership grew to about 1000. A membership directory was being developed, as was a comprehensive directory of all institutions or agencies offering programs at the level of postgraduate training in psychotherapy.

Very active programming was one of the major goals of the section, with workshops and symposia planned for presentation during the APA convention and at regional and other meetings throughout the year to provide quality postgraduate training in psychotherapy. And a commitment was made to work toward requiring training in psychotherapy for accreditation of graduate psychology programs. Even before becoming a section of Division 12, PIAP had begun planning publication of a journal, and efforts had begun to work out policy and structure for the journal for presentation to the APA for final approval of the publication. The decision to pursue establishment of a journal was based in part on the results of a research questionnaire dealing with 11 critical issues in psychotherapy and sent to nearly 4500 psychologists in the APA who listed psychotherapy as an interest in the 1962 APA directory. Only 20% of respondents thought that coverage of psychotherapy topics was adequate in APA journals, and 78% thought that there should be a new journal dealing with psychotherapy.

A letter dated April 8, 1963, from Leonard Pearson, vice president of PIAP, to the publications board of the APA, indicated that PIAP was concerned about the adequacy of publication outlets for theoretical, clinical, and professional articles dealing with psychotherapy practice, teaching, or research. The first issue of their journal, *Psychotherapy: Theory, Research and Practice*, instituted to provide such outlets, was published in 1964, under the editorship of Eugene T. Gendlin. A *PIAP Bulletin* (1964) was discovered that reflected an organization with a membership truly interested not only in the practice of psychotherapy but also in teaching, training, and research.

Despite some differences within the executive board, PIAP continued as an active section of Division 12. But problems were experienced as members had to deal with a 50% rejection rate of the programs they submitted for APA convention presentation, and their frustration increased because of what they perceived as a lack of cooperation regarding PIAP's election ballots, dues billing, and other requests for help. Discussions about the possibility of achieving divisional status, begun in 1960 but tabled when the affiliation with Division 12 was agreed to, resurfaced.

When PIAP's executive board convened on September 1, 1966, Theodore H. Blau led a discussion that culminated in a unanimous vote to draft a petition to be circulated for signature, requesting that the APA Council of Representatives establish a new division of the APA to be known as the Division of Psychotherapy. This petition, with the necessary signatures and proposed bylaws attached, was presented to the Council of Representatives in August of 1967.

A Home of Our Own: The Division of Psychotherapy

On September 4, 1967, PIAP became Division 29, the Division of Psychotherapy of the American Psychological Association (Division 29), and all of PIAP became charter members of the division.

So now we were officially recognized, we were on our way, and—more or less—on our own. Members of the first official board of the Division of

Psychotherapy took their seats following the 1967 council meeting. According to the *Psychotherapy Bulletin* (1968, June), the division by then had its bylaws approved by the membership and was actively engaged in a broad variety of projects. Eugene T. Gendlin was editing the journal, and Jack G. Wiggins was already chairing its Insurance and Related Social Issues Committee. Alvin R. Mahrer was editing a project titled *Creative Directions in Psychotherapy,* and the *Psychotherapy Bulletin* succeeded the *PIAP Bulletin* as the official organ of the division (Mahrer & Pearson, 1973). A 1-day conference on psychotherapy research was planned to precede the 1968 APA convention in San Francisco, as were two all-day therapy workshops. And a booklet titled *Psychotherapy—A Psychological Perspective*, designed to educate the public about how and when to use psychotherapy and where to seek it, was nearing publication. Division 29 was already soliciting input from graduate students relating to their training and providing its membership with critical information concerning matters such as the first freedom of choice law in the United States recognizing psychologists under group major medical policies.

The board did not have sufficient funds to pay for their meeting, so, at the suggestion of Theodore H. Blau, the members held workshops in Tampa, Florida, from which they raised the money. It was these workshops that were, in fact, the forerunners of the midwinter meetings.

Division 29 has had many firsts: first division to hold midwinter meetings, which many other divisions have emulated over the years; first to offer student travel scholarships; first to have a central office; and, thanks to PIAP, which had used this format, the first division to have conversation hours and programs in a divisional hospitality suite. It was a leader in trying to reshape fellowship requirements for practitioner divisions. And it was, according to Ronald E. Fox, Theodore H. Blau, and many others, the first real home for the practitioner within the APA. One of the things that has made it special over the years has been the sense of family in Division 29. In the early years, it was the one division within which the young practitioner would find many role models. In a conversation with Theodore H. Blau (1992), he shared with me his perception that Division 12 did not then represent "real clinical psychology," in the sense that they were a very academically oriented group and not really interested in practice issues. The "real clinicians" belonged to Division 29, where the young, aggressive, independent practitioners, who felt suppressed and ignored by Division 12 came together to act on their commitment to change as they saw change indicated.

Division 29 was also a leader in bringing practitioners into participation in APA governance, on boards and committees, on the board of directors, and ultimately into the presidency of the APA. We were delighted with the election of Theodore H. Blau, our second president, as the president-elect of the APA in 1976. We believe that he was the first practitioner to fill the office. Blau told me that some people considered Abraham Maslow the first practitioner president, but that he—and Maslow—both thought that was ridiculous. Other strongly identified Division 29 members such as Max Siegel, Nicholas A. Cummings, Stanley R. Graham, Jack G. Wiggins, Ronald E. Fox, and Norman Abeles, all were elected to the highest office in the APA.

STRUCTURE OF THE DIVISION

The bylaws accompanying the application for divisional status in the APA were modified many times, particularly in 1981, 1987, and 1993. The changes reflected the changing needs of the division as it sought to serve its members over time. There are four categories of membership in the division: member, fellow, associate, and student affiliate, requiring equivalent membership status in the APA for the first three categories.

OFFICERS AND BOARD

Officers, elected by the membership, consist of the president, president-elect, the immediate past-president, the secretary, and the treasurer. (See Table 33 for a list of division officers from 1967 to 1998.)

These officers make up the executive committee (until 1995 referred to as the administrative committee) of the division, and supervise and transact the business of the division between meetings of the board of directors, which includes, in addition to the executive committee, the division's representatives to the APA council and nine board members-at-large elected for 3-year terms. The number of council representatives has varied over the years, ranging from a low of two to a high of six. The structure has remained the same over the years, except that until 1982 the same individual could fill more than one seat simultaneously. Since 1982 that has not been permitted.

STANDING COMMITTEES AND BOARDS

The standing committees consist of the fellows, membership, nominations and elections, program, finance, gender issues, multicultural affairs, professional awards, education and training, professional practice, and student development committees. Their names have been different but their missions have been consistent. The division has had only one board: the very important publications board.

TABLE 33
Division of Psychotherapy
OFFICERS

Year	President	Secretary	Treasurer
1967–1968	Fred E. Spaner	Nancy Orlinsky	Ronald E. Fox
1968–1969	Theodore H. Blau	Ronald E. Fox	(unknown)
1969–1970	Vin Rosenthal	Leah Gold Fein	Ronald E. Fox
1970–1971	Victor Raimy	Leah Gold Fein	Stanley R. Graham
1971–1972	Max Siegel	Leah Gold Fein	Stanley R. Graham
1972–1973	Jules Barron	Jack D. Krasner	Stanley R. Graham
1973–1974	Gordon F. Derner	Jack D. Krasner	Stanley R. Graham
1974–1975	Arthur L. Kovacs	Jack D. Krasner	Stanley R. Graham
1975–1976	Jack D. Krasner	Gloria Behar Gottsegen	Stanley R. Graham
1976–1977	Carl N. Zimet	Gloria Behar Gottsegen	Ella Lasky
1977–1978	Stanley R. Graham	Gloria Behar Gottsegen	Ella Lasky
1978–1979	Robert A. Harper	Laura H. Barbanel	Ella Lasky
1979–1980	Jack G. Wiggins	Laura H. Barbanel	Mathilda B. Canter
1980–1981	Herbert J. Freudenberger	Laura H. Barbanel	Mathilda B. Canter
1981–1982	Ronald E. Fox	Suzanne B. Sobel	Mathilda B. Canter
1982–1983	Jacob Chwast	Suzanne B. Sobel	Shirley Sanders
1983–1984	Mathilda B. Canter	Suzanne B. Sobel	Shirley Sanders
1985	Ernst G. Beier	Ellen McGrath	Shirley Sanders
1986	Suzanne B. Sobel	Ellen McGrath	Stanley R. Graham
1987	Patrick H. DeLeon	Ellen McGrath	Stanley R. Graham
1988	Donald K. Freedheim	Patricia S. Hannigan	Stanley R. Graham
1989	Aaron H. Canter	Patricia S. Hannigan	Alice K. Rubenstein
1990	Norman Abeles	Patricia S. Hannigan	Alice K. Rubenstein
1991	Ellen McGrath	Patricia S. Hannigan	Alice K. Rubenstein
1992	Reuben J. Silver	Patricia Hannigan-Farley	Alice K. Rubenstein
1993	Gerald P. Koocher	Patricia Hannigan-Farley	Alice K. Rubenstein
1994	Tommy T. Stigall	Diane J. Willis	Alice K. Rubenstein
1995	Stanley R. Graham	Diane J. Willis	Gloria Behar Gottsegen
1996	Patricia Hannigan-Farley	Diane J. Willis	Gloria Behar Gottsegen
1997	Larry E. Beutler	Diane J. Willis	Gloria Behar Gottsegen
1998	Alice K. Rubenstein	Diane J. Willis	(unknown)

Ad Hoc Committees and Task Forces

Over the years many committees and task forces have been formed, done their work, and, as expected, been appropriately dissolved. Others have been maintained as significant work for them continues to surface.

Liaisons and Monitors

Over the years the division has appointed liaisons and monitors to various APA boards and committees, such as the Committee for the Advancement of Professional Practice (CAPP), the Board of Professional Affairs (BPA), the Committee on International Relations in Psychology (CIRP), and so on. At present liaisons have been appointed to the Joint Council on Professional Education in Psychology (JCPEP), to the Interdivisional Task Force on Health Care Reform, and to CAPP, and a CIRP monitor has been appointed.

Sections

The bylaws provide for the establishment of sections. But though some interest groups within the division have talked at times about forming sections, with one exception they have bypassed this option, on their way to divisional status.

ADMINISTERING THE DIVISION

The early leaders assumed the burden of carrying out the clerical and other functions necessitated by divisional status. But increasing activities developed by the division soon made it necessary to consider other arrangements.

Early Arrangements

By 1968, the division was already feeling the need for administrative help in running its affairs, and after a trial period of 4 months using the outgoing president's administrative assistant as a central office resource person, the volume of work was so great that the board agreed unanimously to raise the funds for a full-time executive secretary.

The affairs of the division were being handled well, and it was noted that the division was incorporated on October 2, 1973, and was working on securing 501C(6) status (nonprofit educational organization) from the Internal Revenue Service. Unlike most professional organizations, which are classified as guilds, the division did meet the requirements for 501C(6) status. By August of 1975, the Division of Psychotherapy was taking in a good deal of money, with annual income and expenditures of approximately $50,000. A central office in the New York City area was established to administer its activities, with Jack D. Krasner as administrative coordinator. In 1978, Gloria Behar Gottsegen took over until June of 1979, when she gave up her post to Benjamin Fabrikant.

The Administrators

Dr. Fabrikant died while he was still administrative coordinator, and the central office underwent some times of crisis, as new people stepped in on a part-time basis to try to keep the division afloat, with mixed success. The crisis was weathered, and after much agonizing deliberation, it was decided to contract with a management firm, The Administrators, in Phoenix, Arizona, because of their broad capacities, desirable financial terms, and the presence of a divisional past-president to provide local supervision. In October of 1985 the division moved to a new central office in Phoenix.

Division president Suzanne B. Sobel attended the first Division Leadership Conference sponsored by the APA in May of 1986 and made a presentation sharing the extensive experience Division 29 had accumulated regarding organization of a division. She noted that Division 29 seemed to have much that most divisions did not have—a tax ID number, a central office, a midwinter meeting, and ownership of two publications, while lacking the problems in continuity that plagued many other divisions.

The Administrators have been positioned to provide increased services for the division as membership and activities have grown over the years. They are the archivists, preserving the division's publications, minutes, agendas, correspondence, and so on. Their responsibilities have increased over the years, so that at present, in 1997, they handle the financial end of the journal, are deeply involved in the production and mailing of the bulletin, work closely with the officers and committees needing their services, take care of the accounting with the oversight of the treasurer, make all necessary meeting arrangements, prepare agendas and backup materials for executive committee and board meetings, answer questions from members and others, and so on.

THE STANDING COMMITTEES AT WORK

APA divisions are interest groups. This division's interests are reflected in the committees it has formed to provide structure and to carry on the activities it was created to pursue.

Membership Committee

The entire membership of PIAP had been rolled over as charter members of the division. By 1970, it was more than 1600 strong, and by 1979, it had grown to 3803 (despite an assessment of $25 per year—somewhat higher than other similar assessments—but with the journal included as a member benefit). They have grown gradually over the years (see Figure 2), with slight

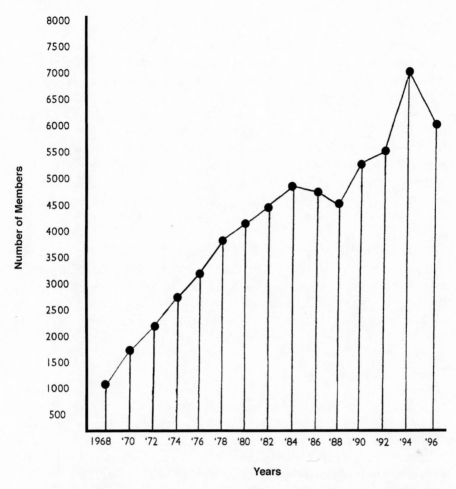

Figure 2. Division 29 Membership Figures From APA Membership Records.

fluctuations, except for a large jump in 1992, a function of a membership campaign involving free membership. The effects are yet to be assessed fully, but it looks like a costly failure because it appears that many did not renew their membership once the free journal and membership offer ended.

One of the problems experienced by divisions in the APA was the time lag for inclusion of applicants for divisional membership created by the APA system. Efforts by Division 29 to change procedures were helpful, and in 1985 it became possible for divisional memberships to be accepted automatically along with APA membership, thus allowing members of Division 29 to receive the journal and participate in divisional activities in a more timely fashion.

A demographic profile of Division 29 compiled by the APA Office of Demographics, Employment, and Educational Research (ODEER) revealed that of the total 1989 membership, more than two thirds were male; 43% of the associate members were female. Mean age of members was 50.5 with 89% having an earned doctorate and a little more than 70% describing their major field as in the health service provider area. Sixty-three percent were employed full time, only six members stated that they were unemployed and seeking employment, and about 4% were retirees or students (but a significant 21% did not specify employment status.) Eighty-nine percent of the members were licensed or certified, approximately 28% stated that they were involved in research, 43% in education, and 93% described their activities in the area of health and mental health services. All APA divisions appeared to have some Division 29 members, 39% of our membership belonged to four or more divisions, and 74% belonged to state psychological associations.

The division remains one of the largest divisions in the APA and probably one of the most active, though divisional representation on council fluctuates between two and six seats. (It was up to three in 1996, but it decreased to two in 1997.) This may be in part a function of the proliferation of divisions tapping the pool from which Division 29 members are likely to come.

Fellows Committee

The criteria used by the APA membership committee for awarding fellow status did not seem to fit for practicing psychotherapists. Rejection of Division 29 fellow applications frequently hinged on publication credits, not the most appropriate measure of practitioner achievement. At a meeting with the membership committee in September of 1974, some criteria were worked out for election of fellows in Division 29. This helped for a while, but Division 29 and other practice divisions continued to have problems with rejection by the APA membership committee of individuals the division deemed worthy of fellow status. In 1982, Division 29 submitted two resolutions to the APA council and some help was forthcoming. Despite the fact that, according to the APA membership committee, the divisions establish their own criteria for fellow status, the acceptance of new fellows by the APA membership committee is still, at times, a struggle, as interpretations differ, but the situation is much improved.

Program Committee

One of the major reasons for seeking to become a division of the APA was to be able to increase availability of convention program time and to provide excellent programs of most interest to the division's membership. In addition the division introduced the use of a hospitality suite for conversation hours that were conducted by some of its most prominent psychotherapists. In 1973, preconvention workshops were held, but in 1974, it was decided to move the workshops to tie in with the midwinter meetings because of the increasing numbers of competing pre-APA offerings.

In 1978, Ellen McGrath and Alice K. Rubenstein instituted a formal procedure for evaluation of submissions for the APA program, each program being rated by three independent reviewers with expertise in the topical area. Their work was of such excellence that in 1979 the APA Board of Convention Affairs requested the forms they had developed to be used as models for other divisions.

In the early 1980s presentations were already focusing not only on the usual content areas of psychotherapy, but also on the need to influence public policy affecting health service consumers and providers, on the promotion of mental health as well as the prevention of mental illness, and on the APA organization and the complex issues facing practitioners of psychotherapy.

Sometimes, with growth come problems. Increasing numbers of submissions and decreasing numbers of program hours available at the APA convention were responsible for a year such as 1985, which was very successful in terms of program quality and attendance but which necessitated a 60% rejection rate of submissions. Effective 1996 the provision of a hospitality suite at the APA for programs has been discontinued, in recognition of the declining attendance there, seen as related to the increased numbers of exciting programs and miniconventions now offered at the APA.

Finance Committee

The finance committee, founded in 1977 and reorganized and chaired by the treasurer effective 1978, is responsible for the financial health of the division. Over the years, the committee has prepared budgets, made recommendations to the board regarding monetary policies and financial needs, and continues to serve with diligence. The division is solvent, but struggling. A drop in membership and increasing numbers of dues-exempt members coupled with growing expenses as needs escalate in our troubled profession and projects develop all make for a real challenge. The division's leaders are taking necessary steps to economize.

Gender Issues Committee

The forerunner of the gender issues committee was established in 1974 as the Committee for Women (CFW), the first such divisional committee in the APA, to the best of our knowledge. Its initial charge included examining what is transmitted to women clients in psychotherapy and helping with the integration of women into a full leadership role in the governance of the division. An active committee, it explored the literature regarding sexual intimacies between therapist and client, devised a questionnaire to be sent to the membership to gather data regarding men's and women's professional lifestyles, and helped women to prepare program presentations (Lee, Resnick, & Clamer, 1982). In 1977, a CFW brochure, "Program Development—Your Guide to Getting It On," written by Mathilda B. Canter and Ellen McGrath was completed, was published in the *Psychotherapy Bulletin* (1978) and in 1978 was printed by the division for distribution. It was also requested by the APA Board of Convention Affairs to use as a model for other divisions.

The CFW was involved in updating and distributing the Hannah Lerman annotated bibliography, *Sexual Intimacies Between Psychotherapists and Patients,* which, since its original publication in 1984, had generated broad interest, was revised in 1990, and has been a consistent source of revenue for the division each year. CFW also drafted a patients' rights statement and worked with the APA's director of Women's Programs and Divisions 35 (Psychology of Women) and 43 (Family Psychology) on the development of resource materials. The CFW surveyed the membership about depression patterns in their individual practices, and a questionnaire was inserted in the *Psychotherapy Bulletin* (1989). A report by Carol Goodheart of the questionnaire findings was published in the *Psychotherapy Bulletin* (1989). CFW also prepared a model letter to politicians on the freedom-of-choice for abortion issue.

The CFW had from its inception been working hard to encourage female leadership roles, and one of its goals was to see appropriate gender balance in division governance. The 17th president of the division, Mathilda B. Canter, was the first woman to hold that office (1983–1984), and there have been 4 women among the 14 presidents elected since. Also, almost all of the secretaries and treasurers have been women, sitting on the executive committee.

Over the years, the CFW continued its educational and political focus, and in 1990 the chair was a liaison to the Interdivisional Task Force on Gender. In 1991, on the recommendation of its chair, CFW was reconstituted as the Gender Issues Committee.

Multicultural Affairs Committee

The precursor of the Multicultural Affairs Committee, the Ethnic Minority Affairs Committee, was established in 1978 and was, it is believed, the first such divisional committee formed. Through the years it was very active and established a newsletter and a network among members interested in minority issues related to psychotherapy theory, practice, and research. The committee was successful in increasing the number of ethnic minority presentations at conventions and enhanced divisional liaisons with other APA ethnic minority bodies. It was instrumental in helping the Massachusetts Psychological Association to form its own committee on ethnic minority concerns and worked on giving input to state legislators regarding the training and licensure of ethnic minority psychologists and any psychologists who would be working with ethnic minority clients.

It was noted that in 1987, 49 new ethnic minority students joined. Lisa M. Porché-Burke, committee chair, was designated to serve as the division's liaison to the new Division 45 (Society for the Study of Ethnic Minority Issues), which planned to cosponsor a social hour at the APA convention for ethnic minority psychologists. In addition to working on student recruitment, the Division 29 committee was collaborating with Division 45 to produce a special collection of papers pertaining to ethnic minority issues in psychotherapy, education, and training, with Division 29 committing $1000 to this project. And the division initiated an Ethnic Minorities Student Paper Competition.

In 1991, the committee name was changed to Multicultural Affairs Committee, a title more in line with changing demographics and goals. The competition name became The National Students of Color Paper Competition.

Professional Practice Committee

Although the origin of the committee title Professional Practice Committee, stipulated in the current bylaws, is not clear, it is eminently clear that the division has been doing the work of such a committee from the start and that a variety of committees, over time, was involved in issues of professional practice, working alone and in cooperation with other practice divisions. Only some of these can be mentioned. In 1967, the division already had a committee on insurance and related social issues. Later on, the division's Committee on Health Insurance (COHI), chaired by Jack G. Wiggins, was busy cooperating with and assisting the APA's COHI in its negotiations with insurance companies and government agencies regarding the use of psychotherapy by psychologists and in negotiating some specific insurance contracts. Out of this interaction the APA developed the Committee for the Advancement of Psychological Professions and Sciences (CAPPS), the forerunner of the Association for the Advancement of Psychology (AAP) with Max Siegel, Theodore H. Blau, and Jack G. Wiggins representing Division 29 and Nicholas A. Cummings, Rogers Wright, and Melvin Gravitz representing the APA's COHI.

The division's COHI provided testimony to the Federal Trade Commission (FTC) regarding psychology's economic losses resulting from the restraint of trade practices of the National Association of Blue Shield Plans and also addressed the complaint of the Association for the Advancement of Psychology (AAP) to the FTC regarding the Joint Commission on Accreditation of Hospitals (JCAH) guidelines for hospital privileges. In 1983 the division had a committee on independent practice, chaired by Stanley R. Graham, because 85% of the division's membership was interested in issues of practice. This committee was focusing on such areas of concern to practitioners as peer review, master's-level issues, and the organization and provision of health services. The marketing committee, established in 1986, directed its energies, among other places, into collaboration with Divisions 42 (Psychologists in Independent Practice) and 43 (Family Psychology) on a project for which Division 42 had received a grant, for the establishment of a corporate consultation service.

By the mid-1970s the division's public information committee had initiated about 70 radio and television shows across the country, featuring members of Division 29. Its work seemed to merge with and be taken over by the division's Committee on Professional Practice, chaired by Ellen McGrath, and the coding of applicants for a media hotline, which had begun much earlier, was well on its way. A referral list was being developed from which the division's central office could provide media representatives with the names of appropriate resource people to contact for professional information. The committee was focusing also on the development of other marketing tools for psychotherapists and conducted marketing training workshops at the midwinter convention, while continuing the development of the media hotline. The media hot line project was completed in 1993 and turned over to the media relations office of the Practice Directorate.

Another professional practice committee, the Committee on Professional Liability, formerly the Malpractice Committee, was at work over the years serving as a resource for members on malpractice issues, surveying the membership to identify areas of concern, publishing relevant informational articles, and seeing to it that programming was provided to members and the profession in general at midwinter and APA conventions.

Student Development Committee

The Division of Psychotherapy recognized very early the importance of reaching out to students, the future of the profession. In 1971, it instituted student travel scholarships, another APA first for the division, and one to which the division points with pride. The division has selected many worthy students for awards over the years, including Nadine Kaslow, who later received the Division of Psychotherapy's early career award.

No applications were received for the 1986 student travel scholarship awards, and an ad hoc committee on student development (now a standing committee) was formed to work on student recruitment and to reexamine the student awards. Ellin L. Bloch was appointed chair. The committees on student development and ethnic minorities proceeded to recruit more than 275 new student members, with 49 of these being minorities. The year before the division had only six student members!

In 1988, an Annual Graduate Student Paper Competition was created. This competition provided that each winner be given a monetary prize plus the opportunity to present the paper at a session during the APA convention. That year the committee reported a student membership of 406, including 100 ethnic minority students and the initiation of a student legislative internship in cooperation with the Hawaii Psychological Association.

Ellin Bloch and student coordinators Scott Mesh and David Pilon met with staff of the APA Office of Educational Affairs (OEA) to investigate the range of possible activities that the APA might consider to increase student membership. Using as a model Division 29's success in recruitment, exciting possibilities were explored. Mesh and Pilon were invited by the APA OEA to address the Division Leadership Conference. And in August of 1988, the American Psychological Association of Graduate Students (APAGS) was formed, with Division 29 (via Donald Freedheim, Ellin Bloch, Scott Mesh, and David Pilon) in the forefront in the formation of this organization. Each year prizes were awarded in the student paper competitions. In 1991 the name of the student paper awards was changed to the Donald K. Freedheim Student Development Award, in acknowledgement of Dr. Freedheim's encouragement, guidance, and his instrumental support for the creation of APAGS.

The Student Development Committee under the aegis of Abraham W. Wolf has continued its successful recruitment efforts and in 1995 alone brought in 205 new student members. The work continues, and as of February 1997, there were 556 student members in the division.

Professional Awards Committee

The division has, over the years, given a variety of special awards to individuals for special service rendered to the division. It also gives student awards, as was discussed previously. There are two major awards for which this committee is responsible, and I will describe them in turn.

Distinguished Psychologist Award

The Distinguished Psychologist Award was established in 1970 to honor psychologists who have made significant contributions to the field. Although it was originally named the Distinguished Professional Psychologist Award, in 1984 its name was changed to the Distinguished Psychologist Award for Contributions to Psychology and Psychotherapy. Nominations

TABLE 34
Division of Psychotherapy: Distinguished Psychologist Award

1970	Eugene T. Gendlin
1971	Victor Raimy
1972	Carl R. Rogers
1973	Albert Ellis and Hans H. Strupp
1974	Haim Ginott (Posthumous award)
1975	Sidney Jourard (Posthumous award)
1976	Nicholas A. Cummings
1977	Gordon F. Derner
1978	Jack D. Krasner
1979	Max Siegel
1980	Jules Barron
1981	Carl N. Zimet
1982	Arthur L. Kovacs
1983	Herbert J. Freudenberger
1984	Robert A. Harper
1985	Stanley R. Graham
1986	Ronald E. Fox
1987	Mathilda B. Canter
1988	Ernst G. Beier
1989	Jack G. Wiggins
1990	Tommy T. Stigall
1991	Donald K. Freedheim
1992	Arnold A. Lazarus
1993	Patrick H. DeLeon
1994	Rachel T. Hare-Mustin
1995	Stanley Moldawsky and Harry Sands
1996	Norman Abeles and Alice K. Rubenstein
1997	Alvin R. Mahrer

are open, and recommendations are made by the awards committee to the executive committee, and then to the voting members of the board of directors, who select the recipients. (See Table 34 for a list of the award recipients.)

The Jack D. Krasner Memorial Award

On the death of Jack D. Krasner, a memorial fund was established, with investment proceeds to be awarded as an annual prize. As formulated initially, the winner was to be a member of the Division of Psychotherapy with a doctorate awarded no more than 10 years prior to receipt of the award, who had made or was making unusually significant contributions in psychotherapy research, theory, or practice. The first award was given in 1981. In 1987, a committee was formed to look into the award criteria, which appeared to be too restrictive. The criteria were modified, and essentially this award is given to people early in their careers and seen as on their way to becoming "distinguished." The list (see Table 35) of awardees suggests that the division has been quite good at predicting.

TABLE 35
Jack D. Krasner Memorial Award Recipients

1981	Annette Brodsky and Gerald P. Koocher
1982	No Award
1983	Jaquelyn L. Resnick and Gary R. VandenBos
1984	Ronald F. Levant
1985	Raymond H. DiGiuseppe
1986	E. Rita Dudley
1987	No Award
1988	Alice K. Rubenstein
1989	Leonard J. Haas
1990	Victor R. Nahmias
1991	Lisa M. Porché-Burke
1992	John C. Norcross
1993	Jon T. Perez
1994	Nadine J. Kaslow
1995	Karen E. Kovacs
1996	Abraham W. Wolf

Nominations and Elections Committee

As its name indicates, the Nominations and Elections Committee, chaired by the president-elect, is responsible for developing slates and announcing election results. It seems to have been able to do its job well enough so that the division has been blessed with excellent officers and board members, under whose aegis its work has prospered.

Education and Training Committee

The division has always considered the education and training of psychotherapists to be among its major concerns, and its programs and publications have reflected this. By 1969 an ad hoc committee on psychotherapy curriculum had been formalized. The division focused on adding psychotherapy to the accreditation requirements for graduate programs, which at the time required only testing and statistics. The division was cooperating with Division 12 and the Board of Professional Affairs of the APA on the Joint Task Force on Evaluation of Psychotherapy Procedures. And it had formed the task force on Developing Minimal Standards for Psychotherapy Education in Psychology Training Programs.

In 1971, the ad hoc Committee on Non-doctoral Training in Psychotherapy was formed and charged with making site visits throughout the country to examine programs training in psychology or mental health. Via its Committee on Education and Training, the division was taking the initiative by working toward the evaluation of postgraduate psychotherapy training facilities. The board communicated to the APA board of directors and the council its support for the prompt implementation and continuance of an effective mechanism for publicly identifying doctoral training programs in psychology, recommending that such a mechanism be based on objective criteria for program evaluation and constituted with interorganizational representation from educational, professional, and credentialing bodies.

In 1983, the Committee on Professional Education and Training was working to put together a list of postdoctoral programs in psychology, particularly psychotherapy, throughout the United States and Canada, and was also exploring postdoctoral clinical respecialization programs. In 1986, the Graduate Education and Training Committee, chaired by Tommy T. Stigall, was formulating and recommending policies concerning graduate education and training to the board, particularly as related to the professional practice of psychotherapy by psychologists. The committee was given the additional assignment of broadly monitoring activities and trends in graduate education and training and serving in an advisory capacity to the officers and board of the division. Stigall was authorized to serve in an observer–liaison capacity with respect to other organizations and units of the APA governance concerned with graduate education and training. In 1987, the committee was active coordinating with counterpart committees of other practitioner divisions on matters of mutual concern, evaluating materials sent to Division 29 by APA groups for consideration, and planning and participating in programs.

During 1989 the committee became part of a Joint Commission on Professional Education in Psychology (JCPEP), established with Stigall as its chair, and including, in addition to Divisions 29, Divisions 42 (Psychologists in Independent Practice), 43 (Family Psychology), 39 (Psychoanalysis), 12 (Clinical Psychology), and 17 (Counseling Psychology), the American Association of State Psychology Boards, the Association of Psychology Internship Centers, and the National Council of Schools and Programs of Professional Psychology. Joint efforts such as this one would, it was hoped by the leadership of Division 29, avoid duplication, enhance communication and clout, and be facilitated via the coalition of practice divisions now in existence. The significance of the joint commission was underscored by a grant from the Practice Directorate to further its work. And Stigall was named a member of the Interim Advisory Committee for an Education Directorate for the APA. In 1992, a subcommittee of the division's Education and Training Committee was formed to make recommendations regarding psychopharmacology for psychologists and psychotherapy with severely mentally ill clients.

In 1994, the Education and Training Committee, chaired by Arthur N. Wiens, presented an excellent and thought-provoking report touching on a broad array of issues concerning psychotherapy training models, facilitation of communication between researchers and clinicians, supervision issues, outcome data collection, and so on. In 1995, the committee was working on training models, staffing requirements, and studying the use of a basic template for therapy outcome.

MAJOR AD HOC COMMITTEES OF THE DIVISION

In addition to the standing committees stipulated in the bylaws, there are ad hoc committees formed to deal with specific matters of interest and disbanded at the end of a year, unless reconstitituted to continue to serve their purposes.

Continuing Education Committee

The division was always concerned about continuing education for its members, and the board had, in fact, taken a position early in its existence, and again in 1990, in favor of mandatory continuing education for psychologists. Workshops were offered at APA conventions, but these were discontinued after some time because of the multitude of competing offerings.

However, at the midwinter meetings, the division was able to offer many quality programs and workshops. In 1984, the division was approved as a continuing education sponsor by the APA, thereby increasing its potential to meet the membership's need for high quality continuing education experiences in psychotherapy that would be honored by state psychology boards. Once again the division's board recommended to the APA Continuing Education (CE) Committee that procedures be developed to grant the APA continuing education credit for attendance at national, regional, state, and midwinter meetings; to substantially reduce fee requirements, reports, and research requirements for APA divisions and state associations, and if necessary to have council intervene in order to make the APA continuing education committee more responsive to divisional, state association, and membership needs. The division's continuing education committee was asked to establish a liaison relationship with the APA's committee in an effort to facilitate better communication and understanding between the two bodies. At the 1985 midwinter divisional joint board retreat, there was a discussion of proposals to promote programs in which all the divisions and state associations have the ability to grant continuing education credit, as does the APA, without our groups having to pay $200 every few years and do an enormous amount of paperwork, as we currently must do in order to grant continuing education credit. In 1993, the division offered continuing education credit for attendance at specifically designated programs at the APA convention. More than 200 psychologists took advantage of this opportunity for learning and for earning continuing education credits without added cost.

Employee Benefits Committee

The Employee Benefits Committee, chaired by Patricia Hannigan-Farley, was formed in 1991 to promote the professionalism of psychologists in relation to employee benefit plans; to educate employers about the appropriate role of mental health in their own and their employees' lives and about the impact of employee mental health or benefits utilization; to promote quality utilization review; to serve as an adjunct to the APA-level efforts in advocacy for mental health coverage; and to serve as an information clearing house for division members on the current topics in health benefits management.

PUBLICATIONS BOARD

The division started out with a publications policy committee but soon put into place a publications board to oversee and facilitate that part of the work relating to the communication of ideas, whether by printed word, audiocassette, videotapes, and so on. The publications board has, in addition to shepherding through the items that will be described in the sections that follow, taken responsibility for producing other materials, such as articles for college newspapers, brochures, and so on.

Divisional Publications and Products

The Division of Psychotherapy, from its inception, has placed great importance on stimulating the exchange of information among psychologists interested in psychotherapy, on furthering research into the nature of psychotherapy, and on generating publications for the membership, to communicate the growing body of knowledge reflected by the data collected. These values have been reflected in the actions taken by the division and the resources that have been devoted to carrying out this commitment.

The Journal

The division considers the journal to be a member benefit and underwrites its cost, though of course nonmember and institutional subscriptions help to defray the expenses. Reflecting a steady growth pattern, by the end of the third year of the division's existence, in 1970 membership was more than 1600, but journal subscriptions were up to 4500 and the journal had doubled in size. In 1975, Eugene T. Gendlin retired as editor, and Arthur

L. Kovacs was selected to replace him. The journal flourished, and in 1978 the division published its first special issue, "Personality of the Psychotherapist," beginning a tradition of publishing that continues to the present. (See Table 36 for a list of journal special issues.)

In 1983, Donald K. Freedheim took over the editorship. Fran Pepitone-Rockwell reviewed all articles going into the journal for gender-biased language and made appropriate modifications. On recommendation of the division's publications board, the name of the journal, *Psychotherapy: Theory, Research and Practice*, was changed in 1983 to *Psychotherapy*, with the words *Theory, Research, Practice and Training* on the lower legend of the page. This recommendation was a result of the change by the APA in the name of its journal, *Professional Psychology* to *Professional Psychology: Research and Practice* and was intended to minimize confusion between the two titles.

In 1985, a book review section was instituted. And in 1987, the president was authorized to sign a contract with a group that would tape-record *Psychotherapy* for a modest annual fee and distribute the material at cost to each visually impaired member of the division. The journal continued to be one of the most prestigious publications in the field of psychotherapy and to publish important and high quality, timely manuscripts with many graduate programs in psychology relying on the journal as a teaching tool.

TABLE 36
Special Issues of *Psychotherapy*

Editor	Date	Title
J. Barron	1978	Personality of the psychotherapist.
S. R. Graham	1980	Values in psychotherapy.
M. Goodman and B. D. Schwartz	1981	Theory and practice of group psychotherapy.
G. B. Gottsegen and P. P. Park	1982	Psychotherapy in later life.
M. F. Shore and F. V. Mannino	1984	Psychotherapy with children and youth.
G. R. Dudley and M. L. Rawlins	1985	Psychotherapy with ethnic minorities.
H. Goldberg and F. Pepitone-Arreola-Rockwell	1986	Gender issues in psychotherapy.
R. F. Levant	1987	Psychotherapy with families.
J. G. Wiggins and B. L. Welch	1988	Psychotherapy and the new health-care system.
D. T. Bradford and M. H. Spero	1990	Psychotherapy and religion.
F. M. Ochberg and D. J. Willis	1991	Psychotherapy with victims.
J. C. Norcross	1992	The future of psychotherapy.
G. DeLeon, H. J. Freudenberger, and H. Wexler	1993	Psychotherapy and addiction.
A. K. Rubenstein and K. Zager	1995	Adolescent treatment: new frontiers and new dimensions.
J. P. Ranier	1996	Psychotherapy outcomes.

Donald K. Freedheim was appointed to a second 5-year term as editor. In his 1991 annual report to the board and membership, he indicated that more than 800 pages and nearly 100 articles had been printed in four issues that year, plus a special issue, adding up to the highest number of articles and greatest number of pages published per year to date. Book reviews were included in each issue.

Wade H. Silverman, who had been *The Psychotherapy Bulletin* editor, was selected to replace Freedheim as editor of *Psychotherapy* for a 5-year term from 1994 to 1999. The transition was smooth, and the journal has continued to grow, with institutional subscriptions increasing in number despite a necessary increase in price. It is regrettable that the unavoidable escalation of costs is such that, starting in 1996, the many dues-exempt members of the division must pay $15 per year (the actual cost of production to the division) to receive *Psychotherapy*.

The Psychotherapy Bulletin

In 1961, before PIAP was even a section of Division 12, it had started to publish the *PIAP Bulletin*, which was a type of newsletter. Publication was continued until PIAP became a part of Division 12, and by 1968 *The Psychotherapy Bulletin* had replaced it as the official organ of the division. Ernst G. Beier was one of its early editors and helped to increase the utility of the bulletin by including in it such items as statements from candidates running for divisional office (1977). On his resignation, in 1980, Benjamin Fabrikant served as editor until 1983, when he in turn handed the reins over to Laura H. Barbanel. On her resignation, Wade H. Silverman was appointed, a position he filled until 1993, when Linda F. Campbell was designated as editor for 1993 to 1996, when she was reappointed for a second term.

Looking through the bulletins of the division over the years, one is struck by the fact that *The Psychotherapy Bulletin* has indeed developed from a one-sheet flyer into a truly substantial publication. In addition to keeping the membership informed about current events, meeting minutes, election results, and the like, it provides substantive articles about issues of concern for the practice of psychotherapy, about computer-related technology for psychologists, about the status of health care reform measures nationwide, and so on. This publication is considered to be essential to the functioning of the division, linking, as it does, the division's governance and its members.

Miscellaneous Publications and Tapes

Although the major publishing efforts have of course been directed toward the journal and bulletin, there are others that warrant mention:

- Between 1967 and 1981, a divisional project titled "Creative Contributions to Psychotherapy" was undertaken and two volumes were edited by Alvin R. Mahrer.
- In 1972, the division released a booklet by Jules Barron, Benjamin Fabrikant, and Jack D. Krasner, titled *Psychotherapy: A Psychological Perspective*, written for students, counselors, teachers, administrators, patients, and the public, providing basic information about psychotherapy and the role of the psychologist and answering some commonly asked questions.
- Frances D. Rothman, chair of the tape library committee, developed a Division 29 audiotape distribution library, which made available to psychologists and allied professionals tapes on psychotherapy by outstanding psychologists.
- In 1980, the publications board completed its public information brochure on psychotherapy, written by Jules Barron and Benjamin Fabrikant, called "Psychotherapy and Psychotherapists." Approximately 20,000 of these public service brochures were distributed to state psychological associations, other organizations, and psychotherapists, for a minimal fee. In 1984, the brochure was revised to take into account state and federal laws regarding confidentiality limits. The brochure was published in the *Psychotherapy Bulletin* (1984).
- In 1990, the division began to offer for sale a 12-cassette tape series library on psychotherapy with families that consisted of a representative sampling of current thinking on the advancing edge of family therapy, featuring philosophical foundations, theory, research, and practice, and representing the emerging maturity of this 40-year-old subfield of psychotherapy.
- As part of the division's contribution to the APA centennial celebration, preparation was begun of a history volume. *History of Psychotherapy: A Century of Change*, edited by Donald K. Freedheim, was published by the APA in 1992 with an introduction by Rollo May and contributions by 63 authors on a variety of aspects of psychotherapy. It was greeted with great pride and enthusiasm for its quality, and ranked in the top five sellers at the APA.
- Mathilda B. Canter (1992), at the division's request, wrote for the APA centennial the book A *History of the Division of Psychotherapy, American Psychological Association*, published by the division.
- The division in 1994 sponsored the APA Psychotherapy Videotape Series, which Gary R. VandenBos, Donald K. Freedheim, John C. Norcross, and the division's publications board con-

jointly completed. This series of 12 videotapes shows prominent psychotherapists from widely differing orientations demonstrating their techniques, with a brochure and teaching guide prepared for each tape. It has been well received, and more products are in preparation—for example, videotapes for undergraduate abnormal and introductory psychology courses demonstrating the basis of psychotherapy.

- In 1995, Patricia Hannigan-Farley spearheaded a division project, in conjunction with the division's publications board, involving the development of a standard outpatient treatment report (OTR) for managed care. The product, because it is being developed under the auspices of a professional organization, could have impact on the standardization of the type of information provided on patients.

SECTION ONE: GROUP PSYCHOTHERAPY

First there was a Committee on Group Psychotherapy. And then, in the 1981 to 1982 year, Division 29 officially established its first—and only—section: Group Psychotherapy. The section developed its bylaws and established liaisons to the executive board, the division's publications board, and the division's program committee. Its main mission was seen as fostering, advancing, and developing the practice and theory of group psychotherapy as an autonomous reparative modality and milieu within the mental health field. The section flourished, providing excellent programs at the APA convention, including an afternoon of conversation hours in the division's hospitality suite. In their first official election the section members chose Arthur Teicher as chair and Jules Barron as vice chair and chair-elect.

In 1984, the section established a peer review committee to define and designate the problems of peer review in group psychotherapy and develop principles related to peer review for group psychotherapy. In 1987, the board gave the section approval to proceed with developing diplomate status for its members. The Section on Group Psychotherapy reported rapid growth and an enthusiastic membership. Its first directory already needed updating, and a newsletter was being published and was well received. Work continued toward the establishment of the ABPP diplomate specialty in group psychotherapy. The section's ultimate goal appeared to be the formation of a separate division of group psychotherapy within the APA. In 1989, the section became actively involved with Division 12's Section VII: Group Psychotherapy; a national conference was being planned; and the newsletter,

The Group Psychotherapist, begun by Division 29, was expanded and became a joint organ of both groups. These two sections, plus sections from Divisions 19 (Military Psychology) and 39 (Psychoanalysis), formed an interdivisional Council on Group Psychotherapy, with Arthur Teicher as president.

The section was working toward applying for divisional status, and their efforts culminated when, at its February 1991 meeting, the APA Council of Representatives overwhelmingly approved the establishment of Division 49 (Group Psychology and Group Psychotherapy). This was a real victory for Division 29's Section 1, which had skillfully shepherded the measure through council. The section voted overwhelmingly to disband and designate the newly formed Division 49 as its successor organization. The section president, Gordon Boals, indicated the intention of the section members to continue as active participants in Division 29. In fact, this seems to have been the case for many of them.

THE MIDWINTER MEETINGS

It was in 1969 that Vin Rosenthal first suggested to the Division 29 board that, in addition to holding a midwinter board meeting, the division consider a full-scale midwinter convention. The idea was greeted with enthusiasm, and agreement was reached to establish such a convention. The first one was held in January 1970 in Tampa, Florida. Two hundred members attended, and it was pronounced a great success and became a model for other divisions that have planned similar events. Attendance seemed to run between 200 and 400, and there was no particular wish to increase the number. What were very much valued, what made the midwinter meeting so special, were its informality and intimacy—the opportunity for interacting with colleagues and friends in a relaxed, comfortable atmosphere. Programs were accepted, initially, without review, and many who were anxious about making presentations at the APA conventions got their feet wet at Division 29 meetings. Programs were exciting, and such opportunities were provided as, for example, in 1977 and 1978, when a consultation–peer discussion format was made available, and attendees could sign up for individual conversation with well-known and respected psychotherapists. In 1980, at the February board meeting, Vin Rosenthal received a special award from the division for his foresight, vision, and dedication in initiating, developing, and nurturing the division's midwinter meetings from 1970 to 1973.

At a board meeting in 1981, a question was raised about exploring the inclusion of other divisions of the APA in the midwinter planning. The chair of the 1982 midwinter meeting was asked to contact Divisions 12 (Clinical Psychology), 39 (Psychoanalysis), and 42 (Psychologists in

Independent Practice), as well as the American Group Psychotherapy Association, to explore the idea of a joint midwinter meeting, especially because many of their members were Division 29 members as well. Division 42 accepted the invitation to join Division 29 in 1982 in Monterey, California, and the meeting was a successful one. As a result, the Division 29 board voted approval, and the 1983 midwinter meeting, held at the Greenbrier resort in West Virginia, was the first one to be officially sponsored jointly by Divisions 29 and 42. Combining forces was an enriching experience, and it was decided to make this joint sponsorship permanent. Guidelines for the establishment and constitution of a midwinter convention committee, with procedures for decision making delineated, were adopted by the boards. And Division 29 applied and was approved by the APA as a continuing education sponsor.

The 1987 midwinter meeting in New Orleans was the first to include Division 43 (Family Psychology) as a sponsor, and a joint retreat meeting of the boards of the three sponsoring divisions, Divisions 29, 42, and 43, was held then, and has been held ever since. With three participating divisions, it was necessary to reorganize. A midwinter conference committee was established, with representatives from each of the three divisions, and policies and procedures were adopted by the three boards to allow the committee to select sites and arrange the meetings and programs. Other divisions—for example, Division 46 (Media Psychology)—meet simultaneously at the same site, but these are not official sponsors.

The midwinter meetings continue to be successful and to meet the needs of some of the major practice divisions by providing opportunities to discuss issues ranging from routine practical administrative details to those of critical importance to practitioner survival, such as managed care problems, access to hospital and prescription privileges, training opportunities, and problematic forensic issues. They have also become a useful format for receiving input from the Practice Directorate and other APA entities.

Vin Rosenthal, recalling his initiation of the midwinter meeting, wrote in *The Psychotherapy Bulletin* (Rosenthal, 1994) that what he envisioned was offering members a small-scale, collegial, winter get-together in a warm climate, at which *anyone* who wanted to could be on the program, and at which people could gather informally, and develop friendships, as well as professional expertise.

SOME MAJOR TASK FORCES

Some of the most exciting work of the division has been accomplished by task forces. These have addressed a wide variety of important issues.

Task Force on Trauma and Research

In August of 1990, Ellen McGrath was asked to run a support group for the spouses of service people at Fort Bragg, North Carolina, for the "Home Show" on the ABC television network. She did so, collecting some research data as well, an analysis of which the division underwrote. Results were summarized in the *Psychotherapy Bulletin* (McGrath & Wexler, 1990) and *USA Today*. McGrath, the division's president-elect, asked that a task force on trauma response and research be established in response to the crisis in the Persian Gulf. The division agreed to form one and to sponsor a project undertaken by Ellin L. Bloch and by Jon T. Perez of LifePLUS Foundation, aimed at delivering psychological support and educational materials, at no charge, to meet the needs of families nationwide. Dependent on volunteer services of psychologists in their own communities who would act as facilitators and resources, this community project generated considerable interest from the U.S. Congress and the Department of Defense. The Task Force on Children and Adolescents prepared materials in conjunction with the Trauma Response Group, on support groups for children of parents deployed in the Middle East. Harry K. Wexler and Wade H. Silverman coordinated the research facet of the work of the task force, collecting and evaluating data from the volunteer psychologists and their support groups regarding the impact of their interventions. The division published, in conjunction with Project Me of Tucson, Arizona, materials that were disseminated through the Family Life Units of the Department of Defense (Embry & Rubenstein, 1991; Rubenstein & Embry, 1991). A pilot study conducted by McGrath and Wexler and funded by Division 29 looked at data collected from military spouses on attitudes and stress reactions.

McGrath started out her presidential year as Operation Desert Shield became Operation Desert Storm, and she facilitated some significant contributions to the government and the public in the name of Division 29. The task force was divided into three sections, as the division's outreach efforts expanded. In the Community Intervention Section, Ellin Bloch and Jon Perez successfully garnered support groups at the community level for families separated by the Middle East conflict, served as consultants for local groups, and served as spokespersons in the media about the plight and needs of these families. In the education section, cochairs Alice K. Rubenstein and Dennis Embry developed a group of brochures for the principals and counselors at schools with a substantial number of children who were coping with military separation (Embry & Rubenstein, 1991; Rubenstein & Embry, 1990, 1991). Their brochures were sent by the Department of Defense to all the military base schools in the United States and Europe in January of 1991, along with a research questionnaire, and were available to other schools and to division members. The division paid approximately $5000 toward the cost of this undertaking. Ellin Bloch was first author of a position paper that was submitted to Congress, the Department of Veterans Affairs, and the Department of Defense outlining recommendations for services and research.

The third section of the task force was on general applications in trauma, and the group planned to work on such areas as how psychotherapists need to respond to natural disasters (e.g., earthquake) and other disasters (e.g., plane crashes). The division worked with the Practice Directorate of the APA to coordinate and develop activities in this area. It should also be noted that a brochure written in conjunction with the Practice Directorate was part of a packet cosponsored by Division 29 that was presented to every member of Congress for distribution to their districts. At the council meeting in August 1991, Ellen McGrath and Ellin Bloch received Presidential Citations from Charles D. Spielberger, the APA president, in recognition of their work in response to the Gulf crisis.

The division's task force was also involved in helping to deal with the Los Angeles riots in April and May of 1992 (Perez, Bloch, & Ernst-Barrington, 1992). The secretary of Health and Human Services and the director of the Los Angeles County Department of Mental Health requested the assistance of the task force in responding to the riots. The task force and Lifeplus Foundation, with which the division had been working, responded, preparing materials for teachers and administrators that were circulated to every school district in Los Angeles County, training trainers, writing grant proposals, and so on. The task force was continuing its activity to include Hurricanes Andrew and Iniki, providing assistance, training, and collecting research data, and was communicating with persons in war-torn Croatia on interventions with children. It was also developing a trauma hotline with Los Angeles print and electronic media to provide psychological support and information during a disaster.

In a personal communication (September 8, 1996), Jack G. Wiggins indicated that it was as a result of working with Ellin Bloch, Ellen McGrath, and Jon Perez that he, in his position as president of the APA, created the APA Disaster Response Network as the APA's centennial gift to the nation in 1992.

Task Force on Children and Adolescents

Formed sometime before 1988 and chaired by Alice K. Rubenstein, this task force planned programs for midwinter and APA meetings and worked on legal and ethical issues in psychotherapy with children and adolescents. In 1988, the focus was on producing a brochure on psychotherapy with children and adolescents to be used by clinicians for parents. Letters of inquiry were written to all state psychological associations regarding confidentiality and ethical issues in psychotherapy with children and adolescents, and the responses received were collated. In 1991 the brochure on "Psychotherapy With Children and Adolescents" was printed and by 1993 had sold 57,800 copies and was the best-selling brochure the division had ever produced.

The task force worked closely with the Task Force on Trauma Response and Research, particularly during the Persian Gulf crisis, providing excellent materials quickly to meet public needs. In 1993, working in conjunction with its counterpart in Division 42 (Psychologists in Independent Practice), the task force initiated a well-received survey on the extent of training in adolescent psychology in graduate, postgraduate, and internship programs. The results of this survey were published in the special issue of *Psychotherapy* on adolescents (Rubenstein & Zager, 1995).

Task Force on Managed Care

In 1994, Stanley R. Graham, the division's president-elect (and the only two-term president in the division) proposed a task force on managed care that he chaired, the purpose of which was to identify through member reports, experiences psychologists have had with health care companies that may have involved questionable policies and practices. The task force planned to compile this information in an attempt to be responsible and search out means by which legal remedies might be pursued. Graham, working with a group that included Harry Sands and Arthur L. Kovacs, addressed many issues concerning managed care and kept the board and membership apprised of the ongoing events involved.

Graham's efforts culminated in May of 1995 in a forum on managed care, a joint venture of the APA Committee for the Advancement of Professional Practice (CAPP) and Divisions 29, 42 (Psychologists in Independent Practice), 43 (Family Psychology), and 39 (Psychoanalysis) leaders, proportionally represented, who met and engaged in dialogue concerning the survival of the profession. It is important to note that for many years, the division had been addressing the felt need to work more closely with CAPP and the Practice Directorate. Progress was being made, concerns of the practice divisions were being addressed by a most cooperative CAPP, and this conference was a landmark event, which, it is hoped, will be the first of a series of annual retreats or forums to provide opportunities for exchanges and brainstorming, to help practitioners and play a role in shaping the APA's practice agenda. At present, a CAPP subcommittee is charged with working on integrating the diverse practice agendas of divisions and with planning another retreat.

OTHER TASK FORCES, COMMITTEES, AND LIAISONS

There is not space to detail all of the work of a group that has been in existence for 36 years. But it seems appropriate at least to indicate the broad spectrum of interests and contributions that have been reflected by the working groups formed by mentioning a few of those created just in the past 10 years.

Task Force on the Elderly and Task Force on Aging

The Task Force on the Elderly was established in 1987. Its follow-up, the Task Force on Aging, is developing recommendations about the education and training experiences needed by trainees to be competent to work clinically with older adults and is working to establish an American Board of Professional Psychology (ABPP) diploma in gerontology.

Task Force on Men's Roles in Psychotherapy

The Task Force on Men's Roles in Psychotherapy has presented programs and linked up with an emerging network of men who treat troubled men. The task force offered information to psychologists to assist men to become less bound up in traditional roles and to become freer, more nurturing, and more oriented toward expressing their feelings. The task force developed, and its chair, Ronald F. Levant edited a special series of seven articles on men's roles and psychotherapy, published in *Psychotherapy* (1990). A drive to form The Society for the Psychological Study of Men and Masculinity was successful (Division 51).

Task Force on American Indian Mental Health

This task force was appointed in 1990 and worked on goals and priorities for meeting the mental health needs of American Indians and determining the need and possible funding sources for a National Conference on American Indian Mental Health.

Committees

A variety of ad hoc committees have been devoted to research, history, ethical issues, committee structure, bylaws, professional standards, international issues, legislation, and so on.

Liaisons

Liaisons have been appointed to other APA governance entities—for example, the Committee for the Advancement of Professional Practice, the Committee on International Relations in Psychology, the Board of Professional Affairs, the Task Force on Scope of Accreditation, the Continuing Education Sponsor Approval Committee, the Committee on Professional Standards, and so forth.

CONCLUSION

The division has always been generous in giving moral and financial support to worthy causes related to the needs of the membership. Its legislative activities were legion, given practitioner concerns in this area, and I might note that of the 57 recipients of the APA Heiser Award for Advocacy given in 1992, 25 were members of this division. Monetary contributions were made both to the California School of Professional Psychology and the Wright State School of Professional Psychology as concrete expressions of support. And $1000 was contributed to the Virginia Psychological Association to help in their battle against the "Virginia Blues" (Blue Cross and Blue Shield), which refuses to make insurance payments for mental health services provided by a psychologist–psychotherapist. The division voted a $5000 forgivable loan to help defray the expenses of the Group for the Advancement of Psychotherapy and Psychoanalysis in their suit against the American Psychoanalytic Association, which was denying psychologists entry into training programs in psychoanalysis. In 1981, $20,000 was donated to the Special Projects Fund of the Association for the Advancement of Psychology (AAP) for legal services in challenging the denial of hospital privileges to psychologists by the Joint Commission on Accreditation of Hospitals. And in 1992 another major contribution was made to the $100 for 100 Days campaign, to raise funds to work on health care reform on the federal level, launched by CAPP.

Keeping in mind the division's multiple interests involving psychotherapy, it was necessary to direct strong efforts not only toward survival in the marketplace but also toward programs involving training and research in the area of psychotherapy. Since 1970, the division has been attempting to form coalitions with other divisions in order to pool resources, ideas, and energy. In 1973, it organized the Interdivisional Committee for Professional and Applied Psychology, composed of ten divisions and representatives from the APA's central office and CAPPS. It tried again in 1980 and 1986, and then in 1988, when, at the midwinter meeting, a coalition of practice divisions was formed. There is now an executive round table of practice divisions in which Division 29 participates.

The division is willing to make changes to accommodate the needs of the profession and the membership. There was a recognition that the division's scholarly activities, particularly its journal, were a great and unique strength of the division. And we recognized that we and the other practice divisions needed to coordinate activities more effectively, develop proactive strategies in the advocacy areas, and unite to define and protect our common interests. And we followed through as best we could.

A self-examination is once again in process, with the executive committee and board of directors taking a critical look at the mission and vision of the division. Brainstorming and thoughtful discussion have led to creative suggestions for reorganization of the division, a reordering of priorities and programs, and a focus on increasing interdivisional activities. Exciting change is in the air.

REFERENCES

Barron, J., Fabrikant, B., & Krasner, J. D. (1972). *Psychotherapy: A psychological perspective*. Division of Psychotherapy.

Barron, J., & Fabrikant, B. (1984). Psychotherapy and psychotherapists. *Psychotherapy Bulletin, 18*(4), 12–13.

Canter, M. B. (1992). *A history of the division of psychotherapy, american psychological association*. Phoenix, AZ: Division of Psychotherapy.

Canter, M. B., & McGrath, E. (1978). Program development—Your guide to getting it on. *Psychotherapy Bulletin, 11*, 12–15.

Committee for Women. (1989). Depression in clinical practice questionnaire. *Psychotherapy Bulletin, 24*, insert.

Embry, D., & Rubenstein, A. (1991). *They're coming home: A guide for parents of infants and toddlers*. Tucson, AZ: Project Me and USO.

Freedheim, D. K. (Ed.). (1992). *History of psychotherapy: a century of change*. Washington, DC: American Psychological Association.

Gendlin, E. T. (Ed.). (1964). *Psychotherapy, 1*, 1.

Goodheart, C. (1989). Practitioners speak out on women and depression: A report on the CFW survey of division 29 members. *Psychotherapy Bulletin, 24*, 48–50.

Lee, S. S., Resnick, J. L., & Clamar, A. (1982). Lifestyle and work patterns of psychotherapists in the division of psychotherapy. *Psychotherapy Bulletin, 16*(4), 17–18.

Lerman, H. (1984). *Sexual intimacies between psychotherapists and patients*. Kinderkamack, NJ: Committee for Women, Division of Psychotherapy.

Lerman, H. (1990). *Sexual intimacies between psychotherapists and patients*. Phoenix, AZ: Committee for Women, Division of Psychotherapy.

Levant, R. F. (Ed.). (1990). Special series on men's roles and psychotherapy. *Psychotherapy*, *27*, 309–349.

Mahrer, A. R., & Pearson, L. (Eds.) (1973). *Creative directions in psychotherapy*. New York: Jason Aaronson Press. [Original issue 1971, Cleveland, OH: The Press of Case Western Reserve University]

McGrath, E., & Wexler, H. (1990). Trauma and post-traumatic stress disorder: New research possibilities for psychotherapists. *Psychotherapy Bulletin*, *25*, 16–18.

Perez, J., Bloch, E., & Ernst-Barrington, S. (1992). The Los Angeles civil unrest: A report from the task force on trauma response and research regarding intervention in large scale disasters. *Psychotherapy Bulletin*, *27*, 6–9.

PIAP Bulletin. (1961, July). Vol 1(1).

PIAP Bulletin. (1963, June). Vol 3(1).

PIAP Bulletin. (1964). Vol. 4(2).

Psychotherapy Bulletin. (1968, June). Vol. 1(2).

Rosenthal, V. (1994). Twenty-nine in the sun: Some reflections on the beginnings of the Division 29 mid-winter meeting. *Psychotherapy Bulletin*, *29*, 19–20.

Rubenstein, A., & Embry, D. (1990). *They're coming home, Vol. 4*. Tucson, AZ: Project Me and USO.

Rubenstein, A., & Embry, D. (1991). *They're coming home: A guide for friends and relatives, schools, employers, co-workers, and the community*. Tucson, AZ: Project Me and USO.

Rubenstein, A., & Zager, K. (1995). Training in adolescent treatment: Where is psychology? *Psychotherapy*, *32*, 2–5.

8

A HISTORY OF DIVISION 35 (PSYCHOLOGY OF WOMEN): ORIGINS, ISSUES, ACTIVITIES, FUTURE

NANCY FELIPE RUSSO and B. ANGELA DUMONT

In 1995, the Division of Psychology of Women (Division 35) became the fourth largest division of the American Psychological Association (APA), its 6043 members a more than six-fold increase over the past 20 years (see Figure 3). Established in 1973, Division 35 has provided a power base and haven for feminists seeking to transform the generation and application of psychological knowledge and to enhance the status of women in the discipline. The creation of an institutional structure within the APA to nurture and support the emerging field of the psychology of women was a landmark step, a virtual paradigm shift, for thinking about the relationship of women and psychology. The words of Elizabeth Douvan, the first president of the division, were prophetic: "We are launched . . . the Division is destined

We would like to express our appreciation to several people for their help with this project: Jennifer Stalteri, a student intern with the Division 35 Archives, assembled and organized some of the material used as sources for this chapter. Arnie Kahn and Joanna Boehnert responded to our call for past issues of Division 35 newsletters, and Darnetta Bascomb provided Division 35 membership statistics. Martha Banks, Ludy Benjamin, Jr., Laura Brown, Gwen Keita, Bernice Lott, Martha Mednick, Naomi Meara, Saundra Murray Nettles, Cheryl Travis, Rhoda Unger, and Michele Wittig provided useful information and feedback.

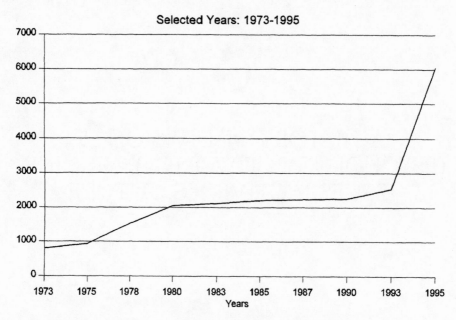

Selected Years: 1973-1995

Figure 3. Membership Growth, Division 35.

to be lively, responsive and productive ... The idea of a Division on the Psychology of women is clearly one of those ideas whose time has come" (Douvan, 1974, p. 3). The division's mission, as stated in the initial by-laws, was,

> To promote the research and the study of women, including both the biological and socio-cultural determinants of behavior. To encourage the integration of this information about women with the current psychological knowledge and beliefs in order to apply the gained knowledge to the society and its institutions. (Porter, 1989, p. 1)

The foothold inside the system was established, and it has been used to good advantage ever since.

Over the years, Division 35 has been so effective in getting things done that in 1993 president Janet Hyde was invited to speak at the APA's division leadership conference titled "How to Be an Effective Division Within the APA." She was told that "Division 35 was without doubt one of the most highly effective divisions within APA, and all the other divisions wanted to know how we did it," and observed "this division has an exceptional record of getting things done, *which is all the more remarkable because many of the things we want to get done are revolutionary and therefore prone to meet with resistance*" (Hyde, 1993, p. 2, italics ours).

ORIGINS

Appreciation of the significance of Hyde's remarks, and of the formation of Division 35 to the field of psychology, lies in understanding the history of women in the discipline. Efforts to raise consciousness about women's issues and to advance women's status in the discipline have been part of the field since its beginnings.

Historical Context

Early women pioneers who wrote and spoke against discrimination and devaluation of women in psychology and society include such luminaries as Christine Ladd-Franklin, Margaret Floy Washburn, Mary Whiton Calkins, Helen Thompson Woolley, and Leta S. Hollingworth (see O'Connell & Russo, 1990; Russo & O'Connell, 1980). Two of these women, Calkins and Washburn, went on to become presidents of the APA, in 1905 and 1921, respectively. The individual voices and accomplishments of distinguished women psychologists did not translate into systematic efforts to eliminate discrimination in the field, however (Mitchell, 1951). Indeed, some academic psychologists even considered it prestigious to belong to networks that explicitly excluded women, such as the Psychological Round Table (Benjamin, 1977).

It was not until World War II that women psychologists officially organized in the name of women's issues. Offended by the APA's failure to include the work of women psychologists in the organization's war efforts, the National Council of Women Psychologists (NCWP) was born "to promote and develop emergency services that women psychologists could render their communities" (Schwesinger, 1943). Although NCWP was successful in promoting women's contributions to wartime activities, it had no lasting impact on women's status in psychology, perhaps partially because of fear on the part of some of its leadership of being labeled feminist (Capshaw & Laszlo, 1986).[1] Its organizers stressed that NCWP should not be militant–suffragist in tone or emphasize the fact it was effectively a one-gender group (Schwesinger, 1943). After the war, the group changed its name to the International Council of Women Psychologists, and, in an attempt to affiliate with the APA, ultimately admitted men and became the International Council of Psychologists (Portenier, 1967). Attempts to affiliate with the APA were rebuffed by the organization, however, at first because it was a

---

[1] For a discussion of a variety of factors that may have contributed to the lack of lasting gains, see Katz, 1991.

"single-sex group" and later because it was an "international" organization. By defining the raising of concerns about women as unprofessional, women were silenced, and the status quo preserved (Walsh, 1986).

Proximate Events

The 1960s were a time of consciousness raising and activism throughout U.S. society. The modern women's movement emerged and began to transform women's ideas of themselves and their relationship to their institutions. Women in psychology were no exception. As president Carolyn Wood Sherif observed,

> Division 35 was formed on the cresting women's movement whose aims are economic, political and social equality. Emboldened to speak out by that historical context, we have continued to gain through the activity of that movement. Whether we were active in it from the Division's beginning, or became parts, or still prefer to regard ourselves as separate, the Division's existence and future are inseparably linked with it. (Sherif, 1979, p. 3)

In 1969, blatant sexism in employment recruitment at the APA convention galvanized women psychologists organizing convention protest action, and the Association for Women Psychologists (AWP—later the Association for Women in Psychology) was born. The AWP became an important voice for feminist psychologists and a critical outside power base for influencing the APA, helping to create the conditions that made establishing Division 35 possible, and providing a dual voice with Division 35 on feminist issues in psychology. Although part of Division 35's contribution has been to reform the APA from within, the division has maintained strong ties and collaboration with the AWP. Joint projects include a student research prize and a hospitality suite at the APA's annual convention that provides a place for conversation hours, book display, meeting and sleeping accommodations, and an annual party (see Tiefer, 1991, for a history of the AWP).

The success of the past two decades of feminist efforts in psychology can be seen in the contrast between yesterday's petitions and today's reality. In 1969, the APA council rejected a petition that asked psychology departments seeking accreditation to avoid "anti-female discrimination" policies on the grounds that it was a political issue and not relevant to assessing professional excellence (Tiefer, 1991). Today, gender-based discrimination is considered unethical behavior, and diversity is an important principle in the APA accreditation criteria. Other "radical" demands—for convention child care, nonsexist language on convention registration forms, and equal treatment in job interviews—are now standard practice. Another sign of change is found in the move from a 50-year absence of a woman president of the APA, from Washburn's term in 1921 until 1971, when Anne Anastasi was elected, followed by Leona Tyler in 1972. Since the founding of Division 35 in 1973, four women have been elected to the presidency of the APA: Florence Denmark (1980), Janet T. Spence (1984), Bonnie R. Strickland (1987) and Dorothy Cantor (1995)—all outspoken feminists and members of Division 35.

Forming the AWP was a courageous action, for raising women's issues brought charges of unprofessionalism. It is ironic to note that sexism did not violate the discipline's professional norms, and stories of disillusioning experiences abounded (e.g., Weisstein, 1971). At the APA convention, for example, "women graduate students were courted, ogled in elevators, invited to the bar and to parties, and pursued by the most eminent of men within our disciplines. . . . These contacts were sexist and shallow. . . . " (Lott, 1995, p. 315). The feminist psychologists who organized the AWP recognized that a fundamental shift had to be made in the definition of appropriate behavior for a psychologist. The APA bylaws professed ideals for promoting psychology as "a science, a profession, and a means for promoting human welfare" (APA, 1973, p. xi). The time had come to recognize that women were in fact human, and a focus on their welfare was an appropriate activity for psychologists.

As Martha Mednick observed in her 1977 divisional presidential address, "We can date the beginning of a necessary set of events for our formation with the start of our sister organization . . . AWP . . . and in particular with its totally unladylike though right-on behavior at the 1969 APA Convention" (Mednick, 1978, p. 124). In response to the AWP demands, in 1970, the APA appointed a task force on the status of women in psychology, chaired by Helen S. Astin. Charged with developing a position paper on the status of women in psychology, the task force undertook a 2-year study to document the disadvantaged status of women psychologists. In its final report, the group made a wide range of recommendations to redress inequities in the field so that women "would be accepted as fully enfranchised members of the profession" (Task Force on the Status of Women in Psychology, 1973, p. 611). The task force pointed out that "according to dominant clinical and therapeutic theories in psychology, women are biologically, intellectually, and morally inferior to men" (p. 613). They underscored the need for curriculum reform to include courses on "the psychology of women and the forces affecting their status" at undergraduate and graduate levels (p. 613). In December of 1972, the APA's board of directors established the ad hoc Committee on Women in Psychology (CWP), chaired by Martha Mednick and staffed by Tena Cummings, to follow through on the recommendations of the task force (the ad hoc committee was awarded continuing committee status in 1973). One of the committee's first recommendations was to establish a division of the psychology of women.

A task force to form Division 35, headed by Helen Astin, and composed of Tena Cummings, Martha Mednick, Lorraine Eyde, and Nancy Anderson, embarked on a concentrated effort to create the division. Anderson headed up the petition drive that culminated with 804 women and men as charter members (Division of the Psychology of Women, 1974). The petition for the Division of the Psychology of Women (Division 35) was formally approved by the APA's Council of Representatives at its 1973 annual meeting in Montreal, despite debate that included concerns about "ghettos" and "segregation" (Mednick & Urbanski, 1991). Division 35 was born, and a pro tem executive board was established with Elizabeth Douvan as president, Helen Astin as president-elect, and Lorraine Eyde as secretary–treasurer. Florence Denmark served as the first program chair for the division. Barbara Strudler Wallston and Rhoda Unger chaired elections and membership, respectively. Its first year, the division was awarded four seats on the APA's Council of Representatives, filled by Nancy S. Anderson, Annette Brodsky, Hannah Lerman, and Georgia Babladelis. Table 37 lists Division 35 presidents and individuals serving on the APA Council of Representatives.

ISSUES

Organizers of the division were aware that legitimizing research on women's lives and issues required directly addressing the societal forces that devalue and disadvantage women (Denmark, 1977). As president Martha Mednick observed, "The goals of expanding knowledge about women, legitimizing the field, and revising our discipline can only be achieved by an understanding of the sexism that is the basis of the exclusion and devaluation of all that is feminine" (Mednick, 1978, p. 134). The division's primary focus was thus to foster and nurture the growth of a feminist psychology of women and to create a knowledge base relevant to women's lives and useful for effecting social change.

Mednick and Urbanski (1991) discussed some of the ongoing issues and concerns raised during the division's formation. Achieving divisional goals required dealing with many issues, some of which continue to be ongoing concerns.

Naming the Division

One of the first issues raised in forming the division was what to call it. Naming the division and articulating its goals was an occasion for lively discussion. Whether or not the term "psychology of women" adequately reflects the nature and scope of the field stimulated substantial debate. A variety of names have been proposed over the years, including Psychology

TABLE 37
Division Presidents and APA Council Representatives

Presidents			
1973–1974	Elizabeth Douvan	1986–1987	Virginia E. O'Leary
1974–1975	Helen S. Astin	1987–1988	Ellen Kimmel
1975–1976	Florence L. Denmark	1988–1989	Nancy Felipe Russo
1976–1977	Martha T. S. Mednick	1989–1990	Lenore Walker
1977–1978	Annette M. Brodsky	1990–1991	Bernice Lott
1978–1979	Barbara Strudler Wallston	1991–1992	Pamela Trotman Reid
1979–1980	Carolyn Wood Sherif	1992–1993	Natalie Porter
1980–1981	Rhoda K. Unger	1993–1994	Janet Shibley Hyde
1981–1982	Michele A. Wittig	1994–1995	Norine Johnson
1982–1983	Mary Brown Parlee	1995–1996	Cheryl Travis
1983–1984	Irene Hanson Frieze	1996–1997	Laura S. Brown
1984–1985	Hannah Lerman	1997–1998	Judith Worell
1985–1986	Jacquelynne Eccles		

APA Council Representatives			
1974	Nancy Andersen	1985–1988	Pamela Trotman Reid
1974	Georgia Babladelis	1986–1989	Vickie Mays
1974	Hannah Lerman	1986–1989	Lucia A. Gilbert
1974–1975	Annette Brodsky	1988–1991	Cheryl Travis
1974–1978	Tena Cummings	1989–1992	Virginia E. O'Leary
1975	Martha T. S. Mednick		(resigned 1989)
1976–1977	Virginia E. O'Leary	1989–1992	Florence Denmark
1976–1979	Rhoda Unger		(replaced O'Leary)
1977–1980	Michele Wittig	1989–1992	Lillian Comas-Díaz
1978–1980	Helen Astin	1991–1993	Hannah Lerman
1978–1981	JoAnn Evansgardner	1992–1995	Nancy Felipe Russo
1979–1982	Lucia A. Gilbert	1992–1995	Gail E. Wyatt
1980–1985	Kathleen Grady	1993–1996	Lenore Walker
1982–1985	Ellen Kimmel	1995–1997	Janis Sanchez-Hucles
1983–1986	Phyllis Katz	1996–1999	Annette Brodsky
1985–1988	Lenore Walker	1997–2000	Nancy Felipe Russo

of Women and Sex Roles, Women, Gender and Psychology, New Psychology of Women, Feminist Psychology, and Psychology and Women (Gardner, 1976; Mednick, 1976; Parlee, 1975). The debate continues.

Inclusion

A central and ongoing concern for the division has been how to develop an organization that would fit into the APA's hierarchical structure yet reflect core values of inclusion, openness, and egalitarianism. Like all divisions, Division 35 has a hierarchical structure, with a board of elected officers and bylaws that set out formal policies and procedures. But within that overall structure, the division has created an internal organization that encourages wide participation.

The executive committee meets twice a year, at the APA convention and at midwinter, typically in the city in which the president resides. Everyone involved in the division is invited to participate in executive committee meetings. This means that in addition to elected officers, meeting participants include editors of the newsletter, journal, and book series, heads of sections, chairs of committees and task forces, and a varying number of individuals appointed to liaison or monitor positions designed to provide links between the division and other groups. Everyone present has an equal voice in the discussion, and typically, decisions are made by consensus. Efforts to maintain openness while respecting the responsibilities of elected officers have led to many earnest but amicable discussions about who gets to vote when in executive committee meetings. Overall, there has been a commitment to the standard, well-stated by Bernice Lott, of "open communication, feminist sensibility, and mutual respect" (1990, p. 2).

Diversity

Achieving the goal of inclusion and respect for all women's concerns has also meant recognizing women's diversity. "Feminism . . . must recognize that women's realities are complex and carry diverse types of oppression" (Comas-Díaz, 1991, p. 597). As O'Connell and Russo have observed, "the feminist task is paradoxical: it involves valuing diverse perspectives and experiences among women, while seeking unity of cause and purpose for women" (1991, p. 677). Struggling with this paradox continues to be an ongoing challenge to the division, with issues raised by diversity stemming from a variety of sources, including age, class, gender, ethnicity, race, sexual orientation, disability, and subfield.

Male Involvement

Given the division's emphasis on inclusion and diversity, it is not surprising that another recurring issue for some has been the relatively low level of involvement of men in the division. Others, however, have argued "our resources and energy are finite. Diverting our resources now into male psychology would be another example of how women are 'supposed' to consider themselves last" (Marlowe, 1976, p. 16). In 1996, about 2% of the division's members were men. One man, Arnold Kahn, has held an elected office in the more than two decades of the division's history (secretary–treasurer, 1977–1980). Table 38 lists individuals holding the position of secretary–treasurer in Division 35.

At one point, the division even had a task force on the male sex role (1978–1979), chaired by Kathleen Grady, charged with recommending a

TABLE 38
Secretary/Treasurer[a]

	Secretary
1978–1989	Dona Alpert
1986–1987	Kathryn Knudsen
1989–1991	Natalie Porter
1991–1992	Margaret Madden
1992–1995	Rosalie J. Ackerman
1995–1997	Mary Gergen
1997–2000	Jan Yoder
	Treasurer
1978–1992	P. Kay Coleman
1986–1987	Sharon Toffey Shepela
1992–1996	Margaret Madden
	Secretary–Treasurer
1973–1974	Lorraine Eyde
1974–1977	Barbara Strudler Wallston
1977–1980	Arnold Kahn
1980–1982	Jeanne Marecek
1982–1985	Charlene Depner
1985–1986	Julia Ramos-McKay

[a] The position of secretary–treasurer was separated into two positions in 1986.

policy on male sex role issues and the division. It concluded that there was little support for a separate section on men's issues but that the APA had an organizational and political vacuum in the area that would increase and ultimately require formalization. In 1995, that vacuum was filled, and the executive committee voted to support the proposal for what ultimately became Division 51 of the APA—The Society for the Psychological Study of Men and Masculinity. A division monitor was also appointed to observe and report opportunities for collaborative activities.

Subfield Diversity

The fact that Division 35's concerns cross-cut psychology's traditional subfields is considered a source of strength and stimulation for the organization. But being part of the APA has meant that at times the division has had to resist becoming embroiled in larger organizational issues that create a divide between science, practice, and public interest concerns. During the 1980s, debates over the organization of the APA became particularly painful for the division, as leaders in Division 35 were on both sides of the issue.

In 1988, in a tense midwinter meeting, president Ellen Kimmel set aside a massive agenda to a discussion of the APA reorganization. In one of the few meetings where an official vote was taken and only the designated voting members of the executive committee cast ballots, the decision was made to support the APA's reorganization plan to be placed as a bylaw vote before the membership. It was a tribute to Ellen Kimmel's even-handed leadership that afterward voices on both sides expressed their belief that the discussion had been fair and respectful of all views. The division's commitment to transforming psychology in all of its aspects, from basic research to all forms of application, continues to be a unifying force across members with diverse backgrounds, work settings, and other characteristics that have proved divisive to the field as a whole.

ACTIVITIES

Becoming a division of the APA meant access to program time at the APA's annual meeting (16 hours the first year), so that feminists "no longer had to beg, borrow and steal from other divisions or a tight-fisted convention board for a chance to present our work" (Mednick, 1976, p. 1). It also made the division eligible for representation on the APA's Council of Representatives and granted the power to publish a journal with the imprimatur of the APA division, confer awards and honors, and establish a newsletter, committees, and task forces to pursue a feminist agenda for psychology.

The first meeting of the division's executive committee focused on crystallizing goals: to "focus scientific and intellectual energies on the psychology of women, sex roles and related topics . . . to stimulate research, facilitate communication of research findings among professionals, and to disseminate information to broader publics" (Douvan, 1974, p. 3). Toward that end, the division launched a newsletter, edited by Tena Cummings and Nancy Anderson. Published four times a year, it provided a means to build solidarity with the membership. In addition to the opportunity for presidents to express their visions in a president's message, the newsletter enabled open calls for nominations, communication about actions taken in meetings, highlights of the convention program, and information on feminist activities and materials. (Table 39 lists newsletter editors.)

In 1995, communication among division members took a technological leap and went on-line with POWR-L, the division's electronic network, moderated by Kathryn Quina. The purpose of POWR-L is "to facilitate discussion of current topics, research, teaching strategies, and practice issues among people interested in the psychology of women, and to publicize

TABLE 39
Psychology of Women Newsletter and
Psychology of Women Quarterly Editors

Psychology of Women Newsletter	
1974–1975	Nancy Anderson, Tena Cummings
1975–1976	JoAnn Evansgardner, Sandra S. Tangri, Tena Cummings
1977–1979	Virginia E. O'Leary, Barbara Reimer
1979–1981	Pamela Trotman Reid, Cheryl B. Travis
1981–1983	M. Marlyne Kilbey, Dorothy Stewart
1983–1984	M. Marlyne Kilbey
1984–1986	Dona Alpert, Nancy Young
1986–1988	Sheryle Alagna, Patricia Morokoff
1988–1990	Sheryle [Alagna] Gallant, Renee Royak-Schaler
1988–1991	Renee Royak-Schaler
1991–1994	Kathryn Quina
1994–1997	Jan Yoder

Psychology of Women Quarterly	
1975–1980	Georgia Babladelis
1980–1985	Nancy M. Henley
1985–1989	Janet Shibley Hyde
1989–1994	Judith Worell
1995–1999	Nancy Felipe Russo

AWP/Div 35 information, conferences, job announcements, calls for papers, publications, and the like" (Quina, 1995, p. 20).

The Psychology of Women Quarterly

One of the executive committee's first actions was to move to establish a peer-reviewed journal. As Mednick and Urbanski (1991) have observed, establishing *The Psychology of Women Quarterly (PWQ)* was "the step most critical to legitimizing research in the field." The first issue appeared in the fall of 1976. Georgia Babladelis, the first editor (1975–1980), set an ambitious course for the journal: "It is time to ask hard questions about established facts and to explore new questions and find new facts. In doing so surely we follow an old tradition of taking nothing for granted, for it is said 'when the Queen of Sheba heard of the fame of Solomon . . . she came to prove him with hard questions'" (Babladelis, 1976, p. 4).

The journal's mandate was to publish "empirical studies, critical reviews, theoretical articles, and invited book reviews" encompassing a wide variety of topics including "psychobiological factors, behavior studies, role development and change, career choice and training, management variables, education, discrimination, therapeutic processes, and sexuality" (*PWQ*, 1976, p. 2). (Table 39 lists *PWQ* editors.)

Book Series

Over the years, *PWQ* published a variety of special issues sold separately as edited books, but they did not fill the field's need for a wide range of publication outlets. In 1990, the executive committee voted to explore the possibility of a monograph series independent of *PWQ*. After extensive deliberations, a contractual arrangement was made with the APA to publish a Division 35 book series, edited by Cheryl Travis. The first book in the series, *Bringing Cultural Diversity to Feminist Psychology: Theory, Research, and Practice,* appeared in 1995. Edited by Hope Landrine (1995), the book is an outcome of a 1990 to 1992 task force on cultural diversity in feminist psychology, which Landrine chaired.

The Convention Program

Program chair Florence Denmark received more than 50 submissions for the division's first program at the APA convention. Elizabeth Douvan delivered a presidential address (Douvan, 1976), Jessie Barnard and Dorothy Robins-Mowry gave invited addresses, and the wide variety of session topics included the psychology of menstruation, mastectomy, gender differences and roles, dual careers, achievement, and women's studies. The convention "brought women together, and . . . provided a place for exchange of ideas" (Mednick, 1978, p. 129). The enthusiasm generated by the division's high-quality convention programming is reflected in increases in program time over the years, from 16 hours in 1974 to a high of 51 hours in 1996 (program time allocation is based on convention attendance).

Program innovations of Division 35 include the open symposium, which was "designed to provide an innovative participative structure for . . . presentation of research. All those who submit . . . will be able to present" (Mednick, 1977, p. 1). A report on the symposium held at the APA meetings in 1979 showed it to be enormously popular (Major, 1979). The division's author's fair in 1979 became widely adopted in the APA as poster sessions. Another innovation occurred in 1983, when the division voted to set aside 20% of its program time for minority women's concerns. In 1984, roundtable discussions were organized (Highlights of the Division 35 Business Meeting, 1984, p. 3), and in 1991 the executive committee voted to eliminate paper sessions entirely from the convention program (Task Force on Policy and Procedures, 1995). Social hours also became occasions for celebrating achievements of members and expressing appreciation for division service. Creative expressions of appreciation, unity, and bonding at these social hours have included poster sales, feminist songs, and huge layer cakes shared by all (in addition, of course, to traditional forms of appreciation such as plaques and certificates).

Not all of the innovations were on the regular program, however. For example, Division 35 joined with the AWP to organize teach-ins on women's issues at the national level and within the APA. The immediate products of these events were resolutions presented at the APA's open forum (Division 35 Newsletter, 1982, p. 8) and fact sheets on critical legislative issues (Wells, 1982).

In addition to participating in the APA's annual meeting, the division has sponsored or hosted a variety of conferences, locally, nationally, and internationally. Such conferences provide opportunities for feminist organizing as well as scholarly exchange. On the local level, annual conferences organized in conjunction with the division's midwinter meeting provide an opportunity to "give feminist psychology" away to audiences who might not typically attend national meetings. On the international level, Division 35 provided key organizing leadership for the First International Interdisciplinary Congress on Women, organized by Marilyn Safir, Dafne Izraeli, and Martha Mednick, and held in Haifa, Israel, in 1981. That successful organization has subsequently met in the Netherlands, Ireland, the United States, Costa Rica, and Australia. The seventh meeting will be held in Norway in 1999.

The APA's Council of Representatives

Being able to participate in the APA's policy-making body, the Council of Representatives, was one of the prime reasons to organize as an APA division. In addition to determining the policies and procedures of the association, the council elects members of the APA Continuing Committees and Boards, including the APA's board of directors. One of the first acts of Division 35 council representatives was to organize a Women's Caucus of Council, seen as an essential step for ensuring women's equal participation in the APA. This was a radical idea. As Mednick and Urbanski pointed out, "in 1974, when the first caucus meeting was called by Division 35 representatives, it was held in secret; some women attended but others refused to do so" (1991, p. 656).

A leader on minority issues in council, in 1985 Division 35 took another radical step: institutionalizing a minority slate for one of its council seats to ensure minority representation from the division. In 1986, Pamela Trotman Reid took her seat as Division 35's first minority council representative.

In 1977, Division 35 council representatives initiated a motion developed by Tena Cummings and Nancy Felipe Russo to establish a women's programs office staffed by a full-time senior-level psychologist whose specialty area was psychology of women. The office was established. The first major task of the newly appointed head of the office, Russo, was to follow up on

Division 35's other successful motion at the meeting: that the APA not hold or negotiate to hold its annual meeting in any state that had not ratified the Equal Rights Amendment (ERA).

The division had decided to play hardball on ERA support, to the point of itself promising to boycott the APA convention, refuse to fill its program hours, and encourage members not to attend should the APA council fail to pass the motion (Wittig, 1977). The resolution's passage, over substantial opposition, was a tribute to Division 35's leadership and the power and organization of the Women's Caucus (Division of the Psychology of Women, 1977). That resolution forced the APA to cancel conventions in Atlanta, Las Vegas, and New Orleans. Later, president Annette Brodsky identified the division's support for the ERA as her most enduring memory. It meant that she was the first division president unable to host the division's midwinter meeting at her home institution (University of Alabama).

Over the years, Division 35 council representatives have been an important voice for public interest issues in psychology. Michele Wittig expressed the division's commitment to these issues in her 1982 president's letter: "Division 35 is determined to build coalitions with other Divisions and organizations that believe psychology must not withdraw from integrating scholarly and professional concerns with those of the public welfare" (p. 1). Implementing this commitment has meant Division 35 has taken leadership on a wide variety of issues, including changes in accreditation criteria to reflect diversity, convention child care, prohibition of sexual intimacy between client and therapist in the APA ethics code, nonsexist language in APA publications, affirmative action, sexual harassment, violence against women, and reproductive choice.

Honors and Awards

Divisional status provided a means to nominate individuals for APA fellow status and confer awards. The decision to do so was not without debate. On the one hand, there was the desire to eschew elitism; on the other was the desire to empower, legitimize, and recognize feminist contributors to psychology. The division came down on the side of conferring status and working to develop award criteria that would reflect feminist issues and priorities. As of 1996, 209 individuals had been elected to fellow status in recognition of "sustained and outstanding contributions to the field."

The division has established several awards to recognize the efforts of feminist psychologists. In 1982, the executive committee agreed to establish The Carolyn Wood Sherif Memorial Lectureship Award to commemorate the contributions of an inspirational Division 35 president (Mednick & Russo, 1983). In 1984, Rhoda Unger became the first award recipient (see Table 40).

TABLE 40
Carolyn Wood Sherif Award and Heritage Award Recipients

Carolyn Wood Sherif Award Recipients	
1984	Rhoda Unger
1985	Nancy Henley
1986	Barbara Strudler Wallston (posthumously)
1987	Kay Deaux
1988	Martha T. S. Mednick
1989	Irene Hanson Frieze
1990	Ravenna Helson
1991	Florence Denmark
1992	Helen Astin
1993	Nancy Felipe Russo
1994	Phyllis Katz
1995	Gail E. Wyatt
1996	Faye Crosby, Bernice Lott
Heritage Award Recipients	
1992	Mary Brown Parlee (Research)
	Florence L. Denmark (Service)
	Carol Ann Tavris (Publication)
	Rachel T. Hare-Mustin (Practice)
	Nancy Felipe Russo (Policy)
1993	Kay Deaux (Research), Nancy Henley, Florence Geis (Policy), Agnes O'Connell (Publication)
1994	Barbara Gutek, Arnold Kahn (Research)
1995	Bernice Lott (Policy)
1996	Janet Shibley Hyde (Publication)

In 1985, a Research Award on Psychotherapeutic Interventions with Women was established, supported by royalties from *Women and Psychotherapy: An Assessment of Research and Practice* (Brodsky & Hare-Mustin, 1980). The book was a compilation of work presented at a joint APA-NIMH conference held in 1979, coordinated by Nancy Felipe Russo through the APA's Women's Programs Office. The idea for the conference began as a Division 35 project by president Annette Brodsky, the first clinical president of the division. Brodsky worked with Irene Elkin Waskow at NIMH, Russo at the APA, and Rachel Hare-Mustin to organize the conference. Brodsky and Hare-Mustin edited the resulting book (1980), and the royalties were designated to support the division. In addition to the substantive impact of this activity, it provides a useful model for revenue-producing divisional projects.

The Barbara Strudler Wallston Award for the Representation of Under-represented Groups in the Publication Process has been developed to recognize journals that show the most progress in this area. It was established in

1988 in memory of Wallston, for whom this issue was of critical importance (Porter, 1989).

In 1991, in response to a recommendation of the Task Force on History chaired by Agnes O'Connell, five Heritage Awards were established (O'Connell, 1990). These awards recognize sustained and outstanding contributions in the areas of policy, practice, publication, research, and APA service. The first recipients of these awards were Florence (Lindy) Geis (Research) and Nancy M. Henley, (Publication). (See Table 40 for a list of Heritage award recipients.)

In 1993, the division received a generous bequest from the estate of Florence Lindauer (Lindy) Geis to establish a fund for scholarships for women pursuing graduate study in feminist psychology. A pioneer in feminist teaching, research, and advocacy, Geis was a woman of strong charisma who inspired devoted students and made important contributions to understanding discrimination and prejudice against female leaders (Eagly, 1994).

In addition, two awards support student efforts. The joint AWP–Division 35 prize to recognize outstanding basic or applied psychological research on women by graduate or undergraduate students, is awarded annually. The eligible areas of research can vary widely, as long as it is significantly related to women's lives or to the psychological understanding of gender role influences on behavior. The division also provides support for doctoral student research projects through the Hyde Graduate Student Research Grants Competition, established in 1996. This program is funded by royalties from Janet Hyde's book, *Half the Human Experience*.

Substantive Undertakings

In 1995, the executive committee reflected on the many activities and issues of the division, "re-visioning" the description of the division's substantive activities used in the APA publications. That description provides a concise overview of the division's substantive work:

> Promotes feminist research, theories, education, and practice toward understanding and improving the lives of girls and women in all their diversities. Encourages scholarship on the social construction of gender relations across multicultural contexts, and applies its scholarship to transforming the knowledge base and practice of psychology. Advocates action toward public policies that advance equality and social justice, and seeks to empower women in community, national, and global leadership. (Worell, 1995)

Over the years, this substantive work has been conducted by a host of divisional task forces and committees focusing on a wide variety of areas related to research, teaching, and practice. A sampling of topics encompasses affirmative action, concerns of women over 40, the Equal Rights Amendment, child custody, lesbian issues, international perspectives, master's-level psychologists, mentoring, poverty, prescription privileges, reproductive freedom, sexual harassment, social class, sociobiology, family and work, religion, technology, epistemology, women and HIV, and teaching and curriculum issues. Although space precludes treatment of all of them, four recurrent themes deserve special attention: research, teaching and curriculum, practice, and diversity issues.

Research

The first ad hoc committee on research was created in 1974 by President Helen Astin. Chaired by Ethel Tobach, the Committee on Research Guidelines identified sexism in the APA's *Ethical Principles on the Conduct of Research With Human Participants* and proposed guidelines for correcting it (Research Guidelines Committee, 1975). Later research committee recommendations included the development of support networks for women researchers, more program time at the APA conventions to present research, elimination of sex discrimination, and grant application assistance networks (Sachs & Vaughter, 1976). One outcome of this work was a report, *Setting Priorities for Research on Women* (Crull, 1976), that articulated a variety of substantive issues and recommended a "clearinghouse for women in research" (p. 6). The following year, the Task Force on Women Doing Research identified gender-specific barriers to research in psychology, emphasizing the need for female role models to aid in acculturation of women into nontraditional occupational roles highlighted in Elizabeth Douvan's presidential address (O'Connell et al., 1978). One outcome of this task force was the organization of a variety of symposia honoring eminent women in psychology, jointly sponsored by Psi Chi and a variety of other divisions (O'Connell & Russo, 1983, 1988).

Other issues have revolved around research methods (Wallston, 1979). In 1980, an assessment of research needs expressed concern about the direction of the field, the generative quality of the work, and the poor state of theory development (Mednick & Urbanski, 1991). In 1981, Rhoda Unger's presidential address tackled these issues from another direction— exploring the extent to which conceptual and methodological issues are related and arguing for a "valued-imbued," reflexive science of psychology (Unger, 1983, p. 26). Concern for methods was also reflected in a 1986 task force on nonsexist research, which created *Guidelines for Nonsexist Research* that were widely distributed (McHugh, Koeske, & Frieze, 1986). Those guidelines were also the catalyst for the APA's task force on nonsexist research (Denmark, Russo, Frieze, & Sechzer, 1988).

In 1988, a task force on feminist research and epistemology, chaired by Mary Crawford, provided an important forum for discussions about feminist methods. It stimulated the development of a special issue of the *Psychology of Women Quarterly* co-edited by Mary Crawford and Jeanne Marecek that included an important task force bibliography (Crawford & Marecek, 1989). This agenda has continued to be pursued by subsequent task forces on innovative research methods. Mary Crawford and Ellen Kimmel are editing a special issue of *PWQ* on innovative methods of feminist research that is scheduled to appear in 1998.

Teaching and Curriculum

Transmission of knowledge—to students, colleagues, and the public—has been another recurring theme throughout the division's history. Several task forces have examined teaching and curriculum issues. In 1979, the division passed a resolution stating that "a core curriculum in the psychology of women be required for psychologists providing psychological services to women" (Task Force on Policy and Procedures, 1989, p. 60). Thus began an ultimately successful campaign to get attention to diversity issues in the accreditation process. Also in that year, a task force on teaching the psychology of women was established, first chaired by Jeanne Gullahorn (1979–1980) and then by Sharon Golub (1983). One product of the task force was a book containing resources for mainstreaming information about the psychology of women into standard offerings (Golub & Friedman, 1987). During this period, *PWQ* sponsored a special issue on teaching, edited by Marilyn Johnson (1982). In 1997, a second *PWQ* special issue on teaching gender and ethnicity is planned, co-edited by Janet Hyde and Margaret Madden.

In 1989, the Task Force on Mainstreaming Feminist Psychology in Education, chaired by Mary Kay Biaggio, highlighted the need to incorporate the "significant scholarship in the area of feminist psychology over the last two decades" (Biaggio, 1990, p. 1) into other, traditional areas of psychology. Following up in 1990, the Gender Issues and Women in Psychology Textbooks Task Force, headed by Ellen Kimmel, analyzed representations of gender in psychology textbooks, presented at the APA meetings as a symposium. Kimmel (1991a) reported superficial changes had occurred in photographs, language usage, and elimination of most sexism and racism. However, the theory and data that make up the substance of psychology—the areas over which publishers have little control—had not changed. The task force concluded that there would be a continued need to monitor textbooks for gender and race bias and to mainstream new scholarship. It developed a scoring manual to "continue to monitor this issue and for comparison purposes over time" (Kimmel, 1991b, p. 1). In 1995, the Task Force on Representation of People of Color in the Curriculum (1995), chaired by Margaret Madden, prepared a pamphlet, "Including Diverse Women in the Undergraduate Curriculum," oriented to serve instructors of lower-level psychology courses.

One of the most well-received teaching activities is a continuing education teaching workshop held in conjunction with the APA's annual convention. First organized by Mary Roth Walsh in 1988, the workshop became an annual event. It is designed for graduate students, beginning faculty, and more experienced faculty who wish to enrich their teaching.

Practice

In 1976, the Task Force on Clinical Treatment and Practice, chaired by Rachel Hare-Mustin, developed a network of regional coordinators for task force activities. One of the enduring accomplishments of the task force was organizing a successful action to change the wording of the APA's ethical standards to clearly state "Sexual intimacies with patients are unethical" (Hare-Mustin, 1976).

An early product of the division was the development of a widely distributed consumer handbook on women and psychotherapy developed by Nechama Liss-Levinson in a joint project between the AWP and Division 35 (Liss-Levinson et al., 1985). This handbook was published and distributed by the Federation of Organizations for Professional Women.

In 1982, the division began steps to reach out to practitioners and clinical students. Barbara Claster and Jeanne Marecek, chairs of the Task Force on Clinical Training and Practice, organized a meeting at the APA convention to devise a plan for outreach efforts. The purpose of the task force was "to improve the treatment of women in mental health settings by helping to disseminate new knowledge about women to consumers, practitioners, clinical students, policy makers, researchers, and other providers of mental health services" (Claster & Marecek, 1983). The work begun by this task force became institutionalized with passage of a bylaw creating a standing committee on clinical issues in 1985.

In 1988, the executive committee voted to establish the Section on Feminist Professional Training and Practice,

> To provide a permanent organizational structure representing feminist perspectives on issues affecting training and practice within APA . . . to develop specifically feminist perspectives on issues affecting training in and practice of professional psychology, creating products which describe and advance the implementation of those perspectives, and advocating for those perspectives with bodies within and outside of APA making decisions on such issues. (Nutt, 1995)

TABLE 41
Section Presidents

Section 1: Section on the Psychology of Black Women	
1984–1986	Vickie Mays
1986–1988	Saundra Rice Murray (Nettles)
1988–1989	Peggy Carr
1989–1993	Veronica Thomas
1993–1995	Martha E. Banks
1995–1997	Lula Beatty
Section 2: Feminist Professional Training and Practice	
1990–1991	Lynne Bravo Rosewater
1991–1994	Norine Johnson & Lenore Walker
1994–1997	Roberta L. Nutt

The subsequent vote on the bylaws was successful, and the new section officially replaced the Committee on Clinical Training and Practice in 1990. Laura Brown and Dona Alpert cochaired the steering committee established to get the new section up and running, and Lynne Bravo Rosewater served as its first president (see Table 41 for a list of section presidents).

In 1993, the division supported the National Conference on Education and Training in Feminist Practice, organized by Division 35 president Norine Johnson and Judy Worell, in collaboration with Mary Brabeck, Jean Chin, and Karen Wyche. Practice was broadly defined to encompass research, teaching, and other psychological applications, and the conference was organized into working groups charged with developing a consensus on the feminist principles and goals in each area. A final plenary session collated the outcome of these groups, resulting in a consensus on feminist principles that can inform a feminist agenda for psychology into the twenty-first century. *Feminist Visions: New Directions for Research and Practice*, edited by Judy Worell and Norine Johnson (in press, 1997), will contain the reports of the working groups (theory, assessment, therapy, curriculum, pedagogy, supervision, research, diversity, postdoctoral training) expanded into chapters that tie the deliberations to relevant literatures. It will appear as the second book in Division 35's book series.

Diversity Issues

In its efforts to make psychology more inclusive and psychological knowledge more relevant to women's lives, the division has taken a broad definition of diversity, one that encompasses age, class, race, ethnicity, sexual orientation, and disability. In addition to having these concerns interwoven into the work of the committees and task forces focusing on other topics, attention to lesbian and ethnic minority issues have been institutionalized in the division's committee structure.

Lesbian Issues

The first task force on lesbian issues was established by President Michele Wittig, in 1983, with Laura Brown as its first chair. In 1986, it was established as a continuing committee on lesbian issues, first chaired by Robin Buhrke (1986–1987). In addition to organizing programs and activities around lesbian issues, the committee was an important source of support for organizing Division 44 (Society for the Psychological Study of Lesbian and Gay Issues), which was established in 1990. In 1996, Laura Brown become the division's first openly identified lesbian president.

Women of Color

As Comas-Díaz observed, "a diverse feminist psychology can afford systemic opportunities for women of color to organize, develop leaders, create their own agenda, and ensure that it is incorporated into the broader feminist agenda" (1991, p. 604). In particular, Division 35 has developed a variety of power bases and centers of activity used by women of color to define and pursue their own goals and enrich and broaden feminist psychology. As Mednick and Urbanski observed, although "painfully cognizant of the persistent gap between its reality and its ideals" (1991, p. 659), Division 35 has labored to make the psychology of women a field that reflects diversity. Division members have been conscious of "the parallels between racism and sexism" and committed to the concerns of minority women (Wallston, 1979, p. 1).

Although individual people of color had central roles in the events that led to the establishment of Division 35, including James A. Bayton and Tressie Muldrow, institutionalization of the concerns of women of color began in 1976 when president Martha Mednick asked Saundra Rice Murray (Nettles) to organize a task force on Black women's concerns. In addition to developing a bibliography of research on Black women, the task force organized APA programs to address concerns of women of color and worked to increase participation of Black women in the APA governance. Although their proposal to further institutionalize their work by establishing a standing committee on Black women's concerns stimulated considerable discussion and controversy (see Mednick & Urbanski, 1991), the proposal was supported and the change to the bylaws was subsequently approved by the membership.

In 1978, the Committee on Black Women's Concerns was official, with Pamela Trotman Reid as its first chair (1978–1980). The bibliography was expanded and a directory on *Black Women in Psychology* (Mays, 1984) was assembled for publication by the APA's Women's Program Office. Subsequent chairs were Gwendolyn Puryear Keita (cochaired with Reid, 1979–1980; chair, 1980–1982), and Vickie Mays (1982–1984).

In 1985, the bylaws were approved for a section on the psychology of Black women to replace the committee:

> The section shall have as specific goals to increase the scientific understanding of those aspects of culture and class which pertain to the psychology of Black women, and to increase the quality of education and training in the psychology of Black women. (Porter, 1989, p. 18)

The Section on the Psychology of Black Women emerged as an important organizing base for Black women, developing its own newsletter and award programs and expanding its convention programming. The section's annual fund-raising dance, held during the APA annual convention, supports a variety of activities, including help for students from South Africa, AIDS research, and the prochoice movement. In 1991, Pamela Trotman Reid became the first Black woman to become division president.

A task force on the concerns of Hispanic women was appointed in 1977. Chaired by Martha Bernal, the task force explored stresses experienced by Hispanic women psychologists and organized sessions on Hispanic women's issues at the APA convention. Hortensia Amaro undertook an ambitious directory project, expanding the initial task force roster into a full-fledged *Directory of Hispanic Women in Psychology* published by APA's Women's Programs Office (Amaro, 1984). The task force also obtained funds from the Wright Foundation to develop an annotated bibliography on psychological research on Hispanic women.

Task force chairs have included Margarita García (1978–1980), Oliva Espín (1980–1982), and Hortensia Amaro (1982–1986). In 1986, the task force became a standing committee, chaired by Angela Ginorio as chair. Subsequent chairs include Mimi Acosta (1990–1991), MaryAnn Santos de Barona (1991–1994), Sandra Pacheco (1994–1997), and Ivonne Romero (cochair with Sandra Pacheco, 1996–1997).

In addition to the Section on the Psychology of Black Women and the standing Committee on the Concerns of Hispanic Women, a series of task forces have addressed concerns of other ethnic minority women (Comas-Díaz, 1991). In 1980, in an effort to "locate and stimulate the interest of Asian American colleagues, both [to] benefit from their contributions and so that the Division could have their guidance in planning" (Sherif, 1979), the division established the first of a series of task forces on Asian women. The initial goal of the first task force on Asian American Women, chaired by Reiko Homma True, was "to form the groundwork of a solid . . . network [of] relationships among individual psychologists and other related people and to create linkage relationship[s] with other Asian American women's organizations" (True, 1980). Later task force chairs included Wanda Lee (1984–1986), Tina Yee and Jan Nakagawa (1986–1990), Jean Lau Chin (1991–1994), Tren Liang (1994–1995), and Sara Miyahara (1996–1997).

In 1984, the first task force on Native American women was established, with Teresa LaFromboise as chair. Subsequent task force chairs include Diane Willis (1992–1997) and Marigold Linton (cochair 1992–1993).

Through these structures, women of color have articulated their issues and concerns. In the words of Lillian Comas-Díaz, "women of color have developed their own agendas and contributed to feminist psychology's progress. . . . As daughters of the legacy of feminism and ethnicism, women of color are collaborating with their feminist sisters and brothers in the transformation of an integrative feminist psychology that will be relevant to all women" (1991, p. 607).

CONCLUSION

As Division 35 president Mary Parlee stated, feminist psychologists see "personal experiences, values, activities, and ways of working . . . as inextricably interconnected with the kind and content of the knowledge produced" (1982, p. 1). Today, Division 35 supports and sustains feminist efforts to move the field forward on multiple fronts, continuing to "boldly assert its identity, significance, and challenge within our primary professional organization as well as within the arenas of scientific scholarship, theory, and practice" (Lott, 1991, p. 1). Using empirical methods to refute sexist assumptions, methods, and findings continues to be an effective strategy to generate knowledge about women's lives and the influence of gender. Developing feminist applications of psychological knowledge in a variety of domains, but particularly in providing psychological services and in educational settings, are areas of lively activity. The division continues to work to translate its commitment to the value of diversity into reality, while maintaining a unity of purpose and providing a power base and haven for feminist psychologists to pursue an evolving, multifaceted agenda. Through that effort, feminist psychologists are gaining a better understanding of the influence of the social context on human behavior and experience across class, culture, and geography. As Corann Okorodudu, chair of Division 35's 1995 Task Force on Global/International Perspectives has expressed, "Feminist psychology will be useful to the degree that it contributes to our understanding and transformation of the daily experiences of the world's women and girls and the communities in which we live" (1995, p. 12). Expanding the division's vision to encompass a global perspective is the next step in the evolution of the division's concerns with issues of diversity.

The area that sparks the liveliest debate, however, harkens back to Rhoda Unger's 1981 presidential address—that is, exploring the relationship between conceptual models and methods (Unger, 1983). How to translate the recognition that individuals' psychological processes are inextricably linked to their social contexts into methods that enable psychologists to study and understand those links is the pressing question. Current empirical methods have their usefulness, but there is a longing for innovation. History suggests that participation in the division will be a source of energy and inspiration for developing creative new approaches and meeting the many challenges ahead.

REFERENCES

Amaro, H. (1984). *Hispanic women in psychology: A resource directory.* Washington, DC: Women's Programs Office, APA.

American Psychological Association. (1950). *Directory of the American Psychological Association.* Washington, DC: Author.

American Psychological Association. (1973). *Directory of the American Psychological Association.* Washington, DC: Author.

Babladelis, G. (1976). Editorial. *Psychology of Women Quarterly, 1,* 3–4.

Benjamin, L. T., Jr. (1977). The Psychological Round Table. *American Psychologist, 32,* 542–549.

Biaggio, M. K. (1990). *Final Report of the Mainstreaming Feminist Psychology Task Force.*

Brodsky, A. M., & Hare-Mustin, T. (1980). *Women and psychotherapy: An assessment of research and practice.* New York: Guilford Press.

Capshaw, J. H., & Laszlo, A. C. (1986). "We would not take no for an answer": Women psychologists and gender politics during World War II. *Journal of Social Issues, 42,* 157–180.

Claster, B., & Marecek, J. (1983). Task force on clinical training and practice. *Division 35 Newsletter, 10,* 4.

Comas-Díaz, L. (1991). Feminism and diversity in psychology: The case of women of color. *Psychology of Women Quarterly, 15,* 597–610.

Crawford, M., & Marecek, J. (1989). Feminist theory, feminist psychology: A bibliography of epistemology: Critical analysis and applications. *Psychology of Women Quarterly, 13,* 477–492.

Crull, P. (1976). Report from workshops III: Setting priorities in research for women. *Division 35 Newsletter, 3*(1), 6.

Denmark, F. L. (1977). The psychology of women: An overview of an emerging field. *Personality and Social Psychology Bulletin, 3,* 356–357.

Denmark, F. L. (1979). Women in psychology in the United States. *Annals of the New York Academy of Sciences, 323,* 65–78.

Denmark, F. L., Russo, N. F., Frieze, I., & Sechzer, J. (1988). Guidelines for avoiding sexism in psychological research. *American Psychologist, 43,* 582–585.

Division of the Psychology of Women. (1974). *Annual Report to the Board of Directors and Council of Representatives.*

Division of the Psychology of Women. (1977). *Annual Report to the Board of Directors and Council of Representatives.*

Division 35 Newsletter. (1982). Division 35/AWP Teach-In: Taking Action on Women's Issues. Division 35 Newsletter, 9(3), 8.

Douvan, E. (1974). President's column. *Division 35 Newsletter, 1*(1), 1.

Douvan, E. (1976). The role of models in women's professional development. *Psychology of Women Quarterly, 1,* 5–20.

Eagly, A. (1994). Gender and leadership: In honor of Florence L. Geis. *Psychology of Women Newsletter, 21*(4), 17, 22.

Gardner, J. (1976). What's in a name . . . *Division 35 Newsletter, 3*(4), 16.

Golub, S., & Freedman, R. J. (1987). *Psychology of women: Resources for a core curriculum.* New York: Garland.

Hare-Mustin, R. (1976). *Report of the Task Force on Clinical Treatment and Practice.*

Highlights of the Division 35 business meeting. (1984). *Psychology of Women Newsletter, 11*(4), 2–3.

Hyde, J. S. (1991). *Half the human experience.* Lexington, MA: DC Heath.

Hyde, J. S. (1993). It's an exciting time to be a feminist psychologist. *Division 35 Newsletter, 20*(4), 1–2.

Including Diverse Women in the Undergraduate Curriculum. (1995). Phoenix, AZ: Division 35 Task Force on the Representation of People of Color.

Johnson, M. (Ed.). (1982). Teaching the Psychology of Women [special issue]. *Psychology of Women Quarterly, 7.*

Katz, P. A. (1991). Women, psychology, and social issues research. *Psychology of Women Quarterly, 15,* 665–676.

Kimmel, E. (1991a) Treatment of gender and diversity in psychology textbooks: Report from the task force. *Psychology of Women Newsletter 18*(4), 9–10.

Kimmel, E. (1991b) Task force on gender issues and women in psychology textbooks, *Midyear Progress Report.*

Liss-Levinson, N., Clamar, A., Ehrenberg, M., Ehrenberg, O., Fidell, L., Maffeo, P., Redstone, J., Russo, N. F., Solomons, H., & Tennov, D. (1985). *Women in psychotherapy: A consumer handbook.* Tempe, AZ: National Coalition for Women's Mental Health.

Londrine, H. (Ed.). (1995). *Bringing cultural diversity to feminist psychology: Theory, research, and practice.* Washington, DC: American Psychological Association.

Lott, B. (1990). Message from the new president. *Psychology of Women, 17*(4), 1–2.

Lott, B. (1991). Message from the president: Transforming the mainstream. *Psychology of women, 18*(1), 1–3.

Lott, B. (1995). Who ever thought I'd grow up to be a feminist foremother. In E. Rothblum, P. Chesler, & E. Cole (Eds.), *Feminist foremothers in women's studies, psychology, and mental health* (pp. 309–323). New York: Haworth Press.

Major, B. (1979, October). Report on the Division 35 open symposium on the psychology of women. *Division 35 Newsletter, 6*(4), 2.

Marlowe, L. (1976). Letter to the editor. *Division 35 Newsletter, 3*(4), 16.

Mays, V. M. (1984). *Black women in psychology: A resource directory*. Washington, DC: Women's Programs Office, APA.

McHugh, M. C., Koeske, R. D., & Frieze, I. H. (1986). Issues to consider in conducting nonsexist psychology: A review with recommendations. *American Psychologist, 41*, 879–890.

Mednick, M. (1976). "From the president." *Division 35 Newsletter, 3*(4), 1.

Mednick, M. (1977). President's column. *Division 35 Newsletter, 4*(1), 1.

Mednick, M. (1978). Now we are four: What should we be when we grow up? *Psychology of Women Quarterly, 3*, 123–138.

Mednick, M. S., & Russo, N. F. (1983). Carolyn Wood Sherif: Teacher, scholar, mentor, friend. *Psychology of Women Quarterly, 8*, 3–8.

Mednick, M. S., & Urbanski, L. L. (1991). The origins and activities of APA's Division of the Psychology of Women. *Psychology of Women Quarterly, 15*, 651–663.

Mitchell, M. B. (1951). Status of women in the American Psychological Association. *American Psychologist, 6*, 193–201.

Nelson, C. B., & Sexton, V. S. (1970). Women psychologists: Psychologists? Militants? *American Psychologist, 25*, 1131.

Nutt, R. L. (1995). Section 2: Feminist professional training and practice. *Psychology of Women, 23*(2), 21–22.

O'Connell, A. N.(1990). Task force on heritage and the APA centennial. *Division 35 Newsletter, 17*(4), 13.

O'Connell, A. N., Alpert, J. L., Richardson, M. S., Rotter, N. G., Ruble, D. N., & Unger, R. K. (1978). Gender-specific barriers to research in psychology: Report of the task force on women doing research. APA Division 35. JSAS Catalog of Selected Documents, 8, 80. Ms. 1753.

O'Connell, A. N., & Russo, N. F. (Eds.). (1980). Eminent women in psychology: Models of achievement. *Psychology of Women Quarterly, 5* (Whole no. 1).

O'Connell, A. N., & Russo, N. F. (Eds.). (1983). *Models of Achievement: Reflections of eminent women in psychology*. New York: Columbia University Press.

O'Connell, A. N., & Russo, N. F. (Eds.). (1988). *Models of Achievement: Reflections of eminent women in psychology (Vol. II)*. Hillsdale, NJ: Erlbaum.

O'Connell, A. N., & Russo, N. F. (Eds.). (1990). *Women in psychology: A biobiographical sourcebook*. Westport, CN: Greenwood Press.

O'Connell, A. N., & Russo, N. F. (1991). Women's heritage in psychology: Future directions. *Psychology of Women Quarterly, 15*, 677–678.

Okorodudu, C. (1995). Envisioning a global feminist psychology. *Division 35 News-letter, 22*, 12.

Parlee, M. (1975). Review essay: Psychology. *Signs, 1*, 119–138.

Parlee, M. (1982). President's letter. *Division 35 Newsletter, 9*(4), 1.

Portnier, L. G. (Ed.). (1967). *The International Council of Psychologists, Inc.: The first quarter century, 1942–1967*. Washington, DC: International Council of Psychologists.

Quina, K. (1995). POWR on line! Psychology of Women Resource List. *Psychology of Women, 23*(2), 20.

Research Guidelines Committee. (1975). Proposed revisions of APA Standards on the Conduct of Research With Humans. *Division 35 Newsletter, 2*(2), 9–13.

Russo, N. F., & O'Connell, A. N. (1980). Models from our past: Psychology's Foremothers. *Psychology of Women Quarterly, 5*, 11–54.

Sachs, S., & Vaughter, R. (1976). APA workshop report: Women doing research. *Division 35 Newsletter, 3*(1), 2–4.

Schwesinger, G. C. (1943). The National Council of Women Psychologists. *Journal of Consulting Psychology, 7*, 298–301.

Sherif, C. W. (1979, October). Message from a new president. *Division 35 Newsletter, 6*(4), 1–3.

Task Force on Policy and Procedures. (1995). *Handbook of the Division of the Psychology of Women of the American Psychological Association*. Washington, DC: APA Division 35.

Task Force on the Status of Women in Psychology. (1973). Report of the task force on the status of women in psychology. *American Psychologist, 28*, 611–616.

Tiefer, L. (1991). A brief history of the association for women in psychology (AWP): 1969–1991. *Psychology of Women Quarterly, 15*, 635–650.

True, R. H. (1980). Task force report, Asian American Women's Task Force. Phoenix, AZ: Division 35 Task Force on Asian American Women.

Unger, R. K. (1983). Through the looking glass: No Wonderland yet! (The Recipro-cal relationship between methodology and models of reality). *Psychology of Women Quarterly, 8*, 9–110.

Wallston, B. S. (1979). Psychology of women: Separation or integration? *Division 35 Newsletter, 6*(3), 1.

Walsh, M. R. (1986). Academic professional women organizing for change: The struggle in psychology. *Journal of Social Issues, 41*, 17–28.

Weisstein, N. (1971). Psychology constructs the female. In V. Gornick & B. K. Moran (Eds.), *Women in sexist society* (pp. 207–224). New York: American Library.

Wells, K. (1982). AWP/Div. 35 Teach-In Fact Sheets, *Division 35 Newsletter, 9*(4), 14–15.

Wittig, M. (1977). APA Council takes brave stand—Cancels convention contracts in non-ERA-ratified states! *Division 35 Newsletter, 4*(4), 1–2.

Wittig, M. (1982). President's letter. *Division 35 Newsletter, 9*(2), 1.

Worell, J. (1995). Revisioning the division. *Division 35 Newsletter 22*(2), 23.

Worell, J., & Johnson, N. (Eds.). (in press). *Feminist visions: New directions for research and practice*. Washington, DC: American Psychological Association.

9

A HISTORY OF DIVISION 38 (HEALTH PSYCHOLOGY): HEALTHY, WEALTHY, AND WEISS

KENNETH A. WALLSTON

Since its inception, the discipline of psychology has been concerned with aspects of health. For example, a number of early figures in the field of psychology—for example, Hermann Helmholtz, William James, Wilhelm Wundt—were initially trained in medicine. However, the predominant focus in psychology up until recently has been on *mental* rather than *physical* health. In the years after World War II, a small, but increasing, number of psychologists began conducting research on phenomena other than strictly mental health concerns. Notable among this work was Neal E. Miller's pioneering research on the conditioning of physiological processes and the resulting flurry of interest in biofeedback. Another example is the develop-

This history is dedicated to the memory of Barbara Strudler Wallston, PhD (1943–1987), who played a key role in founding the Division of Health Psychology and who chaired its Research Committee in the early years. Although she and I were in the process of becoming divorced in August 1974 when we wandered into the meeting of the Task Force on Health Research in New Orleans, it was she who was most responsible for my involvement in this organization.

I am especially indebted to John Linton for providing a complete set of Volumes 1–15 of *The Health Psychologist*, without which this history would have been impossible to write, and to Cynthia Belar, Donald Dewsbury, Joseph Matarazzo, Murray Meisels, and Donald Routh for their comments and suggestions on an earlier draft of this chapter.

239

ment of the Health Belief Model by Godfrey Hochbaum, S. Stephen Kegeles, Howard Leventhal, and Irwin Rosenstock—four psychologists in the U.S. Public Health Service who were trying to understand why people were not becoming vaccinated against tuberculosis.

In addition, more and more psychologists were being employed by Schools of Medicine, Nursing, and Public Health, as well as the Veterans Administration and hospitals specializing in acute and rehabilitative medicine. These psychologists and their university-based colleagues, originally trained in clinical, counseling, experimental, or social psychology, applied their favorite theories and methods to phenomena that had as much to do with the physical as with the mental aspects of health and illness, including the interaction between the brain and the body. Sometimes these theories and methods carried over quite naturally to the domain of physical health. Other times, however, new paradigms needed to be developed, such as the biopsychosocial model that was popularized in 1977 by a physician, George Engel, but that first appeared in an article in the *Journal of Clinical Psychology* 24 years earlier (Guze, Matarazzo, & Saslow, 1953).

Out of all of this activity emerged the Division of Health Psychology of the American Psychological Association (APA). Today, Division 38 can truly be characterized as being "healthy and wealthy," but the gestation of this organization was not without its attendant labor pains. The remainder of this chapter tells the story of how Division 38 was birthed and how it has developed over the past 19 years.

EARLY HISTORY: 1969 TO 1978

Like most gestational periods, the birth of Division 38 did not happen overnight. Instead of taking 9 months, however, it took 9 years.

APA Task Force

In 1969, William Schofield of the University of Minnesota published a landmark paper in the *American Psychologist* on "The role of psychology in the delivery of health services" (Schofield, 1969). This paper caught the attention of members of the ad hoc Committee on Newly Emerging Areas of Research (NEAR) that had been established by the APA's Board of Scientific Affairs (BSA). In 1973, on recommendation by NEAR, BSA established a task force on health research and selected William Schofield to be its chair. "Quite likely in part as a direct response to Schofield's challenge . . . [BSA] sensed the research opportunities for psychology in helping to cut our nation's annually accelerating health costs" (Matarazzo,

1980, p. 808). Other members of the task force were Claus Bahnson, Edward and Miriam Kelty, John Rasmussen, Lee Sechrest, Lisa Schusterman, and Walter Wilkins.

The immediate objective of the task force was to collect, organize, and disseminate information on the status of health behavior research, particularly among American psychologists. This encompassed a review of ongoing health research, sources of research support, and creation of an informal directory of psychologists engaged in health research. Over the next 3 years, the task force held a series of 11 meetings, put together and disseminated a roster of active investigators, published and disseminated six issues of a newsletter, and wrote an article titled "Contributions of Psychology to Health Research: Patterns, Problems, and Potentials," which was published in the *American Psychologist* in 1976. In this article they cited the prior role of psychology in the mental health field, but added,

> There is probably no specialty field within psychology that cannot contribute to the discovery of behavioral variables crucial to a full understanding of susceptibility to physical illness, adaptation to such illness, and prophylactically motivated behaviors. (APA Task Force on Health Research, 1976, p. 272)

Most significant for this history was the open meeting held by the task force at the 1974 APA convention in New Orleans. At that gathering, much discussion centered around forming a new division within APA concentrating on health research. The idea of forming a new division was favorably viewed by those in attendance, but, for a number of reasons, the decision to seek divisional status was put on hold. One of the main arguments for not going ahead with this endeavor was that in August 1974 the APA council voted down proposals to establish two other new divisions.

Section 2 of Division 18

Schofield and some of the other task force members were members of Division 18 (Psychologists in Public Service). Division 18 had recently set up a structure allowing for sections, the first of which was on criminal justice. Schofield approached the executive committee of Division 18 with a proposal that a section on health research be constituted, and, in 1975, 87 new members were accepted into Division 18 expressly to become its Section on Health Research.

The purposes of Section 2 of Division 18 were (a) to increase and improve the application of psychological knowledge and principles to all phases of health research and care and (b) to facilitate communication and dissemination of information among psychologists engaged in health care research. Particular emphasis was placed on relatively neglected and unrecognized areas in which psychologists can make a contribution in health research and care, such as the application of psychological concepts, research methodology, and technical measurement. With the formation of this section of Division 18, the work of the APA task force came to an end in early 1976.

William Schofield was chosen to be the first chair of the health research section and Barbara Strudler Wallston was elected secretary–treasurer. The following year, Wilbert Fordyce, of the University of Washington, succeeded Schofield as chair. In 1977, Stephen Weiss, who had just been made head of the new Behavioral Medicine Branch at the National Institute of Heart, Lung, and Blood, was asked to run for the position of chair-elect. Weiss accepted the nomination but made it quite clear to the membership of the section that, should he be elected, he would devote his energies to the establishment of a new, separate division for health psychologists within the APA. Weiss became chair-elect, and I succeeded my former wife as secretary–treasurer.

Petitioning the APA

In order to garner enough clout within the APA to secure the signatures and political support to begin a new division, Weiss turned to his friend and mentor, Joseph Matarazzo, for guidance and help. Matarazzo had established the first autonomous Department of Medical Psychology at the University of Oregon Health Sciences Center and was widely recognized and respected as one of the pioneers in health research and applied clinical psychology. Because of his belief that health psychology potentially was an area that would attract psychologists whose interests spanned across the many subfields of psychology, Matarazzo invited the following notables from experimental, clinical, and social psychology to join him and Weiss in early 1978 as sponsors of the petition to the APA council to establish a new division of Health Psychology: Joseph Brady, Richard Evans, Wilbert Fordyce, W. Doyle Gentry, David Glass, Irving Janis, Neal Miller, Gary Schwartz, Jerome E. Singer, and George Stone.

More than 600 additional members and fellows of the APA, among them many of the members of the Medical Psychology Network headed by David Clayman and John Linton of West Virginia University and the Society of Pediatric Psychology started by Logan Wright, Lee Salk, and Dorothea Ross, signed the petition for a new division that was subsequently approved by the APA council in late August 1978. Although it took the efforts of many individuals to establish this new division, Steven Weiss would probably win any paternity suit over who could legitimately be called the father of Division 38. Hence, the inclusion of his surname in the title of this history.

MODERN HISTORY: 1978 TO 1996

Division 38 began in 1978. The bylaws were adopted by 175 charter members who attended organizational meetings to form this new division on August 29 during the 1978 APA convention in Toronto. Joseph Matarazzo was chosen to be the first president of the division and Steven Weiss was president-elect. David Clayman was initially both the secretary and the treasurer. Because the division was newly formed, it had no representation on the APA council that first year. (See Table 42 for a listing of all division officers by year.)

Once Division 38 was formed, the *raison d'être* for the existence of Section 2 of Division 18 was no longer compelling. Many health researchers who became charter members of Division 38 retained their membership in Division 18, both out of loyalty to a group that had given a home to health research when there was none and, also, because many, such as Miriam Kelty and Barbara Strudler Wallston, had become active in Division 18. Also, a number of health researchers were committed to the notion of public service, and many were employed in governmental agencies such as the NIH, the armed services, or the Veterans Administration.

However, many health researchers, such as this author, were conflicted about where best to invest their organizational energies. Succeeding Steven Weiss as chair of Section 2 was John Rasmussen, of the Batelle Institute in Seattle. Under Rasmussen's leadership, a ballot was sent to the membership of the Health Research Section, and 78% voted to disband the section and subsume its activities under the banner of Division 38. George Stone, of the University of California, San Francisco, had just been selected chairelect of Section 2 but never got a chance to succeed Rasmussen in office. The Health Research Section of Division 18 was officially dissolved in 1980.

The Mandate of Division 38

The Division of Health Psychology had a much broader mandate than did the Section on Health Research. As stated in the bylaws adopted by the charter members, the purposes of Division 38 were

> (a) to advance contributions of psychology as a discipline to the understanding of health and illness through basic and clinical research and by encouraging the integration of biomedical information about health and illness with current psychological knowledge;
> (b) to promote education and services in the psychology of health and illness; and
> (c) to inform the psychological and biomedical community, and the general public, on the results of current research and service activities in this area. (Matarazzo, 1979, 1)

TABLE 42
Officers of Division 38

Year	President	Secretary	Treasurer	Council Representative(s)
1978–1979	Joseph D. Matarazzo	David Clayman	David Clayman	James T. Webb
1979–1980	Stephen M. Weiss	David Clayman	David Clayman	James T. Webb
1980–1981	Neal E. Miller	Joan Robison	David Clayman	James T. Webb
1981–1982	Jerome E. Singer	Mary Ellen Olbrisch	David Clayman	Joseph D. Matarazzo
1982–1983	Judith Rodin	Mary Ellen Olbrisch	David Clayman	Joseph D. Matarazzo
1983–1984	Gary E. Schwartz	Mary Ellen Olbrisch	David Clayman	Joseph D. Matarazzo
1984–1985	Edward B. Blanchard	Miriam F. Kelty	Mary A. Jansen	Jerome E. Singer
1985–1986	George C. Stone	Miriam F. Kelty	Mary A. Jansen	Jerome E. Singer
1986–1987	Richard I. Evans	Miriam F. Kelty	Mary A. Jansen	Jerome E. Singer
1987–1988	Karen A. Matthews	Miriam F. Kelty	Kenneth A. Wallston	Joseph Matarazzo
1988–1989	Andrew Baum	Miriam F. Kelty	Kenneth A. Wallston	Joseph Matarazzo
1989–1990	Kelly Brownell	Miriam F. Kelty	Kenneth A. Wallston	Patrick DeLeon[a]
1990–1991	Margaret Chesney	J. Gayle Beck	Kenneth A. Wallston	David Krantz
1991–1992	Neil Schneiderman	J. Gayle Beck	Kenneth A. Wallston	David Krantz
1992–1993	Robert M. Kaplan	J. Gayle Beck	Kenneth A. Wallston	David Krantz
1993–1994	Barbara Melamed	Ilene Siegler	Patricia M. Dubbert	Andrew Baum
1994–1995	Suzanne Bennett Johnson	Ilene Siegler	Patricia M. Dubbert	Andrew Baum
1995–1996	Cynthia Belar	Ilene Siegler	Patricia M. Dubbert	Nathan Perry[c]
1996–1997	Howard Leventhal	Edward P. Sarafino	Steven M. Tovian	John Linton

Additional entries under Council Representative(s):
Richard Suinn, Richard Suinn, Nathan Perry[b], [lost seat], Joan Robison, Joan Robison, Joan Robison, Nathan Perry, Nathan Perry, [lost seat]

[a] Chosen by executive committee to replace Joseph Matarazzo when Matarazzo was elected president-elect of the APA
[b] Chosen by executive committee to replace Richard Suinn when Suinn was elected to APA board of directors.
[c] Chosen by executive committee to substitute for Andrew Baum when Baum was unable to attend council meetings

Thus, from its inception, members of Division 38 were as concerned with the practice of health psychology as they were with the conduct of research in health psychology. This dual focus mirrored the parent organization (APA) and has remained a dynamic organizing principle in the division.

DEFINING AND DIFFERENTIATING HEALTH PSYCHOLOGY

The following will explain what is meant by *health psychology* and how it is different from other areas within psychology. Also, how health psychology differs from related fields such as behavioral medicine will be discussed.

Health Psychology

Defining what was meant by this new field was imperative and challenging. The prospect of having to deliver the first presidential address during the 1979 annual APA meeting forced Joseph Matarazzo to face this issue. Matarazzo penned the following definition:

> Health psychology is the aggregate of the specific educational, scientific, and professional contributions of the discipline of psychology to the promotion and maintenance of health, the prevention and treatment of illness, and the identification of etiologic and diagnostic correlates of health, illness and related dysfunction. (Matarazzo, 1980, p. 815)

The next year, that definition was expanded by the addition of the phrase, "and to the analysis and improvement of the health care system and health policy formation," and the full definition was ratified by consensus of the membership in a vote taken in 1980 (Robison, 1981).

Behavioral Medicine

At the same time that Division 38 was being formed, a parallel movement was taking place in medicine and allied disciplines, led by many of the same people who formed the division. At the Yale Conference on Behavioral Medicine held in February 1977, the following definition of that interdisciplinary movement was proposed:

> Behavioral medicine is the field concerned with the *development* of *behavioral science* knowledge and techniques relevant to the understanding of *physical health* and *illness* and the *application* of this knowledge and these techniques to prevention, diagnosis, treatment and rehabilitation. Psychosis, neurosis, and substance abuse are included only insofar as they contribute to physical disorders as an end point. (Schwartz & Weiss, 1978, p. 7)

Although the word *interdisciplinary* was not explicitly contained in the initial definition of behavioral medicine, the spirit of this new movement was meant to be *inter*disciplinary. This is in contrast to health psychology, which was and is *intra*disciplinary, encompassing psychology's role as a science and profession (Matarazzo, 1980). When health psychologists collaborate with colleagues from medicine, nursing, sociology, anthropology, epidemiology, psychiatry, physical therapy, public health, and so forth to work on problems or projects of mutual interest, we are engaged in behavioral medicine. When this collaboration is absent, or when the collaboration is only with others trained in psychology, the most appropriate label for our activities is health psychology.

Not only were health psychologists instrumental in defining and launching the field of behavioral medicine, health psychologists constitute nearly 70% of the membership of the Society of Behavioral Medicine (SBM) and an even higher percentage of its leadership. Health psychologists are also very prominent in the Academy of Behavioral Medicine Research (ABMR), a smaller and very select group of researchers. Both of these organizations began just as Division 38 was being started. There is a great deal of overlap in the membership of these different organizations and it is not unusual to have the same individuals serve simultaneously in leadership positions in Division 38, SBM, and ABMR. Only health psychologists, namely Frances Keefe, Dennis Turk, and Arthur Stone, have been the editors of the *Annals of Behavioral Medicine*, the journal published by SBM, and many other health psychologists serve on the editorial board and contribute articles. In addition, health psychologists, such as Joseph Matarazzo, Donald Routh, and Howard Leventhal, have been appointed to chair the Behavioral Medicine Study Section of the National Institute of Health (NIH), and many other health psychologists have served as members of this study section (as well as other study sections and councils throughout the NIH).

Behavioral Health

Joseph Matarazzo not only helped define and establish health psychology and behavioral medicine, he also is credited with establishing *behavioral health* as

> an interdisciplinary field dedicated to promoting a philosophy of health that stresses *individual responsibility* in the application of behavioral and biomedical science knowledge and techniques to the *maintenance* of health and the *prevention* of illness and dysfunction by a variety of self-initiated individual or shared activities. (Matarazzo, 1980, p. 813)

Thus, when health psychologists join with our colleagues from other disciplines to investigate or ameliorate health or illness, we are engaged in behavioral medicine or behavioral health, or both. When only a single discipline is involved, we are engaged in health psychology. All three of these fields are highly complementary, but only two of them are interdisciplinary.

PUBLICATIONS OF THE DIVISION

As with our parent organization, a major activity and membership service of the division has been its publications. Two of these, the newsletter and the journal, are automatically sent to all members as a basic membership benefit. The other publications, including our book series, are available to members at their request.

The Newsletter

One of the first acts of the inaugural executive committee was to appoint John Linton, of West Virginia University Medical Center, as the editor of the division's newsletter, *The Health Psychologist*, which printed its inaugural issue in the summer of 1979. For 15 years, Linton put in yeoman's effort as the newsletter editor. Volume 1 contained only one issue, but, beginning with Volume 2 through Volume 9, there were two issues per year. Starting with Volume 10 (1988), members received three issues of *The Health Psychologist* each year except for Volume 15, Linton's final year as editor, when there was not enough material submitted to fill the spring 1993 issue. Kevin Larkin, of West Virginia University in Morgantown, became Linton's associate editor in 1988.

In 1993, the executive committee chose me to succeed John Linton as the editor of the newsletter. My first (and possibly best) decision as editor-elect was to select a gifted graphic artist, Kimberly Karl, to be the managing editor. Karl gave the newsletter a whole new look and, through the marvels of desktop publishing, we were able to incorporate many additional features into the publication. Beginning with Volume 18 (1996), *The Health Psychologist* became a quarterly publication.

The Journal

During Neal Miller's presidency of the division (1980–1981), George Stone was selected by the executive committee to become the first editor of a new scientific journal, *Health Psychology*, that would begin publishing as a quarterly in January 1982. Stone had begun the first doctoral program in health psychology at the University of California, San Francisco, and, along with his two colleagues Nancy Adler and Frances Cohen, had published the first handbook in the field (Stone, Cohen, & Adler, 1979). Thus,

Stone was the logical choice to edit this new journal. As associate editors, he chose Clifford Atkinson, Patrick DeLeon, Howard Leventhal, Gary Schwartz, and Shelley Taylor. The division entered into a contract with Lawrence Erlbaum Associates of Hillsdale, New Jersey, to publish the journal on behalf of the division. Beginning with Volume 3, the journal went to six issues a year.

Stone's term of office as inaugural editor of the journal was only for 3 years. Thus, in 1983, during Judith Rodin's presidency, a search began for Stone's replacement. The search culminated with the selection of Neil Schneiderman of the University of Miami as the new editor. Schneiderman was not even a member of the division when he was selected to edit the journal, but his reputation as a first-class, biobehavioral health researcher made him eminently suited to edit what was about to become the premier journal in a new, burgeoning field.

In Stone's last issue of the journal, in a section labeled "Position Statements," was a poem by Thomas Dorsal describing the developmental history of a 55-year-old man whose atrocious habits were what kept clinical health psychologists in business (Dorsal, 1984). Schneiderman felt strongly that *Health Psychology* should be predominantly an "archival" journal—that is, it should contain almost exclusively empirical reports of original research rather than reviews, book reports, editorials, or exercises in "creative writing." Schneiderman began his editorship with seven associate editors, but, by the time his 5-year term was up, he had expanded that number to ten.

It was during Schneiderman's term that the journal began to show a profit, both for Erlbaum, which generously covered the bulk of the start-up expenses, and for the division (which shared the net profits with Erlbaum on a 50–50 basis). Karen Matthews of the University of Pittsburgh was chosen to succeed Schneiderman. Matthews, a former associate editor of the journal and former division president, presided over a number of significant changes in the journal involving its format, its size, the number of articles published each volume, and, most significantly, its publisher. One of the things she did not change, however, was the archival nature of the journal, although she did begin accepting review articles.

The original publishing contract with Lawrence Erlbaum Associates was for a 10-year period. Although the division's executive committee was generally quite satisfied with the job Erlbaum had done in developing the journal, and was deeply indebted to Lawrence Erlbaum for helping to start the journal, there were a few members of the executive committee who felt that it was a good idea to explore the possibility of changing publishers as we negotiated a new contract. For one thing, there was some dissatisfaction at the relatively low number of institutional subscribers to the journal. For another, APA Publications, headed by Gary VandenBos, very much wanted to publish a journal in the field of health psychology and had approached the division with an offer to take over *Health Psychology* and make it an APA journal.

Matthews, in her role as editor-in-chief, was given the assignment of soliciting proposals from prospective publishers. Erlbaum wanted to continue to publish the journal and came up with a generous contract, one that not only would guarantee a higher level of profit for the division than had been experienced to date but would also provide additional expense money for the editor and associate editors and for marketing the journal to individuals and institutions on a worldwide basis. Erlbaum's proposal was matched by one from Williams & Wilkins of Baltimore, best known for their journals in the medical field, who were also eager to have a journal in the field of health psychology. In the long run, however, and not without very serious, protracted, and sometimes painful discussions among its members, the publications committee voted to recommend to the executive committee to accept a unique and financially attractive contract from the APA.

In 1993, beginning with Volume 11, *Health Psychology* became an official APA journal. However, unlike every other APA journal up to that time, Division 38's was a joint publishing venture between the APA and the division. Full and complete editorial control, including the right to select the editor, rests with Division 38's publications committee, not with the Publications and Communications (P & C) Board of the APA. The only concession asked of the division was to allow a liaison member of the P & C Board to sit in on major deliberations affecting the journal.

One of the main reasons the division's executive committee voted to go with APA Publications was to increase the readership of the journal. Within a year of becoming an APA journal, the number of individual subscriptions more than doubled (see Matthews, 1993), due largely to the APA members who could now obtain the publication using the journal credit built into their dues. Although some of these new subscribers did not renew their subscriptions after that first year, many more individuals regularly receive *Health Psychology* now than ever before. Institutional subscriptions were also up, although, perhaps, not as much as originally projected. What has increased dramatically, however, is the number of articles submitted to the journal from health researchers all over the world, possibly due to the added prestige of being an APA journal.

David Krantz of the Uniformed Services University of the Health Sciences was chosen to become the fourth editor of *Health Psychology*. He began his term in 1995 with Volume 14. The extra work involved in handling all of the extra manuscript submissions led Krantz to add an additional associate editor and to renegotiate the contract with the APA to provide more expense money for editorial assistance. Krantz has also put together a number of special issues dealing with such topics as psychosocial and behavioral aspects of genetic testing and assessment of health-relevant variables in natural environments.

The Book Series

At about the same time that the division was negotiating with the APA to publish the journal, the executive committee became aware that some members—those who were not primarily researchers but were engaged full-time in the practice of health psychology—felt the journal was not serving their needs. In an attempt to be responsive to the needs of clinical health psychologists for up-to-date, research-based information that has high practical relevance, the division launched a book series with Andrew Baum and Margaret Chesney, both former presidents of the division, as series co-editors. APA Books was selected to be the publisher. The first volume of that series, edited by Robert Gatchel and Edward Blanchard in 1993, was on *Psychophysiological Disorders*. This was followed in 1995 by a second volume, edited by Perry Nicassio and Timothy Smith, on *Managing Chronic Illness: A Biopsychosocial Perspective*, and a third volume, in 1996, *Adolescent Health Promotion in Minority Populations*, edited by Dawn Wilson, James Rodrigue, and Wendell Taylor. Plans are for one volume to come out each year in this series, for which division members are offered a special 40% discount if they buy the book within a month of its publication date. The division is also supposed to share in the profits of this series, if and when there are any. It should also be noted that the APA also publishes a number of other books on health psychology, many of which are authored or edited by Division 38 members, that are not part of the division's book series.

MAJOR CONFERENCES HELD BY DIVISION 38

In its first 19 years, the division has held three major conferences in addition to participating in the annual APA convention. Those conferences have dealt with education and training, research, and minority health.

Education and Training

One of the first major undertakings of Division 38 was to plan a National Working Conference on Education and Training in Health Psychology, which was held in 1983 at Arden House in Harriman, New York, from May 23 to 27. Originally, the idea for this conference came from a conversation between myself and Gilbert Levin, the developer of the doctoral program in health psychology at Albert Einstein School of Medicine/Yeshiva University. Both Levin and I were members of the division's Education and

Training Committee chaired by Cynthia Belar. Acting as a subcommittee, we developed the initial outline of a conference focusing on training issues in health psychology (see Singer, 1982). The division's executive committee wholeheartedly endorsed the idea for such a conference in August 1982 and selected Steven Weiss to be the overall chair of the event. Weiss and Neal Miller, the president of the division, managed to secure grants from the Carnegie, MacArthur, and Kaiser Family foundations to support the meeting, which was attended by 57 participants.

The Arden House Conference proceedings were published as a supplement to Volume 3 of *Health Psychology* (Stone, 1983). A high degree of consensus was achieved on a number of recommendations, one of which was that "Health psychology is a generic field of psychology, with its own body of theory and knowledge, which is differentiated from other fields in psychology" (Stone, 1983, p. 9). A significant conclusion was that "Health psychology should offer two major training options: scientist and professional . . . [and] the professional path should be based on the scientist/practitioner model as enunciated at the Boulder Conference" (Stone, 1983, pp. 15–16). To this day, the division has steadfastly held to this Boulder model for the education of health psychologists.

Research

Five years after Arden House, the division held a National Working Conference on Research in Health and Behavior at Harper's Ferry, West Virginia (May 15–17, 1988). Originally conceived by Richard Evans in 1985, the task of organizing the conference and coming up with funds to support it fell on Andrew Baum. In addition to financial support from Baum's own department and Nathan Perry's Department of Clinical and Health Psychology at the University of Florida, grants were obtained from the APA's Science Directorate, NIMH, NHLBI, and the Ciba-Geigy and Upjohn corporations. More than 60 attendees heard keynote addresses by Richard Evans and Karen Matthews, listened to five panel presentations, and participated in eight task forces. These latter groups focused on future research "problems and solutions" in the following areas: biobehavioral research and cardiovascular disease; psychoneuroimmunology; cancer; AIDS; smoking; health policy; practice; and child health. The conference proceedings, including the keynote speeches and reports from the task forces, were published in a special issue of *Health Psychology* (Baum, 1989). Although the purpose of publishing the conference deliberations and summaries was to "stimulate research in the area of health and behavior and . . . help us grapple with the problems or obstacles that lie ahead" (Baum, 1989, p. 629), it is extremely difficult to assess what impact, if any, this conference had on the field of health psychology.

Minority Health

From September 17 to 20, 1992, the Division of Health Psychology was the major sponsor of a National Conference on Behavioral and Sociocultural Perspectives on Ethnicity and Health held in Washington, DC. Cosponsoring this conference was the APA, Division 45 (Society for the Psychological Study of Ethnic Minority Issues), Duke University Medical Center, Howard University School of Medicine, NHLBI, NIMH, The Upjohn Corporation, and the Office of Minority Health in the Department of Health and Human Services.

The 3-day conference was attended by approximately 100 invited scientists, administrators, and students, representing such disciplines as psychology, epidemiology, medicine, sociology, public health, nursing and anthropology. The national conference began with and accomplished six objectives, which were to (a) provide an up-to-date summary of the behavioral and sociocultural epidemiology of minority health; (b) delineate the macrosocial and environmental influences on minority health; (c) discuss the current status of research on health behaviors in ethnic minorities, including the sociocultural, environmental, and developmental antecedents and health consequences of those behaviors; (d) produce an agenda for future research in each of the areas named in the proceeding three objectives; (e) address issues in training and career development in minority and health behavior research; and (f) address policy and funding issues of minority health behavior research (Anderson, 1995, p. 590).

The two individuals most responsible for the Minority Health Conference were Neil Schneiderman, who initially proposed the idea when he was president-elect of the division, and Norman B. Anderson, of Duke University Medical Center, who was the conference organizer. Anderson was the guest editor of a special issue of *Health Psychology* that contained reports from six of the panels that presented at the conference and a summary of recommendations from the eight task forces (Anderson, 1995). The impact of this conference will not be known until the turn of the century.

MEMBERSHIP OF DIVISION 38

When the division began in 1978, it had 680 charter members. Not only were APA members, fellows, or associates allowed (and encouraged) to join the division, but, from the beginning, membership was open up to "affiliates," particularly students in health psychology who were not members of the APA. Over the years, affiliate membership has represented approximately 10% of the total membership in the division, about equally split between students and professionals. Some of these professionals are not psychologists but joined the division in order to get the journal at reduced rates. Affiliates who are psychologists are either those who never belonged to the APA or who resigned from the APA but wanted to retain an identity as a health psychologist. The bylaws specify that only (APA) fellows and members have the right to vote.

Throughout the 1980s membership in Division 38 grew steadily. By July 1980, there were almost 1500 members, according to an update on membership by Margaret Chesney and David Clayman published in the summer–fall 1980 issue of the newsletter. By 1985, more than 2500 APA members belonged to Division 38. In 1995, 3356 APA members belonged to Division 38, making it the ninth largest of the APA's then 49 active divisions. The 1996 APA Membership Register, however, only lists Division 38 as having 3062 members, perhaps indicating that the growth phase of the division has come to an end.

MEMBERSHIP SURVEYS

In 1981, Gary Morrow and Paul Carpenter of the University of Rochester, along with division treasurer, David Clayman, surveyed the membership in an attempt to ascertain and establish priorities for the division. The results of this survey were published in the summer–fall 1983 issue of the newsletter. Fifty-seven percent ($N = 1477$) of the members completed and returned this survey. The top three priorities were (a) changing the Joint Commission on the Accreditation of Hospitals' regulations related to psychologists; (b) providing continuing education; and (c) increasing the public's awareness of psychologists' roles in health settings. At the bottom of the list (the 22nd item) was holding social hours at national–regional meetings.

In 1988, the same year as the conference at Harper's Ferry, B. Kent Houston of the University of Kansas was commissioned by the executive committee to conduct another survey of the division's members. Approximately 45% of the members ($N = 1149$) responded. The findings were shared in depth with the executive committee, and a synopsis of the findings was published in the summer–fall 1988 issue of The Health Psychologist. Fifty-five percent of the respondents indicated that their primary work setting was educational, with 42% indicating they worked in some sort of service delivery setting, but 65% indicated that the practice of health psychology constituted a significant part of their workload (compared to 55% for research and 50% for teaching). Sixty-five percent of the respondents indicated that they belonged to some non-APA professional association relevant to health psychology, most particularly the Society of Behavioral Medicine (to which

37% of all respondents belonged). Two thirds of the respondents indicated that, if the APA were to reorganize—a hot topic back in the late 1980s—Division 38 should join a scientific/practitioner unit within the organization. As befit a group of health psychologists, only 6% of the respondents currently self-reported smoking cigarettes, and 77% believed cigarette advertising should be banned from *Psychology Today*.

The first (and, to this date, only) edition of the Division 38 membership directory, edited and prepared by David Schlundt and myself, was distributed in 1991 along with one of the issues of the journal. The plan was to print and distribute a new directory every 2 years. In the summer of 1994, the division's membership committee, under the leadership of Dawn Wilson, attempted once again to survey the membership, partly to obtain updated information to put into the second edition of the membership directory. Less than 10% of the division's members returned this survey, and the data have never been reported. However, according to statistics compiled by the APA Research Office based on the 1993 APA directory survey (with new member updates for 1994 and 1995), 38.3% of Division 38 members are female (up from 26.7% 10 years earlier), and the median age is between 45 to 49 years. Of those specifying their highest degree, almost all (97.8%) earned a doctorate, on average 15 to 19 years previously. Seven-and-a-half percent of Division 38's members hold dual professional degrees in other fields, mainly nursing.

Sixty-eight percent of Division 38's members are classified as being in "provider psychology fields." Of those, more than 71% are identified as clinical psychologists, and only 15% as "health" psychologists. An additional 13% are classified as "research and other psychology." By far, the largest group of these latter members (39%) are social psychologists, followed by developmental (10%) and physiological/psychobiological psychologists (9%). Of the 12+% classified as "other fields" (other than psychology), nearly a quarter were classified as being in behavioral medicine.

Division 38 members overwhelmingly tend to belong to at least one other APA division. Only 16.7% are solely members of Division 38. It is not surprising that 24% of the members also belong to Division 12 (Clinical Psychology), closely followed by 22.3% who are members of Division 42 (Psychologists in Independent Practice). The next most frequent affiliations are with Division 29 (Psychotherapy; 13.7%) and Division 40 (Clinical Neuropsychology; 11.6%). Also noteworthy is the fact that 10.6% of Division 38's members belong to Division 35 (Psychology of Women), followed by 9.9% who belong to Division 8 (The Society of Personality and Social Psychology), and 8.8% to Division 22 (Rehabilitation Psychology). The remaining divisions to which at least 5% of Division 38's members belong are Division 43 (Family Psychology; 7.3%); Division 9 (SPSSI; 7.1%); Division 47 (Exercise and Sport Psychology; 6.6%); Division 20 (Adult

Development and Aging; 6.6%); Division 1 (General Psychology; 6.5%); and Division 17 (Counseling Psychology; 6.1%). Although only 2% of Division 38's members belong to Division 31 (State Psychological Association Affairs), slightly more than half of the members belong to state associations.

In 1995, 354 members of Division 38 held fellow status in the APA, although, according to the 1996 APA membership register, only 211 were fellows in Division 38. Because the leadership in the division, particularly the presidents, often hold fellow status in the APA, it is interesting to note that, aside from Division 38, those holding this status tended to belong to Divisions 12, 8, 9, and 20. To date, about half of the presidents of the division received their basic training in social psychology, with an equal number coming from clinical psychology. There has yet to be a president of Division 38 who was trained at the predoctoral level in health psychology.

COMMITTEE STRUCTURE OF THE DIVISION

No organization comprised of largely academically based professionals could function, it seems, without multiple committees, and Division 38 is no exception. The committee structure for the division can be divided into the executive and functional committees, both of which carry out the "business" of the entire division, and a number of special interest committees.

Executive Committee

The formal executive committee of the Division of Health Psychology is comprised of all of the elected officers. In 1987, based on a bylaws change the previous year, the first two members-at-large (Margaret Chesney and David Krantz) were elected to serve "without portfolio" on the executive committee, joining the president, past-president, president-elect, secretary, treasurer, and representative(s) to the APA council as the official members of this committee. (See Table 42 for a list of presidents, secretaries, treasurers, and APA council representatives.)

The executive committee meets formally twice a year, once at the time and location of the annual APA convention in August and again at a midwinter meeting in late January/early February. Until 1994, when the midwinter meeting had to be canceled because of a blizzard that blanketed the East Coast, this meeting was always held in Washington, DC. In 1995 and 1996 it was held in Florida, partly to escape the snowstorms, but also because the presidents those years (Suzanne Bennett Johnson and Cynthia Belar) were based at the University of Florida.

Appointed committee chairs, editors of the divisional publications, and appointed liaisons meet with the executive committee at these two meetings. It has been a tradition of the division that everyone in attendance at a meeting of the executive committee is allowed to vote on any matter coming before the committee that needs to be voted on. Because most decisions of the executive committee are made by consensus, sometimes after protracted discussion, the actual votes on a given issue rarely matter. During Neil Schneiderman's presidency, however, when the issue of a (new) publisher for the journal came to a vote, it was decided that, for certain *important* issues, such as selecting a publisher, only the votes of the formally elected members of the executive committee would count (see Schneiderman, 1992). Otherwise, everybody present participates equally in the discussions that shape division policies and activities. Therefore, attendance at executive committee meetings has generally been quite high, averaging more than 20 persons around the table.

Functional Committees

The standing committees that carry out the work of the division are Convention Program; Education & Training; Research; Health Services (formerly Health Care); Publications; Finance; Awards; Fellows; Membership; and Nominations and Elections. In the early years of the division, there were also similar committees devoted to Legislation (later changed to Public Policy), Public Affairs (later changed to Public Information), and Scientific Societies (a.k.a. Scientific Liaison a.k.a. Organizational Liaison), but these have disappeared in recent years.

When the division began, it was expected that the president-elect would chair the convention program committee. However, Stephen Weiss, the first person to hold this office, selected Richard Evans to be a cochair. Neal Miller went Weiss one better. Miller asked David Glass to be his cochair, and Glass selected David Krantz, his former student who was just becoming established as a health psychologist, to be *his* cochair. Jerome Singer continued this tradition by asking A. MacNeill (Mac) Horton, Jr., to assist him in putting together the convention program, and Judith Rodin followed this pattern by choosing Karen Matthews to be the cochair. In 1986, when Matthews was chosen president-elect, she asked Ken Holroyd to chair the program committee for the 1987 meeting, and that ended the practice of the president-elect even nominally chairing that busy committee. James Rodrigue of the University of Florida established a record by chairing the program committee 2 years in a row (1995 and 1996).

Although the Committee on Education and Training hit a high point in its third year of operation by stimulating the idea for the Arden House Conference, over the years it has remained active by carrying out such functions as compiling and distributing training directories for predoctoral, postdoctoral, and internship programs in health psychology. Cynthia Belar, Charles Swencionis, Andrew Baum, and Rolf Pederson have been largely responsible for instituting those directories. Edward Sarafino of Trenton State University, Pederson's successor as chair of the E & T Committee, was the driving force behind a brochure titled "Teaching Undergraduate Health Psychology," that has been disseminated by the E & T Committee. Sarafino has also played a major role in putting together an operations handbook for division officers and committee chairs.

The Committee on Continuing Education has ebbed and flowed, despite the fact that in the 1981 survey continuing education was a high priority for the members. For a time, in the mid 1980s, under the leadership of Will Johnson of the University of Mississippi Medical Center, the division offered a number of continuing education workshops at the annual APA meeting. In recent years, however, the division has either been out of the continuing education business altogether or simply involved in cosponsoring such offerings.

The research committee's major activity has been in contributing articles to the newsletter relevant to research funding. Exemplary was the article, "Getting Your Grant Funded by NIH," written by Sheldon Cohen of Carnegie-Mellon for the summer–fall 1988 issue. Cohen followed this up 2 years later with "Funding Your Unfunded PHS Grant Proposal" (Cohen, 1990). The current research committee, under the leadership of Jennifer Haythornthwaite of Johns Hopkins, has instituted a graduate student research proposal competition.

When the division was founded it had a health care committee. The name was changed to the Health Services Committee in 1980. David Engstrom, of the University of California, Irvine, chaired this committee in its early years when it had two major objectives: (a) to serve as a clearinghouse for the dissemination of information about the contribution of psychology to health care, and (b) to provide a system of utilizing outstanding colleagues as teachers and role models in direct consultation to applied settings and in workshops on special areas of health services psychology. From 1981, when Engstrom's term as chair ended, to 1989, when Perry Nicassio of the California School of Professional Psychology in San Diego was appointed chair, the Health Services Committee was essentially inactive. Nicassio helped revitalize this important committee, which had as its mission articulating and serving the needs of the majority of the division's members who were actively engaged in the provision of health psychology services.

The awards committee is chaired by the past-president. The other two members are the president and president-elect. Each year, an average of two awards are given "For Outstanding Contributions to Health Psychology." By tradition, one of the awards typically goes to a "senior" member of the division—in other words, someone who has been a recognized leader in the field for a number of years—and the other award to a "junior" member. The operationalization of this latter designation has generally been roughly less than 10 years post-PhD or younger than 40 years of age. (See Table 43 for a list of the winners of this award by year, beginning in 1980, the first year such an award was made.) In some years only one such award was made; in others, three or four members received this award. To date, Karen Matthews is the only person to win this award twice. Almost always, the contributions that have been recognized have been for the recipient's outstanding program of research and publications; on occasion, other factors, such as the awardee's organizational contributions, have been the deciding factor.

Special Interests

In addition to the standing committees, the division has always had a set of "committees" consisting of members with specific interests in population groups or foci for research–clinical activities. One of the earliest and consistently most active of these groups has been the Committee on Women and Health, the first chair of which was Sharon Hall. The committee was formed after Kathleen Grady, Patricia Keith-Speigel, and Barbara Strudler Wallston developed an initial network of individuals interested in women's health issues and raised with Division 38 leadership the need for recognition of the political and substantive issues relevant to women's health and women in health-related fields. One of the first projects undertaken by this committee was to continue and expand the network of psychologists interested in women's health issues. A number of years later, this committee developed a publication, *Update on Women's Health Issues,* containing abstracts of pertinent studies in this area, which they distributed widely (for a $5 annual charge). They have regularly contributed informative columns on women's health issues to *The Health Psychologist* and have developed and widely disseminated a helpful *Resource Guide to Funding Opportunities in Women's Health.* Many members of this committee, such as Helen Coons, Patricia Morokoff, and Sheryle Gallant, are also active in Division 35 and have been instrumental in helping the APA put on two major research conferences in the area of women's health.

Although few of the special interest committees have been as longstanding or as active as the Committee on Women and Health, it is a model for how these groups get formed and what activities they might carry out. Usually it has been just one or two individuals who have taken the initiative to start such a group and have approached the president with a proposal, which is usually then presented to the executive committee. Sometimes, as with the Committee on Sleep Research and Practice, a whole group of

TABLE 43

Winners of Awards for Outstanding Contributions To Health Psychology

Year				
1980	Patrick H. DeLeon	Judith Rodin	George C. Stone[S]	
1981	David S. Krantz	Joseph D. Matarazzo[S]		
1982	Margaret A. Chesney	Wilbert E. Fordyce[S]		
1983	John J. Conger[S]	Karen A. Matthews		
1984	Kelly D. Brownell	Stephen M. Weiss[S]		
1985	Andrew S. Baum	Neal Miller[S]		
1986	Jerome E. Singer[S]			Barbara Strudler Wallston[S][*]
1987	Sheldon A. Cohen	Robert M. Kaplan	Howard Leventhal[S]	
1988	David C. Glass[S]	Janice Kiecolt-Glaser	Paul Obrist[S][*]	
1989	Neil E. Grunberg	Alan G. Kraut	Richard S. Lazarus[S]	
1990	Neil Schneiderman[S]			
1991	Norman B. Anderson	Thomas J. Coates[S]	John C. Linton[S]	Timothy W. Smith
1992	Richard I. Evans[S]	Robert Klesges	Karen A. Matthews[S]	
1993	Leonard H. Epstein[S]	Dennis Turk[S]		
1994	Abby C. King	James F. Sallis, Jr.	Shelley E. Taylor[S]	
1995	Caryn Lerman	Arthur Stone[S]	Peter Vitaliano[S]	
1996	Karen M. Gil	Rena R. Wing[S]		

[S] Represents a more "senior" member of the Division (at the time of the award)
[*] Posthumously awarded

researchers who had no other "home" within the APA join the division together, much in the same fashion that the Section on Health Research was formed within Division 18 (Psychology in Public Service).

The Committee on Children and Health evolved from a special interest group in Behavioral Pediatrics started by Logan Wright. Members of this group also tended to belong to Section 5 of Division 12. At one point, in the late 1980s, this committee developed and distributed an *Update on Children's Health Issues*, modeled after the publication put out by the Committee on Women and Health. Many of the leaders of this group (e.g., Suzanne Bennett Johnson) have been instrumental over the years in getting Division 38 to cosponsor the biannual Florida Conference on Child Health Psychology.

When Division 38 began in 1978, Raymond Fowler, now chief executive officer of the APA, was active in a group of running psychologists that, for a short while in the early 1980s, was part of the division's special interest group program. Similarly designated groups were the Medical Psychology Network; Psychologists in Family Medical and Primary Health Care; Health Maintenance Organizations; Behavioral Pediatrics; and Students. During this period, A. MacNeill (Mac) Horton was designated the special interest group coordinator and served in that capacity on the executive committee. As noted previously, the behavioral pediatrics group evolved into the Committee on Children and Health, but the others, including the student group, eventually disappeared—except that the HMO group, which began in 1980 as a subcommittee of the Health Services Committee, was resurrected by President Cynthia Belar in 1996.

In 1989, Patrick DeLeon and Angela McBride established the Committee on Nursing and Health Psychology after realizing that more than 100 members of Division 38 were simultaneously nurses and health psychologists. DeLeon, who had headed the division's legislation committee in the early 1980s, was (and still is) an assistant to U.S. Senator Daniel Inouye from Hawaii and was the most influential voice for health psychology on Capitol Hill. I took over from DeLeon as cochair of this committee in 1991 and asked Roberta Smith to be my cochair. Under Smith's leadership, this committee instituted an annual award for outstanding contributions to nursing and health psychology. The first four awards went to Harriet Werley, Jean Johnson, myself, and Angela McBride.

Liaisons

Over the years, various presidents of the division have asked certain members to serve on the executive committee in the capacity of special liaisons. Sometimes, these positions were true liaisons—for example, David Abrams serves as the liaison to Division 50 (Addictions); often, however, they functioned more like ministers "with portfolio." For example, Steven Weiss has been for years the international liaison, linking Division 38 to other health psychology and behavioral medicine organizations around the world. Miriam Kelty, who used to chair the ethics committee, became the ethics liaison when it was realized that she was the only functioning member of the committee. When Margaret Chesney became president of the division, she asked Len Mitnick, who was with the National Institute of Mental Health, to become the health and behavior liaison. This was a timely appointment, coinciding with an increased emphasis on health and behavior throughout the Public Health Service and the Science Directorate of the APA.

MISCELLANEOUS

No history of the division would be complete without addressing long-range and strategic planning, finances, and the division's relationships with other entities within the APA.

Long-Range and Strategic Planning

For the first eight years of its existence, the division engaged in little, if any, long-range or strategic planning. When George Stone assumed the leadership of the division in 1985 to 1986, he became concerned over what he termed "the health of health psychology," so he asked John Linton to chair a committee to do long-range planning (see Stone, 1986). A preliminary report from this committee was printed in the summer–fall 1986 issue of the newsletter. When Kelly Brownell stepped down as president of the division, he suggested that the executive committee should engage in a process of strategic planning. Prior to its meeting in San Francisco in 1991, the executive committee met in Margaret Chesney's suite of offices for a day of strategic planning. Table 44 is a list of the wide range of issues discussed at that meeting, none of which were resolved. Little long-range or strategic planning has occurred since then.

Board Certification

One outgrowth of the Arden House Conference was the establishment of the Council of Health Psychology Training Directors. In 1984, a joint task force of this council and Division 38 established the American Board of Health Psychology (ABHP) as the credentialing body for the specialty practice of health psychology. In 1993, ABHP became fully affiliated with the American Board of Professional Psychology (ABPP). Today, those who

TABLE 44
Strategic Planning Issues: August 1991

1. How can we best assess and meet the needs of our two primary member groups—practitioners/clinicians and researchers/scientists?
2. What is the responsibility of the division toward the development of Health Psychology curricula at the undergraduate and graduate levels?
3. What role should the division play in setting guidelines or standards for practitioners/clinicians or for researchers/scientists? If such a role is defined, how should it be implemented?
4. What position should the division take with regard to informing the public about current research results and service delivery activities in health psychology?
5. What response should we have as other divisions move into health?
6. How important is growth to the division? Is bigger better?
7. How can we best involve our membership in divisional activities?
8. How can we evaluate what we do?
9. What is the role of the division in the international arena?
10. How can we systematically solicit and review proposals for projects that require division funding?

receive the ABPP diploma in health psychology automatically become fellows of the American Academy of Health Psychology (AAHP; see Deardorff, 1996). Starting in 1996, members of Division 38 were offered a 50% reduced application fee ($50) by ABHP. Although there are no formal organizational ties between AAHP and Division 38, almost all of the individuals who are board certified in health psychology are members of the division.

Division Finances

Division 38 is now in a sound financial position (hence the "wealthy" in the title of this chapter), but that was not always the case. When the division was founded in 1978, dues were only $5 per member and $2 for students. Once the division started publishing its own journal and expanded the number of issues of the newsletter, dues needed to be raised to cover those costs, but the dues assessments were still rather modest. As mentioned earlier, in order to hold the three major conferences held by the division, outside grants were sought and secured. In the mid-1980s, when Mary Jansen was treasurer, the coffers were quite tight, partly as a result of the fact that, for a while, many members were mistakenly being mailed two copies of the journal and these costs were being borne by the division, not the publisher. Jansen took immediate steps to rectify the situation and, when I took over as treasurer in 1987, the controls that Jansen had put into place, coupled with a modest dues increase and the division's share of profits from the journal, led to an annual net surplus of income over expenses of approximately $25,000 per year for 6 years. By the time Patricia Dubbert succeeded me as treasurer in 1993, the division had $100,000 invested in treasury notes and bond mutual funds and enough money in reserve to begin thinking about funding special projects (see Wallston, 1993).

Throughout most of my treasurership, I did all of the division's accounting, as had the two treasurers who preceded me. In my last year, however, on the urging of Jack McKay, the APA's chief financial officer, this task was turned over to the APA's divisional accountant, who did the work both professionally and at no cost to the division. It was during this period, also, that the division entered into a contract with Sarah Jordan, director of the APA's Division Services Office, to keep track of the affiliate members of the division and to provide other services to the officers and committee chairs on an as-needed basis.

Other Relationships With the APA

In addition to publications and special conferences, the largest divisional activity each year is the program in conjunction with the APA annual convention. Even though probably no more than 20% of the division's members attend the annual convention in any given year, this activity consumes a great deal of the division's energies and resources. The Division 38 program at the APA has been fairly constant over the first 19 years of its existence. The emphasis has been on a few invited addresses, a number of high quality symposia, and two or three poster sessions. The division does not sponsor any paper presentation sessions at the annual meeting. The summer issue of *The Health Psychologist* always contains a handy pull-out schedule listing the entire Division 38 program.

The presidential address is typically delivered immediately before the annual business meeting and awards presentation, which is almost always held late Saturday afternoon and which is followed by a social hour. Many of the presidential addresses have subsequently been published in *Health Psychology*. The division cosponsors a lot of activities with other divisions, including at least one cosponsored social hour (usually with Division 8— The Society of Personality and Social Psychology). When the APA Science Directorate began science weekend at the APA convention, Division 38 was usually one of the divisions included. In 1995, the entire APA presidential miniconvention, featuring presentations from many Division 38 members, was on psychology's role in health throughout the lifespan.

Although Division 38 has never had more than two seats on the APA council, health psychology has been represented on that body to a larger extent due to the fact that a number of prominent health psychologists have been elected to serve on the APA board of directors. Three former presidents of the APA, Joseph Matarazzo, Charles Spielberger, and Jack G. Wiggins, Jr., had strong ties to Division 38 and Richard Suinn and Patrick DeLeon have been influential board members.

When the directorate structure began at the APA in the late 1980s, Division 38 was "adopted" by the Science Directorate. Barbara Calkins, who was acting director for Science Policy, was the liaison between the Science Directorate and the division, attending the executive committee meetings and contributing columns to the newsletter. During Lewis Lipsitt's years as head of the Science Directorate, it was almost as if the APA was making the division's agenda its own. For a year or two, health and behavior preoccupied the entire directorate. Beginning with Barbara Melamed's presidency of the division, the ties with the Science Directorate have loosened, but the ties with the Policy, Practice, and Education Directorates have strengthened. Throughout the 1980s, the APA tended to view Division 38 as a "science division." In the 1990s, the tendency is more toward viewing Division 38 as a "practice division." In reality, it is both.

This duality between science and practice was never more evident than when, in 1990, various boards, committees, divisions and other groups within the APA hotly debated the issue of whether psychologists should be permitted by law to prescribe medication. Although the majority of Division 38's executive committee was initially opposed to psychologists having prescription privileges, it was Patrick DeLeon, a key member of the division, who was spearheading the effort both within the APA and on Capitol Hill for extending to psychologists the right to prescribe. Because of the respect DeLeon had among the other members of the executive committee, the division ended up strongly supporting additional research and study of the feasibility of providing training to psychologists in pharmacology. The Division of Health Psychology tried its best to make sure that the practice of health psychology would be based on "hard" evidence rather than political expediency.

THE FUTURE

The first 19 years of its existence has seen the Division of Health Psychology take its place as one of the largest and most influential divisions within the APA. There are a few signs, however, that the future for this division might not be as golden as the past. After years of steady growth, membership in Division 38 has begun to recede, a drop of 10% from 1995 to 1996, despite the fact that the APA members who subscribe to *Health Psychology* can get the journal at lower cost by joining Division 38 than by ordering it from the APA at the member price. Other divisions, such as 17 (Counseling Psychology) and 42 (Psychologists in Independent Practice), have started sections on health psychology that may do a better job of meeting their members' affiliative needs than does Division 38. The percentage of division members who responded to divisional surveys went from 57% in 1981, when the division was still new and exciting, to 45% in 1988, when it was entering its adolescence, to less than 10% in 1994, when it was part of the mainstream establishment. Multidisciplinary organizations, such as the Society of Behavioral Medicine, are competing with the APA for the loyalty and energies of health psychologists. Each year it becomes harder and harder for the Nominations and Elections Committee to put together a slate of members willing to run for division offices.

But the most profound factor affecting the future of Division 38 is the fact that with the advent of managed care driving mental health services and companies to redefine and repackage themselves as "behavioral health providers," what was once unique to health psychology has now been adopted and, perhaps, coopted by mainstream clinical psychology, a trend that has been developing for the past 5 to 10 years and may very well threaten the future growth of Division 38 (see Wallston, 1992). Although being part of the mainstream can be interpreted as a sign that the division has been successful in accomplishing its objectives, there is nothing quite as powerful as having "something to prove" to motivate professionals' activity. If the leadership of the Division of Health Psychology is truly "healthy, wealthy, and wise," it will capitalize on the fact that Division 38 is "the only home for the breadth of health psychology within the APA. . . . If our Division is to have a distinctive role in the future, we must continue to support this diversity" (Belar, 1996, 14).

CONCLUSION

In 1997, Division 38 is riding the crest of interest in behavioral aspects of physical as well as mental health. The journal is well respected and well cited, the members are active in the organization and recognized as leaders in behavioral medicine throughout the world. As the division moves out of its teenage years to enter into young adulthood and the twenty-first century, the challenge for us is to remain as vibrant as we have been in the almost-first two decades of our history.

REFERENCES

Anderson, N. B. (Guest Ed.). (December, 1995). Special Issue: Behavioral and sociocultural perspectives on ethnicity and health. *Health Psychology, 14*(7), 587–658.

APA Task Force on Health Research. (1976). Contributions of psychology to health research: Patterns, problems, and potentials. *American Psychologist, 31*, 263–274.

Baum, A. (Special Ed.). (1989). Proceedings of the National Working Conference on Research in Health and Behavior. *Health Psychology, 8*(6), 629–784.

Belar, C. D. (1996). President's column. *The Health Psychologist, 14*(3), 1 ff.

Cohen, S. (1988). Getting your grant funded by NIH. *The Health Psychologist, 10*(2), 3 ff.

Cohen, S. (1990). Funding your unfunded PHS grant proposal. *The Health Psychologist, 12*(3), 6.

Deardorff, W. W. (1996). Board certification: What do you mean you're not board certified? *The Health Psychologist, 18*(3), 10–11.

Dorsal, T. N. (1984). A model for health psychology. *Health Psychology, 3*(6), 583–584.

Gatchel, R. J., & Blanchard, E. B. (Eds.). (1993). *Psychophysiological disorders: Research and clinical applications*. Washington, DC: American Psychological Association.

Guze, S. B., Matarazzo, J. D., & Saslow, G. (1953). A formulation of principles of comprehensive medicine with special reference to learning theory. *Journal of Clinical Psychology, 9*, 127–136.

Matarazzo, J. D. (1979). President's column. *The Health Psychologist, 1*(1), 1.

Matarazzo, J. D. (1980). Behavioral health and behavioral medicine: Frontiers for a new health psychology. *American Psychologist, 35*, 807–817.

Matthews, K. A. (1993). Health Psychology: Journal goes to 8200 APA members. *The Health Psychologist, 15*(1), 3.

Nicassio, P. M., & Smith, T. W. (Eds.). (1995). *Managing chronic illness: A biopsychosocial perspective*. Washington, DC: American Psychological Association.

Robison, J. T. (1981, Summer–Fall). A note from the secretary. *The Health Psychologist, 3*(2), 6.

Schofield, W. (1969). The role of psychology in the delivery of health services. *American Psychologist, 24*, 565–584.

Schneiderman, N. (1992). President's column. *The Health Psychologist, 14*(1), 1.

Schwartz, G. E., & Weiss, S. M. (1978). Yale Conference on Behavioral Medicine: A proposed definition and statement of goals. *Journal of Behavioral Medicine, 1*, 3–11.

Singer, J. E. (1982). President's column. *The Health Psychologist, 4*(1), 1.

Stone, G. C. (Ed.). (1983). Proceedings of the National Working Conference on Education and Training in Health Psychology. *Health Psychology, 2*(Suppl. 5), 1–151.

Stone, G. C. (1986). President's column. *The Health Psychologist, 8*(1), 1.

Stone, G. C., Cohen, F., & Adler, N. E. (Eds).(1979). *Health psychology: A hand-book—Theories, applications, and challenges of a psychological approach to the health care system*. San Francisco: Jossey-Bass.

Wallston, K. A. (1992). Health psychology in the USA. In S. Maes, H. Leventhal, & M. Johnston (Eds.), *International Review of Health Psychology, Volume 2* (pp. 215–228). Chicester, England: John Wiley & Sons.

Wallston, K. A. (1993). Treasurer's report. *The Health Psychologist, 15*(2), 6.

Wilson, D. K., Rodrigue, J. R., & Taylor, W. C. (Eds.). (1996). *Adolescent health promotion in minority populations*. Washington, DC: American Psychological Association.

10

A HISTORY OF DIVISION 43
(FAMILY PSYCHOLOGY):
IT'S ALL IN THE FAMILY

CAROL L. PHILPOT

The Division of Family Psychology (Division 43) is a relatively new division in the American Psychological Association (APA), as is reflected in its number. As this history is written, Division 43 is only 12 years old. Because the division is so young, it is still possible to provide the reader with a chronological review of accomplishments, frustrations, controversies, programs, influential individuals, and structural changes, as well as major themes running throughout our brief history. After a historical review of the roots of the division, this chapter is structured in a year-by-year format. I will identify major achievements and themes on a yearly basis, something that would be impossible if we were 30 or 40 years old, as are many of the divisions discussed in this volume. Although this document will serve as a reference for important events, names, dates, and documents, it is not simply

This chapter has been adapted with permission from *Family Psychologist, 10*(3), © 1994.

Material for this history came from interviews with the division presidents, from documents forwarded by various division members, from back issues of *The Family Psychologist,* and from the memories of the pioneers of the division. I particularly would like to acknowledge George Nixon, whose unpublished history of Division 43 written several years ago (Nixon, 1990) provided a rich and valuable source of information. I would also like to acknowledge Deborah Russo, whose assistance in gathering documentation for this chapter was invaluable.

a dry narrative, a collection of facts with no unifying theme. Indeed readers will discover several common threads throughout the twelve presidencies that continue to be vital issues for the division.

The Academy of Family Psychology gave birth to Division 43 in 1984; this will be discussed in more depth later on. The division began because psychologists with a family systems perspective wanted a home within the APA to share scientific inquiry, promote educational goals, develop therapeutic paradigms, and generate political influence on public policy. This ambitious agenda was undertaken by a dedicated few whose hard work and leadership have made us one of the largest divisions in the APA (APA, 1996). In just 12 years the Division of Family Psychology has come a long way.

THE HISTORICAL CONTEXT

The family therapy movement began as an amalgamation of many diverse disciplines, including social work, sex therapy, marital counseling, anthropology, sociology, and social psychiatry. Most of the pioneers of family therapy (Nathan Ackerman, Murray Bowen, Don Jackson, Theodore Lidz, Salvador Minuchin, Ivan Boszormenyi-Nagy, John Weakland, Carl Whitaker, and Lyman Wynne) were psychiatrists who had become frustrated with the inefficacy of psychoanalysis in the treatment of such problems as schizophrenia, juvenile delinquency, and childhood mental disorders. Independently they began to realize that much of the aberrant behavior and thinking they observed in their patients was in response to on-going interactions among family members, an adaptive response to maladaptive family patterns. Boosted by the seminal work of an anthropologist, Gregory Bateson, and his colleagues, Jay Haley, John Weakland, and Don Jackson, a body of theoretical literature began to emerge in the late 1950s and early 1960s. Most of the clinicians working with families and couples in the field during this time were ministers or social workers; the only theoretical pioneer who was a social worker was Virginia Satir. Nevertheless, due to her charisma and teaching ability, Satir was a major contributor to the popularization of family therapy technique and theory.

There were only a few psychologists represented among the earliest family therapists; the most notable was John Elderkin Bell, who may have been the first psychologist to see families conjointly in therapy. Also notable, in that they developed innovative theories or clinical techniques, were James Framo, Gerald Zuk, Ross Speck, and Carolyn Attneave, all of whom emerged from the Philadelphia area, and Robert McGregor, Harold Goolishian, and Harlene Anderson from Galveston, Texas.

It would be impossible in a chapter of this size to discuss the contributions of each major theorist in the many centers of family therapy that developed throughout the country. The interested reader is referred to "The History of Professional Marriage and Family Therapy" (Broderick & Schrader, 1991) for a thorough and succinct account of the early history of family therapy. However, the story of family *psychology's* development deserves mention. Psychology was relatively late in accepting the value of family systems theory, partially as a result of early psychology's emphasis on traditional assessment as a defining element. Although more recently psychologists (Nurse, in press) have described the use of traditional assessment instruments in systems work and many others (Epstein, Baldwin, & Bishop, 1983; Olson & Portner, 1983; Snyder, 1979; Spanier, 1976) have developed tests designed to look at interpersonal functioning, this was not part of the earlier development of the field. Furthermore, many psychologists were trained to think of family and marital therapy as the province of social work, a field that held less prestige than clinical psychology (D. Routh, personal communication, June 14, 1996). Nevertheless, over the years, psychologists, like the pioneer family psychiatrists before them, began to find that many of the symptoms in the cases they saw were a result of the dysfunctional relationships in which their clients were involved. Furthermore, psychologists who specialized in children and youth found the family system to be critical to effective therapy. Therefore more and more psychologists began to engage in marital and family therapy, employing the same approach to systems work as they had to individual psychotherapy. That is, they generated theory and tested hypotheses based on clinical observation and research findings, they developed and used appropriate psychometric testing, and they implemented therapeutic techniques informed by research (Kaslow, 1991). The difference was their theoretical model—a systemic epistemology that emphasized the interaction within and among systems, the construction of reality within a family context, and the incorporation of such concepts as homeostasis, first- and second-order change, multigenerational transmission processes, triangulation, enmeshment, disengagement, and so forth. (For the reader who is unfamiliar with such concepts, the following brief and oversimplified explanation is provided. *Homeostasis* refers to the tendency of a family system to find and seek to maintain a certain level of interaction in which each family member plays a particular role and gets a payoff. *First-order change* is a change in behavior of family members, whereas *second-order change* refers to a change in the rules that govern family behavior. The *multigenerational transmission* process refers to the tendency of patterns of behavior to be passed down across multiple generations. *Triangulation* is the projection onto or inclusion of a third party into a conflict between two others. *Enmeshment* is the overinvolvement between certain members of the family, which does not allow for independent functioning. *Disengagement* is the total lack of involvement between family members so that there is little interaction between them and very little knowledge of one another's emotional life. These are just a few of the many systemic concepts that family psychologists endorse.)

Those psychologists with a family systems perspective were forced to look to multidisciplinary organizations such as the American Association for Marriage and Family Therapy (AAMFT) and the American Family Therapy Academy (AFTA) for the collegial stimulation offered by a professional organization in the areas of theory, research, and practice. As the professionals trained in psychology grew, they began to long for a home within the APA itself (Kaslow, 1987).

THE EARLY ROOTS

The roots of the Division of Family Psychology began with the formation of the Academy of Psychologists in Marriage Counseling, founded by Lee Steiner at the 1959 annual meeting of the APA in St. Louis. The objects of the academy were

> (1) to promote and advance marriage counseling as a science and profession among psychologists, (2) to set and maintain, among psychologists, professional standards in marriage counseling, (3) to hold meetings, clinical sessions, education and training sessions, conduct research, and institute and carry on other activities common to professional academies to help further the preceding objectives, and (4) to join, by professional means, with other groups and individuals in furthering the objectives of the Academy. (*Constitution of the Academy of Psychologists in Marital Counseling, Inc.*, p. 1, 1960)

Milton Shumsky served as the first treasurer and Hirsch Silverman was president-elect. The academy started with a total of 15 psychologists, dues were set at an exorbitant amount of $1 per year, and a newsletter was established. During most of the next two decades, the academy organized a hospitality suite at the APA convention. In February 1967, the academy began to publish the *Journal of the Academy of Psychologists in Marital Counseling*, edited by Lee Steiner. A formal attempt for division status in the 1960s failed because the academy membership was too small (Nixon, 1990).

In the second decade of its existence, the academy selected Anthony J. Vilhotti to serve as treasurer and executive director, thus centralizing academy operations and providing organization and structure. During this time the academy considered becoming a section of Division 29 (Psychotherapy) but decided that would not provide them with the status they desired (Nixon, 1990). In addition, the members of the academy ran into increasing opposition toward family psychology in the APA (Nixon, 1990). Throughout the 1970s, the academy sponsored a series of APA hospitality suite programs that spotlighted major pioneers in family psychology such as James Framo, whose object relations approach to marital therapy is well known. In 1976, the academy cosponsored the First International Congress of Family Therapy, titled "Coming of Age," in Israel (Dudman, 1976; also D. Araoz, personal communication, September 1996).

MOVING TOWARD THE MAINSTREAM

During the 1979 meeting of the academy in New York City, Daniel Araoz proposed that the academy create the American Board of Family Psychology (ABFamP) to award diplomates in the fields of marital and family therapy and marital sex therapy. It was believed that a cadre of diplomates could serve an important role. A committee chaired by Ronald Levant was established to start ABFamP (Nixon, 1990; *The Relationship,* 1982). It was also due to the urging of Daniel Araoz that the academy recognized the growing importance of sex therapy by changing its name to The Academy of Psychologists in Marital, Sex, and Family Therapy in 1980.

Richard H. Mikesell initiated a comprehensive 4-day hospitality suite program as APA convention chair for the academy in 1980, which was so successful that he was called on to repeat it in 1981. Mikesell went on to serve as academy president from 1982 to 1983. During his presidency, (a) the Academy of Psychologists in Marital, Sex, and Family Therapy changed its name to the Academy of Family Psychology, (b) the *American Journal of Family Therapy* became a member benefit, and (c) the academy was positioned for APA division membership. The term *family psychology* originally coined by Luciano L'Abate (L'Abate, 1983, 1985, 1987, 1992), was adopted by M. Duncan Stanton and Richard H. Mikesell. The name change was considered pivotal to the success of obtaining division status in the APA, as it both emphasized the scientific training of *psychology* and established *family* as the inclusive term that incorporated the fields of marital and sex therapy as well (Mikesell, 1983a; Nixon, 1990).

Lawrence Vogel followed as 1983 to 1984 president. His era was marked by what may have been one of the most extensive and successful lobbying efforts in the history of divisions attempting to join the APA. When the academy first appeared on the floor of the APA Council of Representatives, only three members voted in favor of division status (Nixon, 1990). By the end of the campaign, when the final vote was called, only three members voted against it. Richard Mikesell, Lawrence Vogel, George Nixon, and Don-David Lusterman led the lobbying efforts for approval of the petition for division status by the APA Council of Representatives, and the Division

TABLE 45
Boards of Directors

1985

President	George F. Nixon
President-Elect	Gloria Gottsegen
Past President	Lawrence Vogel
Treasurer	Anthony Vilhotti
Secretary	Florence W. Kaslow

1986

President	Gloria Gottsegen
President-Elect	Florence Kaslow
Past President	George F. Nixon
Treasurer	Ervin L. Betts
Secretary	Patricia Moldawsky
Council Representative	Richard H. Mikesell

1987

President	Florence W. Kaslow
President-Elect	Arthur M. Bodin
Past-President	Gloria Gottsegen
Treasurer	Ervin L. Betts
Secretary	Patricia Moldawsky
Council Representative	Richard H. Mikesell

1988

President	Arthur M. Bodin
President-Elect	James F. Alexander
Past President	Florence W. Kaslow
Treasurer	Ervin L. Betts
Secretary	Josephine P. Beebe
Council Representatives	Richard H. Mikesell
	Harold A. Goolishian

1989

President	James F. Alexander
President-Elect	Alan D. Entin
Past President	Arthur M. Bodin
Treasurer	Ervin L. Betts
Secretary	Josephine P. Beebe
Council Representative	Harold A. Goolishian

1990

President	Alan D. Entin
President-Elect	Josephine P. Beebe
Past President	James F. Alexander
Treasurer	Ervin L. Betts
Secretary	Diana A. Kirschner
Council Representatives	Harold A. Goolishian
	Richard H. Mikesell

1991

President	Josephine P. Beebe
President-Elect	Carol L. Philpot
Past President	Alan D. Entin
Treasurer	Sylvia Shellenberger
Secretary	Diana Kirschner
Council Representatives	Arthur M. Bodin
	Richard H. Mikesell

1992

President	Carol L. Philpot
President-Elect	Robert J. Wellman
Past President	Josephine P. Beebe
Treasurer	Sylvia Shellenberger
Secretary	Gary Brooks
Council Representative	Richard H. Mikesell

1993

President	Robert J. Wellman
President-Elect	Ronald F. Levant
Past President	Carol L. Philpot
Treasurer	James Bray
Secretary	Gary R. Brooks
Council Representatives	Arthur M. Bodin
	Richard H. Mikesell

1994

President	Ronald F. Levant
President-Elect	James Bray
Past President	Robert J. Wellman
Treasurer	James H. Bray
Secretary	Louise Silverstein
Council Representatives	Arthur M. Bodin
	Richard H. Mikesell

1995

President	James Bray
President-Elect	Gary R. Brooks
Past President	Ronald Levant
Treasurer	Louise Silverstein
Secretary	Marsali Hansen
Council Representatives	Richard H. Mikesell

1996

President	Gary R. Brooks
President-Elect	Louise Silverstein
Past President	James Bray
Secretary	Michele Harway
Treasurer	Marsali Hansen
Council Representatives	Arthur Bodin
	Richard H. Mikesell

of Family Psychology was born in 1984 in Toronto (Nixon, 1990; *Proceedings of APA, for the year 1984,* 1985). This was particularly noteworthy because it was a time during which the general direction in the APA was toward not approving any new divisions at all. In fact, a moratorium had been placed on accepting new divisions (Mikesell, 1983b) and was lifted in January 1984, partially in response to letters of support for a division of family psychology (*Proceedings of APA, for the year 1983,* 1984). George Nixon assumed the presidency of the division in Toronto and began the process of organizing the new division from the Academy of Family Psychology, which ceased to exist at this point.

WHY A DIVISION OF FAMILY PSYCHOLOGY?

In the *Petition in Support of the Creation of an APA Division of Family Psychology* co-authored by M. Duncan Stanton and Richard H. Mikesell (Table 45), the purposes of the Division of Family Psychology were established as the following:

> (a) to advance the contributions of psychology as a discipline to the understanding of family psychology through basic and applied research;
> (b) to promote the education of psychologists in matters of family psychology including the appropriate use of psychologists in the field of family psychology
> (c) to inform the psychological communities and appropriate institutions, and the general public, of current research, educational, and service activities in this area. (*The Relationship,* 1983, p. 7 ff)

THE NEXT TWELVE YEARS

This history chronicles the efforts, successes, and frustrations of the first 12 years of the division as the leadership and members struggled to accomplish and enlarge the vision of its creators.

August 1984 to January 1986: Solidifying the Division

George Nixon served as the first president of the division from August 1984 until December 1985. As Nixon described his term as president, it was a period of time during which the organization evolved from a small group of activists with a tight-knit leadership involved in a social revolution into "an institutionally viable member of the mainstream of psychology" (1990, p. 11). Nixon believed that the primary accomplishment of his presidency was the creation of a broad-based system that would lead to democratic elections within the Division of Family Psychology. The transition period was painful because not all members of the academy were pleased with the change in standing and size resulting from division status. Although it was difficult to do, Nixon was satisfied that the division met all of the personal and political commitments made by the former leadership of the academy during his presidency. Much of the energy of the division went into establishing the structure of the organization according to APA formats. During Nixon's tenure (a) the publication of the bulletin, *The Family Psychologist*, began, with Robert Wellman as founding editor; (b) the decision was made to publish a division journal, *The Journal of Family Psychology*; (c) a publications board empowered to develop and oversee a broad range of publication activities was created; and (d) the division began negotiations toward becoming a full member of the midwinter conference with Divisions 42 (Psychologists in Independent Practice) and 29 (Psychotherapy). Nixon was particularly pleased that the division survived on a shoestring budget ($19,170.36) for a year and a quarter and did not leave the next administration in debt (Minutes of the Board of Directors Meeting, 1985).

Nixon (1990) lamented the loss of members who had signed the petition for the new division during this transition period. Many did not become members of the division. He expressed concern that many people in the academy disagreed with the decision to become a division or got lost in the shuffle. He was also disappointed that it proved to be difficult to recruit a large number of senior members of the field into the division or to establish interorganizational relationships with AFTA and AAMFT, other influential and respected groups in the field of family. He believed that these failures were due to a concern among many individuals that the formation of the division posed a risk of dividing the family field. However, members of the APA with a particular interest in family who had never been a member of the academy, (i.e., members of the Division of Child, Youth and Family Services), became interested in the new division and joined at this time (D. Routh, personal communication, June 14, 1996).

1986: Establishing the *Journal of Family Psychology*

In 1986, Gloria Behar Gottsegen took over the presidency. Gottsegen cited two major accomplishments of the division under her tenure. The first was the negotiation of the contract for the first *Journal of Family Psychology (JFP)* with Sage Publishing and the selection of the first editor, Howard Liddle (Gottsegen, 1986). The first publications board, with Arthur Bodin as chair, was instrumental in overseeing the policies and principles followed in getting this journal off the ground (Bodin, 1986). According to Howard Liddle (Liddle, 1986), the creation of *JFP*, unlike other existing family journals, provided a forum that could represent the family systems perspective to mainstream psychology and inform—and perhaps influence—the relevant developments in that field. Liddle called for articles that would create a lively interchange of critical thinking and analysis and that challenged perspectives and conclusions from different vantage points. The broad scope of the journal was expected to include family counseling and therapy, education, family theory, assessment, research, public policy, family and community, pediatric and geriatric family psychology, the impact of illness on the family, forensic family psychology (custody matters, family violence and other abuse, termination of parental rights), ethics, book reviews, and reviews of audiovisual materials (Liddle, 1986).

The second major accomplishment during Gottsegen's presidency was the successful negotiation with Divisions 29 (Psychotherapy) and 42 (Psychologists in Independent Practice) to become a full member of the annual midwinter meetings (Gottesegen, 1986). Several years earlier Divisions 29 and 42 had combined their efforts to hold a miniconvention in a warm location approximately midway between APA annual conventions. This is a very successful collaborative association that has continued to produce excellent educational and networking opportunities each year. In addition, a successful campaign landed the division a second seat on the Council of Representatives of the APA, which unfortunately began a continuing pattern of gaining and then losing the council seat. Liaisons with other groups, both within and outside the APA, began to develop. In support of the American Board of Family Psychology, the division adopted *The Knowledge Base in Family Psychology* (Kaslow, 1986) as a working document to substantiate to ABPP the existence of the specialty of family psychology. Committees were established and evolved from the membership to function as working groups. These included administrative committees such as archives and history, awards, bylaws, continuing education, election, fellows, finance, membership, program, and publishing board, as well as special interest committees such as aging, clinical training, *DSM-IV*, ethical issues, gay and lesbian family issues, mediation, minority issues, research and women's issues. Division 43 was able to nominate and confirm a cadre of existing APA fellows during this first year of eligibility, as well as develop policies and procedures to elect new ones. Invited addresses by Carolyn Attneave, noted for the development of networking family interventions, and David Olson, known for the circumplex model of family functioning, and conversations with Murray Bowen, multigenerational family theorist, and Paul Dell, systems epistemologist, were highlights of the APA convention during Gottsegen's term.

Disappointments during Gottsegen's term included a lack of membership growth and a failure to make much impact on the APA boards and committees. Another area of concern was the decline in the attendance at the hospitality suite that had previously been a vital educational organ of the division. Gottsegen felt some of the enthusiasm had gone out of the division by the time she assumed the presidency. In retrospect, this might have been a developmental stage, the let-down after such a concerted effort to become a division (quoted in Nixon, 1990).

In looking toward the future, Gottsegen recommended a policy and planning committee to address the issues of structure and long-term planning. She also reiterated the importance of developing a presence in the APA and increasing the membership of the division (Nixon, 1990).

1987: Increasing Visibility

Perhaps the hallmark of Florence Kaslow's tenure as president was the increased visibility of the division both within and outside of the APA. Due to Kaslow's influence and contacts and the careful groundwork laid by previous presidents, a number of things were accomplished that contributed to this outcome. These included

- broadening the membership to include a number of outstanding senior family psychologists such as Alan Gurman, noted author, editor and marital therapist;
- establishing liaisons with AFTA and AAMFT;
- creating liaisons with relevant APA committees and other divisions in order to contribute a systems perspective to their deliberations;
- enhancing the connection with the academic and research wings of the profession;
- initiating the Task Force on Classification and Diagnosis, which began to grapple with the issues of relational diagnoses;
- expanding the Women's Issues Committee into a Gender Issues Committee to include men's issues and gay and lesbian issues as well;
- creating a State Legislative Committee chaired by Irene Goldenberg;
- the recording of the contributions of *psychologists* to the family field in education, theory, research, and practice which culminated in the publication of a two volume book, *Voices in Family Psychology*, in 1990 (Kaslow, 1990).

This was also the first year that the division cosponsored the midwinter conference with Divisions 29 and 42 and the year that the first volume of the *Journal of Family Psychology* was published. A number of new committees and task forces were established, a policy and procedure manual was written, the divisional bulletin, *The Family Psychologist*, was expanded, a past president's cabinet was created, an official liaison with the American Board of

Family Psychology was established, and the membership was increased to almost 2000 members. Division 43 was successful in supporting candidates for APA boards and committees by working with other divisions. For example, Arthur Bodin was successfully nominated to the APA publications board, Gloria Gottsegen to the membership committee, Jack Wiggins to the finance committee, John Curry to the board of convention affairs, and Sylvia Herz to the Board of Social and Ethical Responsibility for Psychology (BSERP). Kaslow, as president of the Division of Family Psychology, was invited as a guest of the president of AAMFT to its annual meeting, which began a tradition between the two family organizations. Also during 1987, the practice divisions established the practice roundtable, annual meetings among the leadership of the applied divisions in which Division 43 was a participant.

In spite of these successes, Kaslow (personal communication, September 1993) cited disappointments in two areas: (a) limited participation by major family researchers in divisional activities, presentations, and publications and (b) the lack of impact on the APA in general or the Practice Directorate in particular. As for future opportunities, the promotion of the division and the journal remained a priority, as did continued effort to attract the research contingent of family psychology. Finally, Kaslow pointed to the potential development and field testing of a family diagnostic manual as a major contribution of Division 43 to the family field (Kaslow, personal communication, September 1993).

1988: Expansion Into the Larger World

Among the major accomplishments during Arthur Bodin's term as president was the continued growth of the *Journal of Family Psychology (JFP)*. Probably because of the active effort on behalf of the division to get *JFP* in as many libraries as possible, it became the fastest growing journal in the history of Sage Publications. The division began offering *JFP* as a recruiting incentive for individuals who were applying for membership. In addition, a new membership flyer was produced to assist in the recruitment of members, and a student affiliate category of membership was created. Division 43 became an active member of the Joint Council for Professional Education in Psychology (JCPEP) and exerted substantial influence in the development of the final document emerging from this commission (JCPEP, 1990). The leadership also took an active role in mobilizing diverse interests within the division to work against the political move to split the APA into separate academic and practitioner societies (Bodin, 1988). Other organizational activities that took place through Bodin's guidance and support included

1. The development of a state networking committee to influence public policy;

2. A survey by the ethics committee addressing both members and state licensing boards;
3. A survey of family psychology graduate programs that was instrumental in assisting the American Board of Family Psychology in its negotiations with ABPP;
4. An assemblage of the chairs of family psychology programs;
5. The development of "Principles of Gender-Sensitive Psychotherapy" (Brooks & Philpot, 1988), an expansion of feminist psychotherapy to include sensitivity to men's issues as well;
6. The establishment of a student research award, designed to attract young family researchers and their dissertation directors (See Table 46);
8. The expansion of the Classification and Diagnosis Task Force into an interorganizational task force, with Florence Kaslow as the first chair.

It was during Arthur Bodin's presidency that the APA dealt with the restructuring proposal by the Group on Reorganization (GOR), scientific and academic psychologists in the governance of the APA who felt that the needs of scientists were not being met by the APA under its present structure. The board of directors of Division 43 unanimously opposed the GOR plan to reorganize the APA with the following resolution:

> Division 43 has always valued and represented the integration of science and practice within the Division of Family Psychology. We have studied the GOR Report and conclude, with regret, that it is inconsistent with that aim. (Board of Directors, 1988)

One major area of disappointment for Bodin was the difficulty encountered in attempting to influence state and national policy on family issues. Because of the logistical problems in coordinating efforts in a national organization, he found that the division did not have the same impact as state psychological associations have had. It was to overcome this difficulty that the state networking committee was developed, but it ultimately had little influence over policy-making bodies. A second area of disappointment was the failure, despite major effort, to involve minority and ethnic groups in the governance of the division. Finally, like the presidents before him, Bodin expressed concern that despite a successful expansion of liaisons with APA boards and committees, the division still was ineffective in making major changes in the policies and activities of these groups (Bodin, personal communication, September 1993; quoted in Nixon, 1990).

Consistent with his desire to affect public policy, Bodin envisioned the development of a system within the division that could affect family policy by serving as a source of information to national policy makers and the

TABLE 46
Awards

Family Psychologist of the Year	
1984	Richard H. Mikesell[a]
1986	Florence W. Kaslow
1987	Don-David Lusterman
1988	George Nixon
1989	Harold Goolishian
1990	Arthur Bodin
1991	Howard A. Liddle
1992	Carolyn Attneave
1993	James F. Alexander
1994	Luciano L'Abate
1995	Susan H. McDaniel

[a] Awarded by the Academy of Family Psychology

The Division of Family Psychology has several different categories of awards including certificates of appreciation, president's commendations, Distinguished Service Awards, the Family Psychologist of the Year Award, the Student Research Award, and the Carolyn Attneave Award. The first three of these awards are presented to people who have served the Division or family psychology in some capacity. The recipients of these awards are too numerous to list, although I have included the most recent Distinguished Service Awards. The Family Psychologist of the Year Award is presented to a member of the division for sustained outstanding contributions to the field of family psychology, in either education, research, or practice. The Student Research Award is presented to a student whose research (thesis or dissertation) is on a topic relevant to family psychology research. The Carolyn Attneave Award recognizes psychologists who have made significant contributions to diversity in family psychology.

Student Research Award (established 1988)

Year	Recipient	Institution	Advisor	Paper Title
1991	Alice Newberry	University of Utah	James Alexander	"Gender as a Process Variable in Family Therapy"
1992	Guy S. Diamond	California School of Professional Psychology	Howard A. Liddle	"Process Study of Therapeutic Impasses Between Parents and Adolescents in Family Therapy"
1993	Mitchell Dickey	Yale University	Alan E. Kazdin	"Therapist Experience and the Process of Family Therapy"
1994	Alice Burr-Harris	University of Missouri	Charles Bourduin	"The Ecology of Violent Offending in Early Adolescence"
1995	Diana M. Doumas	University of Southern California	Gayla Margolin	"The Relationship Between Marital Interaction, Daily Experiences, and Health Behaviors: An Extension of the Work-Family Spillover Model"

Carolyn Attneave Award (established in 1994)
1995: Nancy Boyd-Franklin

media. Other opportunities for future development included participating in achieving the inclusion of family systems in educational policies, spreading family systems concepts throughout the APA, and developing systemic diagnoses (Bodin, personal communication, September 1993).

1989: Integrating Research, Education, Practice

The election of James Alexander as the first full-time academician and researcher to be president of the division highlighted the systemic values of Division 43 that research, education, and practice should support and enhance one another. Indeed, if he were to select a theme for his tenure as president, it might be the integration of practice, academics, and research (J. Alexander, personal communication, September 1993; quoted in Nixon, 1990). It was during his presidency that the division took a leadership role at the Division Leadership Conference and in the Practice Coalition that had been initiated in previous years. It was also during this year that family psychology was recognized as an American Board of Professional Psychology (ABPP) specialty, entering the vestibule period on August 2, 1989 (Gottlieb & Nixon, 1989). During the period from August 1989 until October, 1991, individuals who had become diplomates under ABFamP had the opportunity to sit for the ABPP exam in family psychology. The achievement of ABPP specialty status was accomplished under the leadership of Michael Gottlieb, then ABFamP president, George Nixon, executive director of ABFamP, and Gerald Weeks, senior author of the specialty document submitted to ABPP.

In addition, in 1989, Florence Kaslow received the APA Award for Distinguished Professional Contributions to Applied Psychology as a Professional Practice (*American Psychologist*, 1990, pp. 471–472). Division 43 continued to participate in substantive interorganizational activities such as the Joint Council on Professional Education in Psychology (JCPEP) and the Task Force for Classification and Diagnosis. The systemic values of gender-sensitive psychotherapy began to affect other divisions through liaisons and presentations. Liaisons with boards and committees within the APA and with other family organizations were strengthened. Alexander (personal communication, September 1993) felt that these events indicated that Division 43 was beginning to make an effective impact on the APA and other national groups. During his administration, the bylaws of the division were revised, an update of the policy and procedure manual was begun, and a reorganization of board structure took place, which was designed to help the division coordinate its resources more efficiently in supporting the work of the proliferation of committees and task forces.

The APA annual convention programs in New Orleans in 1989 reflected Alexander's concern with integrating research and practice. Family researcher Neil Jacobson, known for his process research on couple interaction, presented "Depression, Marital Interaction & Marital Therapy," and Robert Geffner brought together an outstanding group of experts who discussed the application of recent research on treating incest victims and offenders. Alexander was particularly pleased that Henry P. David, who received a division award for his distinguished contribution to research in public policy, presented an invited address on unwanted pregnancies and the effects of abortion, a result of his cross-cultural research on this topic.

In spite of his own stature as a researcher in the field, Alexander was frustrated that family researchers were not more active in divisional activities and hoped that in the future family psychology would be able to get research and politics more closely integrated. A second concern for Alexander was the lack of financial resources to fund all of the worthy activities undertaken by the committees and task forces existing during his term, because nearly one third of the yearly budget (approximately $85,000) went toward producing the *Journal of Family Psychology* (Minutes of Board of Directors Meeting, 1989). Because raising dues, then set at $32 per year, did not seem to be a desirable solution, the division would need to find some other means of accomplishing its mission. He envisioned opportunities for the division in addressing issues of family violence, longitudinal research, the self in the system, and computerized behavior analysis in process research (J. Alexander, personal communication, September 1993; quoted in Nixon, 1990).

1990: Defining the Division

Alan Entin's year as president began with a strategic planning retreat for board members, past presidents, and administrative committee chairs, conducted by Raymond and Sandy Fowler. The following mission statement was produced by this retreat:

> Family psychology integrates the understanding of individuals, couples, families and their wider contexts. The Division of Family Psychology seeks to promote human welfare through the development, dissemination, and application of knowledge about the dynamics, structure, and functioning of families. (Entin, 1990)

In addition, the participants at the retreat generated a list of goals for the division, primary among which were increasing the membership and developing a more efficient governance structure and accounting system.

A major change that occurred during Entin's presidency was the transfer of the division's journal, *The Journal of Family Psychology*, to the APA convention in August. This transfer freed the division from a heavy financial obligation and allowed the reduction of dues for the membership to $29.00 per year. The transfer of the journal to the APA at the end of the contract with Sage Publications was ably negotiated by Richard Mikesell, with the help of committee members Josephine Beebe and James Alexander. As both Alan Entin and Richard Mikesell stated, the transfer of the journal to the APA was the most effective strategy to achieve the goal of bringing family psychology into the mainstream of psychology and infusing psychology with a family systems perspective. This transfer was made possible because Howard Liddle, as editor of the journal, had crafted an excellent publication that the APA perceived as very marketable. Ronald Levant was named editor-elect to follow in his footsteps. Circulation of the *Journal of Family Psychology* increased from approximately 3000 to 7000 after it became an APA journal (Levant, personal communication, September 1996).

The revision of divisional bylaws that had begun during the previous year was completed and they were ratified by the board. The update of the policy and procedures manual was nearly completed. Jon Carlson became editor of *The Family Psychologist*, and the bulletin was substantially expanded in size and content, becoming one of the finest in the APA. The division's stationery and bulletin cover were redesigned by Chuck Scalin at the Virginia Commonwealth University. This design provided the division with the logo still being used today. The division also joined the "Gold Circle" (financial contributors to the 1992 celebration) for the APA centennial and the monies were raised from the sale of Division 43 t-shirts that sported the new logo.

Daniel Levinson, noted Yale psychologist, was the invited speaker at the APA annual convention in 1990 where he presented his research on the stages in a woman's life, titled "The Seasons of a Woman's Life: Implications for Women and Men." The speech attracted an audience that filled the grand ballroom of the hotel in Boston and was one of the most requested audiotapes of sessions offered for sale by the APA convention office. Also presenting at the APA convention that year was Douglas Snyder, developer of the Marital Satisfaction Inventory (Snyder, 1979).

Frustrations for Entin included the continued cumbersome board meetings that needed somehow to be more streamlined and efficient. In spite of an attempt to deal with action items only, the meeting remained a 9-hour ordeal. Also disappointing was the slight decline in membership despite major efforts made at recruitment (A. Entin, personal communication, September 1993).

1991: Establishing a Place Within and Outside of the APA

Josephine Beebe's presidency literally started out with a war—Operation Desert Storm. The focus of the first board meeting in January was the development of the Task Force Family Shield in response to the needs of families during the Persian Gulf War. Beebe was instrumental in creating with the APA a fact sheet for public dissemination titled *Helping Kids Cope* (APA, 1991) and Arthur Bodin developed *Family Shield: Psychological Support for Families Stressed by the Gulf War* (Bodin, 1991), both of which were submitted to the midwinter joint board meeting for use in helping soldiers of the Gulf War and their families.

In an attempt to pursue the division's long-term goal of having a greater influence within the APA, Beebe appointed liaisons to the APA Directorates of Science, Public Interest, Education, and Practice. She also initiated and cochaired the Task Force on Collaboration: Family Psychology Practice and Family Psychology Research. The objective of this task force was to facilitate collaboration between researchers and practitioners with the ultimate goal of developing research-informed clinical practices and clinically relevant research in the field of family psychology. Other accomplishments included (a) the identification of graduate schools and departments of psychology that offer programs in marriage and family; (b) the establishment of a task force, chaired by Michael Gottlieb, to develop specialty guidelines for family psychologists; (c) the celebration of Division 43's seventh year with a panel of the seven presidents discussing the birth, evolution, and mission of the division; (d) the reduction of dues to $29 per year for members, fellows, and associates and $15 for students, in view of the fact that members no longer received the *Journal of Family Psychology* as a member benefit in 1992; and (e) the streamlining of the executive committee to five members.

One political issue that occurred during Beebe's tenure as president was the application of the American Association for Marriage and Family Therapy (AAMFT) to the Council on Postsecondary Accreditation (COPA) as an accrediting body for marriage and family training programs. The initial reaction of many members of the division was alarm over the potentially disastrous effects to family psychologists if psychologists who had not graduated from an AAMFT-approved program were not allowed to practice in their specialty area. For that reason, Division 43 formally opposed AAMFT's application and gave testimony to that effect at the hearing in October 1991 (Fox, 1992). This was a painful time for many members of the division because of their split loyalty to two family "therapy" organizations.

Beebe has said her fondest memory of her administration was the sponsoring of a celebration that linked the APA's centennial kick-off with the birth of Division 43 (J. Beebe, personal communication, September 1993). It was also during her presidency that Harriet Goldnor Lerner, author and syndicated columnist, was guest speaker at the APA convention. Other invited addresses were presented by Patrick Carnes who spoke on sexual obsession and family life, and Bernard Murstein who presented on love and marriage.

For Beebe, as for the presidents before her, one unfulfilled goal was that of making a real impact on the thinking and decision making of the governance of the APA. She stated that future challenges for the division would include (a) increasing the division's visibility and influence in the APA, (b) introducing a systemic perspective to the APA boards and the council, and (c) achieving the inclusion of the interests and concerns of families and family psychologists in APA deliberations (J. Beebe, personal communication, September 1993).

1992: Establishing Long-Range Goals

The theme of my presidency seems to have been organization and planning. The year's activities began with a retreat at midwinter to Amelia Island, led by Lee Grutchfield. Those present shared in a vision of restructuring the division governance so that the committees fed into the four areas represented by the directorates of the APA (practice, science, public interest, and education) and developing both short-term and long-range goals in each of those areas. I appointed a task force on long-range planning chaired by Ronald Levant. Using the Harbridge House Planning Model, this task force consulted with every committee, board member, and task force in the division to define objectives and develop strategies to achieve objectives. The resulting 7000-word, 50-page document (Levant et al., 1992) was approved by the board at the August APA meeting, the objectives were prioritized, and budgetary decisions for the coming year were made based on those priorities. In this process it became clear that the division was an organization with multiple and varied purposes, serving researchers, educators, practitioners, and political activists in family psychology. A secondary result of the process was a renewed enthusiasm and participation of the membership. The long-range plan was the hallmark of this year, serving as a map to guide division activities for many years to come.

Those activities in the areas of science, education, practice, and public interest supported by the division during the 1992 year included

- *Science:* (a) Funding a survey of Division 43 members on research utilization, (b) promoting research-based programs for the APA convention, (c) providing a research/practitioner forum at the hospitality suite, (d) nominating family researchers to serve on national committees, (e) awarding a student research award for family research;
- *Education:* (a) Appointment and funding of representatives to both the American Board of Professional Psychology and post-doctoral accreditation councils sponsored by the Association

of Psychology Post-doctoral and Internship Centers, (b) cooperation with the APA and Association of Psychology Postdoctoral and Internship Centers (APPIC) to identify family psychology tracks within clinical and counseling psychology programs, internship sites with family emphasis, and family postdoctoral programs in existence, (c) continued participation with JCPEP, (d) recruitment of student members.

- *Practice:* (a) Continued support of the Diagnosis and Classification Task Force in its work on establishing relational diagnoses for use in *DSM-IV,* (b) development of specialty guidelines for family psychologists, (c) promotion of age, gender, and ethnic-sensitive family therapy practices;
- *Public Interest:* (a) Continued support of the Critical Issues Task Force that developed position papers on AIDS, family violence, aging, trauma, and at-risk children, (b) invited speakers at the APA convention focused on gender issues and ethnic diversity; Ronald Levant and Marlin Potash, *Men and Women: The Crisis of Connection,* and Nancy Boyd-Franklin, *African-American Families in Therapy,* (c) nomination of Irene Deitch as representative from the division to the APA Board of Applied Psychology in the Public Interest (BAPPI).

Another task force emanating from the midwinter meeting on Amelia Island was that chaired by Richard Mikesell that investigated the feasiblity of centralization of services, particularly finances, membership enrollment, and publications. The committee recommended that we contract with The Administrators (a management company based in Arizona) to serve as a central office, provide membership enrollment services, process mailings to the division, and provide data entry and dissemination of the newsletter. The hope was that a central office would greatly improve member enrollment processes and services as well as reduce the cost of production of the newsletter.

It was during my administration that the division struggled with the continuing issue of AAMFT's application to COPA for accreditation privileges of freestanding marriage and family therapy programs. Many members of the division were concerned that licensing boards would make graduation from an AAMFT-accredited program a requirement for state licensure, which would put family psychologists out of business. In an effort to find a resolution to this issue, James Alexander and I represented Division 43 at the Joint Council on Family Therapy Training on Amelia Island at AFTA's invitation. Representatives from AFTA, AAMFT, AAMFT-COA, Family Systems Nursing, The American Psychiatric Association Family Therapy Caucus, National Association of Social Workers, and the Council of Social

Work Education also attended. The joint council agreed as a body that training needs are diverse across disciplines and that it was premature for COPA to grant accrediting privileges to any one organization (Walsh & Bloch, 1992). The APA received written assurances from AAMFT at the executive-director level (Bowers, 1992), from legal council (Newman, 1992), and on a presidential level (Benningfield, 1992) that AAMFT recognized the APA's privilege to accredit professional psychology programs and that they would help educate licensing boards that psychologists were qualified to treat families and couples.

Other developments occurring during the 1992 year included (a) the selection of a new editor-elect for *The Family Psychologist*, Terry Patterson; (b) the decision to increase the term of the continuing education chair to 3 years to allow for continuity and planning of continuing education programs; (c) completion of a telephone survey of former members to determine their reasons for leaving the division; (d) the invitation and hosting of the International Academy of Family Psychology at the APA annual convention at the recommendation of Florence Kaslow; and (e) a divisional networking ceremony conducted by Uri Ruveni in celebration of the APA centennial.

The major frustration during my term as president was the lack of financial and personnel resources to accomplish all of the worthy goals that the membership would like to have seen initiated. The solution to this continuing problem was the development of a long-range plan that gave each worthy goal its chance for future funding. These future directions for the division were clearly articulated and prioritized in the long-range plan.

1993: Inclusion, Diversity, and Outreach

Robert Wellman's term as president was centered around themes of inclusion, diversity, and outreach. He instituted an open forum at the membership meetings at both the midwinter and APA conventions. This prompted lively discussions of issues of concern to members, such as licensure of marriage and family therapists and its implications for psychologists, managed care, and insurance reimbursement for couple/family therapy, education and training, sources of research funding, and so forth. Also, he introduced a "response card" in *The Family Psychologist* whereby members could communicate directly to the president their likes and dislikes and suggestions regarding the division. The response rate, however, was somewhat disappointing. In addition, a gathering of committee and task force chairs was begun at the midwinter convention, facilitating communication and cooperation among chairs and giving them a unified voice at the division's board of directors meetings. This resulted in the board's voting, for the first time in division history, to fund fully the requests made by committees.

Many of the division's programs at both the midwinter and the APA conventions concerned issues related to diversity in ethnicity, race, gender, and sexual orientation. An invited panel on "Considerations in Working With American Indian Families" was presented at the APA convention in honor of Carolyn Attneave, an American Indian who developed a networking intervention in family therapy. The presidential invited address, "Who's Parenting the Parents: Shattered Scripts, Missing Models, and AIDS," was given by Terry Tafoya, an international expert on AIDS and a storyteller from the Taos Pueblo and Warm Springs Indian Nations.

1993 was the first *full* year during which the division's organization and activities were driven by the long-range plan. Under this plan, the division funded initiatives in each of the APA directorate areas. During 1993 these initiatives included

- *Education*: (a) Cosponsorship, with the Academy of Family Psychology and the American Board of Family Psychology of ABPP, of the Committee on Family Psychology Accreditation of Postdoctoral Training Programs. The committee reviewed the policy statement of the 1992 National Conference on Postdoctoral Training in Professional Psychology and made comments and recommendations to the Interorganizational Council for Accreditation of Postdoctoral Programs in Psychology (IOC) regarding the statement's potential impact on postdoctoral programs in Family Psychology; (b) development of plans for a National Conference on Family Psychology, which was held in 1995.
- *Practice:* (a) Continued funding of the Task Force on Specialty Guidelines, which developed a draft document. Feedback on the draft and the changed political climate within the APA with regard to guidelines in general and specialty guidelines in particular, led to the likely conclusion that now is not the time to move forward. This is a source of frustration, because the task force spent several years of hard work. (b) Continued funding of the Task Force on Diagnosis and Classification; (c) continued lobbying of the APA to recognize family psychology as a specialty area in the APA directory survey and other such documents.
- *Public Interest:* (a) Funding a new initiative to enable our Committee on Lesbian and Gay Family Issues to create a liaison with the national organization, Parents and Friends of Lesbians and Gays (PFLAG). This liaison will lend the expertise of family psychologists to the efforts of PFLAG to educate state and provincial psychological associations and state mental health

associations about issues concerning lesbian and gay families, and families with lesbian and gay members. This is the first true outreach effort by the division. (b) Participation in the 1993 APA Convention Miniconvention on AIDS, through symposia, papers, and the invited address by Tafoya. (c) The development of a book by the Committee on Current Critical Issues in Families (Harway, 1996). The book emphasizes the latest research and intervention strategies covering issues such as addictions, aging, AIDS, at-risk children, chronic illness and disability, family violence, mental illness, and trauma as they affect families.

- *Science*: (a) Continued support of a liaison to the APA Board of Scientific Affairs; (b) presentation of the Student Research Award to Mitchell Dickey.

Robert Wellman (personal communication, September 1993) suggested that, in the future, the division maintain a balance between internal professional concerns and external, real-world issues. For example, additional initiatives like the PFLAG effort should be devoted to applying family psychology's knowledge base and expertise to areas of human concern. Also the division continued to struggle with finding additional ways to attract and retain family psychologists who work primarily in academic and research settings. The delicate balance between scientists and practitioners continued to be a challenge to maintain during Wellman's presidency. Finally, getting feedback from members about what the division is doing right and wrong continued to be a concern.

1994: The Tenth Anniversary Year

August 1994, marked the 10-year anniversary of the Division of Family Psychology. President Ronald Levant addressed the membership with his summary of the past in the tenth anniversary edition of *The Family Psychologist*:

> I have the good fortune of serving as President during the tenth anniversary year of the Division. This is a very important milestone. Those of us who remember the last few years of the old Academy of Family Psychology, the precursor to the Division of Family Psychology, when we were working so hard to gain APA Divisional status and it was not at all clear that we would succeed, realize just how far we have come in a relatively short time. The major achievements that stand out from the array of divisional accomplishments include: (1) the establishment of the Division, (2) the launching of the *Journal of Family Psychology*— at first as a divisional journal published by Sage, and now an APA primary journal, and (3) the formation of the American Board of Family

Psychology, which gained acceptance as one of the specialty boards of the American Board of Professional Psychology. This is an impressive trio of achievements, that together have put family psychology on the map as a new specialty in psychology. (pp. 16–17)

To celebrate this milestone, a tenth anniversary task force, chaired by J. Renae Norton, planned a number of events designed to commemorate the division's tenth anniversary. The first of these was a special panel discussion at the midwinter convention in which former presidents passed on the history of the division by way of reminiscences and recollections, both substantive and humorous. Second, in a more scholarly vein, a series of symposia on family psychology was planned for the annual convention. Each symposium included invited addresses from leaders in the field, which took stock of our accomplishments over the past 10 years and outlined what we needed to do in the next 10 years. The symposium on family psychological science was chaired by James Bray; the practice symposium was chaired by Richard Mikesell; the symposium on family psychology in the public interest was chaired by Louise Silverstein; and the education and training symposium was chaired by Ed Bourg. Third, celebratory events were planned for both the midwinter convention and the annual convention. Fourth, I prepared a special history of the division (Philpot, 1994).

During Levant's presidency, a major membership recruitment campaign was launched by Richard Mikesell, who, as chair of the 1994 membership campaign used a carefully developed marketing approach that he had found to be very successful in prior campaigns for two other divisions and for APA's second century membership campaign. The membership increased from 1600 to 3784 due to Mikesell's campaign (See Figure 4) (Mikesell, 1994). This made Division 43 the sixth largest APA division in 1994.

Plans to develop a conference on family psychology were begun during Levant's term. A planning committee for a national conference in family psychology was appointed, including James Alexander, Ed Bourg, James Bray, Ross Carter, Ana Gardano, Michele Harway, E. Mavis Hetherington, Nadine J. Kaslow, Howard Liddle, Susan McDaniel, Roy Scrivner, Louise Silverstein, and Guy Diamond, who acted as coordinator for the project. The successful national conference on outcome and process research in marital and family therapy took place in May 1995. The conference addressed not only the scientific foundations, but also the applications that family psychologists have developed in practice and in the public interest. Education and training of family psychologists were also part of the agenda.

The year 1994 was declared by the United Nations to be the International Year of the Family (Levant, 1994). The APA Council of Representatives adopted a resolution in support of the UN proclamation and directed that the annual convention contain programs that reflect this theme. Ronald

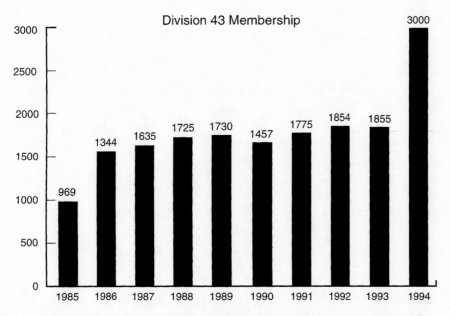

Figure 4. Membership Graph, 1984–1994.

E. Fox, president of the APA and a fellow of Division 43, sponsored a presidential miniconvention on the family, with 20 hours of programming. The miniconvention was kicked off with a session titled "Psychology Looks at the Future," followed by programs on "Women, Men, Change and the Family," "Families and Violence," "Child Rearing Challenges for Families of the Future," "Aging and the Family," and "Families, Health and Illness." In addition, Richard Mikesell, in his capacity as chair of the APA Board of Convention Affairs, created a special program to commemorate the International Year of the Family. The presidential invited address given by poet and author Robert Bly drew the largest audience of the convention, with 800 attendees. Without a doubt the 1994 annual convention of the APA emphasized *family psychology*, which gave tremendous visibility and recognition to the division.

In addition, Ronald Levant set in motion the process of filing an application for specialty status for family psychology with the Commission for the Recognition of Specialties and Proficiencies in Psychology (CRSPP). The division created a new award during Levant's administration, the Carolyn Attneave Award, to be given to persons who have made significant contributions to diversity in family psychology. The successes of this year indicated that the Division of Family Psychology had truly come of age.

On a negative note, the division struggled with two issues, one specific to family psychology— AAMFT's title certification law—and the other a problem faced by all of professional psychology—managed health care.

Regarding the first issue, many members of Division 43 became concerned about the effect of the title certification law on psychologists' ability to practice marital and family therapy. Levant clarified for the membership that the law did not restrict the scope of practice of family psychologists, merely their use of the title "Marital and Family Therapist" without holding such a license (Hinnefeld, 1994). The other issue was not so easily resolved. It is clear that practitioner psychologists will have to adapt in order to survive the multiple changes taking place in the health care industry. The advice coming from those in the know indicates that the most survivable model is an interdisciplinary group practice and the flexibility to share the financial risk with the third-party payor through capitation (Newman, 1996). This challenge is not one that is likely to go away in the near future.

1995: Surviving Managed Health Care, Advocacy, and Research

The specter of managed health care loomed over all of professional psychology during the 1995 year. Dealing with the potential consequences of changes in the health care industry to practice, research, and teaching took priority over all other projects during James Bray's administration. The division was fortunate to have Bray, a politically savvy advocate who kept us apprised of issues as they developed nationally and who met with legislators on Capitol Hill to lobby for family psychology.

Three presidential initiatives were implemented to address the problem of managed health care. The first of these was a task force on collaboration with primary care health providers. The division cosponsored the first annual collaborative family health care coalition conference, "Transforming the Practice of Health Care: The Collaborative Solution" in July in Washington, DC. James Bray explained that "the work of the Coalition emphasizes three key principles of practice. First, teams of health and mental health professionals work in concert. Second, the bio-psycho-social aspects of treatment are given equal importance. Third, the patients' family is included as a crucial component of treatment" (Bray, 1995, p. 4). The task force on collaboration developed and distributed materials to facilitate partnerships with primary care health providers, developed linkages with other primary care organizations, and worked with the APA to expand the scope of psychology further into the general health care arena. The coalition completed a demonstration project for the development of collaborative practice between psychologists and family physicians and provided the membership with tips regarding the do's and don't's of a collaborative relationship.

The second initiative to deal with the managed health care crisis was the creation of a task force on advocacy for family psychology issues. This task force educated division members about the need for advocacy and lobbying efforts by providing articles and materials on advocacy in the *Family Psychologist*. The task force also labored to increase the influence of family psychology on social policy by working with the media to provide commentary and information regarding changes that may affect families.

Third, James Bray spearheaded a special initiative to increase the participation of academic and research family psychologists in the division. The division offered a 1-year free membership in the division to family psychologists in academic settings. The first Marital and Family Therapy Outcome and Process Research Conference was held in May 1995, at Temple University, cosponsored by Division 42 (Psychologists in Independent Practice), Division 43, and the Philadelphia Child Guidance Center. The conference addressed "a systemic appraisal of marital and family therapy's empirical contributions; its major conceptual, empirical, and methodological challenges; and needed directions and emphases." (Marital and Family Therapy, 1995, p. 7). An edited volume from the conference is being developed and published by APA Books. John Gottman agreed to spearhead an effort to make the family psychology research conference an annual event, and the division agreed to cosponsor such an event annually. In 1996, the conference was in Seattle and was cosponsored by the University of Washington. Another positive result of the conference was the agreement among researchers that Division 43 provides a home for family-based process and treatment researchers and that the *Journal of Family Psychology* has become a major outlet for their work.

It was also during 1995 that Richard Mikesell developed a miniconvention on family systems therapy for the APA convention. The symposia were presented by the contributors to the new APA volume edited by Richard Mikesell, Don-David Lusterman, and Susan McDaniel, titled *Integrating Family Therapy: Handbook of Family Psychology and Systems Theory* (1995). Although not a division project, the miniconvention represented, in the opinion of many, the high-water mark of family therapy in the APA. The vast majority of contributors to the book and presenters at the miniconvention were Division 43 members.

Also at the APA convention, John Gottman, Judith Wallerstein, and James Bray provided the results of their research on "Families in Transition." Jim Coyne and Don Bloch presented an invited symposium on collaborative health care. Bray presented his presidential commendation awards to four family psychologists who have contributed to advancing family psychology research: James Alexander, John Gottman, E. Mavis Hetherington, and Judith Wallerstein. It is clear that the emphasis during 1995 was two-fold: advocacy and research in the service of family psychology. Bray was very successful in accomplishing his goals.

1996: Achieving Specialty Status

The APA created The Commission for the Recognition of Specialties and Proficiencies in Professional Psychology (CRSPPP) in 1996. This has afforded the division the opportunity and challenge of establishing family psychology as having "a distinctive core of scientific and professional knowledge" and becoming a specialty recognized by the APA. Gary Brooks, president during the 1996 term, made the achievement of specialty status his number-one priority. To that end, a task force headed by Roberta Nutt, has been working on the petition. Robert Jay-Green drafted a history of the status of specialty education in family psychology, which was published in *The Family Psychologist*, and provided the members with examples of model programs throughout the United States, both predoctoral and post-doctoral (Jay-Green, 1996). In addition a national survey on graduate training in family psychology has become a priority of this administration. The strategic plan calls for development of a national network of university and professional school training opportunities and APPIC-approved internship training opportunities as well as greater divisional involvement in continuing education activities. Brooks continued the advocacy initiatives instituted by his predecessor, maintained the researcher–practitioner collaborations, and continued to endorse increasing awareness of diversity issues within family psychology.

OVERVIEW

The rapid growth and achievement of this division can be summarized in six categories: membership, administration, finances, publications, organizational relationships within and outside of the APA, and other accomplishments.

Membership

In 1979, the Academy of Family Psychology consisted of about 150 members. In the division's first year as a division of the APA (1985), the membership stood at 950. For the next 9 years the membership hovered between 1500 and 1900, a phenomenon that resulted in Division 43 gaining and losing a second seat on the Council of Representatives repetitively. In 1994, Richard Mikesell's membership campaign produced a growth spurt, giving the division more than 3000 members and making it the sixth largest division in the APA (Mikesell, 1994). However, the surge was short-lived and the membership had dropped back to 2522 when the *1996 APA Membership Register* was published (*APA Membership Register*, 1991, p. viii). Nevertheless, this still represents a maintained increase of close to 60%, and makes Division 43 the twelfth largest division in the APA as of 1996.

Administration

The first goal of the new division was to restructure its administration to correspond to that of other APA divisions. For many years the governance struggled with what appeared to be a cumbersome and sometimes frustrating board structure that made accomplishing goals more difficult. A number of measures were taken over the years to facilitate a smoother operation. These included reducing the number of people on the executive committee, structuring the board to correspond to APA directorates, limiting board meeting discussion to action items only, providing social time at conventions for committee chairs to generate ideas, turning membership meetings into open forums, developing a long-range plan to guide decision making, and centralizing operations by hiring The Administrators to handle inquiries, mailings, conventions, and newsletter publication.

Finances

The division never has enough money to do everything it would like to do, like most other organizations. Dues were initially set at $25 per year, but as the division began to offer the *Journal of Family Psychology* as a membership benefit, the dues were raised to $32 per year. For several years the journal required almost a third of the annual budget to operate, but when it was sold to the APA, this drain on finances was eliminated and dues were reduced to $29, where they remained in 1996. Operating budgets hovered between $60,000 to $80,000 for many years. The frustration expressed by most presidents regarding financial restraints reflect a desire to fund many worthy projects at once, rather than having to make difficult choices. The adoption of the long-range plan was intended to resolve this problem by prioritizing and scheduling the funding of various projects in all four interest areas: practice, research, training, and public interest.

Publications

The Academy of Family Psychology published a newsletter titled *The Relationship*. In 1984, the Division of Family Psychology began publishing a bulletin, *The Family Psychologist*, with Robert Wellman as its first editor. This publication has also changed over the years as editors have changed. During Jon Carlson's years as editor, *The Family Psychologist* increased in size and quality, becoming a 60-page publication that offered substantive articles on clinical, research, and training issues, book reviews, and regular columns on subjects such as computerized assessment or forensic and ethical issues, in addition to division news. Although the publication was laudable, it was also very expensive in this format and the division found it necessary to curtail some of the features. Under Terry Patterson's editorship, it has downsized somewhat, but it continues to offer substantive articles of interest to the membership and regular featured columns.

The other major publication initiated by the Division of Family Psychology was the *Journal of Family Psychology*. Originally published by Sage Publishing and edited by Howard Liddle, this journal provided a forum that represented the family systems perspective to mainstream *psychology* and created an interchange of critical thinking and analysis, which challenged perspectives and conclusions from different vantage points. As a result of its high quality and popularity, the division was able to transfer the *Journal of Family Psychology* to the APA in 1990, which proved to be the most effective way to achieve the goal of infusing psychology with a family systems perspective. Ronald Levant then became editor, and circulation of the *Journal* increased more than twofold (Levant, personal communication, September 1996).

Relationships With Other Organizations

When the division was first formed, there was a great deal of controversy regarding how it should relate to other family therapy organizations, such as AAMFT (Minutes of the Executive Committee, November 1984; Nixon, 1990). Because the APA supports the doctorate as a terminal degree and most of the other organizations in family therapy require only the master's, it was originally felt that any liaison with these organizations was equivalent to condoning their lower standard of credentialing. Therefore, despite the fact that many members were supportive of other family therapy professional organizations, the official position of Division 43 was that they have no formal contact. This attitude was difficult to maintain for several reasons. It was in some ways like endorsing the Monroe Doctrine during the electronic age. Organizations such as AAMFT, AFTA, and NASW (National Association of Social Workers) were simply too large, active, and powerful to ignore if the division wished to have any influence on the family field at all. Furthermore, many members of the division retained dual or triple memberships, and found themselves torn between the APA's stated position and their own loyalties. As a result, over the years Division 43 developed formal liaisons with AAMFT, AFTA, and Society of Teachers of Family Medicine. When the crisis arose among family organizations regarding AAMFT's application to COPA for sole accrediting privileges, Division 43 participated with nine or ten other family organizations on the Joint Council on Family Therapy Training under the leadership of AFTA. This cooperative effort brought Division 43 into a closer relationship with family organizations outside of the APA.

Within the APA, Division 43 established formal liaisons with numerous other divisions, including the Divisions of Psychotherapy (29), Child, Youth and Family Services (37), Psychology of Women (35), and Psychologists in Independent Practice (42). Furthermore liaisons were created with various APA boards and committees such as Board of Applied Psychology in the Public Interest, Board of Scientific Affairs Committee on Divisions/APA Relations (BSA), Council on Divisions and APA Relations (CODAPAR), and with all of the APA directorates. In 1987, the division began to cosponsor nominees to various boards and committees, which provided a forum for influencing APA policy. Division 43 also participated in joint efforts such as the Joint Council on Professional Education in Psychology, the Task Force on Classification and Diagnosis, and the Interorganizational Council for Accreditation of Postdoctoral Training Programs in Psychology.

Other Major Accomplishments

Other major accomplishments that illustrate the success of Division 43 include (a) the development of the American Board of Family Psychology, which gained ABPP status in 1989, (b) the cosponsoring of a major national conference on research in family psychology in 1995, (c) the coordination of an APA Board of Convention Affairs miniconvention on family psychology in 1995, and (d) the application to the Commission for the Recognition of Specialties and Proficiencies in Professional Psychology for specialty status for family psychology.

CONCLUSION

The dream of establishing a division of the APA that endorses a systemic perspective as its unifying force has been achieved. The Division of Family Psychology has come a long way in a relatively short time, from its inauspicious beginnings of 15 psychologists with a systemic perspective supporting and stimulating one another at annual APA conventions to one of the larger divisions of the APA with 2500 members and national influence. The past 12 years have seen tremendous change in the amount of influence Division 43 has on the larger field of psychology as evidenced by the existence of the *Journal of Family Psychology*, an official APA journal; the acceptance of family psychology as an ABPP specialty area; and the sponsoring of a presidential miniconvention on the family by the president of the APA at the 1994 annual convention. An important work, *Voices in Family Psychology* (Kaslow, 1990) was published in 1990. In 1995, *Integrating Family Therapy:*

Handbook of Family Psychology and Systems Theory, (Mikesell, Lusterman, & McDaniel, 1995), which most observers see as bringing a new definition to the field, was published. In 1995, the first Marital and Family Therapy Outcome and Process Research Conference took place in Philadelphia, and an APA Board of Convention Affairs Miniconvention on Family Psychology was held in New York City. The division has reorganized its structure to best facilitate its many goals and projects in the areas of science, education and training, practice, and public interest. It continues to sponsor a rich variety of programs at the midwinter and APA annual conventions and to produce important documents and publications in each of these areas. It has adopted a long-range plan to guide its activities in future years in order to best serve the interests of its diverse membership. It has centralized its administrative functioning to make it more efficient and effective. It has developed task forces that are designed to deal with larger issues of the survival of psychology and political advocacy. It is presently striving to achieve specialty status for family psychology from the APA. It is an enthusiastic organization with multiple and varied purposes, serving researchers, educators, practitioners, and political activists in family psychology. It shows what great strides can be made within a supportive and challenging family of professionals.

REFERENCES

American Psychological Association. (1991). *Helping kids cope*. (Factsheet). Washington, DC: Author.

American Psychological Association. (1996). *1996 APA Membership Register*. Washington, DC: Author.

American Psychologist. (1990). Vol. 45(4), 471–472.

Benningfield, A. B. (1992, November 17). Letter to Division of Family Psychology. *The Family Psychologist*, 9(2), 7.

Board of Directors, Division of Family Psychology. (1988). *The Family Psychologist*, 4(2), 1.

Bodin, A. (1986). Howard A. Liddle named editor of the Journal of Family Psychology. *The Family Psychologist* 2(3), 1.

Bodin, A. (1988). Can we help APA avoid being GORed? *The Family Psychologist*, 4(2), 1.

Bodin, A. (1991). *APA's Division of Family Psychology presents family shield: Psychological support for families stressed by the Gulf War*. Unpublished manuscript.

Bowers, M. (1992, July 31). Letter to Russ Newman, Assistant Executive Director, Practice Directorate, APA.

Boyd-Franklin, N. (1992, August). *African American families in therapy*. Invited address at the annual APA convention, Washington, DC.

Bray, J. (1995). Working together in our second decade. *The Family Psychologist*, *11*(2), 1, 4–5.

Broderick, C., & Schrader, S. (1991). The history of professional marriage and family therapy. In A. Gurman & D. Kniskern (Eds.), *Handbook of family psychology, Vol II*, 3–40. New York: Brunner/Mazel.

Brooks, G., & Philpot, C. (1988). *Principles of Gender-Sensitive Psychotherapy*. Unpublished document.

Constitution of the Academy of Psychologists in Marital Counseling, Inc. (1960). Unpublished document.

Dudman, H. (1976, March 1). The family as a unit. *Jerusalem Post Reporter*, p. 5.

Entin, A. (1990). President's address. *The Family Psychologist*, 6(3), 1.

Epstein, N., Baldwin, L., & Bishop, D. (1983). The McMaster family assessment device. *Journal of Family Therapy*, 9(2).

Fox, R. (1992). Opposition to separate accreditation: Division 43 and APA speak out. *The Family Psychologist*, 8(2), 8–9.

Gottlieb, M., & Nixon, G. (1989). Family psychology recognized as ABPP specialty. *The Family Psychologist* 5(2), 1.

Gottsegen, G. (1986). Family intimacies. *The Family Psychologist* 2(3), 1.

Harway, M. (Ed.). (1996). *Treating the changing family: Handling normative and unusual events*. New York: John Wiley.

Hinnefeld, B. (1994, April 20). Memorandum to Russ Newman re: Marriage and family therapist licensing/certification.

Jay-Green, R. (1996). Education in family psychology: History, current status, and the future. *The Family Psychologist*, *12*(2), 10–15.

Joint Council on Professional Education in Psychology (1990). *The Report of the Joint Council on Professional Education in Psychology*.

Kaslow, F. (1986). *The knowledge base in family psychology*. Unpublished document.

Kaslow, F. (1987). Trends in family psychology. *Journal of Family Psychology*, *1*(1), 77–90.

Kaslow, F. (Ed.). (1990). *Voices in family psychology, Vols. 1 & 2*. Newbury Park, CA: Sage.

Kaslow, F. (1991). Organization and development of family psychology in the United States: An overview. *Family Therapy*, *18*(1), 1–10.

L'Abate, L. (1983). *Family psychology: Theory, therapy and training*. Washington, DC: University Press of America.

L'Abate, L. (1985). *The Handbook of family psychology and therapy*. Washington, DC: University Press of America.

L'Abate, L. (1987). *Family psychology II: Theory, therapy , enrichment and training*. Lanham, MD: University Press of America.

L'Abate, L. (1992). Family psychology and family therapy: Comparisons and contrasts. *The American Journal of Family Therapy*, *20*(1), 1–12.

Levant, R. (1994). Diversity, the division, and the gathering storm. *The Family Psychologist, 10*(2), 1, 6–7.

Levant, R., Bray, J., Bourg, E., Deitch, I., Ginsberg, B., Gottlieb, M., Peterson, F., Philpot, C., & Wellman, R. (1992). *Division of Family Psychology: Strategic plan.* Unpublished document.

Levant, R., & Potash, M. (1992, August). *Man and woman: The crisis of connection.* Invited address at the APA annual convention, Washington, DC.

Liddle, H. (1986). *Journal of Family Psychology* to debut in 1987. *The Family Psychologist 2*(3), 4.

Marital and family therapy outcome and process research conference: State of the science—May 5, 6, 7. (1995). *The Family Psychologist, 11*(2), 7.

Mikesell, R. (1983a, January 20). Letter to Academy of Psychologists in Marital, Sex and Family Therapy.

Mikesell, R. (1983b). President's message: A healthy family. *The Relationship 9*(1), 3.

Mikesell, R. (1994). Council representative's message. *The Family Psychologist, 10*(2), 5.

Mikesell, R., Lusterman, D.-D., & McDaniel, S. (Eds.). (1995). *Integrating family therapy: Handbook of family psychology and systems theory.* Washington, DC: American Psychological Association.

Minutes of the Board of Directors Meeting, Division of Family Psychology. (1985, March 1), 1.

Minutes of the Board of Directors Meeting, Division of Family Psychology. (1989, March 9), 2.

Minutes of the Executive Committee Meeting, Division of Family Psychology. (1984, November 9), 2.

Newman, R. (October, 1992). Letter to Council on Postsecondary Accreditation.

Newman, R. (1996, January 24). *The changing face of practice: A conversation with Dr. Russ Newman (Practice directorate, APA).* Presented at the National Council of Schools and Program of Professional Psychology Midwinter Meeting, Clearwater Beach, FL.

Nixon, G. (1990, March). *Family psychology: Psychohistory and its lessons.* Invited address presented to the Division of Family Psychology at the 29th Midwinter Convention of the American Psychological Association, Divisions 29, 42, and 43.

Nurse, R. (in press). *Using psychological tests with families.* New York: John Wiley.

Olson, D., & Portner, J. (1983). Family adaptability and cohesion evaluation scales. In E. Filsinger (Ed.), *Marriage and family assessment: A sourcebook for family therapy* (pp. 299–316). Beverly Hills, CA: Sage.

Philpot, C. (1994). A history of the Division of Family Psychology. *The Family Psychologist, 10*(3), 10–23.

Proceedings of the American Psychological Association, Inc. for the Year 1983. (1984). *American Psychologist, 39*(6), 622.

Proceedings of the American Psychological Association, Inc., for the Year 1984. (1985). *American Psychologist, 40*(6), 638.

The Relationship. (1982, October). Vol. 8(3), 9.

The Relationship. (1983, March), Vol. 9(1), 7–9.

Snyder, D. (1979). *Marital satisfaction inventory.* Los Angeles: Western Psychological Services.

Spanier, G. (1976). Measuring dyadic adjustment. New scales for assessing the quality of marriage and similar dyads. *Journal of Marriage and the Family, 38,* 15–28.

Tafoya, T. (1993, August). Who's parenting the parents: Shattered scripts, missing models, and AIDS. Presidential invited address, APA annual convention, Toronto, Ontario, Canada.

Walsh, F., & Bloch, D. (1992, July 8). Letter to Council on Postsecondary Accreditation.

NAME INDEX

Those entries that appear in italics refer to listings in the reference sections. Entries with an "n"
following indicate listings in footnotes

305

Beer, Bernard, 162, 171
Behrens, Peter, 147
Beier, Ernst G., 182, 192, 198
Belar, Cynthia, 239n, 244, 251, 255, 257, 260, 265, 266
Bell, John Elderkin, 66, 74, 270
Bellack, Alan, 68
Bellows, Roger W., 112, *124*
Benis, Warren, 99
Benjamin, Ludy, T., Jr., 5, 103, 104, *124*, 131, 143, 144, 145, 211, 213, *234*
Bennett, George K., 94, 107, 110, 122
Bennett, Leila, 98
Benningfield, A. B., 289, *300*
Benton, Arthur, 65, 66, *79*
Berger, B. D., 158, 164, *176*
Bernal, Guillermo, 66
Bernal, Martha, 232
Berry, Charles S., 58, 72
Bettelheim, Bruno, 66, 74
Betts, Ervin L., 274
Biaggio, Mary Kay, 228, *234*
Bickel, Warren K., 162, 171
Bickman, Leonard, 12
Bieliauskas, Vytautas, 94, 99
Bigelow, J. George E., 161, 162, 172
Bills, Marion A., *104*, 107, 108, 109, 110, 111, 115, 122
Binet, Alfred, 56, *79*
Bingham, Walter Van Dyke, 106, 107
Bishop, D., 271, *301*
Blain, Daniel, 63
Blanchard, Edward B., 244, 250, 266
Blau, Theodore H., 71, 94, 121, 180, 181, 182, 189
Bloch, Don, 289, 295, *303*
Bloch, Ellin L., 191, 203, 204, *209*
Blount, Ronald, 68
Blumenthal, Arthur, 147
Bly, Robert, 293
Boals, Gordon, 201
Bodin, Arthur, 274, 275, 277, 280, 281, 282, 283, 286, *300*
Boehm, Virginia R., 110
Boff, E., 157
Boren, John, 155, 158, 162
Boring, Edwin G., 2, 7, 128, 129, 130, 131, 132, 136, 137, 143, 144, 150, *151*
Borman, Walter C., 111
Boszormenyi-Nagy, Ivan, 270

Bourduin, Charles, 282
Bourg, Ed, 292, *302*
Bowen, Murray, 270, 278
Bowers, M., 289, *300*
Boyd-Franklin, Nancy, 288
Brabeck, Mary, 230
Bradbury, Thomas N., 75
Bradford, D. T., 197
Brady, Joseph V., 155, 159, 162, 242, *300, 301*
Bray, Douglas, 99, 116, 119, *124*
Bray, James, 275, 292, 294, 295, *301, 302*
Brayfield, Arthur, 26, 133, 134
Bregman, Elsie, 104
Breuer, J., *79*
Brewer, Marilynn B., 12, 49
Bringmann, Wolfgang G., 143, 144, 147
Broderick, C., 271, *301*
Brodsky, Annette, 193, 216, 217, 224, 225, *234*
Bronner, Augusta F., 58, 70, 72
Brooks, Gary, 275, 281, 296, *301*
Broskowski, Anthony, 98
Brotemarkle, Robert A., 70, 94, 105, *124*
Brown, Andrew W., 70, 230
Brown, Laura, 211, 217, 231
Brownell, Kelly, 244, 259, 261
Brozek, Josef, 136, 137, 138, 143, 144
Bruner, Frank G., 58
Bruner, Jerome S., 12
Bry, Ilse, 136
Bryan, Alice I., 94
Bryant, W. H. M., 104, *124*
Buck, Mildred, 97
Buckley, K. W., 104, *124*
Buhrke, Robin, 231
Burnham, John C., 129, 147
Burr, Emily T., 93, 94
Burr-Harris, Alice, 282
Burtt, Harold E., 106, 107, 108, *124*
Byrd, Larry D., 153, 160, 162, 167

Cadwallader, Thomas C., 2, 7, 143
Calkins, Barbara, 264
Calkins, Mary Whiton, 213
Campbell, John P., 110
Campbell, Linda F., 197
Campbell, Richard J., 116
Campion, Michael A., 111
Cameron, Norman A., 70, 74
Canter, Aaron H., 182

Fryer, Douglas H., 86, 94, *100*, 107
Fromm, Erich, 74
Fuerstnau, Lynda, 14
Furumoto, Laurel, 139, 143, *151*

Gallant, Sheryle [Alagna], 221, 258
Galton, Francis, 56, *79*
Gamzu, Elkan, 162
Garber, Judy, 75
García, Margarita, 232
Gardano, Ana, 292
Gardner, J., *235*
Garfield, Sol L., 71, 73, 74
Garmezy, Norman, 71, 75
Garner, Ann Magaret, 73
Garrett, H. E., 24, *50*
Gatchel, Robert, 250, 266
Gault, Robert H., 58
Gavin, Eileen, 143
Geffner, Robert, 284
Geis, Florence Lindauer, 225, 226
Geller, Irving, 162
Gendlin, Eugene T., 179, 180, 192, 196, *208*
Gentry, W. Doyle, 242
Gergen, Mary, 219
Gersoni, Charles, 135
Gesell, Arnold L., 58, 59, 66, 70, *79*
Ghiselli, Edwin E., 110, 111
Gibson, James, 147
Gil, Karen M., 259
Gilbert, Lucia A., 217
Gilbert, William M., 97
Gilbreth, Lillian, 104
Ginorio, Angela, 232
Ginott, Haim, 192
Ginsberg, B., *302*
Glaser, Edward M., 94, 95, 98, 99
Glass, David, 242, 256, 259
Goddard, Henry H., 56, 58
Gold, Martin, 13
Goldberg, H., 197
Goldstein, Irwin L., 110
Golub, Sharon, 228, 235
Goodchilds, Jacqueline, 12, 43
Goodheart, Carol, 188, *208*
Goodman, Elizabeth S., 143
Goodman, Lisa, 45
Goodman, M., 197
Goolishian, Harold, 270, 274, 282
Gopland, Eric, 98

Gorman, Margaret, 136
Gottlieb, Michael, 283, 286, *302*
Gottman, John, 295
Gottsegen, Gloria Behar, 182, 183, 197, 274, 277, 278, 279, *301*
Gould, Laurence J., 99
Gowing, Marilyn K., 110
Grabowski, John, 162, 172
Grady, Kathleen, 217, 218, 258
Graham, Stanley R., 181, 182, 190, 192, 197, 205
Grant, Donald L., 110
Grant, Harold, 129
Graumann, Carl, 147
Gravitz, Melvin A., 93, 94, 189
Gray, Philip, 136
Greaves, George, 97
Greene, Edward B., 72
Greene, Katharine B., 93, 94
Gregory, W. Edgar, 129, 136
Grossman, S. P., 157
Grunberg, Neil E., 259
Grutchfield, Lee, 287
Guion, Robert M., 110, 119
Gullahorn, Jeanne, 228
Gutek, Barbara, 12, 13, 225
Guttentag, Marcia, 12, 29, *50*
Guze, S. B., 240, *266*

Haas, Leonard J., 193
Habbe, Stephen, 122
Haber, Leonard, 68
Haines, Thomas H., 58
Hakel, Milton D., 110
Hale, M., Jr., 103, *125*
Haley, Jay, 270
Hall, C. C., *126*
Hall, Douglas T., 119, *125*
Hall, G. Stanley, 2, 102, *125*
Hall, Sharon, 162, 258
Halpern, Florence C., 71, 72, 74
Hamlin, Roy M., 98
Hannigan-Farley, Patricia S., 182, 200
Hansen, Marsali, 275
Hansen, William, 98
Hanson, Harley, 156, 158, 166
Hardin, Carolyn, 129
Harding, John, 43
Hare-Mustin, Rachel T., 192, 225, 229, *234, 235*

Johnson, Suzanne Bennett, 244, 255, 260
Joiner, Thomas E., 75
Jones, Robert, 77, 80, 96
Jordan, Sarah, 83n
Jourard, Sidney, 192
Jung, Carl, 67

Kahn, Arnold, 13, 218, 219
Kahn, Robert L., 12, 13
Kalinkowitz, Bernard, 74
Kaplan, B. H., 29, 50
Kaplan, Norman, 88, 93, 100
Kaplan, Robert M., 244, 259
Karl, Kimberly, 247
Karnes, Merle B., 98
Karpf, Faye, 129
Kaslow, Florence, 271, 272, 274, 278,
        279, 280, 281, 282, 283, 289,
        299, 301
Kaslow, Nadine J., 190, 193, 292
Katz, Daniel, 11n, 12, 13, 118, 125
Katz, I., 49
Katz, Phyllis A., 12, 24, 31, 43, 50, 213n,
        217, 235
Katzell, Raymond A., 101, 102, 110, 112,
        119, 125
Kazdin, Alan E., 75, 282
Keefe, Frances, 246
Kegeles, S. Stephen, 240
Keita, Gwendolyn Puryear, 126, 211, 232
Keith-Speigel, Patricia, 258
Kelleher, J. C., 126
Kellerman, Jonathan, 75
Kelley, Harold H., 43
Kelley, Robert E., 98
Kelley, Noble H., 74, 94
Kelly, E. Lowell, 71, 74, 80
Kelly, George A., 66, 67, 68, 71, 74, 80
Kelman, Herbert C., 12
Kelty, Edward, 241
Kelty, Miriam, 241, 243, 244, 261
Kemp, Hendrika Vande, 143
Kenkel, M. B., 126
Ketcham, Warren A., 99
Kiecolt-Glaser, Janice, 259
Kiesler, Charles, 17
Kilbey, M. Marlyne, 153, 161, 162, 172,
        221
Kimmel, Ellen, 217, 220, 228, 229, 235
Kimmel, Paul R., 5, 13, 45, 50
Kinder, Elaine F., 72

King, Abby C., 259
King, D. B., 134, 149, 151
King, Martin Luther Jr., 21–22
Kirby, Kimberly, 162
Kirschner, Diana A., 274, 275
Kirscht, John, 13,
Klesges, Robert, 259
Klimoski, Richard J., 110
Klineberg, Otto, 11n, 17, 24, 25, 26, 47,
        51,
Klopfer, Bruno, 74
Kluger, R., 18, 51
Knapp, S., 60, 80
Knudsen, Kathryn, 219
Koch, Helen L., 93
Koeske, R. D., 227, 236
Kohout, J., 126
Koocher, Gerald P., 68, 71, 73, 182,
        193
Koppes, Laura, 101, 116, 125
Korchin, Sheldon, 74
Kornhauser, Arthur W., 107, 108
Kornetsky, Conan, 155, 158, 162, 164,
        171, 176
Kovacs, Arthur L., 64, 80, 182, 192,
        196–197, 205
Kovacs, Karen E., 193
Kraemer, Doris R., 88, 93, 94, 100
Krantz, David L., 137, 138, 143, 244,
        249, 255, 256, 259
Krasnegor, Norman A., 163, 171, 172
Krasner, Jack D., 182, 183, 192, 199
Krasner, Leonard, 77, 81
Krech, David, 10, 12, 15, 51
Kubena, R. K., 158, 166, 175
Kuhlmann, Frederick, 58, 70
Kunert, Kenneth, 129
Kurpius, DeWayne, 99

L'Abate, Luciano, 98, 273, 282, 301
Ladd-Franklin, Christine, 213
LaFromboise, Teresa, 233
Lah, Michal, 98
Laird, Donald A., 104
Landrine, Hope, 222
Landy, Frank J., 104, 110, 116, 125
Larkin, Kevin, 244
Larsen, Stephen W., 98
Larson, Cedric A., 129, 132, 135, 136
Lasater, Thomas M., 98
Lasky, Ella, 182

May, Rollo R., 66, 74, 199
Mayer, Ronald W., 6, 129, 132, 133, 135, 136, 140, 143
Mayo, Clara Weiss, 12, 47
Mays, Vickie, 217, 230, 231, 232 *236*
Mazure, Carolyn M., 161
McBride, Angela, 260
McCormick, Ernest J., 113
McDaniel, Susan, 282, 292, 295, 300, *302*
McFall, R. M., 76, *80*
McGehee, William, 110
McGrath, Ellen, 182, 187, 188, 190, 203, 204, *208, 209*
McGrath, Joseph E., 12, 17, 42, 43, *51*
McGregor, Robert, 270
McGuire, G. R., 128, *151*
McHugh, M. C., 227, *236*
McKay, Jack, 263
McKearney, James W., 172
McNeill, Harry V., 72
McPherson, Marion White, 143, 144, 149
McReynolds, P., 55, *80*
Meara, Naomi, 211
Mednick, Martha T. S., 12, 33, *51, 126*, 211, 215, 216, 217, 220, 221, 222, 223, 224, 225, 227, 231, *236*
Meehl, Paul E., 74, 75, 77
Meichenbaum, Donald, 98
Meisch, Richard, 161
Meisels, Murray, 239n
Melamed, Barbara, 244, 264
Mello, Nancy K., 172
Meltzer, Hyman, 58, *80*, 94, 96, 97, *100*
Meltzer, Malcolm L.
Mensh, Ivan N., 71, 72
Mesh, Scott, 191
Meyer, Herbert H., 110, 115, 116, *125*
Miczek, Klaus A., 162
Mikesell, Richard H., 273, 274, 275, 276, 282, 285, 288, 292, 293, 295, 296, 300, *302*
Miles, W. R., 154, *176*
Milgram, Norman, 68
Miller, D. K., 11, *51*
Miller, George A., 15, 42, *51*
Miller, James Grier, 63, 71
Miller, Neal E., 154, 155, 160, *176, 239*, 242, 244, 247, 251, 256, 259
Miner, James B., 58, 70, 72

Minton, Henry, 143
Mintz, Alexander, 129
Minuchin, Salvador, 270
Mischel, Walter, 66
Mitchell, David, 58, 66, 70, *81*
Mitchell, Mildred, 147, 213, *236*
Mitnick, Len, 261
Mittlemark, Maurice, 98
Miyahara, Sara, 233
Mold, H. P., 111, *126*
Modawsky, Patricia, 274
Moldawsky, Stanley, 192
Moles, Oliver, 30
Moore, Bruce V., 107, 109, 110, 122, *125*
Morawski, Jill G., 143
Morgan, Clifford T., 67, *81*, 131
Morgan, L., 89, *100*
Morokoff, Patricia, 258
Morrow, Gary, 253
Moskowitz, H., 158, *176*
Mountjoy, Paul, 129
Mowrer, O. Hobart, 70, 74
Muldrow, Tressie, 231
Münsterberg, Hugo, 103, 104, 123, *125*
Murphy, Gardner, 11n, 25, *51*, 129, 130, 137, 143, 144
Murray, C., 24, *50*
Murray, Henry A., 66, 67, 74, *81*
Murray, Saundra Rice Nettles, 211, 230, 231
Murstein, Bernard, 286

Nakagawa, Jan, 233
Nahmias, Victor R., 193
Napoli, D. S., 103, 105, *125*
Nathan, Peter, 66, 71
Neisser, U., 25
Nelson, C. B., *236*
Newberry, Alice, 282
Newcomb, Theodore M., 11n, 12,
Newman, R., 294, *302*
Nicassio, Perry, 250, 257, 266
Nichols, J. R., 157
Niemark, Hedwin, 44
Nixon, George, 269n, 272, 273, 274, 276, 277, 279, 281, 282, 283, 284, *301, 302*
Noblitt, Robert, 98
Nolen-Hoeksema, Susan, 75
Norcross, John C., 193, 197, 199
Normandin, Jo-Anne, 98

Rehm, Lynn P., 71
Reid, Pamela Trotman, 217, 221, 223,
    231, 232
Reimer, Barbara, 221
Renault, Pierre, 171
Resnick, Jaquelyn L., 188, 193, *208*
Resnick, Jerome H., 68, 71
Resnick, Robert J., 75
Reymert, Martin L., 70
Rice, B., 24, *51*
Rich, Gilbert J., 93
Richardson, M. W., 109, *236*
Rigby, Wilbur K., 5, 83n, 87, 89, 93, 94,
    100
Robins-Mowry, Dorothy, 222
Robinson, Daniel N., 143, 147
Robison, Joan T., 244, 245, 266
Rodin, Judith, 244, 259
Rodnick, Eliot H., 69, 74, *80*
Rodrigue, James, 250, 256, *267*
Roe, Anne, 65, 71, 72, 74, *81*
Roesch, Ronald M., 98
Rogers, A. M., 103, *124*
Rogers, Carl R., 64, 66, 67, 70, 74, 107,
    192
Rogers, D. K., *81*
Rokeach, Milton, 12
Romero, Ivonne, 232
Rose, Jed E., 171
Rosenberg, Allison, 45
Rosenbaum, A., 103, *124*
Rosenstock, Irwin, 240
Rosenthal, Robert, 97
Rosenthal, Vin, 182, 201, 202, *209*
Rosenzweig, Saul, 75, 129, 150
Rosewater, Lynne Bravo, 230
Ross, Alan O., 71, 75
Ross, Barbara C., 143, 144
Ross, Dorothea, 77, 242
Ross, Harvey L., 98
Rothman, Frances D., 199
Rotter, Julian B., 68, 71, 74
Rotter, N. G., *236*
Routh, Donald K., 5, 55, 56, 57, 59, 60,
    61, 67, 68, 71, 73, 75, 76, 77, *81*,
    239n, 246, 271, 277
Royak-Schaler, Renee, 221
Rozelle, Richard M., 98
Rubenstein, Alice K., 182, 187, 192, 193,
    197, 203, 204, 205, *208*, *209*
Ruble, D. N., *236*

Ruch, Floyd L., 107, 109, 110, 118, *126*
Ruml, Beardsley, 104
Rundquist, Edward A., 94
Rush, Craig, 161, 168
Russell, R. W., 157
Russell, Wallace, 136, 143
Russo, Deborah, 269n
Russo, Nancy Felipe, 6, 117, *126*, 213,
    217, 218, 221, 223, 224, 225,
    227, *235*, *236*, *237*
Ruveni, Uri, 289

Sachs, S., 227, *237*
Sackett, Paul R., 111, 121, *126*
Saenger, Gerhart, 18
Safir, Marilyn, 223
Salk, Lee, 77, 242
Sallis, James, F. Jr., 259
Sanchez-Hucles, Janis, 217
Sanders, Shirley, 182
Sands, Harry, 192, 205
Sanford, R. Nevitt, 12, 74
Sannerud, Christine, 161
Sarafino, Edward P., 244, 257
Sarason, Seymour B., 66, 71, 74
Sargent, Helen D., 73
Sargent, S. Stansfeld, 12, 13, 20, *51*
Saslow, G., 240, 266
Satir, Virginia, 270
Scalin, Chuck, 285
Scarborough, Elizabeth, 135, 139, 143,
    150, *151*
Scheckel, Carl L., 155, 156, 157, 158,
    162, 163, 172
Scheerer, M., 68, 79
Schein, Edgar H., 99
Schlundt, David, 254
Schmitt, Clara, 58
Schmitt, Neal W., 110
Schneck, Jerome, 129
Schneider, Benjamin, 110
Schneider, Stanley F., 74
Scrivner, Roy, 292
Schneiderman, Neil, 244, 248, 256, 259,
    266
Schofield, William, 7, 73, 240, 241, 242,
    266
Schrader, S., 271, *301*
Schroeder, Carolyn S., 68, 69, 73, *81*
Schroeder, D., 90, *100*

Sutherland, Arthur H., 58
Swencionis, Charles, 257
Swenson, Clifford, 94, 96
Sylvester, Reuel H., 58

Tafoya, Terry, 290, 291, *303*
Tangri, Sandra S., 221
Tapp, June Louin, 12
Tavris, Carol Ann, 225
Taylor, Dalmas, 12
Taylor, Erwin K., 110
Taylor, Harold, 112
Taylor, Samuel N., 98
Taylor, Shelley E., 248
Taylor, W. C., 250, *267*
Teicher, Arthur, 200, 201
Tennov, D., *235*
Tenopyr, Mary L., 110
Terman, L. M., 58
Terrell, D. J., 139, *151*
Teska, James, 98
Thaw, Jack, 99
Thayer, Paul W., 101, 110, 121, *126*
Thomas, Veronica, 230
Thompson, Travis, 155, 162, 167, *176*
Thorndike, Robert, 96
Thurgood, D. H., 139, *151*
Tiedke, Jean, 14
Tiefer, L., 214, *237*
Tiffin, Joseph, 110
Tippins, Nancy T., 111
Titchener, Edward B., 2,
Tobach, Ethel, 24, *52*, 227
Tobias, Lester, 98
Tolman, Edward, 11n
Tolman, R. S., 69, *80*
Tomkins, Silvan S., 74
Toomey, Laura C., 73
Tovian, Steven M., 244
Town, Clara H., 58, 70, 72
Travis, Cheryl B., 211, 217, 221
Triandis, Harry C., 12
Trow W., Clark, 131
True, Reiko Homma, 232, 233, *237*
Tuma, June M., 73
Turk, Dennis, 246, 259
Turner, Samuel, 68
Tyler, Leona, 215

Unger, Rhoda K., 31, *52*, 211, 216, 217,
   224, 225, 227, 234, *236*, *237*

Urbanski, L., 33, *51*, 216, 221, 223, 227,
   231

Valkenburgh, Lois Van, 30
VandenBos, Gary R., 193, 199, 248
Vaughter, R., 227, *237*
Verhave, Thom, 147
Vilhotti, Anthony J., 272, 274
Vitaliano, Peter, 259
Viteles, Morris S., 105, 107, *126*
Vogel, Lawrence, 273, 274
Vroom, Victor H., 110

Waldrop, Ann, 15
Walfish, Steven, 98
Walker, Lenore, 217, 230
Walker, Ronald, 129
Wallace, S. Rains, 110
Wallerstein, Judith, 295
Wallin, J. E. Wallace, 57, 58, 70, 82
Wallston, Barbara Strudler, 216, 217,
   219, 225, 227, 231, *237*, 239n,
   242, 243, 258, 259
Wallston, Kenneth A., 6, 244, 250, 254,
   260, 262, 263, 265, *267*
Walsh, F., 289, *303*
Walsh, Mary Roth, 214, 229, *237*
Warren, Melissa, 45
Washburn, Margaret Floy, 213, 214
Waskow, Irene Elkin, 225
Watson, Goodwin, 10
Watson, John B., 104
Watson, Robert, I., 128, 129, 130, 131,
   132, 133, 135, 136, 137, 143,
   144, 150, *151*
Weakland, John, 270
Webb, James T., 244
Webb, Wilse B., 143, 150
Wechsler, David, 66, 70, 74
Weeks, J. R., 157
Weichlein, Caroline, 14
Weidensall, Jean, 58
Weigel, Richard, 93
Weiner, N., 157
Weinman, J. M., 139, *151*
Weiss, Bernard, 153, 155, 162, 165, 168,
   174, *176*
Weiss, Stephen M., 242, 243, 244, 245,
   251, 256, 259, 261, *266*
Weissman, Albert, 155, 157
Weisstein, N., 215, *237*

SUBJECT INDEX

319

National Council of Women Psychologists (NCWP), 213
National Institute of Health (NIH), 246
The No-Name Group, 115–116

One-Percent Rule, 133
Operation Desert Storm, 285–286

Parents and Friends of Lesbians and Gays (PFLAG), 290, 291
Peace Psychology. *See* Division 48.
Pharmacology societies, 174
Physiological and Comparative Psychology. *See* Division 6.
Practice, psychology as a, 119–120
Psychoanalysis. *See* Division 39.
Psychological Round Table, exclusion of women in, 213
Psychologists in Independent Practice. *See* Division 42.
Psychologists Interested in the Advancement of Psychotherapy (PIAP), 6, 178–179
Psychologists in Public Service. *See* Division 18.
Psychology of Women. *See* Division 35.
Psychopharmacology, growth of, 154–156
Psychopharmacology and Substance Abuse. *See* Division 28.
Psychotherapy. *See* Division 29.

Regents of University of California v. Bakke, 16, 51
Rehabilitation Psychology. *See* Division 22.

Science, psychology as a, 119–120
second-order change, 271
Sexism in employment recruitment, 214

Social Science Information Service (SSIS), 29
Society for Behavioral Medicine (SBM), 246, 253
Society of Experimental Psychologists, 2
Society for Industrial and Organizational Psychology (SIOP). *See* Division 14.
Society of Personality and Study of Social Issues, The. *See* Division 8.
Society for the Psychological Study of Ethnic Minority Issues. *See* Division 45.
Society for the Psychological Study of Lesbian and Gay Issues. *See* Division 44.
Society for the Psychological Study of Men and Masculinity, The. *See* Division 51.
Society for the Psychological Study of Social Issues (SPSSI). *See* Division 9.
   50th anniversary, 13
Southern Christian Leadership Conference (SCLC), 22
State Psychological Association Affairs. *See* Division 31.

Task Force on Trauma and Research, 203–204
Theoretical and Philosophical Psychology. *See* Division 24.
Therapeutic agents, 164–165
triangulation, 271

UNESCO, 25–26
U.S. Food and Drug Administration, approval of drugs, 154

Vietnam War, 26

ABOUT THE EDITOR

Donald A. Dewsbury was born in Brooklyn, New York, grew up on Long Island, and received an AB degree in psychology from Bucknell University in Lewisburg, Pennsylvania. After completing his PhD is psychology at the University of Michigan with Edward L. Walker, he spent a year as a postdoctoral fellow at the University of California, Berkeley, with Frank A. Beach. Through much of his career he has been a comparative psychologist with a special interest in the evolution of reproductive and social behavior. In recent years, his interests have shifted so that he now works primarily in the area of the history of psychology, with a secondary interest in comparative psychology. He is the author or editor of eight books, including *Comparative Animal Behavior* (1978) and *Comparative Psychology in the Twentieth Century* (1984). In addition, he has published more than 260 articles and book chapters. He is a fellow of the American Psychological Association's Divisions 1, 2, 6, and 26, the American Association for the Advancement of Science, the American Psychological Society, and the Animal Behavior Society. He has served as president of the Animal Behavior Society and APA's Division 6 and is currently president-elect of APA's Division 26.